Self Empunishment

by

Brian Walsby

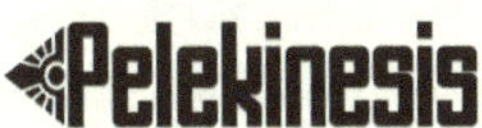

Self Empunishment by Brian Walsby

ISBN: 978-1-949790-42-9

eISBN: 978-1-949790-20-7

Artwork by Brian Walsby

Additional artwork used by permission, rights retained by the artists: Michel Langevin, Todd Kowalski, Errol Engelbrecht, Chris Shary, Dale Flattum, Steve Shelton, Ryan Case, Tom Hazelmyer, and Kristin Smith DeBockler

Layout and book design by Mark Givens

First Pelekinesis Printing 2020

For information:

Pelekinesis, 112 Harvard Ave #65, Claremont, CA 91711 USA

Library of Congress Cataloging-in-Publication Data

Names: Walsby, Brian, interviewer, artist.
Title: Self empunishment / [interviews and artwork by] Brian Walsby.
Description: Claremont : Pelekinesis, 2020. | Includes index.
Identifiers: LCCN 2020022514 (print) | LCCN 2020022515 (ebook) | ISBN 9781949790429 (paperback) | ISBN 9781949790412 (epub)
Subjects: LCSH: Rock musicians--Interviews. | Artists--Interviews. | Rock musicians--Anecdotes. | Artists--Anecdotes. | Rock musicians--Portraits. | Artists--Portraits.
Classification: LCC ML3534 .S447 2020 (print) | LCC ML3534 (ebook) | DDC 780.92/2--dc23
LC record available at https://lccn.loc.gov/2020022514
LC ebook record available at https://lccn.loc.gov/2020022515

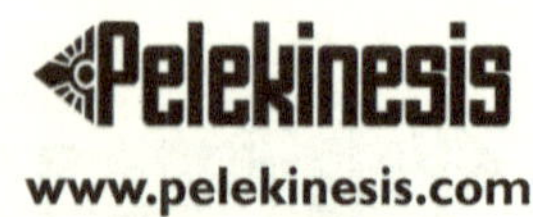

www.pelekinesis.com

Self Empunishment

by

Brian Walsby

CONTENTS

FOREWORD BY BOB DURKEE

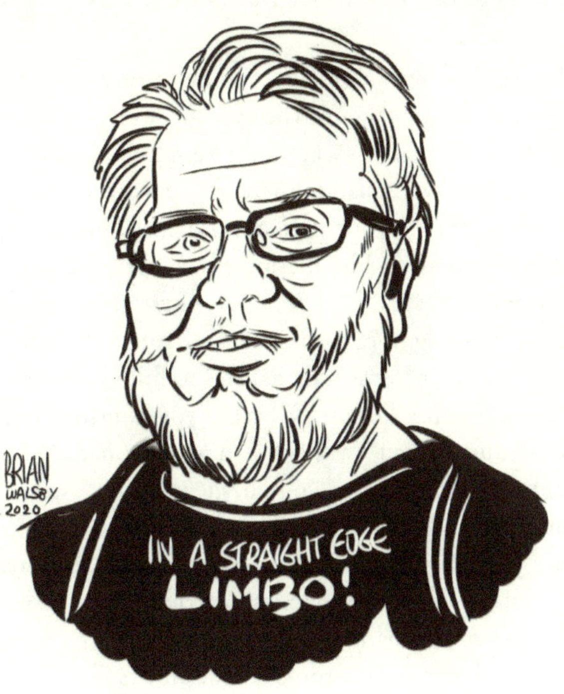

I first met Brian Walsby sometime in 1984. Having started to get seriously involved in the punk/underground music scene in 1981, I started seeing some of his comics in various fanzines, and later his artwork started showing up on some of Mystic Records early Nardcore releases for the Oxnard-based hardcore bands. It's a little hard to comprehend today how small the punk and hardcore scene was in those days. If you involved yourself in any way—whether writing for a fanzine, taking pictures, or playing in a band—people who were contributing to spread the word would gravitate toward the people that were making things happen and spreading the word. My initial impression was that Brian was kind of a goofy young kid (he was probably only a couple years younger than me at most, but when you're 20 that can seem like a lot), but one who was also very passionate about the bands and the music. I think it would be very fair to say that that passion continues to this day, hence this book that you are now holding in your hands.

This book is both a profile of some of Brian's favorite artists as well as an examination of the type of resolve it takes to make a living out of your art—whether it be music, art, writing, photography, or some combination thereof. It may seem more than logical to want to pursue your passion and work hard enough at it to make a living at it. The difficult part for most artists is seeing that through, especially in America where artists can spend many, many years struggling to find an audience for their work. When you are young, it seems only natural to follow your passion and to see where it will take you. Whether you continue to live at home or strike out on your own, you can usually manage to get by with a menial part time job as you pursue your art, especially with the encouragement of your friends and peers. It also helps if you can share a living arrangement with some of them! The real challenge is as time passes, it can be more difficult to continue following your muse when financial considerations become more important. If an artist begins to see some actual profits from their endeavors, they usually face a turning point when they have to decide if the time has come to pursue their art full time. Also as the artist gets older, they find that many of their less successful peers have given up on the hopes of making a living out of their art. I know from my own personal experience that I almost always held down a full time day job as I pursued first a side career as a musician and the owner of a small record label, then as a recording engineer. Even with the job and a somewhat steady paycheck, I was always pouring every last available dollar into trying to build something where I could leave the day job behind and pursue my real love.

Another important consideration for many artists as they get older is the conundrum of pursuing their art versus the impact this has on their personal lives. Many people enter into a relationship as they reach their 30s and suddenly it becomes important to re-evaluate their goals for their art in the terms of how it will impact the people they love, whether it be a husband/wife and/or children. In our capitalistic society, unfortunately, a steady paycheck that allows someone the ability to pay for things like housing, food, and medical care can become far more important as one gets older than it is when you are starting out. All these considerations aside, for some artists it is somewhat of an easy decision if they have never felt comfortable being stuck in a 9-to-5 day job while trying to pursue their art at the same time. In this book you will find multiple examples of what it takes to pursue your art and make a go of it, not only as a labor of love but also as a vocation. Be prepared to work hard, but also to have some fun! On top of all that, there are many great stories in here. I hope you enjoy this book as much as I have and can use it for some helpful tips in pursuing your own artistic destiny. Enjoy the stories, take some notes, and hopefully this will help you as you embark on your own artistic journey.

Bob

INTRODUCTION

This book was written about artists, musical and visual, who have chosen careers outside the commercial mainstream, outside of the box.

But what happens after the counterculture you were involved in—that changed your life and turned you into the weirdo that you were already—eventually goes away? You still have to live and provide and survive and pay the bills while hurtling into middle age, knowing you can't turn back. Maybe you didn't get that college degree or set yourself up with a regular, steady profession with benefits like most normal people. Yeah, maybe.

That is what this book is about.

Let me describe two typical days to you real quick:

One day I wake up and everything is great right away! The t-shirt I made with that kind-of-popular band is doing well, and I will eventually get six hundred or seven hundred dollars put into my bank account by my business partner! I received a few inquiries about some freelance art assignments that won't take long and are even fun to do. Someone ordered a few prints already and it's only 10:00 a.m. I have enough time to work on that other project for a few hours before I have to run errands and go to the post office to mail a few things from yesterday. I have already made enough money to not worry about anything for at least one week, tops!

Life is good!

Here is another day:

No one seemed to like the prints I just did. I probably missed the interest level of the subject matter, or it was just too obscure for anyone to care about. That one company isn't interested in working with me after all. The jig is up, no one is going to buy any of my shit anymore. Why didn't I get a normal profession twenty years ago when I was young? What if I get sick tomorrow?

Why didn't I buy insurance like I should have when I had the extra money? I must be a miserable failure. What if I have to get a job in a kitchen again? I am too old for that shit! Fuck, now I am too depressed to create. I hate peddling my shit on social media, I am in front of this fucking screen too much. Think I will lay down for a while.

Life blows!

Welcome to the world of the self-employed. This is the story and I am sticking with it:

THE STORY.

My mother said I drew the zodiac signs when I was three years old. I don't remember any of that at all. It did seem that as long as I could remember, I was always drawing or doodling or doing something. Discovering Charles Schultz's *Peanuts* and the Mad Magazine of the early seventies and all of the guys that worked on that blew me away. There were other cartoonists that I liked as well, but those two were the main influences for sure. I didn't understand everything I was looking at or reading as a small child, but it all still had a profound effect on me. Strangely enough, I was never attracted to superhero comics as much. I got into those later because my little brother Marc was into them. But that was definitely later. Thanks, Marc.

I remember sixth grade in 1975/1976 being bitten by the rock and roll bug when the band Kiss and their *Alive!* album came out. I was hooked. Before that, it was AM radio and the Jackson 5. Next it was these four scary looking guys in clown makeup singing about blowjobs and partying. And from there I sought out other rock and roll acts from the time period. One day in sixth grade I tried to copy Paul Stanley from the front of the *Alive!* album. I drew it at school, and lo and behold, it was the first time that something I drew sort of looked like what it was that I was copying.

Lightbulb moment.

Throughout my adolescence there were only two things that I

seemed to care about. One of them was listening to music. The other was drawing stuff.

My deep-dive into compulsive drawing started when I found the counterculture of my time in the form of the early to mid-eighties hardcore punk rock scene. I don't know of any way to call it anything other than that. Everyone has their entrance into some sort of counterculture and for me, this was mine.

Through reading early issues of *Maximum Rock N Roll* and *Flipside* fanzines, I was plunged into an exciting world of weirdos and rebellious music and attitude. It was pretty mind-blowing to say the least, reading about all of these exciting bands and people that were all over the globe. I soon realized that it was also very easy to tap into the beneath-the-surface lifeblood of everything, which was the letter-writing/tape-trading aspects of both the punk rock world and the parallel world of underground metal music. For all of the differences, there was a lot that both worlds shared as well. And people both liked and needed artwork. So it was very easy to get in touch with like-minded bands, artists, fanzine makers, poets, and any other weirdo that wanted to participate and be a part of it somehow. That all started around early 1983.

I actually got stuff printed in *Flipside* and *MRR* before I had a chance to go to my first show. That was sort of funny, I just had to *imagine* what punk shows were like. My first actual show that I was able to attend at the end of 1983 was 45 Grave, Redd Kross, Tex and The Horseheads and D. Boon of the Minutemen playing a solo set. I didn't know what to expect. I even brought some paper and some pens.

That was a good show.

I started to see a lot of my cartoony work all over the place—in fanzines, magazine covers, and even, eventually, singles and album covers. People seemed to like my stuff. When I say it was "all over the place," it wasn't. It was just noticed in this really, really small underground world at the time. Looking back, it seemed obvious that I just dashed off all of it with the sheer enthusiasm of a fan. But that's okay. I started to build a little initial name in the underground, which resulted in relocating to the east coast when I was nineteen years old. So the years 1984, 1985 and 1986 were really neat.

I suppose the apex of that underground "early fame" was the year 1985. I drew a lot. I was receiving packages and letters from countless people and pen pals around the world, every single day. I even played in a local band called Scared Straight that even managed to tour a bit. I was in awe of those guys, and eventually they let me join their band on drums. Back in 1985, the punk rock hardcore scene was in full swing. You could be anyone holding an instrument and people would come and see you. Our band went to Lincoln, Nebraska, and people came from four states to see us and meet us. It was all kids doing things for other kids. It was very cool and very exciting. You felt like you were part of something very special. Scared Straight and the band members—Scott Radinsky, Dennis Jagard, Steve Carnan, and Eric Swift—were sort of my little group. Touring with them a couple of times was a real kick. Our parents bizarrely let all of us go. That is pretty funny when I look back on it now. (There is a story I wrote about the second tour in here.)

Back home, strangers would show up at my door because they read scene reports I had written in *MRR* which printed my address. Some of these people came from Australia and Italy. I would invite them in and some would stay for a day or two. My family was a little bemused, but it was all in the name of punk rock.

I was introduced to a lot of the artists of the day and even met some of them. I met the late Mad Mark Rude once. He drew Misfits and Battalion Of Saints album covers and was an accomplished artist. He was really punk rock looking and pretty nice, as I remember. I never met Raymond Pettibon but of course was a huge fan, seeing as he was the main artist behind all of those Black Flag covers and flyers. Everyone knew Pettibon. I would have been scared to meet him anyways, so it is just as well. Brian "Pushead" Schroeder was really cool the first time I met him. We rapped in the Cathay de Grande one night. The second time I was in his company, Scared Straight was playing in San Francisco. We stayed at the *MRR* house and he refused to talk to me. I found out through the late Tim Yohannan that Pushead was mad at me for not spending enough time on my art. Which was true, I guess. But the idea of a highly accomplished illustrator like him —years beyond anything I could do at the time—getting weird over me and my little doodles remains one of my strangest experiences of that time. And it was my first encounter with someone acting weird for whatever reason, which really stood out. There would be much more of that kind of stuff to come. I think I was pretty naive about stuff like that. I thought everyone was friends in punk rock, but when I look back, I question why I thought that in the first place. A lot of what people thought punk rock was, or what it was supposed to represent, was stuff that I hated and still think is stupid. I was attracted to the weird music and the weird creativity attached to it. I wasn't sitting on the train tracks drinking a forty with a ten-foot mohawk, bumming for change afterwards. Maybe I should have tried it? (Much too late now)

In any event, all of these guys were a huge influence on me, big time. They had tapped into the counterculture in their own unique ways and a lot of the amazing work they did was done for very little or no money. Sometimes that would come back and haunt you. In any event, needing money would come later in life.

I moved to Raleigh, North Carolina, in the spring of 1986. I lost interest in drawing a few years after I relocated, being more interested in living a carefree and super cheap life as a young adult. I hung out and played drums in mostly local bands that maybe a hundred people in Raleigh might remember, and eventually burned out of drawing and the punk rock scene in general. It was the end of the eighties and drawing cartoons about uniting the scene wasn't very appealing anymore. It never occurred to me to maybe, you know, try drawing something else or whatever. Who knows. Times just changed.

The next couple of years were sort of my wilderness years. I played music, wasn't very ambitious with anything else, and worked in a restaurant for a long time. I didn't spend a lot of time drawing. I regret having that down period, but looking back, it was sort of necessary. At least that is what I tell myself now.

One of the guys in this book, Chris Shary, somehow found my number and called me out of the blue. This must have been in the early nineties. I didn't know who he was but it turned out that he was an artist who was a lot like me and did a lot of the same things that I did. He wondered what had happened to me since I sort of disappeared. And on top of all of that, he was a really nice guy. It was his phone call that made me decide to get back into drawing, take what I do a little more seriously, and try and get better. So I did.

In the mid-nineties, I started to draw my socks off and sort of rebuilt my name and started to get work freelancing and drawing all manner of things. I noticed that I had made a jump in my abilities when I switched to using an ink brush and India ink.

Things really kicked off with the invention of the internet and social media. There is a powerful downside to it, but the genie is out of the bottle. It is good for networking but a poor substitute for human contact and it seems to bring out the worst in people at times. I try to keep it light but I am no stranger to social media, which makes me really cringe at times.

One thing about the times that we live in that is kind of funny is this: at times, the stuff I drew was very sarcastic and ridiculous. Back in the eighties and early nineties, if I drew something that was silly and offended someone I would hear about it half a year later in some sort of awkward meeting with someone. That kind of sucked, because usually I was just kidding around in a *Mad Magazine*-type of fashion. I wasn't drawing cartoons about wishing people would get sick and die, but I found out the hard way that sometimes people were sensitive, or took themselves too seriously. Actually, when I look back, A LOT of people seemed to take themselves VERY seriously. And this would usually be with people that I liked. But this hasn't happened in the decades since the invention of the internet, because now everyone is potentially an asshole twenty four hours a day. Well, not really, but you know what I mean. It's not real life, it is more of a hyper-accelerated fake life with online people that aren't really your friends. I question this a lot as time goes on but I still think that, for my purposes, it still has more positive things than negative things.

Did I also say that I played drums off and on for a long time? Yeah. I did. I played a lot of music over the years—for thirty-plus years actually—but I think I have probably retired from playing drums. I consider musicians to be artists as well, and many of them are trying to do the same things as someone like me—carving out an alternate way to make a living with the skills that they possess. I don't know how musicians these days get to the point of making money, getting a fan base, touring successfully, and being able to do it on a consistent level. Some of the musicians I interviewed have somehow made it work for them. Some struggle. But they are all in here nonetheless with some interesting stories.

SELF EMPUNISHMENT was written about artists, musical and visual. Some of these people have done this for a long time. Some haven't. Some go back and forth between freelancing and having a "real" job. And a few of the people here aren't at all self-employed or never had to hustle for a living but still had stories that I thought would be interesting enough to include.

As I assembled this book, I talked to a variety of people that I know, plus a few that I didn't. I wanted to get their perspectives from being either artists or musicians or both. I wanted to see how they got by and balanced things while either being self-employed or semi self-employed. There are all kinds of stories here. The idea is to describe what it is like to try and earn a living and/or spread their work and talents through nontraditional means.

As the interviews continued, another theme developed: nerdy music-related shit! Since I am a nerd who grew up in the eighties and has talked to a lot of people with this same background, it's going to make sense that there will be some deep nerdy music-related stuff thrown in along with the roller coaster ride of hustling and being self-employed. What does nerdy music shit have to do with being self-employed? Well, maybe not a whole lot. But nerdy music shit is forever intertwined with what I do. Hopefully the end result will be interesting as well as entertaining.

As for me, not a whole lot has changed even though everything has changed, and continues to change. I have a partner these days. We also have daughters. And we are both self-employed, for the most part. But in the center of everything there is the reality that I still draw all of the time and still listen to music all of the time. I did this in junior high school and to this very day, I do the same thing. That hasn't changed.

Thanks for reading,
Brian Walsby

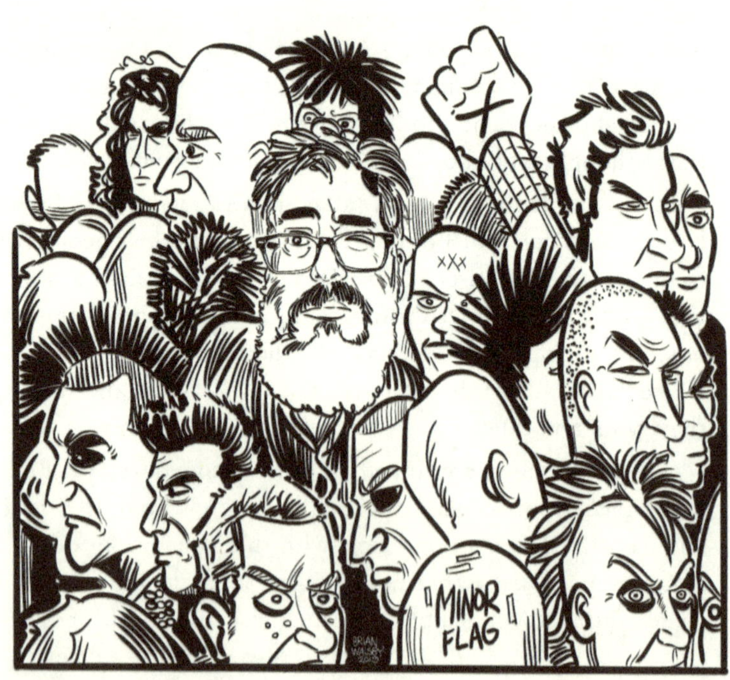

STEVEN McDONALD

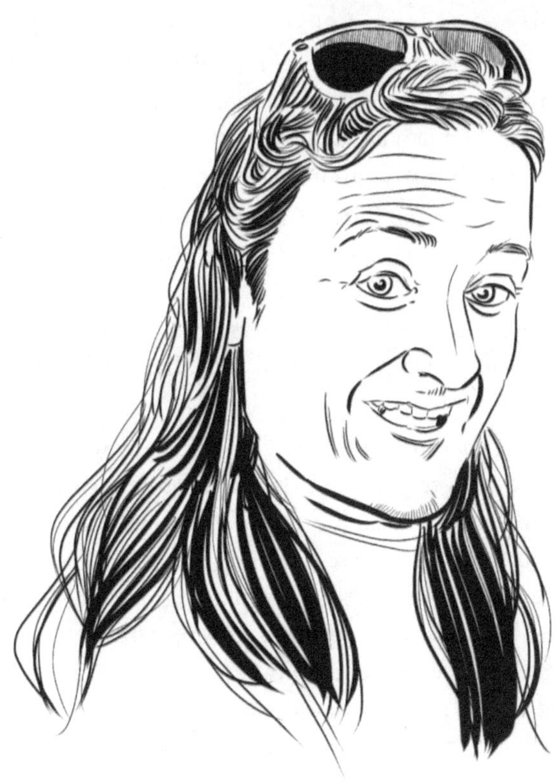

Steven McDonald was one of the first people I wanted to talk to for this book.

Steven formed his band Red Cross (later changed to Redd Kross for obvious reasons) with his older brother Jeff at the end of the seventies, inspired by the Runaways and the Ramones. The McDonald brothers were swept up in the new weird world of punk rock music when Steven was 11 years old and Jeff was 14. Red Cross were among the first handful of "punk" bands that I had ever heard of, courtesy of the first Rodney Bingenheimer *Rodney*

On The ROQ compilation album. Rodney has a radio show in L.A. and he was a real pied piper for thousands of kids in the Southern California area. That first record boasted Black Flag, Adolescents, Minutemen, the Circle Jerks, Agent Orange, and more cool bands that were under the umbrella of whatever they were calling this punk rock thing. Red Cross had the song "Burnout," which I loved as much as the rest of those other bands. So Steven McDonald was in my consciousness right away.

I bought that first Posh Boy twelve-inch the band did, I eventually bought the *Born Innocent* album (recorded in a little town called Moorpark near where I grew up, oddly enough, in Simi Valley, California) and loved both. *Born Innocent* had a trashy and snotty vibe. The band was obviously different than the other bands.

They also didn't look punk rock and actually were amongst the first of those kids to grow out their hair and do their own thing. They unashamedly rocked out and cited older rock and roll as being important. They were fun and smart. The first punk show I was able to go to featured them playing, and they were great. It was the *Teen Babes from Monsanto* version of the band, but with Dez Cadena on second guitar. That was 1983. Not too long afterwards, the *Teen Babes* covers-only album came out and that was a big deal. Redd Kross introduced me to a lot of music that I really didn't know about. They were sort of pied pipers themselves. They have had a very long up and down career and have put out a lot of great music.

I eventually met Steven for real about three or four years ago when he was brought into the Melvins. He and Dale Crover hit it off in a big way when Dale was playing with OFF!, the punk rock supergroup that I am sure you have heard of. Steven turned out to be a really great guy and we got along right away. His love of music is very deep. It's a very pure thing. He is also one of the best musicians I have ever seen, easily. Everything he plays is perfect. Like, if Paul McCartney joined your band or something. He has a lot of skills in a lot of assorted areas, and he is no stranger to hustling and being self-employed. His profile as a musician is at the highest it has ever been, not just through Redd Kross but also via his involvement with OFF! and the Melvins. He also has a lot of stories and history.

I talked to Steven last year over the phone for this project. Sit back and enjoy one of the nicest guys on earth, Steven McDonald.

♫

Brian: When you were a kid what was your first job?

Steven: I was a paperboy. I was about ten. I was a paperboy for the *Daily Breeze* newspaper in the South Bay Area of Los Angeles. I don't think it is exists anymore but it was the most popular newspaper in the South Bay.

Brian: How long did you do that?

Steven: Probably about a year. It came at a weird time because it was right around the time where Jeff and I were starting Redd Kross. I think a standard juggling act for a paperboy would be baseball practice and homework. I was juggling starting a band and playing with Black Flag and going to Hollywood on the weekends and still getting up for the Sunday paper—Saturday morning paper too. So what I am saying is, I think that my paperboy job would have lasted a bit longer if I wasn't doing all of that kind of stuff.

Brian: To me, that all sounds like a very exciting life for a paperboy.

Steven: What was funny is that I sort of paid for the first Redd Kross recordings. I was responsible for paying Spot to engineer our first recordings. Spot, the same engineer who recorded all of those early Black Flag Records.

He recorded our demo. When you hear the word "demo" you assume it is like someone using GarageBand on their computer, but we were in a real studio—the same studio where Black Flag recorded their *Nervous Breakdown* single. It was called Media Art in Hermosa Beach, California.

I was the youngest member of the band at eleven. I think Greg

Hetson might have been eighteen years old, yet the eleven-year-old is the one who coughed up the money, got the money together for the recording.

Brian: What exactly was your brother Jeff doing during this time? Did he have a job?

Steven: Maybe he chipped in, I don't know, I could be exaggerating but I paid the lion's share. Jeff might have still been working, Jeff had a paper route before me at the *Herald Examiner*, which was the other competing paper for the *Daily Breeze*. We didn't work at the same time, that is how I got the idea for my *Daily Breeze* job.

Brian: I want to ask you about the Posh Boy recordings. How did that come about? Did you have a manager?

Steven: No. (laughter) Greg Hetson's father was a lawyer so we might have deferred to Greg a lot on stuff, you know. And he had been in a band before. Evidently Greg's father wrote us the contract that we signed with Posh Boy. I didn't know that until recently—Greg told me that. I don't remember any of it, I doubt that my parents co-signed it. I would like to stand on a soapbox and declare that the contract is null and void because I was twelve years old.

Brian: It won't stand up in court. So there was no money but hey… "Annette's Got The Hits!" "Cover Band!" You guys were being played on Rodney!

Steve: Yeah! True, and I settled with that for years. (laughter) Exposure as payment. It is hard to cash in exposure. I wish I could have controlled how it was exploited.

Brian: I understand that. There are very few people from back in those days that own what they created.

Steven: And also the idea that is has been exploited continuously for forty years, and I have never seen any money from it. But you know… whatever, I am not a lawyer.

But Posh Boy[1] left the country. I talked to him once about fifteen years ago when he was living in South Africa. I did receive some money from Posh Boy once, and this is my memory of it. The one time I received some money from Robbie Fields, my brother and I were playing at the Cuckoo's Nest in Costa Mesa, and we were at a liquor store down the street from the Cuckoo's Nest and we ran into Robbie Fields and he looked like he had seen a ghost.

And he just started throwing cash at us. He gave us like forty bucks, and we were like, "what was that?" and this is two years after that record, probably. And then we found out when we got back to the Cuckoo's Nest that TSOL had shook him down, did something to him and really put the fear in him. So when he escaped that situation, he went to the store and then me and my brother walked in....not that we would have been very imposing figures, not next to TSOL, not next to these athletic-looking...

Brian: ...giant guys who would torture people in their parent's garages!

Steven: Yeah, they were kind of punk thugs. Maybe he thought we were coming in to finish the job, I have no idea. And then we got forty dollars out of that! (laughter)

And then flash forward to when I called him in South Africa... I was just talking about getting control of those recordings and he was like, "that is cool, that is fine and if you ever do anything with them just cut me in." That is what he said. So... whatever that is worth, I have no idea. (laughter) so for years and years and years I just looked at the exploitation as free promotion. But these days, no young musician gets money for recordings anyways, it's all promotion for the shows.

Brian: Right. So, after a reshuffling of the lineup you were able to get more free exposure in the form of the *Born Innocent* record, which was the first album by you that I heard—well, back then

---

1 "Posh Boy" is the name of the record label and the nickname of the founder, Robbie Fields.

it was your only album—and I very much enjoyed it. I enjoyed how trashy it was, I loved the song "Linda Blair," and the song "Kill Someone You Hate."

Steven: And that record was recorded right down the street from you. We were in Moorpark, which is kind of part of Simi Valley, right?

Brian: Yeah, it is sort of the same thing, just separated by a few rolling hills and farms. That is crazy. Anyways, I didn't know if I am remembering this right but didn't you tell me that there were actually some demos for the *Born Innocent* album?

Steven: Yeah, we recorded demos.

Brian: Were you working part time jobs to pay for it?

Steven: We actually probably had just saved up some money from playing shows at that time. The demos were recorded at the Kitchen Sink Studios in Hollywood, which is where the majority of the Dangerhouse records were recorded. So that was kind of a neat thing for us back then because all of those bands who did those Dangerhouse singles were like idols to us.

Brian: And the demos have never come out?

Steven: In our minds at the time, we were probably feeling competitive towards the Circle Jerks… Greg Hetson was in Redd Kross but quit the band when we didn't want to hire Lucky Lehrer as our drummer. Jeff and I just didn't think it was going to work. Lucky was twice my age and had been to law school, I was barely out of junior high, I just looked at him the same way you would have looked at any adult if you were my age back then, you know? Whatever, it just felt awkward to me. And Keith Morris and Greg had just formed the Circle Jerks and the Circle Jerks kind of exploded on the scene, they were immediately popular, they were also instantly infamous amongst their peers—meaning Black Flag and Redd Kross—because Greg had been in Redd Kross and Keith had been in Black Flag.

A bunch of their initial songs that they were playing out live were kind of like a revamp of Redd Kross and Black Flag songs, which really pissed us off. I think it pissed off Black Flag, too. Then they put out a record on Frontier Records, they might have changed some of their stuff but one of riffs still made it onto the record, a riff an eleven-year-old wrote.

Brian: And it is one of the Circle Jerks most famous songs,"I Just Want Some Skank"!

Steven: That used to be a Redd Kross song called "Fun With Connie" which is about... uh... I don't even know how to describe it... it was about Connie Francis.

So you know we thought, that record label seems to be happening, I don't know if the Christian Death record had come out yet—they had put out TSOL—and we turned in some demos with the hope of being on Frontier, and Lisa... I think she was polite about it, but she passed. Which of course was just outrageous to us.

Brian: Sure, but she would eventually release the extended version of the *Born Innocent* album years later.

Steven: Yes, so the *Born Innocent* album came out on a little record label called Smoke Seven Records from Simi Valley. And ten years later, he sold the record, probably for next to nothing.

Brian: Right. More exposure. It's gotta be worth something, right? Anyways, this is part of why I liked Redd Kross. I knew I was NEVER going to be a cool looking, muscle-bound punk rocker who was going to slam in the pit, and you were completely rejecting the punk rock conformist thing— growing out your hair and stuff and saying that even before punk rock happened, people were putting out some really great music.

And obviously before the hardcore explosion, every punk band was different sounding and maybe some of it was kind of arty. And then with the hardcore punk rock explosion all of these people are pretending that all of that earlier rock music never existed. So I always thought that you and your brother, and maybe Black Flag to a certain degree, were rejecting a lot of that stuff, the rules.

Steven: Once the Hollywood punk thing got more evolved it started to morph into a post-punk thing. And then the people that were our age, our peer group, like the Orange County scene, that became this place where if you wanted to go to a punk show, that is where it would be at. There was also that place in the Valley, Godzilla's—run by the Stern Brothers, who now do Punk Rock Bowling— that became more where we were invited to play. And that is when it started to be a really big turnoff for us because it was supposed to be this rebellious subculture where you are spitting back at the norms of society but it all became more regimented in a lot of ways.

It was like junior high school but with a crew cut. (laughter) You would dress in punk gear with spiky hair and yet all of your friends look just like that. It used to be a melting pot and it became a suburban pissing match in a punk rock costume.

Brian: When I think about what you are describing, I always think of the record *Reagan's In* by Wasted Youth. It was hilarious, it was totally the soundtrack for what you just described.

Steven: There is also early Redd Kross alumni in Wasted Youth. So I still feel a connection with them. And the most accomplished musician from our neighborhood at the time was the drummer, Allen Stiritz. I see him nowadays, he lives in Europe. And Chett Lehrer, brother of Lucky Lehrer from the Circle Jerks, had wanted to play guitar for us and he was very persistent. He wanted to join Redd Kross for a long time and we kept putting him off. Eventually he played a few shows with us and I don't know… Jeff and I were probably too stoned to be interested. (laughter) I mean, we were burned once, you know. The way that the first lineup fell apart was… hurtful. And Dez Cadena was playing guitar at the time, too. That was just before he was in Black Flag, and after he quit them, he rejoined Redd Kross.

I think that my brother was probably grossed out by their rapid success, too. Yeah, it was probably around that time where Jeff stopped cutting his hair, and I had just gotten comfortable with my punk look. So Jeff was the one who initiated all of that, around '82. He never told me that I had to do it. The last time I heard those *Born Innocent* demos they were much more in line with the hardcore thing that was happening around 81 and 82. By the time we had recorded the actual album it seemed less of a punk record and more of a proto-indie rock album. It resembled more of what bands like Pavement would be doing.

Brian: Except I enjoyed your version of that sort of thing.

Steven: You mean you enjoyed a fourteen-year-old's version in Moorpark more than an arrogant college graduate?

Brian: Well, when you put it that way then it really is no contest.

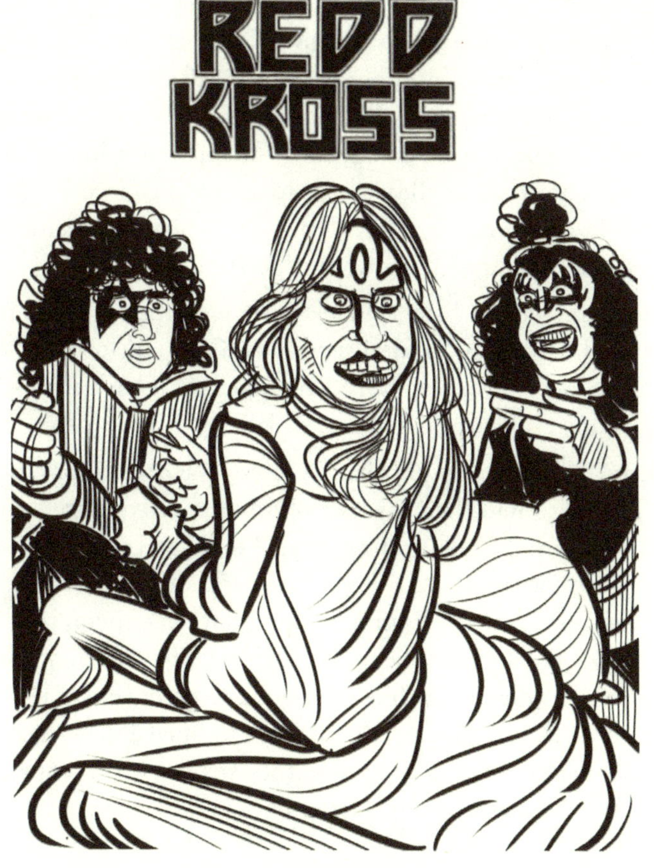

Brian: Why did you guys never release anything on SST Records? You knew all of those guys and played shows with them and were friends with some of the bands in that scene, like the Descendents, who were your peers and stuff. Why was there never an SST Redd Kross release?

Steven: Well, when we went and made our first record, they weren't really a record label yet. They were pressing up their *Nervous Breakdown* single. You know, SST didn't put out the first Black Flag album. We didn't view them as a record label even though they put out those early singles before they did *Damaged*. I don't know when they had started to put out albums by other bands, but by the time they did, we might have played the odd show with them but we were no longer a part of their core crew like we were during our first year. I don't know if they ever wanted to make a record with us but at other points we definitely didn't want to make a record with them. We really admired them and we appreciated them putting us on bills early on especially, but I think we also thought that we didn't want to get too involved because we wanted to do our own thing. They were almost like mentors on a certain level, and SST had a very specific… language.

Brian: Yeah, when I listened back to some of the radio interviews they did back then, it almost sounds like a cult or something. Which I never ever would have thought about back then when I was young and worshipped Black Flag.

Steven: We never thought that we weren't accepted, or a part of it. They also had their own set of criteria, or whatever, and we had our own ideas of what we wanted to do and one of them was putting on a show and living out a rock and roll fantasy. And at that point, we knew from hanging out with them, they were reacting against that. They were older than us and they thought that you could cross the line from punk to poser very quick doing some of that stuff. And I didn't want to be judged that way. Originally for sure, it was just because they weren't really a label, and Posh Boy happened really quick.

The first time we had played a real club was opening for Black Flag in Chinatown, and Posh Boy was there, and he offered us a deal right then and there. It was almost embarrassing because these guys were older than us, but suddenly we were getting opportunities tossed at us. We were going to record and we didn't have to pay for it.

Brian: The Janet Housden/Tracy Lea era came next and that was kind of short-lived but that was also when you guys got the front cover for *Flipside* fanzine! You recorded a handful of songs.

Steven: That lineup is on the cover of *Flipside* and on the first repressing of the Frontier version of *Born Innocent,* but in all reality, the album was recorded predominantly as a three piece—my brother, myself, and John Stielow. John kind of quit during the making of the record, and Tracy Lea was in the band when we went in to make the *Born Innocent* record but she only showed up for a little bit of it, so she is kind of like the Brian Jones of the band.

You know it is funny, because I have been playing with Janet and Tracy lately because we are doing a reunion gig with that lineup, and it has been awesome playing with them. Tracy has that sound that is very unique, the way she forms her barre chords. But she is on half of the record. So that lineup you could say is kind of responsible for the *Born Innocent* album. That lineup only did a handful of songs for compilation albums.

Brian: After Tracy bowed out, Dez rejoined. That version was the first punk band that I saw, man. I will always remember that. But, the lineup records nothing except for that awesome cover of "Out Of Focus" by Blue Cheer that Dez sings. Even more bizarre is that it isn't even online anywhere.

Anyways, Dez left and that was around the time you guys recorded the *Teen Babes From Monsanto* mini album. Why did you guys decide to do an all covers record at that point? I should also point out that it was that record and those covers that sort of turned me on to checking out The Stooges and David Bowie more—it was a gateway into a whole lot of stuff that I really didn't know about in 1984. And I think that, based on talking to some people over the years, that record was also other people's introductions into those kind of bands.

Steven: You could say that a part of it was that we were lazy and didn't want to write any songs. But Jeff always said that he thought of it as sort of a history lesson. Which is funny, it is a little arrogant that you want to give your peer group a lesson, but it was true. It baffles me when I think about what I was exposed to at a really young age musically and that it is all stuff that I still really love today. It was really important music and it wasn't like I had a much, much older sibling that was ten years older from another marriage... no, he was three years older than me and on his own he was reading about the New York Dolls, reading about Patti Smith, reading about the Velvet Underground and he was bringing home Lou Reed records. He was bringing home that and Patti Smith's *Easter* album, alongside Aerosmith's *Rocks*, along with the stuff that was very popular and mainstream... he was checking out the weird ass shit that Lester Bangs was trying to turn kids on to. I think about the comp tape that we made and listened to on these road trips when we were kids. It had Johnny Winter live, which was classic blues rock, into "Chatterbox" by the New York Dolls. And there would be the Ramones on there right alongside Aerosmith. So, you know, it is very legitimate that my brother should give his peer group a lesson in rock history around that time. He was knowledgeable and he did have great taste and I think he was really passionate about that stuff.

Another part of the puzzle for us was that we grew up loving David Bowie—we got *Hunky Dory* when I was five years old, the year it came out. I don't know how a nine-year-old knew to get it but Jeff knew how to get it. And Bowie did that record *Pin Ups* during the Ziggy era, and that was the first place that we heard a lot of that stuff, like Syd Barrett-era Pink Floyd or the Pretty Things. So Jeff said that he wanted to do our version of that record so we could turn kids on to what we knew about.

Buzz [Osborne] has brought up that record to me, we heard about it from the Mudhoney guys and others so that record might have had an impact on some people, who knows.

Brian: Not too long after that, Robert Hecker joined the band and you got to go on your first tour of the United States. I think that was at the end of...1985?

Steven: Yeah, we had a tour booked by the Global Booking agency, which was Chuck Dukowski of Black Flag.

Brian: I bet it was exciting to finally tour.

Steven: Yeah, it was exciting. There were lots of big surprises and you know... humbling moments. It was the typical story of a young band's first tour.

Brian: Did Roy McDonald play drums for that tour across the country?

Steven: No, Dave Peterson, the drummer on the *Teen Babes* record, did. Dave was out of the band prior to that and we had this heavy metal drummer named Glenn Holland, and Glen quit the band on the eve of leaving for this tour. Dave didn't want to be in the band but he said he would do the tour.

Brian: so this sets the stage for the next phase and the *Neurotica* album.

Steven: At this point I am eighteen years old, or seventeen. And I wanted to be more serious about doing this thing. You had to set your goals higher, and we wanted to get signed to a label and get more money, and go into the studio for a whole month, or something like that.

Brian: My perception of that period of the time was that it was a complete step up, more into the big leagues. I remember the reaction to the record was that it universally went over really well. You were in the pages of *Creem*, it seemed like your profile really jumped up. A lot of people really loved that record. They certainly did in Raleigh, North Carolina, where I lived. It was a good sounding album, full of some really catchy songs. It certainly didn't sound like anything the band did before that.

Steven: We weren't living the high life but I remember...we had fifty grand to make the record,—fifty grand in 1986—and that was considered respectable, but kind of moderate. Which says a lot about the recorded music industry.

Brian: Especially when you look at it now these days. Did you guys spend all of that money on the recording?

Steven: We would have made that mistake, that would have been one thing that someone like Buzz Osborne would have made a much wiser decision in that situation. We relied on managers. We never looked for a manager, but we always had these people that wanted to manage us. And these people were persistent, they would call us on our parents' phone. They wouldn't leave us alone and we were passive about it. Me and my brother never had a passion for the business side of it. Part of that was because we had very supportive parents. We definitely were not raised with a silver spoon in our mouth. My dad has always owned his own small business, kind of a blue collar thing but at the same time, a step up. Maybe they overindulged us, I don't know, but I probably would have been a much shrewder business person if I didn't have that much support? But then again I might not have had the guts to pursue this thing.

Brian: You reshuffled the lineup for the *Third Eye* record.

Steven: Every album has to have a different band lineup and at that time we were signed to Atlantic Records. Part of this story—what is relevant—is that you know we grew up in Los Angeles, we grew up in the suburbs, so we weren't like industry insiders in any shape or form. But at the same time we were part of a scene, a community, you know. You are going to see the same faces over and over playing at the same clubs. And so when the eighties rolled around, Los Angeles was the capital for the rock music industry, this is where everyone moved to get big and try to get into the mainstream.

So I think that it is going to just be natural to be competitive with people from the scene, to take note about what people are doing in the scene and in our world. We were watching people—people that we thought were totally talentless—overnight becoming really popular and accepted by the mainstream. It happened several times. Sometimes they were talented, some of the time they weren't talented at all.

We were running neck and neck alongside these kind of bands a lot, and I have to put some things into perspective on how I arrived where I am at now. And that is a unique part of the lens that I looked through, the opportunities, the possibilities to do it that way seemed like very distinct possibilities. So when we were given the opportunity, we took the chance.

Brian: *Third Eye* sort of sidestepped to where you had gone before, it certainly was different than whatever, or whoever, it was that you were watching and being competitive with.

Steven: Yeah, we certainly didn't think that we had the formula for becoming successful from watching these hair metal bands. We weren't taking cues from anyone creatively. I just think it is

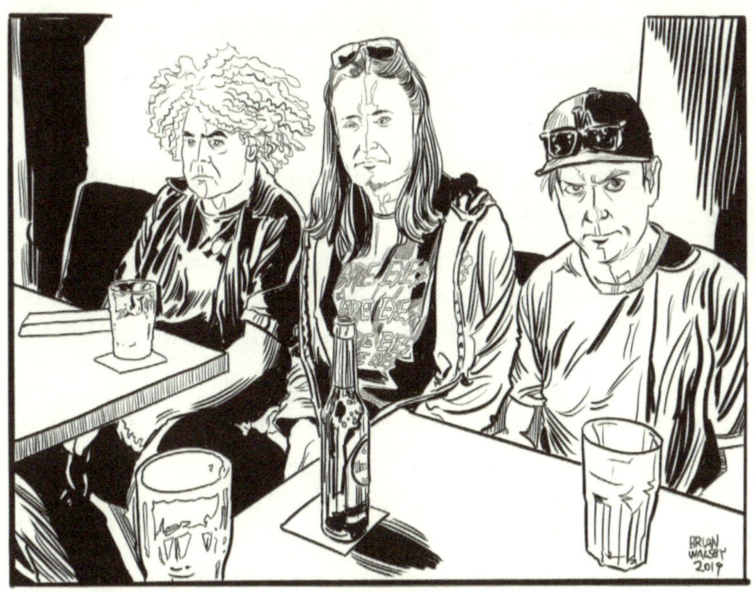

worth noting that when you think about the history of a band, it is just natural that you would aim for certain things, like you would aim to be on Atlantic Records. And you know talking to Buzz, I have been in the Melvins for three years and so we have that experience in common and we know some of the same stories and his perspective was always like a pessimism. The way he tells it is like he would have never expected or tried to get on Atlantic Records, you know. They came to him and he always viewed it like, "Really? Okay. If you want. If you insist." In other words, "...but I'm not trying, I don't think it is going to succeed, I am going to do what I am going to do. I am going to try because that is how I do things, but if I am not next year's Nirvana then that is on you."

Brian: Which is a good attitude to have about that kind of thing.

Steven: It's the best attitude that a young artist could ever have in that kind of environment but I didn't even know about that attitude. (laughter) And I definitely took it on. It didn't inform the music that we made, we always aimed to love the music that we made. Sometimes we would have a frustrating experience that we might have made with a choice of a producer, the band might have imploded during the icing of the record, whatever. But the one thing I will say, when I look back on that experience with a little bit of regret, was how much I would take on myself, and feeling like a failure. Like with the Atlantic thing—not becoming a mainstream known name.

Brian: Since I have gotten to know you over these last three years, sometimes when you talk about some of those experiences, I can't help but think that maybe you're being just a little too hard on yourself.

Steven: I thought, in a way, it was being more courageous. I am setting myself up for potentially being a failure, which is a brave thing to do. It can really fuck you up.

I mean, the chances of hitting a chord with millions of people is very rare. You are asking millions of people to exchange money for something that you created, which is asking a lot. And it is very, very rare. But I was willing to take the chance, as they say, and go for it. But the fallout of not breaking into the mainstream and feeling like a failure lasted years.

Brian: I was just thinking about the shadow that Nirvana cast, or before that, when all of a sudden there was an industry for punk rock and Green Day and Epitaph Records and all of that stuff.

Steve: It is very rare to be in that position. Most people aren't.

Brian: So then you re-shuffled the lineup and did the next record, *Phaseshifter*, which was more of a rocking record. There are some big rock songs on it but there is also this pop songwriting style that is coming in the picture. So during that period, did you ever have a job between all of that activity? Did you have a manager?

Steven: Yeah we had the same manager from pre-*Neurotica* all of the way through…I guess from '86 to '97. John Silva, he later managed Nirvana and Sonic Youth. He now manages Foo Fighters.

Brian: So, the band was taking a break, or laying low, and you were stating how you had been in Redd Kross up until this point and you eventually decided that you wanted to go to school and do other things.

Steven: Well, yeah. By the time I was thirty-one, I had been doing Redd Kross for twenty years and so… you know, turning thirty… it was this milestone year. And I tend to take stock a lot more and I sized myself up and determined whether or not I had been achieving enough. And I felt really paranoid about continuing on after thirty, I don't know why…(laughter) When I think about it now I am like, "what a fucking little ageist asshole."

Brian: Ha ha. That is pretty funny, especially considering how busy you have been in the last five years. Your profile is higher than it has ever been and you are doing more stuff then you have ever done and playing in more bands.

Steven: Yeah. I definitely have made more money as an artist then I ever have, that is for sure. And I have been way more busy, and

I definitely have a few people to thank for it.

Brian: And you are completely self employed.

Steven: Yeah. Well, part of it was that is was the pre-internet age. Very few people then controlled the information line. I don't think that I had even understood it enough to even look at it that way but it was like… if the industry wasn't even interested in you and your stocks were low then you were really fucked, you know? You didn't have a lot of opportunities to try to reach potential audiences on your own, like you do now.

But then, I felt that I wasn't very marketable in the eyes of the industry, which I probably internalized and felt like I wasn't marketable, you know? I just took it on, .and I felt like a failure. When I was sizing up my efforts, as the kid who paid for the demo tapes when I was eleven with my paper route money, I worked hard and I think that I had a certain expectation for myself. It is hard being in a career where you are trying to market yourself, it does a fucking number on your brain you know? Your ego, your sense of self. It's hard to be constantly trying to… what's the word? Commodify yourself, because even the most in-love-with-themselves person is bound to get embarrassed by the process after a while. And then you take a healthy amount of self-deprecation and you throw that in the mix and it is just painful.

Brian: I have some of that, I am not "Mister Confident" but I just do what I do. And I think that the jig is going to be up any second. I always think that.

Steven: Right. I guess that is a good way to be. But anyways, around that time I had thought that perhaps the career plans that I had made for myself at ten years old, or eleven, should be re-examined a little bit. Because I had been going up there with such fervor and such tunnel vision for two decades solid, you know? And I had found myself broke, too. I mean, that is always the hardest time with this whole independent contractor self-employed thing is that when you got some money in the bank, then you are the smartest person in the world and you are so glad you made all of these choices. But then you are once again broke, it gets harder and harder, you know? It is really hard not to give yourself a major lashing. That is what was going on when I turned thirty.

Then someone hired me to produce a record in the mid nineties and I thought that maybe there was something in that for me so I was going to go learn. I wasn't giving up on music, I just wanted to learn how to speak about music. So I went and studied theory. I just wanted to know the rules more. Not that I wanted to abide by them, I just wanted to understand how classical music theory worked. I guess it would be sort of like if you went to art school to learn some kind of basic classical art techniques in your thirties. So that is what I did. And you know, I ended up producing and I ended up being a side guy, playing for people like Beck, and Sparks.

But on the topic of how I supported myself even before this time, I would always supplement my income with whatever kind of odd work that I could find. Redd Kross, we would take whatever advance we would get and we would put it in a bank and we would take a shitty little stipend a month. And I lived very cheaply, and I could just kind of get by. And once that was gone then I had to find other ways, or I would get more in debt, too.

Brian: I had a period where I lived off of credit cards and it sucked. It only happened once, luckily.

Steven: Yeah. And I can't say that I am completely debt free today, so that is one of the reasons why when you had hit me up to talk to you for this book, I was like, "don't ask me, I don't know fucking shit."

Brian: A lot of people I have talked to are in the "one day at a time" thing, just like me. I am going to hustle tomorrow because I didn't do anything today.

Steven: A lot of my life in these last couple of years has been this idea that I don't know where this is going to take me, but I am open to more new interesting places that I haven't known about yet. On a good day I look at it like, "all of the new things I get to learn how to do!" And then when I am in a shitty mood, I think about all of the fucked up shit I have to learn how to fucking do, you know?

I guess that gratitude is the secret there. Be grateful for what you have.

Brian: You learned how to record and engineer music, too.

Steven: Yes. And I was also involved in the business of it. That was always something that was in the back of my mind. Living in L.A., I always had this thought, I had it as a teenager and I don't know why, it was really dumb. I thought, "Well, if it doesn't work out for me playing in a band, I probably could get a job at one of these fucking record labels." And there used to be millions of these people at these record labels and as I later learned, people would float from one label to the other and it went on for years and years. And a lot of it would happen through personal relationships, you know?

Brian: Hard to believe! Who would have thought it was about who you knew?

Steven: Well, but who would have...Yeah, I know. I know. But in the back of my mind, when I was a fifteen-year-old, I was thinking, "by the time that I am an adult, I will probably know so many people just by doing what I do, then those answers will become clear to me when I get there if I need something." And it did happen—it totally happened—but it was funny because it was at the end of... I probably caught the tail end. I was off by about five years. And so I caught the tail end of anybody even imagining that anything could come from underground rock and roll, was shit. Without any reason why mainstream America should be focusing on what would be bubbling up from that underground. I caught the tail end of any kind of interest in that.

So it was weird, it was hard. It was a weird time trying to initiate yourself into a major label environment, a major label corporate office.

Those environments have always had the reputation of being

brutal shark tanks anyways. And I think I had got there right when Rome was totally burning.

It was kind of nasty and it left a nasty taste in my mouth. So I produced a few records and I ended up consulting for a few labels. And consulting was great. It just meant that you had to know one guy at a label, and you would just call that person and talk to him once a week and tell him what you were doing.

I just recently got into sports—my nine-year-old is heavily into NBA—and I never cared anything about it. But at any rate, he has gotten me into it, I actually really enjoy the NBA. And now he has gone beyond that, he is into college sports, and he is all about trying to figure out who is going to be the great rookie for next year. And he is really looking for the diamond in the rough.

So now I totally get sports and why people would be enthusiastic about it because I felt that exact same way about thinking about young artists, and I had fun doing it and I really did think that I had a talent for it It wasn't a soul sucking thing to do, I actually enjoyed it. But ultimately I ended up at an office, one of the last times that I had done one of those jobs. I worked for about five different labels, the last one I worked at was in the office and that was horrible. But the beautiful thing was that OFF! kind of took off, my punk rock supergroup with Keith Morris. That sort of took off and became this big splashy thing. Right in the middle of my stint with a corporate record label.

Brian: Didn't Keith work at one of those places too?

Steven: Yeah, Keith did too. He said it in his own book that he worked for V2 Records. I used to see him at South by Southwest and we were both checking out bands, and that was how we both rekindled our friendship.

Brian: The thing I liked about OFF! was how you were gung-ho about playing a sort of Dee Dee Ramone role in this supergroup that played aggressive punk rock music. You told me these funny stories about talking to aggressive looking, punk rock hardcore kids who were namechecking all of these bands, but in all honesty, you didn't know who they were talking about because you were never a hardcore kid. Your roots were before all of that stuff, before hardcore and certainly before hardcore bands influenced by other hardcore bands.

Steven: Well, yeah. I have already talked about how many of the choices that Redd Kross made was to go against the stuff that even Keith did. We were reacting to the success of the Circle Jerks when we decided to stop cutting our hair. And we very much immediately distanced ourselves from a lot of that genre, some of which is now considered seminal. (laughter)

Brian: In the last four or five years you have worked your ass off, playing in a lot of bands and staying very busy. That must feel sort of good, especially thinking about what your game plan was when you were an eleven-year-old. It must be satisfying on some level.

Steven: No, it is. It totally is. Of course it is. I mean, I don't want to totally judge myself on where I think I am financially, although I am not in a bad place financially, either. Financial security is so elusive, it is always a struggle. But I will say that I can look at my accomplishments much more these days. And the thing is, the big surprise is, that I know that I am better at what I do now then I was at twenty five years old. And when I was twenty five, I didn't even think that I could be doing it when I was my age now. And not only can I do it, I am way better now. I feel way more confident that I am going to be consistently at a certain level. So I have to acknowledge and be grateful for that.

Regardless of whether or not I am hitting certain marks that I have set for myself, I am still part of a very elite group of people that get to be in a functioning band, much less three functioning bands, that people will come and pay money for.

Brian: You have a studio, you are hustling, you have a couple of Redd Kross reissues coming out on Merge Records, there is a new Redd Kross album coming out… Plus, you have played with Dale Crover in all of these bands and you seem to have a good thing going. And speaking of Dale, how did the Melvins thing happen?

Steven: The real catalyst was when Mario couldn't go on a tour with OFF!, Mario Rubalcaba. And Dale was available and open to doing it, so Dale went out on a two or three week tour with OFF!, in 2015 maybe and that just kind of led to further discussion. But I think the real genesis of me playing with Melvins goes back to the early nineties when Buzz moved to L.A. and he and I would rap on the phone for hours at a time. And knowing Dale.

And we had Bill Bartell in common, who was the guy from White Flag, he was a real weirdo. He had a knack for annoying people, like a gnat flying around your head. And he also had an amazing knack for bringing people together. And that is the part that I think everybody really misses about Bill and that definitely had a bit to do with me playing with the Melvins.

And also, Redd Kross had done an album in 2012 that I think that those guys kind of liked. I ended up in their consciousness so the next time they needed someone, my name came up. Those guys have a long, very interesting past, a decorated past. So I think that it is probably hard to find people that you can relate to, and that they could relate to my situation too, and I would like to think that they thought of me as someone that could make sense in their world, you know? So that is how we arrived there.

Brian: What have you taken away from the experience? I owe a lot to the Melvins. It is a fortunate thing to have been friends with them for so long. I try to learn a few things from watching how they operate and how a few people around their orbit operate, and as these tours keep going on, I seem to appreciate them more and more.

Steven: Buzz talks about this stuff a lot. When you are in a new environment or you are meeting new people, try to look for something that you can learn from them. That is one thing that I have taken away from it. And with those guys, there is tons. The main thing is their ability to make this format—which could be pretty limited, it's a rock band—how you can make it work; how to make it financially work, how you can make it creatively work, how to have longevity with it. For years I didn't even think that was a possibility. All of those years where I was doing my band, it was always about investing in the band because the only way we could make money from the band would be to break into the mainstream.

I mean, that is one way. You can make money but you are also making a lot of other people money. But I don't think I even knew it was possible to do it more of a DIY way. I think that the process of being in the Melvins... Buzz is an extreme guy. And he can be challenging but more than anything it has been this really welcome lesson about how to make something sustainable. It is a very difficult thing to wrap your head around. I really have learned from them what not to sweat so much. They can really make a living doing this, and I think that they have taught me to really believe that. It is weird; Buzz is a pessimist but he also exhibits the power of positive thinking.

It has been fun to learn from him, and here I am. I feel like I am learning to take more chances about being an artist myself.

Like, I am making a Redd Kross record right now and I have had more songs on this Redd Kross record than any of the records before. I am finishing the album now and right now I am deciding if we need a few more songs that I have been writing for it in mind. I have always been more of an accompaniment guy, so taking on more of the writing stuff is probably a result of being around Buzz and Dale.

Brian: Well, I really liked your Melvins solo album that you did.[2]

Steven: Oh, thank you.

Brian: I don't want to say that I was surprised it was as good as it was but those were four really good songs in a row.

Steven: Yeah, thanks. Well, it was a fun thing for me to do. A lot of it is just like... those guys have been living in their routines

---

2 The *Steven McDonald* EP (2017) is one of four EPs recorded and attributed to The Melvins à la the KISS solo albums.

for so long that they invite change in certain areas. When they invite change into it, you get different results. Now they have two bass players in the lineup, or they had two drummers for awhile or whatever.

Before I was with them, I would have never thought that it would be okay to do that because somehow I would think that it was wrong, but now I can understand the process with them because they are in it for the long haul each time. There might be a change, but there is going to be a hundred and fifty shows on it. It's going to get to this place where it is unique. And I think that taking those chances is good. And that has influenced me into thinking that it is okay to take more chances, and to take more chances with writing, writing songs and lyrics. Of course I can do it. Why not? You cannot be afraid if it's just fine. Maybe playing at the Casbah in San Diego is just fun because it's the first show on the tour. But by the time to wrap it up back in L.A. at the end of the tour, it's fucking brilliant. And that can happen in other areas, you know?

Redd Kross will work more this year than we have in years. I am finding myself more ways to make myself more of my own boss. And I am grateful for that. That is a real gift. And I will always credit those guys and Buzz.

Brian: I think one time Jeff Pinkus said of Buzz something like, "we are pretty lucky to be in this position where we can all benefit from this guy's obsessive qualities."

Steve: Yeah, he is talking about Buzz and his crazy OCD-ishness that makes him an insane workaholic and creates jobs for all of us. And opportunities, and he is very open about wanting to put a spotlight on you and help you out and fan the flames of your own potential. And I see him doing it and I will always give him that. And it makes me want to do more of that myself.

KEITH MORRIS

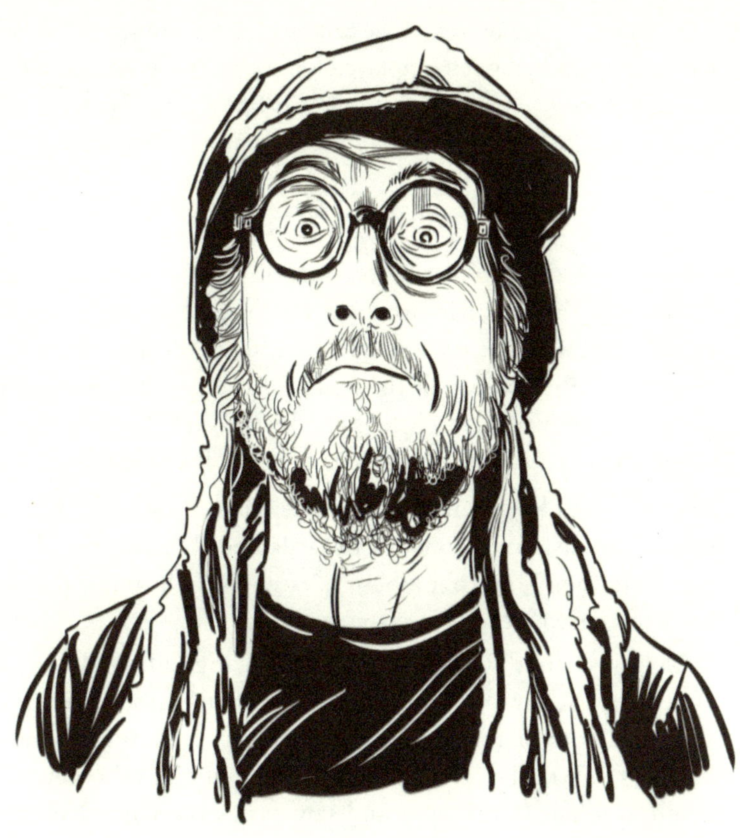

Keith Morris is someone that everyone who is reading this knows full well about, so let's get the credentials out of the way. He was the first singer of Black Flag and sang on the classic debut seven-inch *Nervous Breakdown*. He then formed the Circle Jerks with ex-Redd Kross guitarist Greg Hetson where he sang for a very, very long time.

In recent years, he has been the singer for the band OFF!, has written a book[1] with another one on the way, and this year it looks as if the Circle Jerks have reformed. Every single punk rock history book on earth seems to have an interview with Keith in it, and now it is my turn!

In reality, I have no real sense of knowing how much of his time has been spent being self-employed but we do touch on that a little bit here. Mostly, our conversation reads like a sort of entertaining stream of consciousness rambling over many different subjects.

♫

Brian: Can I ask you about the one job that I know you had, working in the music industry? It was pivotal because you also reconnected with Steven McDonald during that time, which kind of led to the formation of the band OFF! And that band came about because you were a little tired of the Circle Jerks being sort of secondary to your guitarist's other band, Bad Religion.

Keith: Yes, it's okay to mention Bad Religion. People think that I have a bad taste in my mouth towards Bad Religion, and I love Bad Religion. That first album is essential L.A. punk rock, or hardcore, or whatever you want to call it.

Anyways, since we are talking about being self-employed, we are talking about all of the different jobs and I was offered the opportunity to be the A&R boy at V2 Records on the west coast here in Los Angeles. I was allowed to go out and be a scout and listen to music and I went and saw bands play live. I went to South by Southwest and some other music festivals. I remember one of my assignments was to go and see Vampire Weekend. They became a big hit amongst the hipster indie crowd and it was like, "What the fuck?" I had a rule—I would allow a band a certain amount of songs, and by the fourth or fifth song, if they aren't rocking or moving me, I am the fuck out. Some of the people I

---

1 *My Damage: The Story of a Punk Rock Survivor with Jim Ruland* https://www.dacapopress.com/titles/keith-morris/my-damage/9780306824074/

knew who were also scouts, some of them were my friends, some of them were actually really cool people but for the most part... Steven [McDonald]—I don't even know how long he was there but he would get in a room and all of a sudden there would be all of these other A&R people who had been there six months before him telling him that he couldn't talk to certain bands. He was not swimming in a pool full of sharks, those people busting out knives and razors and fucking were slicing at his ankles and stabbing him in the back and then pushing him into a pool full of piranhas. I felt bad because I realized that these people, for a lot of years, just sneezed millions and millions of dollars. It was a dying breed. There are still some good people and labels out there but they aren't throwing the money around the way they used to.

Brian: Steven said it was like arriving when Rome was burning. But he also said that it led to OFF! forming, which was a good thing for all concerned. OFF! made a lot of waves in the post death-of-the-record-industry world.

Keith: We just got into survival mode, and we just went out there and did what we did. Maybe we had pressed some of the right buttons. We just went out and played, and we are going to play with whomever we can play with.

Brian: What is going to happen in the future with OFF!? I know that Dale [Crover] has stepped in for Mario [Rubalcaba] and they played me a few tracks without vocals, and you said you had to work on that a while ago. What is up?

Keith: We have twenty five songs, some of which need proper recording. A lot of those that you heard were like, "let's spend a half an hour to record this song and then play it." It's all going to be for a soundtrack to a movie that we are filming. We have some people set up to produce the movie, we don't know when we are shooting but we have some stuff attached to that. I am also sitting on a couple of scripts for movies, one involves Chuck Bukowski.

Brian: How do you feel about the legendary status that Black Flag has? It has lasted beyond anyone's imagination and now people debate which version was the best. For instance, Ron Reyes was in the band for six months—which is a really short amount of time—but because of the internet and because of how slow time seemed when you were a youngster, everything is massively discussed. What do you think about all of that? I mean, you were a big part of it because you were the first guy singing for Black Flag.

Keith: Well, the thing is, when we started the band we weren't a band. It was Greg Ginn and I in a room with him playing and me singing through the same amp and speakers. He was playing these songs and teaching them to me, and I was just floored by

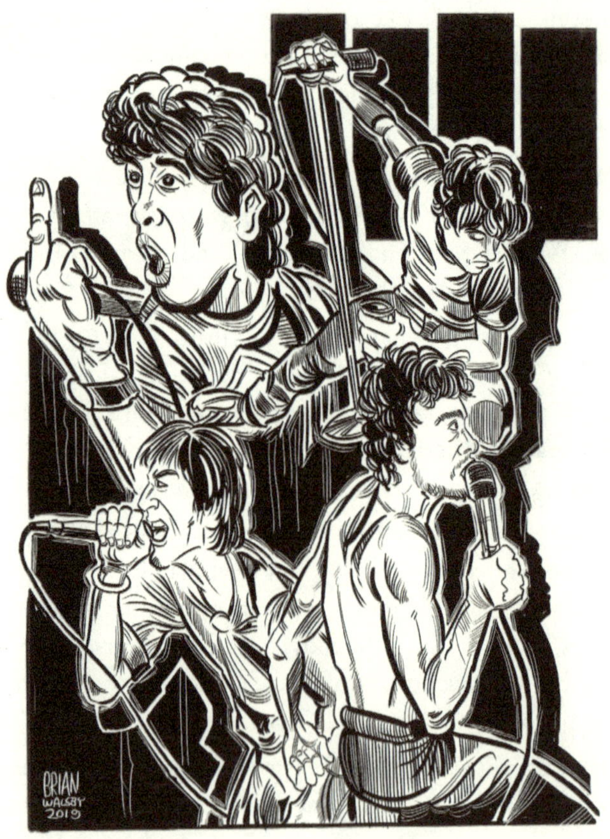

what I was hearing. This could not have been more perfect or more fitting for what we were going through, because we were in a situation where in Los Angeles... there was a point in musical history where there were only a handful of bands. In the late seventies there were about six dozen bands and a lot of them were just not worth listening to. And we were putting a lot of this stuff under a microscope and then we would have a band like the Dogs from Detroit, who were a three piece who were just like somewhere between the MC5 and The Who. We loved this. And then all of a sudden, down by where we were at, there's The Last. That is an island of what we wanted to hear. They were perfect for us. I would be sitting with Joe Nolte and we would be listening to Steeleye Span, which is electrified folk music. We would be listening to Golden Earring. At this time, this was the best stuff that we had that was available to us.

If we went up to Hollywood, maybe we would see The Quick, who were an amazing pop band. Or maybe we would see the Runaways, who were a bunch of snotty-ass girls who were totally rocking. There was no musical compass. What made what we were doing so... I can't say outstanding because all of the people that wanted to kill us—there were these jock cowboy "Hooray for the U.S.A."-types who wanted to bomb the fuck out of everybody—I guess we just stumbled upon something. There was no formula. There was no big book about how your band could become bigger than everybody else, no map from point a to point b, it was just the blind leading the blind.

Brian: What I think is really interesting about how—by the time you guys started Black Flag, as well as all of those other bands—it all almost follows this unconscious idea of the next thing. I mean, I am younger than you guys, and when I was a kid I grew up on seventies hard rock music and was into bands like Aerosmith. And I know from talking to Steven McDonald and a few other people I knew, that you had seen probably every early seventies rock band that I would have been too young to see, all before punk rock started.

So when all of the bands that I liked as a kid started to suck, like from '77 or '78 onward—maybe not really suck but you know what I mean, like when it wasn't as interesting anymore, like Kiss and Aerosmith and Ted Nugent—and all of a sudden here comes this new world of music and you guys were a part of it, and it was just kind of funny how it all started around '77 going into '78.

Keith: I guess we kind of got sucked into a vacuum. When all of these bands started sucking, normally a decent band is good for three or four records.

Some of these bands that you rattled off were on their what, fifth albums?

Brian: Aerosmith *Draw The Line* or Kiss *Love Gun*, perhaps.

Keith: Yeah, but the *Love Gun* album has quite possibly the greatest Kiss song on it, and that would be "Christine Sixteen," which is one of the greatest fucking pop songs ever written. Maybe the scenario with Kiss was that they were paying too much attention to Cheap Trick. The first time I saw Kiss, they opened for Savoy Brown and Manfred Mann's Earth Band. The second time I saw Kiss, they had blown up. They were playing at the Long Beach Arena, they were the middle band slot, and that was Camel, Kiss, and Wishbone Ash.

All of the bills back then were great because you would always see three different bands on a bill together. Nobody cared. You see, one of the things that happened to me over the years was that I just burned out on the punk rock thing where you would go in and all of the bands are like, "Oh boy, another punk rock band." It's kind of like a metal show.

Brian: You mean five bands that all basically sound the same.

Keith: Yeah, they come from the same genre. I saw Graham Central Station at the Whisky a Go-Go opening for Lynyrd Skynyrd. And Lynyrd Skynyrd had just been the opening band on The Who and their Quadrophenia tour in North America. And I got to actually meet all of those guys, and they were ecstatic to be in Hollywood. It was pretty cool. Now that I have talked in circles because this is what I do, I got away from what we were talking about.

Brian: Ha ha… it's okay.

Keith: We just burned out on our heroes. They got too far away from what they were doing and were not doing it in a very creative way. Some of them not even in a good way. I did see a ton of those bands back then, except for Rush which I am glad of. (laughter) I was thankful.

Brian: Dude! I love Rush! Did you see Angel?

Keith: I did see Angel. In fact, my next door neighbor managed Angel for one night. They did a dress rehearsal in downtown L.A., in a place called the Hope Street Theater. And they rocked, they were cool. They were obviously Casablanca Records' good guys as opposed to Casablanca's bad guys, who were Kiss! I love the song "The Tower." That was a good fun song.

Brian: The first two records are good. I love Steven McDonald's story about seeing Angel. His brother told him that they had a choice of seeing two shows one night. One show was The Damned, the other was Angel. And what did they pick? Angel.

Keith: Ha ha ha ha ha ha!!!!

Brian: I love that story. I am actually kind of jealous, because I love The Damned, of course, but I actually think I would have rather gone to see Angel! It's still an entertaining consolation prize.

Keith: Well, that's typical of those brothers. Oh, brother.

Brian: Let me ask about Flag then. If you don't mind.

Keith: I have no problem talking about them, they are some of my favorite people.

I got to reconnect with Chuck Dukowski. When I left Black Flag, I did not like Chuck Dukowski. Chuck Dukowski just got under my skin, rubbed me the wrong way, really irritated me, but also you have to understand that when Chuck the Duke joined the band, he said that we had to start rehearsing and behaving like a real band. And that was the reason why we got into this rehearsal groove. We could rehearse for an hour and then jump in the van and go see AC/DC at the Whisky. Or we would have nothing else to do that night, so we are rehearsing for three or more hours. So it turned into a job. A lot of the adventure was kind of taken away.

So, for years and years I would have horrible thoughts about Chuck Dukowski. And when we got back together to do Flag, I discovered that he is one of the nicest and sweetest \ you are going to meet. He is very opinionated with what he likes, but Chuck is a really great guy.

And just like Steven McDonald, I had always loved Billy [Stevenson]. He would come into my dad's store when he was eight years old. At one point when he started experiencing some growth on his testicles, he would say, "Keith, what am I supposed to be listening to? What music should I listen to?" And we are standing in my dad's store, everyone is gone so I can play whatever I want to play on the radio, and I am listening to Cheap Trick. And I said, "Billy? This is a good place for you to start." (laughter) Obviously they made an impact on him, listen to the Descendents. These guys are like my brothers. We argue and fight and have our differences but so be it. This is life.

Brian: There was some forward motion after your lawsuit in reference to reissuing Black Flag material and nothing seemed to happen. Can you elaborate on any of this?

Keith: I am not going to mention any names, I am just going to say that three of us got in a room. It was almost decided for us by one of the three guys that we were going to contact Spot, who has some master tapes. Spot was never paid for the work that he did, and if he was paid, it was fucking dog food and cat food. So apparently Spot had held on to the master tapes and the idea was, we were not going to run around asking permission from all of the people who had participated in this music. It would have turned into a clusterfuck.

One of the three guys said that we were meant to gather all of this stuff and then go to everyone to explain what we were doing.

One of the things that had happened that bummed me out is that there are all of these authoritative figures that think they know the history of the band, that think they know all of the personalities of the band, they think they know who is cool and who is not cool, and there was all of this talk about me like, "Well, Keith Morris he tried to rip everybody off." And you know, I am not going to respond to that. And when I am talking about these people, these are people on the internet. Now everyone can chime in, thanks to the internet, and it got ugly. We found out the name Black Flag belongs to a Japanese clothing company. (laughter) So we got the four bars. We had to give that up in the lawsuit. We never had the name so we didn't have to give it up.

So in the process, two of us told the third member that we were going to go out and play. Me, Chuck, Billy, and Stephen [Egerton] from the Descendents went out and played the *Nervous Breakdown* EP and there was great energy there. People lost their minds, so we decided to go out and do it. We knew we would be stupid to not pursue this, and we earned the right to do whatever the fuck we wanted to do. Anyways, we won the lawsuit. I am going to get into more details in my second book, I have been asked to write a second book. I am extremely fortunate because the people who put out my book didn't expect my book to get past the first pressing.

Brian: When the Melvins went on tour the last time, we got a hold of your book on a tape, but it was someone else reading it, not you, and we listened to the whole thing. So I learned a little above it your father and his bait shop. Was there really a rift between you and your father about you not wanting to step into the family business? Also, was that your first job?

Keith: My first job was having a paper route. Which I failed miserably, because who wants to deliver papers in the rain, or the fog? All of that fun stuff, all of the lousy weather that comes to the beach instead of the sun. I also, at one point, swept the floor of the barbershop across the street from my dad's store before I started to really work for my dad. I would sweep it twice on Saturdays and I would get paid fifty cents each time I had swept the floor. And then I went to work for my dad.

In that process, I learned how to deal with the California Department of Fish and Game. I learned to do accounting, and dealing with the Bank of America on Friday afternoons and Monday afternoons—Friday afternoon being when I deposited all of the money from the week and having enough change on hand, and on Monday afternoon after school, depositing all of the money that was made over the weekend, because we would have pretty busy weekends. So I was learning all of this, and I was also in charge of inventory and ordering and filling things that were sold, shipping and receiving.

At one point, my dad said, "There is no one that I could hire to fill your shoes." So I was allowed carte blanche, I could make my own hours. But I had to be there x amount of hours. And when I had my scholarship for the Art Center in Pasadena removed by one of my teachers at MiraCosta out in Manhattan Beach, I thought that I would cruise through some classes at El Camino Real community college. And while I was going to junior college, I was working a minimum of thirty or forty hours a week. While I was still going to school. At that time, I was getting paid sixty dollars a week. That was my cash. Granted, I was given a charge card to put gas in the car. I was actually allowed to take money out of the cash register. Which I never knew.

For years and years, I would be shifty and seedy and looking around to make sure that no one could see me removing the cash from the cash register or selling something and not putting all of the money in the cash register. Just being a really shitty little slimeball. And I would eventually be told by my dad when I sat with him and said, "Look I probably embezzled about sixty or seventy thousand dollars." He said, "No no no, because it is your business. The cash register was your bank." Yeah.

Brian: You weren't expecting that.

Keith: I was not expecting that. That was completely mind boggling to me. Being self-employed, working those kind of jobs. Being in a band is being self-employed—it's not a nine-to-five—it could be a six thirty in the morning till six thirty the next morning kind of thing, depending on if you are partying, depending on how long your drive is, depending on how much time you have for a load in and how much you have for a sound check and how much time you are allowed on stage—because I love the forty five minutes to fifty minutes amount of time. Because of the internet and everyone wanting instant access and not having a lengthy attention span, it is just "get the fuck up there and blow up and get the fuck off" and "see you later, hope you had fun."

Brian: After you left, how long did your dad have his business?

Keith: You know, for years I lost track of my dad. Because when I left, we were not getting along, we were not on good terms. It's like hating the authoritative figures, and he was always the one who would be, "Well, how much money do you have in the bank? Are you keeping your nose clean?" My friends were all just heroin addicts and drunks and fucking cokeheads, just lowlife scumbag motherfuckers. So he was always coming from that angle, coming from a very conservative angle. Maybe he was caring, but it was never encouraging.

Whereas my mom, my mom was like, "Go out and see the world and fucking kick ass and have fun and party and do your thing. And don't fuck with anybody. Don't fuck with anybody."

Brian: Cool. So let's talk about self-employment. You have been a singer off and on for a long time.

Keith: That's a misnomer calling or referring to me as a singer. I gotta have some loud wild crazy musical garbage going on behind me. For years and years and years, we didn't even know what a stage monitor was. So the lead vocalist had to scream and yell as loud as the guys playing behind him. To this day I really don't care about doing a sound check. It is what it is.

Brian: How are your ears?

Keith: I have got two wasp nests duct taped to each side of my head. Just wrapped with duct tape. I am ringing and buzzing right now.

I have to sometimes sleep with the TV on, it's so loud. I think Bob Mould does the same thing.

Brian: It seemed like every Circle Jerks album came out on a different label. I am going to assume that money was tight because it was in the pre-internet, pre-Epitaph, pre-actual industry here where people will actually make money doing that. So you guys along with Black Flag, Bad Brains, DOA, and a million other bands are touring. Is this what you are doing as a living during the eighties?

Keith: Well, we would work odd jobs. The song "Beverly Hills Century City" was based on all of us working in Beverly Hills and Century City. We worked for a law firm where we were just filing papers in a massive lawsuit. We would party there on the weekends after the legal people left, we would invite all of our friends down there.

We also worked for a real estate firm that sold timeshares (laughter) Yeah. We did goofy shit like that. I also bartended, I bussed tables…

Brian: You had Chuck Biscuits and Earl Liberty in the band.

Keith: That lineup was one of my favorite lineups. Chuck Biscuits is undeniably like a brilliant drummer, a pummeling drummer. He is going to beat it into your head, he is playing with tree trunks for drumsticks. And he had this thing where if somebody threw something at him—because people would throw things at us and if he got hit by a bottle or if he got hit by a can and if he saw who threw it—he had the uncanny ability to just fucking rocket the drumstick right at the person who tossed whatever they tossed at him.

Brian: Why did you not record anything with those guys, other than that *Repo Man* thing?

Keith: Would that be the missed opportunity? That lineup was great and we spent so much time touring. I mean, we would go out on a tour and leave in our van and we wouldn't come back for four months. And we would come back and we had been in each other's faces for all of that time.

Brian: You need to get the fuck away from everyone!

Keith: Yeah, I need a vacation! I need to get away from this. So getting back to your question, one recording with Earl and Chuck, for the *Repo Man* soundtrack. Where we didn't even have Chuck Biscuits playing drums, he was playing acoustic guitar, playing to a drum machine. That's just one of those odd scenarios that is just the Circle Jerks—whatever happens, happens. I think throughout the history of the Circle Jerks we might have had three or four managers. And some of them weren't really real managers. We had one manager, she managed the Germs. And that had to be a nightmare headache experience. We had one manager who was a sound man, who because he knew all of these people in Hollywood, he knew who to talk to. We had some stop gap managers who actually were a part of the industry, but you know.

So we had one recording with two amazing musicians. And then right after Earl left to be born again, right after the end of one of our tours that was just... everybody was in each other's faces. Earl at one point, we were done in Florida, Earl left the van with all of the windows rolled down and left the van running parked in a parking lot in a supermarket and I just happened to be walking across the lot. And there is the van. And I hear the motor running, but where is the guy who is driving the van? This is not supposed to happen. I got in the van and I drove back to the venue. And that was when Earl came fuming playing the role of Godzilla wanting to beat the fuck out of King Kong. That was Earl's epiphany of him not wanting to do this anymore.

BOB BERT

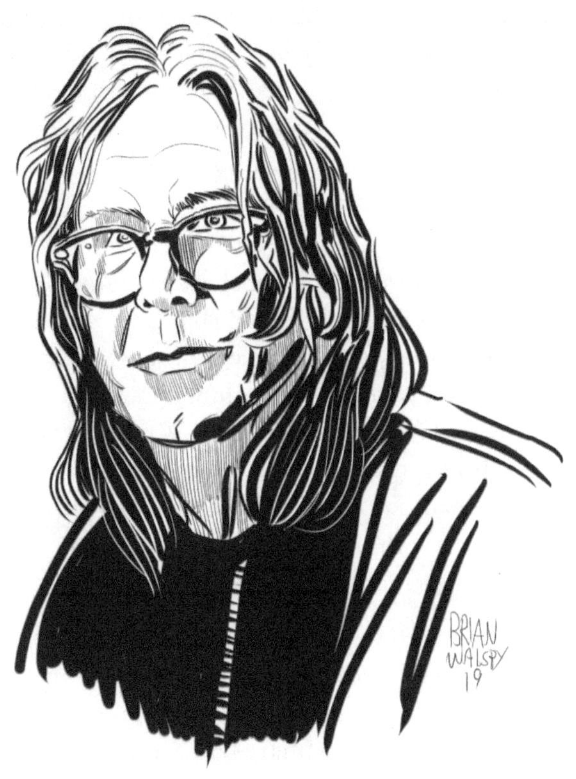

As usual, I met Bob Bert in the flesh during a Melvins tour. This tour had Jon Spencer's new solo band opening up for the Melvins. Bob was playing "metal," a metal and aluminum-based drum kit. It was a throwback to the metal he used to play with Jon back in the band Pussy Galore. Bob was very nice and immediately friendly and approachable. The band was totally winging it, with very little practice under their belt when they showed up for their leg of the tour. You wouldn't have noticed any of that, they were whipped into shape in no time.

Bob, of course, has a very long history as a musician, as well as a music fan. He has roots going back to hanging out at CBGB's and seeing tons of weird bands. He played drums in bands like the aforementioned Pussy Galore and Sonic Youth (that is him drumming on *Bad Moon Rising.*) He spent a lot of time in the Chrome Cranks, and besides playing with Jon these days, he also backs up Lydia Lunch and has a cool project with Kid Congo Powers (Gun Club, the Cramps) and Mick Collins (The Gories) called Wolfmanhattan Project.

Bob has a book out that is recommended[1]. Like Eugene Robinson before him, I somehow thought that Bob was also on more of the self-employed side but he revealed that he didn't do that very much, and it was only for a very short time when he was able to live off of his drumming and the royalties that came with that. He worked for Andy Warhol in the seventies doing screen printing and he is an artist himself! So he can slide by on that alone, as far as I am concerned. He even commissioned me to draw a few things for him. That was cool.

Bob: I grew up in New Jersey about ten miles outside of Manhattan and my father owned a few liquor stores so I grew up clerking in the liquor stores. But I have had every job that you could think of and I have hardly ever really been self-employed, even though it might look that way. I have had every job, from working at the liquor store on and off for years, and a lot of times I did that mainly to get health insurance. And then I have worked in record stores, I have worked in a Doc Marten store, I worked in a book factory. The last real job that I had was working for this company called SST. Which has nothing to do with the record label but it is this equipment band rental rehearsal recording studio, which

---

1 *I'm Just The Drummer: My Time behind Sonic Youth, Pussy Galore, Chrome Cranks & BB Gun Magazine* by Bob Bert https://hozacrecords.com/bob-bert/

was right outside of Hoboken.

I think the first day that I had worked there I was delivering something to Bjork's house, and the van I was driving Norah Jones around and all kinds of stuff like that. It was a pretty cool place. Everyone rehearsed there, from Alicia Keys to Black Sabbath to The Rolling Stones. It was a really interesting job. Sometimes it was a drag schlepping these assholes around, you know. And actually thinking to myself, "they are being such dicks and I have been in better bands then they were." (laughter)

Brian: How long ago was that?

Bob: That was after 9/11. I worked there a few days a week. Part of the reason that I did it was for the health insurance.

Brian: playing in a succession of bands alone wasn't enough to pay all of the bills?

Bob: Oh, no. Not at all. There were a couple of years in the eighties when Pussy Galore was doing well and I was starting to get some money from Sonic Youth because they were getting bigger at the time. I got by for, like, two years maybe, without working but I wasn't living high on the hog by any means. I was scraping by. It was cool not to have to work for a little while.

Brian: Did you quit any jobs that you had in order to go on tour?

Bob: You know, I had no plans on being a musician. I am in my sixties and I was around when the Beatles were on Ed Sullivan and stuff, so I took drum lessons when I was twelve. And then, when I moved out of my house at eighteen, I was going to lots of shows and I was a big music fan and luckily I was around to see like the New York Dolls in 1973 and catch on to the whole CBGB's/Max's scene in 1975. The first time I went to CBGB's was in 1975 and it was Television opening for Patti Smith and there was fifteen people there. So I just started going there four times a week and discovered this new world.

I went to a school of visual arts because I had wanted to be an artist. I worshipped Andy Warhol. So I learned how to be a silkscreen printer and I became a fine arts silk screen printer and I did that for like fifteen years, mostly through the Sonic Youth and Pussy Galore time and I ended up actually printing Andy Warhol's artwork up until he died in 1987.

Brian: Oh man. How did you meet those sort of people?

Bob: When I was in high school *Ziggy Stardust* came out and Lou Reed's *Transformer* album came out. And T. Rex and Roxy Music, I started getting into all of that stuff. I was fourteen in 1969, that is when I started smoking pot and experimenting with psychedelic drugs and stuff. In my high school art class we took a field trip to the Whitney Museum to see an Andy Warhol retrospective. And that was a big influence, and around the same time I went to see the film *Trash*. I don't know, I was just really into that stuff. People always say stuff like, "Oh, I wish I was around during that time. I would love to be involved in that Factory scene," and I was only off by a few years. But luckily I got interested in the CBGB's scene.

Brian: You timed it pretty well. I gotta say, it took a long time for me to understand Andy Warhol but I always liked the Velvet Underground. I thought they were the backdrop for that scene but it was sort of the other way around.

Bob: Right. I learned how to silkscreen print and I got into working for these places that ran print editions. Then I was looking for a job, and I knew about this place—it wasn't the actual Factory, it was this guy named Rupert Smith. That is where they did all of Warhol's printing—and so I just went there one day and showed them my portfolio and they hired me. It was great because at first it was in Rupert's loft and I was working the night shift by myself or with one assistant so, you know, I was helping myself to some things once in awhile. (laughter)

But then they got this whole big building right off of Canal Street so it was three floors of screens being shot, screens being printed. We ran off all of his editions and they would come and bring canvas over like portraits of just faces in the background painted over and we would screen on top of it. All the stuff that has camouflage in it, I was part of that. Those really gigantic Last Supper paintings, I was involved with that.

In fact, I just went to see his recent retrospective at the Whitney and also I went to the museum when I was on tour with Lydia Lunch in Pittsburgh, and there were so many things, "Hey, I did that."

Brian: We went to the museum in Pittsburgh a while ago on tour, so I guess we saw all of your stuff without knowing it.

Bob: Yeah. Totally. And they were flexible too. I was able to take off time and go on tour and come back. I really, really enjoyed it and it was fun doing that art. The only downside was breathing in all of those ink fumes and stuff. I was careful, I wore a mask, but that stuff is pretty brutal.

Brian: Did anyone get sick from that?

Bob: No. It was very gay, so some of the people I worked with died of AIDS. In fact, Rupert died from AIDS. Three or four people. But I am still friends with some of the people I met that worked there. Everyone seems fine. That is where I met Matt Verta-Ray from the band Speedball Baby. He has a recording studio here in New York, that is where I met him.

I was a silkscreen printer for a long time, but once Warhol died in '87, I didn't do it again. Going into the nineties, I don't remember what kind of jobs I had, I probably worked at the liquor store here and there. I was touring with the Chrome Cranks a lot, and I had my own band, Bewitched, and I was playing with the Action Swingers a little bit, but my decade was the eighties. The first half was Sonic Youth and the second was Pussy Galore. And then the nineties weren't that great. And in the early 2000s, my wife's health started failing. I inherited some money because my father died. And from about 2006 on, I guess I was basically taking care of my wife, I didn't tour or go anywhere for a good ten or eleven years. She passed away in 2012. We bought a condo in 1990 in Hoboken—I sold it two years after she died and I made a ton of money, which is why I don't have to work now. I am still living off of that money and it allowed me to tour like crazy with Lydia for the past six years without a job.

Brian: Wow. That is an intense story. I guess that is why you have been so busy lately.

Bob: Yeah.

Brian: How did you get back in touch with Jon Spencer and pick up that metal kit again? I know that you are playing the metal in Jon's band and not the drums, but when we met you on the Melvins tour, we were all looking at your metal stuff and wondering if it was the same stuff from back in the Pussy Galore days.

Bob: No. (laughter) Jon went and recorded the solo album that I don't play on that we are promoting now and then all of a sudden he started showing up to my shows and stuff. We were always friends—we always saw each other out a lot—so he just asked me and I listened to the record and really dug it, so I said yeah. When I first joined Pussy Galore, I was living in Hoboken. Back then, there was actually a junkyard in Hoboken where there were a lot of gas tanks piled to the sky.

I went through about four or five in the period of Pussy Galore. Those things get beat up and have to be replaced. We did a one show reunion in 2011 with Yo La Tengo. The gas tank that I was using on tour with the Melvins is from then. But everywhere we go—we are flying to Japan on Monday—I am bringing my metal snare kit over but they have to have everything else ready for me. When we travel we always have to have something arranged.

Brian: Since you are playing with actual hammers and wearing gloves, was that something that took a while to get used to?

Bob: Yeah. Everyone has been asking me, "how is your wrist?" It's fine, you know. It's not that bad. Even with my custom made ear plugs, it seems like my ears are ringing more just from hitting that stuff.

I don't know if I will be doing it for several years, I also have an album coming out that I made with Mick Collins and Kid Congo Powers, the Wolfmanhattan Project, and I want to do some support for that. I also have my book.

Brian: Can you talk about this book ?

Bob: My book is not a memoir, it is basically a photo book. I took a lot of photos of the music scene before I was even involved in it. And also, I took a camera on tour with me on the very first Sonic Youth tour and various Pussy Galore tours. The book sort of starts off with me writing a couple of little essays about me growing up and stuff but it is mostly photos. And then it goes up to the nineties. When my wife was alive we had a fanzine called BB Gun, so there are a lot of photos and interview excerpts from there. I am really psyched, it came out well. It is going to be 8″×10″, lots of color photos, and I think anyone that picks it up will dig it. In a way, it is like my whole life.

Jeff Pinkus

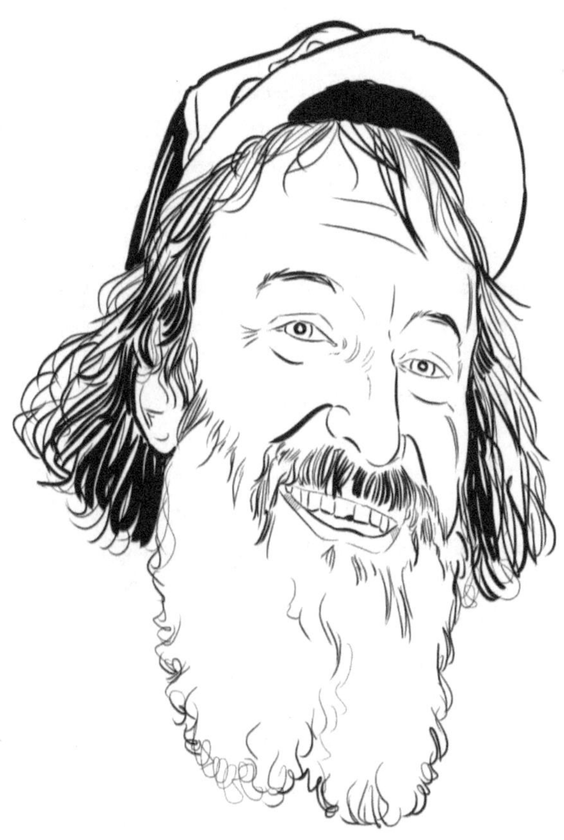

I met Jeff Pinkus when he joined the Melvins. We toured together a bunch and I grew quite fond of him. Besides being a nice guy who was whip smart, he was also definitely a total weirdo in the best sense of that word. Coming from the Butthole Surfers and being whisked into that band at a very young age for ten years is also pretty interesting. I just figured he might have some stories and of course he did. Settle back for a nice interview, and get the popcorn ready.

Jeff Pinkus was by far the most social person I have ever seen in the Melvins, ha ha. Take it away, Jeff.

♬

Brian: On the second tour that I went out with you playing bass in the Melvins, you revealed a fondness for Marginal Man and you also let it be known that you remembered seeing the Atlanta band Neon Christ a lot. I didn't even know that you had that sort of background before you joined the Butthole Surfers.

Jeff: Yeah. I talk to Randy (DuTeau, singer of Neon Christ) now and then and I bring up those guys because they were like the house band—them and DDT opened for everybody. And DDT were also part of my link to the Butthole Surfers. But I was playing in bands and I left home kind of early and traveled around. I went up to D.C. when I was fifteen during the summertime and kind of floated in and out of my parents' house for a couple of months. I had a great childhood, but I left early because it was one of those "if you can't live by the rules in our house, you can't live here" things and I said, "Oh, okay."

I left home on fairly good terms. It wasn't pretty at first. My dad came down for me downtown at the Metroplex—he drove all of the way down there—and people were saying, "Pinkus, your dad is here."

He said, "You know I can take you home right now," and I said, "Yeah." And he said, "Alright. Well, I am not going to, but take care of yourself." (laughter) So I was living downtown. I spent a lot of time in Downtown Atlanta, I lived in a warehouse on Edgewood St, I lived with a bunch of people in an apartment. I played in a bunch of bands back then that no one would have ever heard of. I got turned on to the Butthole Surfers. Me and my friend went down to their show for the first time on blue gel acid. I remember the blue gel was around a lot back then. I saw

Flipper, Black Flag, Butthole Surfers, and a bunch of bands on it. But I went down there and my mind was pretty blown. Terence [Smart] was playing bass for them and it was an amazing show.

So I started listening to them and they came back through with a different bass player. We didn't have any money to get in and we were sitting outside and we got somebody's Vespa and we got some of the grease off of the Vespa and put it on our wrists where everybody would put a stamp. We just waited for everybody to come out between the bands and we went in with everyone else. But we went to see the band and it was Trevor [Malcolm] on the bass and he was playing the tuba. And I remember I didn't like him playing bass nearly as much because he actually used a capo to play the song "Cherub," which is really not a hard song to play. I wasn't very impressed.

He was only in the band for six months and according to them, especially now, they don't blame him for leaving the band because as King [Coffey] put it, "We didn't even have any furniture,we were living outside of Athens, Georgia." They spun a globe and basically it landed on Georgia. They went there because REM were close by. They went to Winterville, Georgia, and then they came down to Atlanta. They had Kramer in the band instead of Trevor, just to do a tour. It was their first tour of Europe. He had already been there in a band called Shockabilly and so when the Butts went over there, everyone thought it was Kramer's new band.

I came in after they parted ways with him. They were in Atlanta, and there was this thing downtown. I was living in an apartment with seven people. I had a pay phone that was down by the convenience store on the corner and I would give that number out to people if they needed to contact me. I went down there and it was actually Jimbo [Yongue] from DDT who was also in Daddy Longhead with me. He suggested me to them to join the band when they were looking for a bass player. I was told to go out by the pay phone and I thought it was Jimbo fucking with me but it was actually Gibby [Haynes] saying, "Yeah, come on down and play," and I said, "Yeah, whatever man." And I didn't realize it was really Gibby, but it was.

I brought a pint bottle of Heaven Hill whiskey and went over there and played Blue Cheer and Black Sabbath songs with King and Paul [Leary], and played "Mexican Caravan" because I knew that one, and a couple of other ones. And Paul said, "This is cool. Do you want to go to Europe?" And I said, "Sure." And at the end of that tour he said that I could stay in the band for as long as I wanted. So that was my tryout. (laughter)

Brian: So you were in!

Jeff: Yeah, it was pretty perfect. At the time I was homeless, I didn't mind leaving my girlfriend behind, I didn't have many possessions to leave behind. I left behind a record collection and a bass amp.

Brian: How old were you when this was going on?

Jeff: I was seventeen when I first started practicing with them. I just turned eighteen when I played the first show. My first show was January 10th of 1986.

Brian: So these guys are older than you and sort of like your mentors?

Jeff: It is hard to say mentors because I didn't really have any mentors back then. Watching people like Randy, he was more of a mentor to me. Gibby and Paul were ten years older than me and King is about five years older than me. And Teresa [Nervosa] was not with us at this point, she had left the band.

And so this girl named Cabbage [Kytha Gernatt] started jamming with us, and she almost accidentally in the band. She ended up leaving the band. At the end she just quit doing her laundry or wearing clean clothes, she started to get kind of red and lumpy and stinky, and acting a little weird. We tried to drive her to an airport but ended up stopping at a bus station in Alabama and dropped her off there. And then, at that point, we were a four piece. And then Teresa came back to the band.

I came from Atlanta and now we were sleeping on people's floors and living on the road. Austin was our home base.

Brian: You joined this noteworthy band that was pretty bizarre at a very young age and now here you are traveling with them…

Jeff: Yeah, I didn't know how popular they were.

Brian: When did things settle down enough for everyone to go, "Hey I need my own place to live at?"

Jeff: Man, that took awhile. We rented a house with a studio and all of us lived there, except for King, who was going to school. I lived in the master bedroom closet, and we had a mattress for King in the jamming room, and Paul had built a loft over the studio room, and Gibby had a loft in the hallway. So we didn't make a living doing it, we actually kept all of the money in one pile. We all ate together, we did everything together which was the only way that we could make it work. I think it might have been a lot tougher on those guys than it was for me, being ten years younger. I was looking at everything wide-eyed.

When we started to actually make money, my way of doing things was not to eat better, it was to eat two Big Macs instead of one Big Mac. I gained some weight there.

Brian: From what I understand, Paul and Gibby were accounting majors?

Jeff: Oh yeah, both of them. Paul's dad was the dean of the business school at Trinity University. He named Gibby the accounting student of the year. He was also the captain of the basketball team down there. Paul dropped out with, I think, two semesters left before he graduated which didn't make his dad very happy, I am sure.

Brian: Did the business savvy of Paul and Gibby come in handy during these years?

Jeff: I will tell you the first lesson that Paul ever gave me in business on the road. When we were asked if we wanted to get a guarantee or do a door deal and get a back end off of it if so many people showed up, Paul said, "Business 101: money in my pocket is better than money in yours." So we took the guarantee, we didn't want to chance anything. But yeah that definitely came into play. We got ripped off for a lot of money, so even with that business training, it didn't necessarily help.

Brian: There was the whole lawsuit brouhaha between the band and Corey Rusk, the head of Touch And Go Records. Were you in the band during all of that?

Jeff: That's a part of the whole thing and what it's about, making it self-employed and trying to run a business. It is really tough in the music business when you are trying to be on that level as well, because nobody wants you to make money. Most bands don't stick around for thirty years. They are around for two, three, four, five years tops, make their money, and then move on to another project. So people don't like seeing a band go from a minor label to a major label. The whole idea of selling out is really a strange concept when you are a musician and you want to just eat food and stuff.

Brian: It is less strange to the musician and more important to the people outside of it who have nothing to do with it.

Jeff: Right, Yeah. And when we signed the contract with a major label we had full control of what came out of it, that was part of our thing. And that is what the independent music scene is about, having full control of your stuff. We were just able to make money off of it for once. Corey treated us good when we were with it, I was involved with it on the periphery because there wasn't much going on in the band at that point in time. I was not called in to talk to a lawyer for a deposition—they didn't take a deposition from me—but I was involved in it as far as getting paid and not getting paid with the Touch And Go stuff. Basically, what it boiled down to at the end was, the judge in his words quoted Yogi Bear and said, "A handshake deal is only worth the paper it is written on."

Basically, it was a handshake deal between the two parties instead of a contract. Corey didn't like the band's decision, obviously, because he burned all of the Butthole Surfers' stuff.

Brian: Like how people in Alabama burned Beatles records after John Lennon said they were bigger than Jesus Christ?

Jeff: Exactly. He gave us a lot of hatred, obviously. As far as me leaving the band, those guys have never ripped me off—those guys have been nothing but solid to me. Even through those times. I have no bad things to say about them as people. The thing that got me was who we should play with, or what direction we should go into. There was management that was pulling us towards stadium shows which I wasn't very keen on. We just finished one that didn't work out. Well, it wasn't a stadium tour, but we worked on a tour with the Mighty Mighty Bosstones—they booked us a tour with them—it didn't work out well.

It lasted two shows. We canceled the tour. I remember me and Paul went out there to check them out, to try and be nice to them, and these guys just started dancing. And me and Paul just looked at each other and said, "What is going on here?" (laughter) At the end they made a press statement that said that all of The Butthole Surfers were jerks, except for me. And I was really upset because I didn't want to be the nice guy, because I didn't like them either.

After that, our manager wanted to go through his tour plan, which would have made money. But this is where my integrity showed up. I didn't like it, but it was to open for Mötley Crüe with John Corabi singing. Then it was Type O Negative, the Ramones, and us. I didn't really dig that because people that were already our fans were alienated enough by who we were playing with on these tours. And when I was asked what I would rather do, I told them I would rather play with the Meat Puppets or Ween. I remember Tom [Bunch] the manager telling me that that would be the difference between playing stadiums or playing theaters. I wasn't looking at the money side so much, I just didn't really like these tours that alienated our people.

No one wanted to get into a room and write songs together, and Gibby was not in very good shape at that point in time, so he wasn't very productive. There was even talk of doing something different without him at one point. I probably said some things in that meeting that probably alienated myself away from the other guys, too. So it was just more of a mutual departure, it just wasn't working out. But I am very glad that I remained friends with them and when they started playing again in 2008, Gibby kind of laughed maniacally and said, "My plan is coming to fruition," because he was trying to get Paul in on it. Paul agreed to do it and we played some shows, so it's good to be on that kind of level with those guys again, and the past is the past. I am really happy to be good friends with all of them.

Brian: Awesome. What about what came afterwards? You spent a lot of time doing other musical projects.

Jeff: This part is good for anyone who plays music. When we released records, we didn't have credit on any of the album sleeves that said who did what. People thought that we were extremely mysterious but the truth is we were kind of lazy and we didn't have any way to do the typeset stuff, we just sent in the pictures and let them finish it out. People thought we were mysterious about not having information on who was in the band. Well, that didn't really help me a lot when I left the band. I thought, "Oh, well I have been in this band for almost ten years, people will definitely come out and see what I am doing."

Well, no one knew who I was. (laughter) it didn't really help out too much and I had to start from scratch again. I had a kid around that time as well. So it was taxing, I did have a studio in my garage because I used the money from Lollapalooza to buy a house. That is when I put a down payment on a house out in the country in San Marcos, Texas, outside of Austin. I lived there for ten years. I kept my band going, I recorded some bands, I got a job at a ranch and worked as a handyman carpenter out there. I was also doing sound at clubs. I was also a part owner of Emo's when they opened up. That was in '93, I was still in the Butts at that point and so I would do sound out there as well for extra dough. I sold my shares out of that.

I felt entitled at that point in my career. I felt like I should have a step up on people but that is when I realized, unfortunately, that I had to start from scratch. You are only as good as your last record. All of those things came into play, it was a rude awakening.

It put me in scramble mode for years, trying to make ends meet. You really feel entitled when you have some success and I see it now in other people, you really, really lose a little touch with reality. I think it is really good to be humbled, and looking back at it, I wouldn't change anything. I definitely have had all kinds of doors open for me when other ones were shut, and you just have to keep flowing with it. And if you fight it, you are going to lose every time.

Brian: You are hustling with the experience of everything that you have learned.

Jeff: When I had my divorce, which was amicable, we sold the house and I took my share of the money and went to Arizona and went to audio school in 2000. I already had been recording but I wanted to learn the physics of recording and the physics of sound. Things like that. And I got really into that and learned a lot about it. A lot of it is probably outdated now but it was a big investment in something that I had wanted to do.

Brian: The last musical project that you did—the one that not only got you some attention, but ended up being how you met Buzz and Dale—was the band Honky.

Jeff: I met them when Daddy Longhead was going on, it was actually the drummer who introduced me to them, I never really heard them until *Stoner Witch*. That was the first time I had heard the band. But yeah, Honky did shows with Altamont and that was back when Carson [Vester] was in the band, pre-Bobby [Landgraf]. I kept in touch with Dale especially, and when they came through I said, "If you ever need a second bass player, let me know. I will gladly play rhythm." And I guess they kept that in the back of their head. I played a Honky show opening up for Down and Buzz came out to the show. It was in Orange County and he was coming out to watch me, and they needed someone to play bass because Jared (Warren) was going to have a baby, it was on their 30th anniversary tour. Buzz came out and said that Honky was like ZZ Top mixed with Van Halen. I think he wanted to come out to see if I could sing and play, just to watch me play before he asked me anything.

So I was very happy that they did ask me to play. I was very happy about that. I thought that tour might be it for me but we recorded a lot of stuff and it was fun. And then they asked me to come back and do a run. They asked about Honky opening and without talking to anyone, I said sure and that meant Dale would be playing drums. Bobby became the guitar tech on that tour and we did some of our fastest shows. And then after that, they got Steven [McDonald] in the band. And then after about two years the double bass thing came up. It was mainly about recording at first, but the shows came into play.

This is the mellowest band I have ever been in as far as touring goes, nobody gets upset with anybody.... unless someone's hula hoop gets stolen or screws up at the border (not going to name any names there.) But other than that, nobody raises their voice.

Brian: I couldn't help but notice on the first tour you were on, when Coady Willis was on it—it was good of course, two drummers and all—but for some reason, on the second tour you went on, when it was the three of you, it felt like you kind of came into your own.

Jeff: Well, thanks. The thing is, I didn't really know what my place was when I first started playing, it was really easy to fit in because of the two drummers, because everyone is watching them. I was just providing the low end and didn't really figure that I was a featured part of it as much as I was filling in for Jared. And on the second tour, I realized that I was a third of the stage. And on the first couple of shows I was a little confused about what my role should be. I kind of restrained myself a little I think. I didn't want to distract people for them coming to see Buzz, and I couldn't have been more wrong about how Buzz felt about that—that Buzz and Dale *wanted* me to be myself and to do what I do.

And when I felt more comfortable with that, that is what I did. I love the fact that they encouraged that.

Brian: And you said my favorite quote ever about Buzz and being involved in the Melvins universe, something like, "we are pretty lucky to be in this position where we can all benefit from this guy's obsessive qualities."

Jeff: Yeah, totally. But it's the truth. If someone is willing to drive the car, and to drive it with such care, and to carefully route everything that they are doing, and you just get to go along for the ride they are smart about it, they aren't trying to be rockstars about it—you know, vans instead of buses, hotel rooms instead of sleeping in a bunk on a bus. It's a lot smarter, and being with someone who has taken that care is definitely a treat. And it does make you soft. (laughter)

Brian: Your banjo-only solo record is something I really liked a lot[1]. As a representation of you and your personality and your songs, I think it is a really good representation.

Jeff: Thank you. My kid said, "Dad, that is the most *you* that you have ever sounded."

I think when I listened back to it after it was mastered, I laughed and I cried and I couldn't believe that I put all of myself out there, but it is definitely more *me* than anything I have done. I was encouraged by my friend and banjo mentor Danny Barnes. When it is all said and done, whether people like it or not, it is all me and for the people that I have been losing left and right as I have gotten older, when I am gone, I love the fact that if someone wants to have a cup of coffee with me in the morning and put on one of my songs in the five minutes they got before they have to go to work, that I could be in their kitchen and play a banjo song to start their day. It's nice to be able to leave something that is that personal around, whether it is a piece of crap or not. (laughter)

---

1 *Keep on the Grass* by JD Pinkus [https://jdpinkus.bandcamp.com/album/keep-on-the-grass]

LORI BARBERO

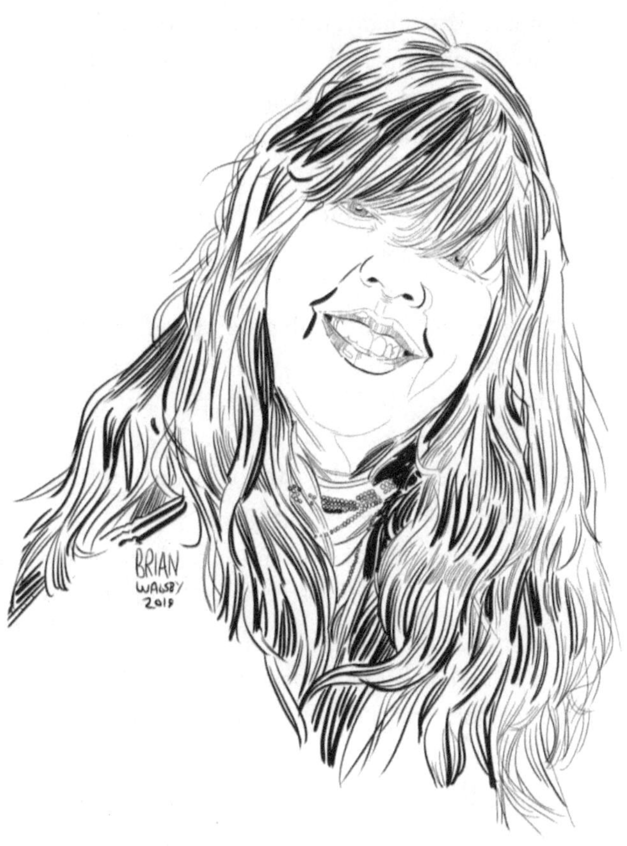

Over the years through the job I have had with the Melvins, I have gotten to know Lori Barbero a little bit and she is a really cool person with a big heart. I think most people will recognize her as the drummer for the band Babes In Toyland. Not too surprisingly, as it turned out, Lori was a behind-the-scenes person in Minneapolis for ages, and has done a lot of neat stuff and has A LOT of interesting stories under her belt.

Brian: I am going to guess that you really aren't much of a nine-to-five type of regular job person.

Lori: No. I have never worked a nine-to-five job in my entire life. I am very fortunate. Back many, many years ago, my friend's family owned a printing company and I worked at the front desk I think for maybe two days. And I quit. I think it might have been one or two days but I know that I didn't make it even a week.

I am just not that personality. I need to be a bartender, I need to be a deejay, I need to be a musician. Right now I am organizing a big flea market that happens once a month, and I organize that and I am not getting paid for it, it is a labor of love at the local VFW that I bartend at. It's becoming very popular and successful. I think about that, about how I have been able to survive without taking a nine-to-five job. I respect people that can do it, but there is no way in the world that I could ever do it. I never have. Literally, I lasted one or two days and that was probably back in the early eighties. That is how long ago it was.

So I have learned how to survive with just wheeling and dealing. I sell things, I have had antique stores, I sell things off of Craigslist, eBay, flea markets… .

Brian: I jumped off the cliff eight or nine years ago. Eight years of not having a real job, and now it has gone so far and I am too old, that there is no way that I could go back to working in a kitchen.

Lori: Some people in that situation are like octopuses, with eight arms feeling everything around them, and they make those choices and they are really smart. People have said to me, "Oh Lori, you are so smart, you could do anything, you could do art, you could do great art." You know, I am planning on doing a coffee table book with all of my thousands of photographs but right now I am just concentrating on getting rid of stuff because I bought land in Yucca Valley. I bought two and a half acres and hopefully we will build a house out there. I want to sell this monster that I have—I have a four thousand square foot house in Minneapolis with a four car garage. I don't need ninety five percent of this stuff, or want it.

Brian: I like having as little stuff as possible because it gives me the illusion that I could pick up and leave if I wanted to.

Lori: Minneapolis is getting too big for me. It's turning into this metropolis, they are tearing down residential homes and building condos, just like what they are doing everywhere. Even in my little tiny neighborhood where I live, it used to be called Crack Alley. I bought my house and people were like, "where do you live?" They just couldn't believe I bought a house in this neighborhood twenty six years ago.

I just turned fifty eight last week and I tell you—I love maturing, it really doesn't bother me. I don't fear it because my life has been great and it's really cool getting older . It is just more calming, and you know, I got my house which is my nest egg. When I sell it, I can do whatever I want. I mean, I am not going to get millions of dollars or anything but I have nothing else but the stuff in it. And I have that land. Which is a lot! I own my house, and there are not that many people that own their house in the United States.

And so I was lucky. Well, not lucky, I just really concentrated on just making sure I was secure somehow because I don't have an IRA. I don't have a 401K.

Brian: It sounds like you were smart and lived within your means and was careful with money which is what most artistic and creative people tend to do. Certainly most of the people I have talked to for this.

Lori: You have to be smart with the money you get in that situation. I don't know if you know this, but they have done brain scans of artists—you know, people that do art for a living—and people that have a nine-to five-job, and that the two brains are way different. And I don't know if you are born into it and you just can't *not* do it, or if it changes as you create, as you change your life. That I don't know, I haven't gotten that far into it but it is just how it is.

Brian: For me it has turned into a trade where I can make money, but it is also always something I just have to do.

I played music for a long time and it was successful, in terms of working with some talented people and playing some good stuff, but a long time ago it was obvious that drawing and making art was the better option for me.

Lori: I am glad that you stuck with it because for both Jack and I, it lights me up because it is something that is just creative, artistic, and positive and funny and great, and it's just really needed. If you didn't do that, there would be this little hole in my soul.

Brian: Thank you. That sounded like a compliment.

Lori: Happiness is more important than anything, I am telling ya. How can people think that success is fame or fortune? To me, success is surviving and living happily. I don't care if you don't have any money, I don't care if you are washing the toilets at White Castle, if you are happy and you are content and you feel great, that is all that matters. And that is being successful, living the life the way you want to live it. It doesn't mean that you have to have money or that you have to be famous. I am living the life that I want to, and I am really happy about it and life is good.

Brian: I wanted to ask about your early life a little bit. As I understand you were a big music fan, a punk rock sort of person who knew a lot of people. Did you ever promote shows?

Lori: I did do that, way back in the early eighties—the early eighties punk rock, hardcore sort of world. I brought Minor Threat to Minneapolis, the only time they ever played here, but I rented a hall. I was twenty one years old. I rented a hall, I had to get insurance, I made tickets, I promoted it, the tickets were black on black. I got support acts and I organized the whole thing. That was really one of my first times I did that, and went at it and it was really great because I loved Minor Threat, I wanted them to come to Minneapolis and I did it.

Brian: That stuff and that world was such a pure and innocent thing back then. It was such a different universe.

Lori: It really was. It was much more simple. Technology and everything has made everything untouchable and unreachable. I have friends that are super, super famous and I used to be able to just call them and they would call me back. Now it's like you can't even touch anyone anymore because it is so much like an illusion now. It is just crazy because now people have to seclude themselves more than they used to because of all of that. You have to hide to be more anonymous and untouchable.

But it started when I was really young. I just really loved music and I would drive to New York when I was a teenager. My dad got transferred and I lived in a little place outside of New York City and I used to go into the city all of the time. I mean, I was sixteen or seventeen and I was going into the city all by myself and it was insane and I think about that now, you know... I don't know.

Brian: I was in a band, my first band, and I was eighteen years old and we tried to tour the country with another band and our parents let us all go, which looking at it now, seems fucking crazy because anything could have happened to us.

Lori: I graduated from high school in 1978. I was hanging out in New York City in 74, 75, 76. Omigod, I had no fear. I went to see Patti Smith on New Years Eve, I saw Queen at Madison Square Garden, I saw David Bowie. I used to go into the city with a few older guys who were my neighbors and my friends. My parents never said no and I never had a curfew. I think about this now, I was sixteen years old and I was going to New York City by myself. I would just spend the day walking around and then maybe I would go and see a show and then I would take the train back at one thirty in the morning or whatever. It is just crazy.

Brian: The excitement of doing that stuff is way more on your mind then any fear you have of it.

Lori: I was never afraid. If I was afraid then I probably just wouldn't have gone. I remember going back to my high school and talking to my friends about it, and there were kids I knew that had never been to New York City but could see the skyline from their house.

And people would just never go there. It was just so unbelievable. I would tell these people what I did and they would look at me like I had just landed from Mars. I couldn't fathom why these kids didn't go. You live in a one high school town, get the John Jacob out of here and spread your wings. I just can't fathom that.

I hung out with Johnny Thunders and Alan Vega. And then I went to Key West, Florida, and was living down there by myself.

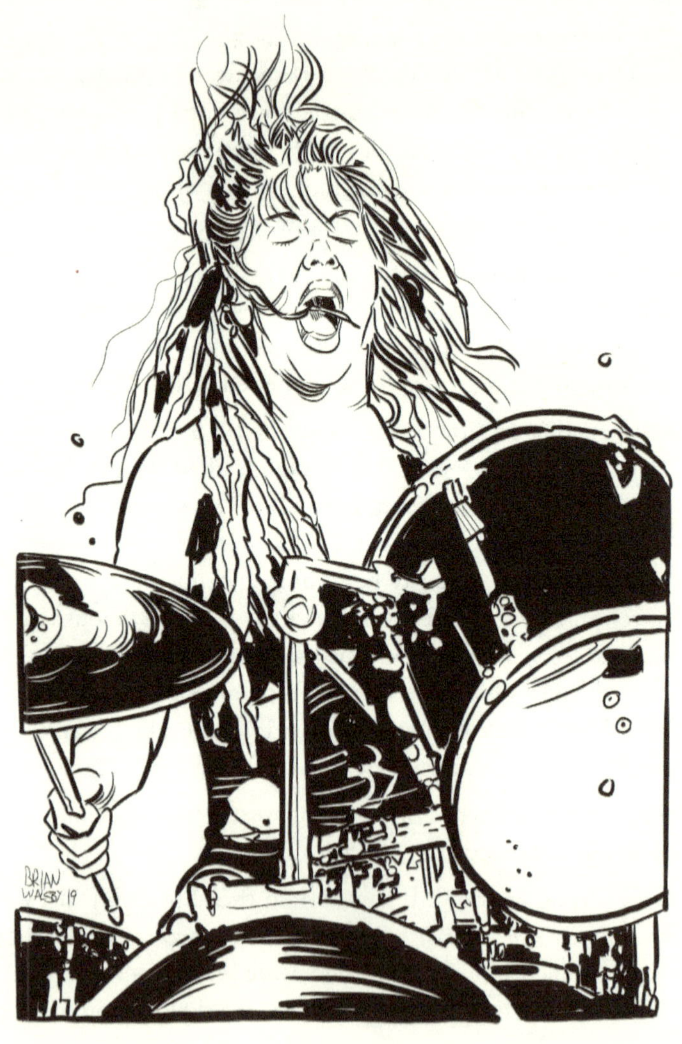

I lived on a houseboat. Oh man, the stories from that, are you freaking kidding? I turned eighteen down there. And then my parents moved back to the Twin Cities where we were from. I told them to get my brothers out of where they were living, a small town where all people would do is drink and smoke pot. And I don't know what happened—I think something happened to my dad—I don't know what happened, but they all came back. Then I came back and I lived in South Minneapolis and got a job at a punk rock bar. And that is where it all started, I worked at the Longhorn. The Plasmatics played there, the Stooges, 8 Eyed Spy, the list could go on and on. I have so many photos. That was maybe 1980, and that is when music was everything. Seven nights a week. Omigod.

Brian: I knew that you were an early supporter, friend, and fan of Hüsker Dü, who I still think of as one of my favorite bands.

Lori: Yup. Me too, they are still one of my favorites. They were from St. Paul and I remember them playing at the Longhorn and it was so, so rudimentary. It was slow and drudgy and Bob (Mould) would sing out of key, but it kind of like *fit* at the Longhorn.

Brian: I liked pretty much all of their phases, and I was also pretty amazed at those stories about your friendships with all three of them, and then how, at some point, you became sort of a mediator between them.

Lori: In a power trio, there is always a third person. There are the two who are either closer or they have a conflict, and then the third is always not a part of that, and it seemed like that a lot and Greg (Norton) was very non-confrontational and he was great and even-keeled. Grant (Hart) and Bob were way more bull-headed and had their own things going on—their own things together and separate, you know? And Greg was neither here nor there. I really didn't have any of that with him, it was just with the other two. "You go tell him," and I would go and tell him and then the other would be like, "You go tell him this." I was friends with both of them, so I didn't take sides either, I would just be like,

"Come on you guys," you know, just being the devil's advocate and the meeting of the minds just kind of like balancing them out.

Brian: I only met Grant once and he left a very big impression. I didn't recognize him at first, he looked like a total freak. "Who is this freak? He is being really nice... oh shit, it is Grant Hart!" Grant Hart, drumming hero of my youth, who sang and wrote and played great and never seemed to use a hi hat. Just a ride cymbal. After he passed, I felt...I honestly wasn't up on everything that he had done since Hüsker Dü, which was, like, thirty years ago. I was familiar with *Hot Wax* and *The Argument*, which sounds like a David Bowie record to me. So I was amazed that everything else I had listened to since, I instantly really liked and I felt bad that I didn't know how good all of his stuff was.

Lori: Yeah, a lot of people don't. You know, the thing was, there was a lot of animosity because Bob went on to do great things and had world tours, and Grant never did. He could have, but Grant was not proactive. He didn't go anywhere because he wasn't proactive. It is not that he didn't work hard, he just didn't move forward. Trying to finish his last record, it took him over three years and it still wasn't finished. That is just Grant. And that is the difference between those two right there. That is just the big picture summed up very small, I mean that very simple, you know? You said the two record names, and I got goosebumps from my toes to my eyeballs. *Hot Wax* and *The Argument*. It just happened again.

Bob was so hard working. And Grant was more of a homebody, a recluse, a creature of habit. He loved to go to this local music store a few blocks from my house, Twin Tone Guitars—I think he went there, I don't even know how many days of the week—and just hang out and talk to people. He would stop at places, he had favorite places. He just had a very simple and happy... well, not really happy, he got dealt a really bad hand, you know. He loved his parents so much and he lost his parents. And after they died, the house he grew up in, his house, it burned down. And then he got cancer. He had it real tough. I mean, everyone has their own stories but he just really... he lost his brother when he was really young, all kinds of things.

We really miss him so much. I hang out with his wife pretty often, we are very close. I had known her for many, many years and they were really great friends, they were super close. I knew all of these people, but now that Grant has passed, we are just really close. Like, really great things come from tragedy, you know, and I just really love them. We get to spend a lot more time together, I just wish we would have hung out a lot more when Grant was alive, but everyone is living their life and then a huge black cloud blew everything away from us so now we kind of look for each other, and it's just really great.

I get to see them really often and it's comforting and really nice. I started an all girl music studio, this gentlemen Chris Larson did this thing at the Walker Art Center, which is a world famous art museum in South Minneapolis. He did this thing with Grant Hart called "Land Speed Record." And Chris is very famous—he has art in every famous art gallery in the world—and he is very humble. He approached me when I was DJing an art opening at my friend's studio, and he said, "I have this idea and I will get a hold of you."

I was like, "Omigod Omigod." The guy goes to Berlin, and then he goes down to Brazil, and I waited almost a year for him to reach out to me again. I didn't want to bother him.

Brian: Is this the guy who did the thing for what Grant plays on *Land Speed Record* and then made an art thing out of it?

Lori: Yeah. And he did this film thing but, unfortunately, I was on tour so I didn't get a chance to see it. He brought Grant into the Walker Center.

So his thing was that he wanted to have an all girl music studio and wanted me involved. There was another woman that he works with, one of his assistants, and it's us three who do it. And he built the studio and it's really, really great. We just ended our first session with girls aged six to nine. And we got like five or six songs out of two bands. We don't teach them their instruments, we show them the fundamentals of it but they just went in there and did it, they wrote these songs and it's unbelievable. It is great that they did it all by themselves. I've wanted to do this sort of thing for a few years and then Chris invited me to do this with him. I wanted to do a safe place to empower a young girl to create, and it is exactly what Chris came to me for. And I am not kidding, sometimes when you just put it out there, it comes back to you. It's just really strange. I was telling Jack about it for a couple of years, the year before it or whatever.

Brian: There is way, way more about you than just the fact that you were in Babes In Toyland, but I still have some questions about the band. What was it like, looking back at things, when it was a different world, and you had a lot of albums, and tours, and videos on MTV. What was it like to live in that sort of bubble?

Lori: Okay well, we rehearsed a lot a lot a lot when we first got together. Kat [Bjelland] and I went through this lineup and that lineup and then got Michelle Leon, who was pretty much our solid bass player. I used to have bands play in the basement of the house that I lived in, it was pretty punk rock. And so, like, Die Kreuzen played in my basement, and Tar Babies and Mecht Mensch, all of those guys. So when Die Kreuzen were going out on a tour—I was pretty close to them, they became good friends of mine, I would go to Wisconsin and stay with them…

Brian: That first record is one of the greatest records.

Lori: It certainly is. So when they were going on tour, Dan got a hold of me, Dan Kubinski. And he was like, "Hey Lori, we are going on tour and there is this band that we are taking with us, White Zombie. Do you want to come with us?" And I was, "sure."

We didn't even have a van at that point. We needed to buy a van. This was, like, 1987. We had been playing for maybe a year. But we had songs—we didn't have to play that long—and because I had known Dan so well, he had just asked us to go with them, so that was the beginning. It was just crazy you know, with White

Zombie. And then White Zombie ended up taking us out on tour with the Melvins. I don't know if you know about that tour.

Brian: Yeah, I heard some good stories. Not about you guys, they all like you a lot of course. They didn't have a lot of good things to say about White Zombie's fearless leader.

Lori: It all goes in circles. But we toured for many years, we lived in London for a little while in the early nineties, and there is nothing better than traveling. I am a Sagittarius—I have wings on my heels and I just love adventure. We worked very hard, we travelled eight months a year for ten solid years. It was crazy, but we could do that. We were young, it was really fun and we did it. And it was great, I wouldn't change anything about that to be honest, and then an incident happened where Kat pulled out a wild card, pulled out a handful of Jokers and threw them at me and I severed my everything with her—my friendship, my music, my business, everything. And we didn't speak for many many years and then there were these gentlemen in California that were friends with our other bass player, whose name I won't say.

Brian: Uh, yeah.

Lori: I can't even say her name at this point. But anyways, these gentlemen were just about the best guys, I think about them so much and I really miss them. But they were like, "We will do anything for you to get the band back together." And I was living in Austin Texas, Kat was living in Minneapolis, and the bass player was living in California. We had to go there because she had a daughter. So we went there once a month for a week or so, and rehearsed every day. They paid for everything, I still admire them and I am very grateful for everything that they did. They were just philanthropists who were kind and humble and wonderful and they really helped us get back on the road again. And it was pretty good while it lasted. Last October we played at the Dave Grohl concert, Cal Jam. That was the last show we played. We were going to play some shows when the Super Bowl was in Minneapolis and they had to be canceled, Kat was very sick and we haven't played since then and I don't think that we will.

Addiction is a bitch, it destroys. I've been around it for decades and I am no better than anyone else but...

Brian: You have been around enough to see how shitty that stuff is, drugs and alcohol, all of that abuse, it destroys people... but you got property in Yucca Valley. The future is great!

Lori: I do. And people are like, "what are you going to do?" I get by. And it's fine. I don't mind bartending at a VFW and seeing a bunch of people.

Brian: Maybe you are a little more extroverted than some other artistic sort of people.

Lori: I do love people but it depends on where I am at, what people are around me.

Brian: I am sure your bullshit detector is finely tuned.

Lori: Yes! But...it really doesn't bother me. Being a drummer is not my identity, I mean, it is and I am proud of it—it was more than half of my life, I worked really hard, it was great, it really helped shape me into who I am—but it doesn't mean that I can't move forward or live my life without it.

Michel Langevin

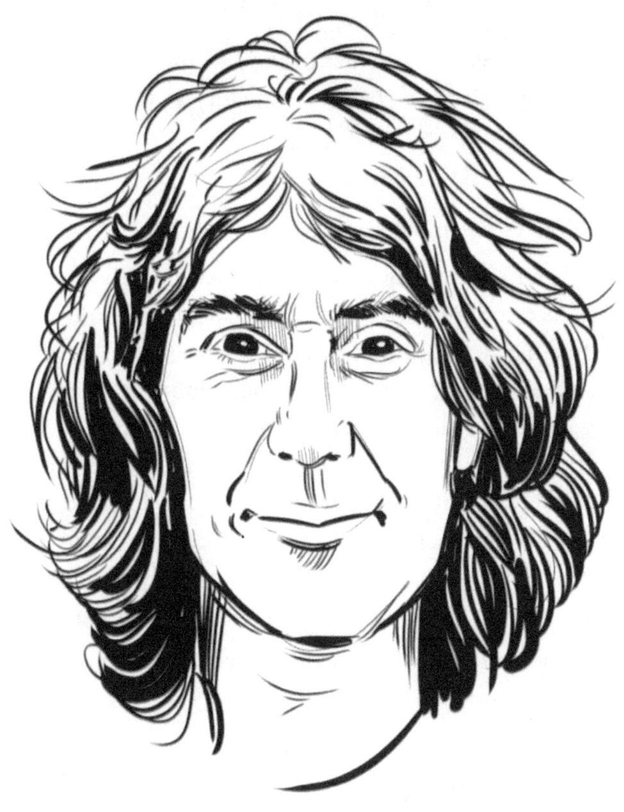

Michel Langevin is not only one of my favorite drummers, he is one of my favorite artists. In both cases, he has his own unique voice. Sometimes when I talk to him, I feel like I am talking to a sort of French Canadian doppelgänger of myself, in terms of influences and our backgrounds. I have a lot of respect for him as an artist.

Over the years his band Voivod have done some of my favorite heavy metal-based music and his album cover artistic efforts are heralded as classic rock and roll artwork. I have followed every single thing that Voivod has done since their debut album *War and Pain* and their catalog reaps many rewards, both in terms of classic recordings (the holy trinity of *Killing Technology, Dimension Hatröss* and *Nothingface*) and holding their own as a current entity. Last year's album, *The Wake*, is as good, and as current, as any of those classic recordings. Next to the Melvins and the Descendents, I would put Voivod in the same category as influencers and lifers.

♫

Brian: How old were you when you started drawing?

Michel: The first drawing that I remember doing was Atom Ant and I was super young, like four or five. I must have drawn before that time like many kids do, but the oldest memory I have of drawing was Atom Ant. He was a super cool Japanese cartoon from the sixties. I went with my family to my uncle's place and my cousin had drawn it on some cardboard and had another one on his wall and I asked him if he could give it to me. He said no, but that he would show me how to draw it. And that is why I remember drawing Atom Ant. For the *Negatron* album, it was almost a homage to that first drawing, that mechanical ant.

Brian: So you stuck with drawing as you were growing up. What inspired you to keep drawing?

Michel: There was an artist from France or maybe Belgium called FRED. His comics were really poetic and visually stunning, so I started to copy him. I had access to this library when I was at school when I was very young, so my style was influenced by him a lot. Shortly after that, in the mid-seventies maybe, I saw the first issue of *Heavy Metal* magazine, but at the time it was called *Métal Hurlant*[1]. That really blew my mind. So I totally changed my style to a more pointy style with a lot of pointy metallic structures because I was so influenced by the artists in the magazine.

I am still a really big fan to this day.

---

1 In France it was called *Métal Hurlant*, in the United States the title was *Heavy Metal*, and in Germany it was *Schwermetall*.

Brian: That makes sense, A lot of your artistic style has this very strange, almost angular, sort of thing. And I remember when the Voivod records started to come out, the idea that the drummer of the band did the album covers was pretty cool.

Michel: Well, at first I wanted to be an artist for *Heavy Metal*, so until we formed the band I had already developed the character of Voivod, the planet and everything, and it was for the purpose of doing comic books and hopefully becoming an artist for *Heavy Metal* magazine.

When we formed the band, especially when Snake joined in early 1983, at that point the Cold War atmosphere was full on, and I really learned a lot about nuclear weaponry.

Brian: And don't forget that in the early eighties, the punk rock that had started really reflected the fact that everyone thought that the world would just explode any second in a nuclear war disaster. And bands like Crass and Discharge made a huge impact because that was what every kid thought.

Michel: Yeah, and actually because of hardcore and thrash metal appearing—that many of these thrash metal bands were talking about the destruction of our planet and there was a nuclear fear—visually my style went along with that, totally. There was some space stuff but mostly it was nuclear disaster, post-apocalyptic orientated. And at the same time, there were a lot of bands using that same imagery that I loved, like Icons of Filth or Amebix. That influenced my style as well.

Brian: When did music come into your life? How did you discover all of that stuff in the small town in Québec that you and your band mates lived in? How were you guys able to discover all of that weird music so far away from everything?

Michel: At first I listened to the Beatles when I was nine or ten. And then I discovered Kiss, and then right after that Deep Purple, Black Sabbath, and Alice Cooper. I remember reading in a rock magazine at the library about the Sex Pistols. That was something that took me awhile to get a copy of, I couldn't wait to get it.

And that really really changed my style of drumming. Some of the stuff that we were listening to we could find, but other stuff we had to hitchhike to Montreal. We all hitchhiked to Montreal to see Iron Maiden on the *Killers* tour.

Brian: That is amazing. The first two records by Iron Maiden were so great, and Clive Burr was such a great drummer, really influential.

Michel: Yes, Clive Burr, Philthy Animal Taylor and Terry Bozzio would be my three favorite drummers. For sure. And after that Guy Evans from Van der Graaf Generator and Paul Cook from the Sex Pistols. We also went to see the *No Sleep 'til Hammersmith* tour in 1981.

Brian: That is my favorite record by Motörhead.

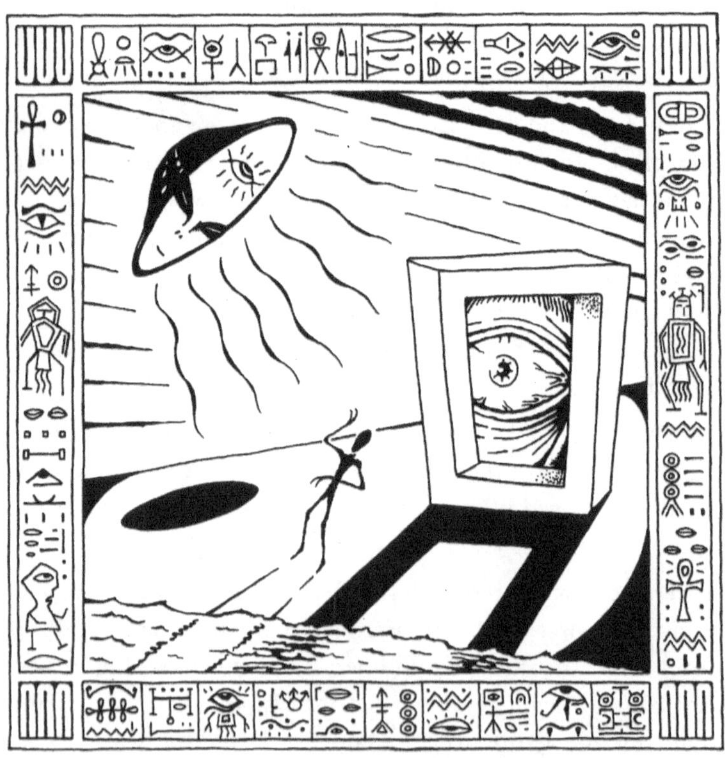

ARTWORK BY MICHEL LANGEVIN

Michel: Oh, me too. And when I came back from that trip from Montreal to see Motörhead, that is really when I was convinced I should give being a professional drummer a try. We got all of these records and we really learned a lot from going on those trips to Montreal. In terms of music, in 1980 when I heard the first Iron Maiden album, it totally changed my life. I saw the cover and I immediately thought that they would be my favorite band without knowing the music.

Brian: I had the same experience, but I bought *Killers* first. I looked at the front cover, I looked at the back cover, and I thought that there was just no way that it wasn't going to be something that I didn't like a lot.

Michel: Exactly! And when I put it on, the first song "Prowler," they instantly became my new favorite heavy metal band. They had everything—punk, metal, prog rock, everything that I loved. But we had to travel to Montreal to get these records, these NWOBHM albums and bands. Up north we could get stuff like the AC/DC albums but that was it.

Brian: I have heard a lot about the factory up near the town that you guys lived in. Was there any pressure for you guys to look to something like a factory job as something that you would eventually end up doing? When you formed Voivod, was there a thought of, "we have to do something like this so we don't end up doing something like that."

Michel: Yes, I am sure of it. I lived by the paper mill factory. Not too far from everyone else in Voivod was the aluminum factory, the biggest one in North America, and the smog is pretty intense. There is a red lake by the factory that we used to go to. It is a strange situation because it is a great part of Quebec, with lots of wood. But all of a sudden you hit these two towns that are connected together, where we come from, and there is this huge factory. There is a beautiful river but it is probably very polluted and all of that.

I personally wanted to move from where we lived because

slowly, at the end of the seventies and the early eighties, all of the computers got into the factories and all of a sudden there were all of these people getting laid off and things there were getting more computer-oriented. We could tell that there was going to be less and less jobs for everybody and that was an incentive to form the band. But we actually waited for our first album, *War and Pain,* to come out in 1984 before dropping out of school. It had a very big impact on the thrash metal scene and the punk scene as well. So we thought that maybe we did have a chance to have a career. At first it seemed impossible because we were French Canadian from up north in Quebec and I barely knew how to speak English, as you could tell on the first couple of albums.

Brian: But that is part of the charm, though. How did you get signed to Brian Slagel's Metal Blade Records? You were on one of those *Metal Massacre* compilation albums and then all of a sudden the debut album was released. How did that happen?

Michel: There was a friend, Wayne Archibald, and he was really into the NWOBHM.He had all of the demos of bands like Raven, Tank, and Angel Witch before they recorded their albums and he always had their new stuff. He had the Metallica demos with Dave Mustaine and he was a pen pal to everyone on earth, and he was writing to Brian Slagel back then. We had a demo in very early '84, the one that was eventually released by Jello Biafra, and he sent that to Brian, and Brian asked us to go record "Condemned To The Gallows." I think we actually recorded "Blower" and "Iron Gang" as well, three songs.

So Brian put the song on *Metal Massacre Five* and we got a great reaction, and immediately he asked us to record an album. So that was what we did and it happened fairly quickly. By 1984 we already had the first album out.

Brian: Writing letters, either in the punk rock scene or the young metal scene, was a very powerful thing because it was usually the only way to really get information about what was going on. That was totally what I did—I had a lot of pen pals and drew a lot of stuff for people because of it, heard a lot of music and got a lot of fanzines, too. That is how I heard about you guys and pretty much everybody in either world. That was like the lifeblood of both of those scenes.

Michel: Yeah, I think Wayne might have sent a demo to Brian as early as 1983, and back then it was really the only way. It was really a long process when you think about it because we used to send the demos to fanzines, and they would send an interview and we would answer, and we would get the fanzine back a few weeks later or a few months later. Now it is just insane how everything is so instantaneous.

Brian: I heard you painted some of the album covers on pizza boxes?

Michel: Ha ha. Well, in 1984, Blacky and Piggy had dropped out of school, at least before Snake and I did. And when we decided to quit it was a big deal for everyone's families. Everyone in the band had a classic dinner conversation with their families about how we were joining this heavy metal band and quitting the university or college or whatever.

It was clear that we had to move from our parents' places. And just to accelerate the point that we wanted to pursue a career and find proper management, we decided to make that move in 1985 to Montreal. And at this point we only had a deal for one album for Metal Blade. We were in Montreal living off of the government, we got fifty dollars a month to live off of. We would get a burger the first day of the month and after that it was Kraft macaroni and all of that. The four of us lived in one apartment in eastern Montreal infested with cockroaches and all of that. It was out of the question for me to afford a canvas for the *Rrröööaaarrr* cover, so I got this cardboard and cut it up and painted the cover on it, and it was a really bad idea.

Brian: Okay, so it was the second album where you painted on the back of a piece of cardboard, not *War and Pain*.

Michel: For *War and Pain*, we were still living at our parents' places up north and my mother bought me a canvas, and tubes of paint.

Except for one painting for my grandmother that I did in art class in high school, it was my very first painting, the *War and Pain* cover. I had to be pretty bold to tell Metal Blade, "Okay I will do the cover." I actually learned many, many years afterwards and put it in my Worlds Away[2] book, that when they received it at the office of a Metal Blade, the staff all gathered around the office and were like, "Uh oh. The drummer did the cover." (laughter) I put a lot of work into it, which is the same story for the first four album covers that I did for Voivod, I used acrylic paints and a little bit of airbrush. I had no training and it took me months, which is why I switched to digital art in the mid-eighties.

Brian: *Killing Technology* and *Dimension Hatröss*, the covers that you did, really stood out from the rest of the other bands.

Michel: It probably stood out in the early thrash metal scene, but a little after that I started to see some Carnivore or Nuclear Assault art that was in the same vein.

Brian: When was your first tour of the United States?

Michel: When we first moved to Montreal, we got some of our gear stolen. We were halfway through recording the second album, we needed to mix it, and we didn't know what to do. So, with the management that we found, we decided to organize this festival called World War Three in 1985. It was with Celtic Frost, Possessed, Nasty Savage, and Destruction. We were headlining, and tons of people showed up!

Brian: It's a legendary show, I read about it in a few metal fanzines back then.

Michel: Yeah, I think it was, like, three thousand people. For us, it was a huge show. People came from the U.S.A. and from Europe and it was super amazing. So we got some money and the recording was done but we had to mix the album. We gave the rough mix to Martin Ain from Celtic Frost. And with the money we made

---

2 *Worlds Away: Voivod and the Art of Michel Langevin* by Martin Popoff https://voivodmerch.com/en/products/worlds-away

from the festival, we used that to mix the album.

Martin brought the rough mix back home to Switzerland and I think that he copied it and sent it to Noise Records. And then we got an offer from Noise for three albums. And they offered us a chance to tour the U.S.A. with Celtic Frost and Europe with Possessed. And this was 1986.

The thrash metal movement was really exploding and it was super intense with riots in Europe. We got attacked by a gang in San Diego. In many parts of the U.S., we would leave the club after the show and there were like forty or fifty cars following our bus to the hotel and there were all of these people in the pool, super drunk, and the police showed up. We ended up doing a European tour the next year with Kreator for the *Killing Technology* album and the same thing would happen, with riots in Germany. So it was a very intense time and really exciting for us, because we were all in our twenties and we were part of this exploding movement. At this point, Metallica were huge and everybody knew about thrash metal, you know? So I have very fond memories of all that.

Brian: When *Killing Technology* came out, I thought that was really the record where you guys made a quantum leap. From literally the first few minutes of hearing it and Piggy's guitar playing, I thought right away that there was a little bit of a Die Kreuzen influence in here. It was just the kind of chords that Piggy used and how it mirrored some of what Brian from Die Kreuzen was doing.

I learned later that it probably really was these sort of prog rock King Crimson sort of chords. But I thought that *Killing Technology* was unique and it was one of my favorite metal records of that time period.

Michel: I got Piggy into Die Kreuzen. The record *October File* really did it for him. He became a HUGE fan of Brian, and when we met them on the Celtic Frost tour in '86 in Milwaukee, Brian told Piggy that he was a huge fan of Voivod, so they were fans of each other, which was great. We probably share a mutual admiration for Alex Lifeson and Robert Fripp and stuff like that.

Brian: After that, you guys did *Dimension Hatröss*, which was completely something that was your own. And then when the next album, *Nothingface,* came out, that seemed to be, and forgive me for saying this but, that might have been the commercial peak. You already had made videos for some *Dimension Hatröss* songs, then the Pink Floyd cover and video got a lot of attention. You guys had a pretty big profile and that was really exciting. But when I listen back to *Nothingface,* thinking about the commercial popularity for it, it is still this really strange uncommercial music; it is still really out there.

Michel: Between the time that we had signed with Noise and the time we signed to MCA, it was a short time. We were doing an album a year with a world tour afterwards. We gave Noise the second album and then we did all of this touring, stopping in a Berlin at the end of the tour to record the *Killing Technology* album. We wrote *Killing Technology* before going on tour for *Rrröööaaarrr*, and then we got to do the same thing again for *Dimension Hatröss*! And so we wrote the material for *Dimension Hatröss* before going on tour for *Killing Technology* and so on and so on.

Brian: That is fucking crazy.

Michel: We were all still living together in the same apartment and we were really developing the Voivod thing together. We rehearsed every night. We did that from '84 all the way through to '89. So that is why there is such a difference between *War and Pain* and *Nothingface*, really. And also, I had developed the Voivod concept for comic books but Snake really sat down with me to really develop the concept for the band. So we really had a great time expressing these ideas, I was more into outer space and Snake was more of a street guy, really punk and all of that. By living together like that, the four of us were really able to match everything musically, lyrically, and visually. And it was at a very fast pace. We were doing these videos at a very low budget, these low budget special effects...

Brian: Yeah, but they are still cool! Like the video for "Ravenous Medicine?" That is a great video. Part of the charm of it is that it is low budget but it still looks really cool.

Michel: So all of the work that we did started to really pay off, we got bigger and bigger. By the time that we had done the video for "Tribal Convictions," we really had a pretty good sized fan base, and the video had played enough so that MCA noticed us.

At this point, it was towards the end of the eighties and it seemed like there was a new sort of alternative scene forming, with Jane's Addiction and Soundgarden and Green River—anything that sort of became grungy. All of a sudden, all of the major labels wanted their alternative heavy act. The majors were after that kind of stuff, so we just got picked up by MCA. It was quite a step up in terms of everything—recording budget, touring budget, promotion…

Brian: You can definitely hear the step up in terms of the production on *Nothingface,* for sure.

Michel: Yes, and all of a sudden we are recording at the Record Plant in L.A. so it elped for us to go for this psychedelic sound with lots of layers recorded in these really big studios. For the *Outer Limits* album, we really went far into this psychedelic pop metal direction.

Brian: I loved the *Outer Limits* record when it came out and I loved your artwork on it, too, with the 3-D glasses that came with it. And the artwork was obviously different. Was the concept for that record something that MCA was into?

Michel: Yeah, they were into it but they were reluctant because of the cost of the 3-D glasses that came with the record. It actually delayed the release a couple of months. But one of the guys from the art department had really gotten into it and helped me to understand the process and technique of 3-D design. I was super happy when they agreed to do it. When I was a teenager that Grand Funk album *Shinin' On*, had a 3-D cover with the glasses and all of that. I had always wanted to do that. They were a band that really influenced Piggy and I as kids.

Brian: When *Angel Rat* came out, I think I was one of the few people that dug it right away. After three pretty complex records I thought that a simpler, stripped down Voivod record was still a Voivod record. And the colors that you used for the cover, with all of the blue and purple, I thought fit the music perfectly. People seem like they enjoy that record more as time has gone on.

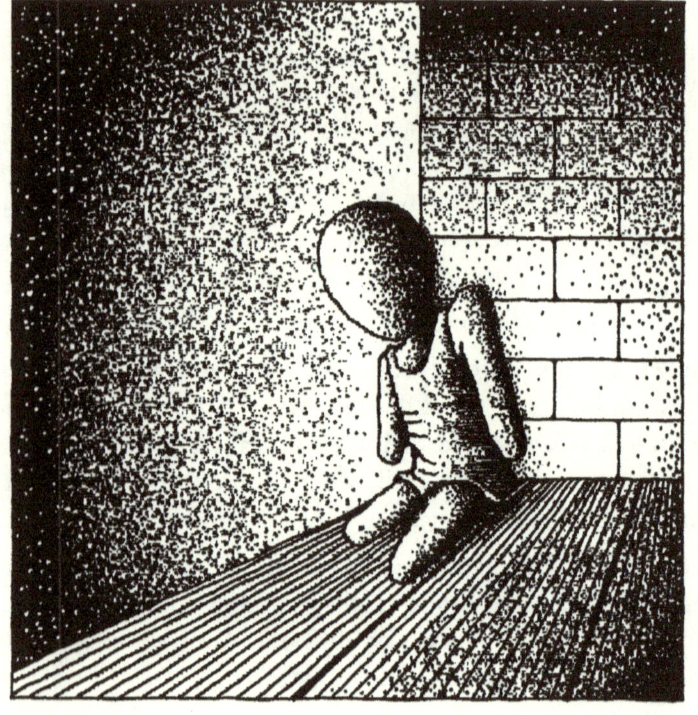

ARTWORK BY MICHEL LANGEVIN

Michel: Well with Voivod, we actually never really sat down and discussed how we needed to be more commercial or more this and that. It was really just a progression, we just wanted to have this emo, moody metal album and that is why we hired Terry Brown. But at this point, the band was sort of crumbling in a way, and Blacky left during the mixing of the album and it was a very strange time. When it came out, everybody had their eyes turned to Seattle. So, it was kind of crushing in a way. I don't know, we really didn't stop and moan about it or anything like that.

During those years, and when we did *Outer Limits*, heavy metal had a smaller following in America but it was still huge in Europe. We were doing big festivals there and packing clubs and all of that. And we would do the odd U.S. tour that was going okay, so it was just business as usual for us. The good thing was when *Angel Rat* came out, it didn't do that great but we were still able to do the *Outer Limits* album, and we had a little bit more budget and all of that, and it was really kind of a relief that we weren't dropped by the label.

Brian: I love the way *Outer Limits* sounds. What is going on with the drum sound? They sound really odd, in a way that I like. Is that computer stuff?

Michel: Yes, it is actually. It was an engineer that was using Q Bass, and we spent a lot of time sampling my drums. They are actually sampled acoustic drum sounds. I played on an electronic pad drum kit, even the cymbals. And it went into Q Bass and then when I showed up at the Record Plant in L.A. I had two tapes with all of my drum tracks on them. It was an experiment to make that record sound really, really big. But I would never do that again. (laughter)

Brian: I saw you guys in Raleigh on the *Negatron* tour. The Eric Forrest period, to me, is almost what people thought about *Angel Rat* at first. I remember buying *Negatron* and liking it instantly, it was cool that Eric did two jobs at once, bass and vocals. I thought he was good live. His harsh voice, I really liked it, especially the second record, *Phobos*. That might be in my top three of all of your records. That is your most terrifying sounding album, for whatever reason.

Michel: Yeah, it is super dark.

Brian: And Piggy's guitar, it is just a wash of terror. I think people are starting to really enjoy the trio version of the band, mostly because of *Phobos*.

Michel: Yeah, *Phobos* didn't sell very well but now people really, really love those two albums. We really worked hard on it, as much as *Dimension Hatröss* and the new album, *The Wake*, almost. It was a lot of effort to make it into a long journey. I am really proud of *Phobos*, it has parts that remind me of Tool because Piggy was a huge fan of Tool. The Eric Forrest period was great for touring as well, and we toured as a trio a lot between '95 and '98. Then we had that bad van crash in Europe and that really put a stop to touring for a very long time, and that is when I became more available for artwork and started doing a lot of stuff.

We waited for Eric to come back after the crash. He was very seriously injured in the crash so it was about a year before he was able to go back on stage. We opened for Iron Maiden and did a tour with Neurosis and then went to Australia. That was all after the accident. But we sort of lost momentum, and Piggy and I decided to split the band in 2000.

Brian: Is there ever going to be a chance for that stuff that you were demoing with Steve Albini, the missing third album of the Eric era, to see the light of day?

Michel: Actually, nobody has that except for me and Eric. When Eric was at the hospital in '98 and '99, Piggy and I wrote a whole album and when Eric came out of the hospital, he added his vocals and bass and we were supposed to record in 2000 with Steve Albini. I had spoken to Steve on the phone and he was a huge fan, I knew him from his Big Black days and I was a huge fan of his sound. When I spoke to him he told me that he actually had a *Nothingface* cassette in the car and a *Nothingface* CD at home, so I was really pleased that he was aware of Voivod.

We did twelve songs that were supposed to be the last chapter of the Voivod story, based on Eric's recovery. There is supposed to be a box set with all of this unreleased material, and there was an invitation for me to do the bonus DVD, similar to what Noise did with our older material last year—for every album there was a DVD added from the Voivod archives. So that is in the works right now. What is going to end up happening is that recording is going to be on the DVD along with some live footage, like the Dynamo Festival in Holland, or something like that. There is also talk about licensing the MCA material as well. So *Angel Rat* and *Nothingface* and *Outer Limits* might come out, with bonus material. So that if that all happens then everything will be available. I know that someone wants to rerelease the first album we did with Jason (Newsted) on vinyl, so all of the missing pieces are getting out back togetherI. It is a lot of work but it has to be done. The *War and Pain* reissue and then the *Killing Technology* And *Dimension Hatröss* reissues were ten years in the making. We actually started working on that in 2007, and it came out last year.

What is missing now is the *Warriors On Ice* live album. Someone in Europe wants to do it, so that is really the last one that wasn't available. I think that we are going to have to be patient for the MCA catalog. I have been working on that case for years.

Brian: And you did more artwork in the down period of the band following the crash.

Michel: First of all, in the mid-nineties I learned how to do 3-D design, so that was how I was able to do the cover for *Negatron* and the video for "Insect". So after the crash in '98, it was the first time where...we did have a big scare in 88 when Piggy had his big scare with a brain tumor and we canceled the *Dimension Hatröss* world tour. He was able to find the proper pills so everything was stabilized and everything was cool, but it was really the first time, when Eric was at the hospital, because he was so seriously injured and we had no idea if he was ever going to come back at all, it was the first time where everything really stopped, and I was confronted with the fact that I had to make a move quick. I took a traditional 2-D animation course and I was hired to do some coloration for educational DVDs. So I was coloring frame by frame in 1999 while Eric was at the hospital, and at this point I had made myself more available by people to do more work. I did stuff for the band Non-Fiction, and that got me more work. All of a sudden, Dave Grohl wanted me to do the Probot cover. I did tons of work for Danko Jones, tons of work for him.

But it didn't take long before I really got antsy. And so in 2001 I phoned Piggy. We already wanted to do something but we had broken up the band. We got together with Snake and recorded the vocals for the Probot song—I don't remember when it came out, maybe 2004—so in 2001, the three of us gathered and Snake played us the song that he was doing for Dave Grohl and it was amazing. We were like, "Wow," because Snake had left the band in 1994, so it had been a while. We decided that we should do something, we started to write some music and called Jason Newsted. Piggy and I had recorded music with him, we had a project with him in the eighties and nineties called Tarrat and had recordings we had done at his studio in California. So we found Jason and asked if he wanted to do the bass on the album. He was super excited and he ended up joining the band.

Brian:: You did a tour with Sepultura.

Michel: Yeah, we did a tour with Sepultura. Jason had joined Ozzy and we were touring with Ozzy, so the whole year 2003—or the whole summer, actually—Jason was playing two shows a day, and the Ozzy one was two and a half hours or something. So we were openeing for Ozzy and we did the Ozzfest. Jason was such a warrior. This brought a lot of attention to us and we became high profile again. It was going great and all of a sudden in 2005, Piggy was struck with colon cancer.

Brian: It happened very quick. I had a friend for a really long time who passed away last year in a similar scenario, which was really terrible.

Michel: Exactly, the strangest part for me, after he passed in 2005, was we used to have a daily phone call to discuss Voivod matters and I was always waiting for the call. It was very strange and it went on for a long time. In 2004, it was Snake, Jason, Piggy and I, we had written a double album Piggy and I had done some very cheap demos where we put a couple of mics in my drum kit. I recorded the drums for the songs alone, singing the songs in my head and then he went back home and did some Pro Tools guitar recordings on top of it, and then he sent it to Jason, he did some very quick bass recordings, he actually recorded it on his porch.

These demos for the double album we actually turned into two albums, *Katorz* and *Infiniti*, after Piggy passed. We just re-recorded and added a whole bunch of stuff, I redid the drums. Snakes vocals for the demos were recorded in Piggy's bathroom, so he went into a professional studio to do the real vocals. At this point we were on a mission to finish these two albums—Snake, Jason and I—aand it was all we were going to do.

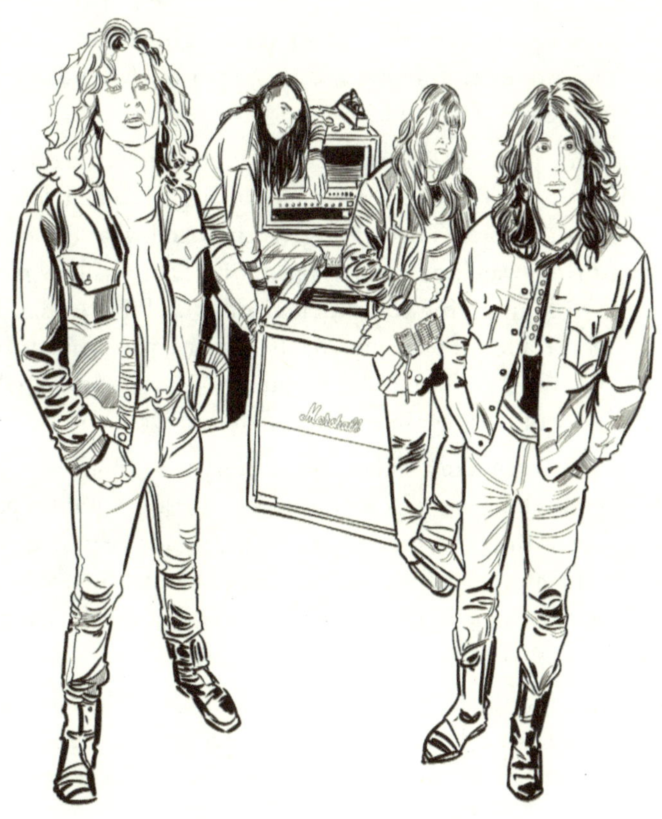

But in 2007, there was a celebration in Montreal. They were celebrating heavy metal in Quebec and Piggy was to be featured in part of the ceremony. Piggy's family was there. And Blacky and Chewy (Dan Mongrain, Piggy's replacement in Voivod) were playing a medley with people from many bands in town, many heavy metal bands. And they were playing a medley of Voivod songs. Snake and I were there, and we noticed that Blacky and Chewy had a great chemistry and were playing really well together.

Chewy was playing Piggy's chords perfectly and all of that, so when we were asked to reform for the Heavy Montréal, a big festival in 2008, we thought it would just be for one show, and we phoned Blacky and Chewy. And from then, it really never stopped. The word spread and soon enough we were asked to open for Testament in Japan and then opening for Judas Priest, and it kept going and going.

Brian: I remember that you were nice enough to let me and my friend Justin see you a few years ago in Virginia when you were touring with Kreator. That was a great show and what I remember the most from watching you guys play with Dan was how perfect he was, without trying to be a clone of what Piggy did. There seemed to be a lot of pure joy. Maybe because you went through such a horrible thing losing Piggy, and now here you guys are back with Blacky on bass again and having found Dan.

Michel: It has been like a rollercoaster. Every time that I have been able to go back on the road and travel, it is really what keeps me going—traveling and meeting up with friends year after year, playing the music that we like across the planet. So every time that I get the chance to go back and travel, I am super happy. It must show for sure.

Brian: You guys, to me, have pulled off the impossible. How many bands have replaced their main songwriter and managed to find someone that can do the job but still has his own flavor, who liked the band as a kid? And it is too bad about Blacky bowing out, but Rocky is a more than capable replacement.

Michel: The chemistry is fantastic. Now we somehow have bounced back in a big way with the new album having these reviews where it is 9 out of 10 or 4 out of 5 in every review and all of that. Everyone loves it. We are really enjoying the momentum now. The last tour we had in Europe last year, all of the places were super-packed and the album is doing really good. So this year we booked really solid touring, starting mid-January with going to Japan and Australia, and then we are going to go to the U.S.A. two times, and then Europe two times, and also try to make it in South America and Southeast Asia. Between all of that, I am squeezing recordings for Tau Cross and touring for Tau Cross and this is great.

Brian: This seems like you are the busiest that you have ever been.

Michel: It has been a bit difficult for me lately, because for the past three or four years we have been playing lots of shows. So it has been difficult for me to do any artwork, commissioned artwork. I do a lot of book covers these days, which is great. But it has been difficult for me to keep my website updated and keep up with the conversations,but I am doing my best.

The one thing about being a freelancer is that you have to really learn to discipline yourself and actually put the alarm clock on and everything. Otherwise, you just lose control.

Brian: So, because the band is doing so much stuff, your other life as an illustrator has diminished. Is the *Worlds Away* book still available, and are you planning to do another book in the future?

Michel: The Worlds Away book is at www.voivodmerch.com, and there is a book in the works[I]. It is all of the work that I do on the road, I have like thousands of them since we have reformed in 2008. It kind of picks up from the first book but it is mainly road art, because every time we play a city, at the end of the night I draw my impression of the city. We have done so much for the past eleven years and I have so many drawings. So that is my next project with the same publisher.

Even though I am super tired at the end of the day on the road,

I really force myself to do a little doodle or anything. Sometimes it is very elaborate but sometimes it is very quick. I have tons of that. There has been some talk online about how I should buy an iPad.

Brian: You gotta get one. You obviously bring a few pads of paper and some pens on tour.

Michel: Yes, I always have a toolbox full of art and a couple of good pens.

Brian: You have played with one band for so long, and you have been an artist for so long, and you have been self-employed for almost all of that time. What do you think about the path that your life has taken since Voivod started?

Michel: If anything, it took a lot of perseverance and at times it was borderline crazy to keep going. Many, many people would tell me that I should know when it is time to let go. It is just that doing that for that many years has given me such liberty. Even though there were some dreadful moments where I didn't know if Voivod would be popular ten years down the road, or if I would be totally forgotten and all of that. I realize now that we have jumped into this classic thrash metal thing where people will always know about Voivod and if anything, it is gaining momentum.

Even though it doesn't mean super financial security or a huge retirement plan, the fact that I am able to spend half of my life playing music and the other half doing art at home, it is just really amazing for me—the best of both worlds—and I feel really lucky that now I am an established artist. There will always be some tech metal band from Finland who will want me to do some art for their next album, or a t-shirt, or tattoo design. I am just impressed that thirty five years down the road, I can still rely on that. It is amazing.

SCARED STRAIGHT

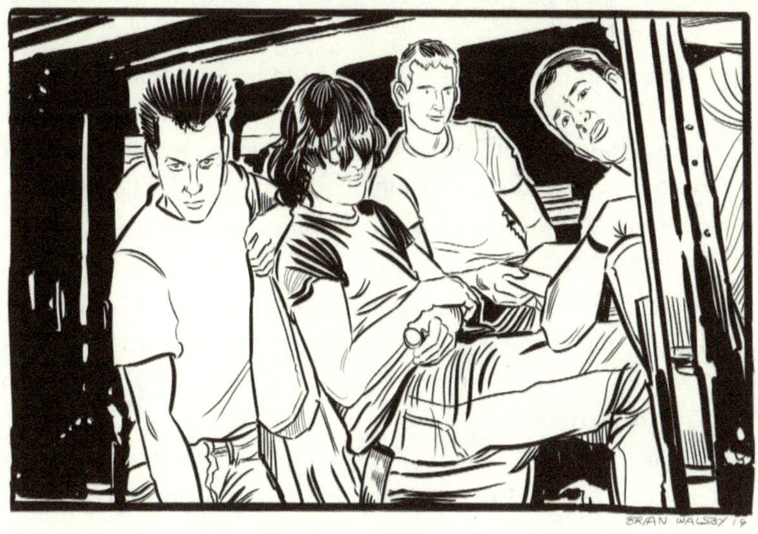

Scared Straight had an opportunity to go on tour in December of 1985. It was a quick week or so worth of shows across Arizona, New Mexico, Texas and then working our way back to California. Scott Radinsky, the singer of the band, had become friendly with the singer of the San Fernando Valley band, The Grim. The singer's name was Tim [McDuffee]. Some of you might remember that both bands were part of the legendary label, Mystic Records. There are a thousand stories that could be told about Mystic and their deservedly unsavory reputation.

Led by an odd older Englishman named Doug Moody, by the 1980s Mystic got this not-so-great reputation of putting out tons of records by a lot of bands that weren't ever going to be courted by SST, Dangerhouse, or anyone else. Mystic had a bizarre studio in Hollywood next to the Cathay de Grande where everything and everyone that recorded there ended up sounding like total shit. So even though, in all fairness, even if the band DID sound good (and quite honestly, a good amount of those bands did sound good live) they would all come out sounding really crappy in the same exact way. There were stories about bands honestly getting paid in PIZZA. I don't know if any of that was true but that is still really funny.

But in all honesty it was thrilling to be on a record, no matter how shitty the end result. Scared Straight had a single. The Grim (or as they spelled it out "Getting Revenge in 'Merica") had a twelve-inch. And at this time, it seemed like ANYONE could go on a tour and have SOMEONE come out to a show. It was still that climate.

I still have no idea what motivated the likes of Doug Moody to start Mystic Records. The whole thing seemed so strange looking back, but now it is a bit of a hyped up history note for someone to find on the internet.

The tour was basically, as I remembered it, booked due to Tim's contacts, but I think Scott helped him out. I can't be sure. It was a long time ago.

Scared Straight at that time consisted of Scott, guitarists Steve Carnan and Dennis Jagard, bassist Eric Swift (from nearby Newbury Park), and their new drummer Tim Williams. Tim couldn't go, and Tim had replaced me when our previous summer's tour with Ill Repute (another in the Mystic stable) got destroyed after someone ripped off ALL of our stuff in Pittsburgh. A legendary story to this day. I went to North Carolina and hung out with COC for the rest of the summer.

But afterwards I was back, and lo and behold, they were all still my friends and didn't hate me. I continued to hang out with them but I didn't play with them. I didn't even have a drum set when I was in the band, I had borrowed Scott's. But Scott's drumset was stolen in Pittsburgh that previous summer. Soon enough, after hearing about this tour, I think I volunteered to play on it, or maybe they had asked me. I don't remember. I don't even remember practicing for it although we might have. I do remember sitting in my bedroom with chopsticks going over everything in my mind and hitting pillows for drums, and trying to get a handle on whatever new songs they had. But I honestly do not remember if we ever even played together before that tour. All I knew is I was going. If we just left without me even playing with them once to get ready, I wouldn't be surprised.

We got the van and were meant to pick up the Grim. I didn't know them at all. Besides Tim there was this guy Shawn [James] on bass. If I remember correctly, I didn't seem to like him very much but looking back I don't remember why. He smoked and drank and had a poofy sort of punkish haircut. I have to point out that this is literally all I remember about Shawn, even though I would be in his company every day for the next week and a half or whatever. He was probably a nice guy, who knows. Tim seemed alright and was pleasant enough. The drummer, Jordan Lieberman, had this super nice, expensive drum set that was huge. I ended up using it on the trip. That was nice of him. Jordan is a fantastic drummer but I couldn't seem to remember any of that since what he was playing in the Grim was a lot of basic slower sort of stuff. Or at least slower than the usual hardcore type of stuff we all tended to like. And he was also a pretty nice guy.

The guitarist of the band, Bob [Oedy], travelled separately from us and even had his own personal roadie with him. I don't even remember his name. We all thought that was hilarious and probably made fun of that a little bit. Looking back, Bob was probably the smartest man on the tour.

Joining both of our bands on most of the shows would be two other bands from the L.A. area, Entropy and NOFX. We sort of knew both of them, NOFX more than Entropy.

Entropy were a four-piece hardcore band. I think it was Dave [Hinnebusch] singing, Nick [Chavez] on guitar, another Nick [Fitarelli] on drums and occasional singing, and I think Evan [Shanks] on bass. I had seen them a few times, when they had an extra surfer-looking guitarist which they now had shed. I liked them and thought they were the best band on this tour. They had a neat trick where the drummer Nick would sing along with Dave, or alternate the singing duties. They were nice enough guys. I don't think they ever put any records out but they were sort of known. Perhaps they didn't want to be on Mystic Records.

We knew NOFX, mainly guitarist Eric [Melvin] and bassist Mike [Burkett] (Fat Mike). I saw them every punk show that I could go to with Scott, so we were friendly. We all thought that NOFX were a pretty lousy band at the time. But it is not like any of us could really throw stones in their direction—since we were in Scared Straight and Getting Revenge in 'Merica, if you what I mean. They had a singer during that period who died in a car accident, and a drummer who I also do not remember at all. All I remember is Mike, Eric, and a girlfriend Eric had that seemed like she was there to fight with Eric all of the time and that is pretty much it. They played at most of the shows on this trip. Four bands. Sometimes there would be a few openers. Any punk hardcore show seemed to only be able to work out if there were at least five or six bands on the bill. Industry standard or whatever.

So here is what I sort of remember. If I think I am full of shit, then I won't put it in here.

TUCSON, ARIZONA.

Both bands played at this house party. I seem to recall it went well, but all I really remember is that afterwards, outside, someone ran up to us and told us that the Minutemen's guitarist, D. Boon, was killed in an van accident somewhere in Arizona. I don't know how he got this information or how old the news was. It may have happened the day before we left California to go on this thing. I remember being bummed out but I don't recall anyone else in the band especially liking the Minutemen or getting them but I know everyone was familiar with them. They were sort of a hard sell to the thrashing punk crowd and honestly it took me a little while to get them but when I did, I was a big fan. So that is what I remember—D. Boon passing away in Arizona while we, too, were in Arizona. I think we left and drove onward. When we woke up, it was freezing outside and all of the windows were frozen.

EL PASO, TEXAS.

All four bands played in this giant frozen tin shack to nobody. I watched everyone chain smoke and drink beer, both foreign concepts to me at that point. After the show, the promoter was nice enough to let us and the Grim and, I think, NOFX crash at his apartment where he lived with his girlfriend. We had a whole day to kill the following day. Some of the guys wanted to go to Juárez, which didn't interest me probably because I was sort of a pussy and scared of the idea. Before anyone could leave for that adventure, one of the guests tried to steal a leather jacket from the girlfriend of the promoter. There was an uncomfortable standoff. No one could go anywhere until it was found. It turned up in a nearby dumpster on the apartment property and I think we knew that it was Eric's girlfriend who did it. For whatever reason, the promoter STILL let some of us stay there afterwards. Most everyone else went to Juárez. Later that evening, we went to the border to meet everyone and get going. A lot of the touring party were pretty well lit. We said goodbye to NOFX while Eric screamed at his girlfriend who wouldn't shut up and Mike just rolled his eyes.

Having no experience being around drunk people, I had no idea what was going on until we took off away from El Paso driving east. A few minutes later, a calm Jordan Lieberman, who was sitting in the front passenger seat quietly rolled down the window, stuck his head out and violently threw up whatever he had ingested in Juárez, all while screaming at the top of his lungs. It seemed to go on for days. He sprayed the side of the van with the gnarliest puke ever, a sort of purple chunky spray. It was amazing.

An hour or so later I was in Jordan's spot. I had lost my voice. Eric Swift was driving. We pulled off at some agriculture checkpoint. The man there asked Eric a few questions and then leaned towards me and asked if I was from this country. My hair had grown out, I was wearing a ski hat and was unshaven. He thought I was an illegal immigrant from Mexico. I sputtered out my reply in a hoarse whisper as he looked at me like I was a total idiot. He let us proceed.

AUSTIN, TEXAS.

Both bands played to no one at our show. There were maybe two people there, at most. So we played to each other and recorded the show. I still have the tape somewhere. After the show we went outside to see both Tim Kerr and Chris Gates of the recently defunct BIG BOYS walking by. We bugged them and they were real nice, talking to us about whatever. I don't think they knew there was a show, or who we were, they were just literally walking by when we saw them. But it was still neat to meet people you admired. Afterwards I think we were all allowed to crash in a musty bookstore on these hard, wood floors while it was freezing outside.

SAN ANTONIO, TEXAS.

All four bands met at this big show where we also played with the Fearless Iranians from Hell, who we all liked. I remember NOFX had a rough night but played some Rudimentary Peni covers. Apparently they were even less prepared then we were. When Entropy played, their singer, Dave, lit off a mega smoke bomb that filled the club with this thick toxic smoke and cleared the club of everyone. Later that night, as we were crashing at someone's dirty crusty punk rock shithole house, I got up in the middle of the night and ran outside into a nearby field violently throwing up as a result of the smoke bomb.

DALLAS, TEXAS.

It was bone-chillingly cold and we were playing at this giant brick warehouse in the scary industrial part of Dallas. Since it was New Years, the show promised bands playing all night, and that is what happened. There was this giant, scary-looking heat generator jutting out of the ceiling that pumped out a massive amount of heat and looked like it could fall from the ceiling and hurt a lot of people. There was one band called the Party Owls, who were really, really good—a fun party band with a two man horn section that you couldn't hear. They all ran all over the stage and went apeshit and threw beer cans all over the place. I will always remember the Party Owls. Scared Straight played well and basically had a giant pit of kids. I guess when that happens you sort of know that you must be doing something alright.

AMARILLO, TEXAS.

After getting lost, driving all over this weird frozen town, and wondering who in their right mind is going to actually go to a punk show here, we finally show up—after the show is almost over. Back then there were no cell phones or social media or devices for directions. It was a different world, one where we drove seemingly for hours lost in Amarillo, Texas. There was even the tiniest amount of snow on the ground.

I seem to recall that no one was there and it was another frozen looking metal shack.

Afterwards we were allowed to crash in someone's motor home and eat cold food while listening to some BGK or COC record.

ALBUQUERQUE, NEW MEXICO.

All four bands played this night. NOFX had a song mocking "straight edge," so being the outraged geniuses that a few of us were, we made paper airplanes writing stupid messages to them and threw them at the band while they were playing. They looked at them and shrugged their shoulders. We sure showed them. Entropy were good. We did alright. The Grim were The Grim, I guess. We played in a nice little room for a change instead of an unheated tin shack. There was a fairly decent sized crowd who came out and I seem to remember that there was a healthy sized crowd of Hispanic metal heads who were there for some reason. I don't remember anything else about this night.

PHOENIX, ARIZONA.

We showed up only to find out that the show was cancelled, or was never happening. In another strange moment, the guitarist of the local band Mighty Sphincter was walking down the street and, in no time at all, we all went back to his Goth death rock punk rock house, where it was cold, looked like the set of the Munster's household, and where he had his oven door open to heat the place. Somehow he was nice enough to set up an emergency, last-minute show for both us and The Grim. Everyone was a potential friend in punk rock it seemed. "Sure, I will set up a last minute show for a bunch of strangers."

I don't remember anything about the show in Phoenix other than someone filmed it. Aside from that, who knows? We drove to Las Vegas the following morning and sat in a restaurant buffet in some casino and ate casually for many hours because we didn't know anyone or have anywhere to go. I don't think I brought along much money because I didn't really have any. I quit my busboy job at Simi4Deli to go on this tour.

LAS VEGAS, NEVADA.

The last show of this tour was in Las Vegas. All four bands played and there was a good crowd of punker types. It was at a Moose Lodge, with actual moose heads mounted on the wall behind the stage. Later that night we crashed at some punker chick's house, where there was lots of beer drinking and chain smoking. Someone probably got laid. Definitely not me. I was sort of a goody goody who just liked the music and was probably afraid of anything else. I seem to remember that my parents were in town and I told them about the show and that they should come. I had mixed feelings about that. On one hand, it would be sort of neat for them to see what their son could do. On the other hand, I was somewhat embarrassed about that same idea and worried about them embarrassing me, or whatever. I need not worry, they never showed up, and to be honest, I was a little relieved. To this day, neither of them have ever seen me in public playing music and only my brother Marc has ever seen me drum—decades later, when I was in the band Polvo.

Looking back, the funniest thing about the time period, this tour, and the culture surrounding it was how much partying and beer drinking and chain smoking was going on, and how I knew nothing about any of that. Most of Scared Straight didn't drink beer. But that was all it was—not drinking a beer, not for any real reason. Steve drank, he partied. At the time, Eric and Dennis were Mormons. They did nothing. I didn't even know what a Mormon was. And it wasn't that everyone we encountered was troubled, scary, or dangerous but that element was always there. For the most part, we were always able to avoid that element.

It is also really funny to look back and think that none of our parents had any problem with us—at eighteen or nineteen years old—just leaving to go on tour and do god knows what. Anything could have happened, and if you remember, we already did that aborted summer tour where something DID happen. We were totally ripped off for everything, and yet here we were again. Somehow, all of that was really exciting.

We were constantly surrounded by sketchy people in weird locales and we never batted an eye towards any of it. Punk rock always attracted damaged people and damaged kids. Anyone could walk in off the street to these things and you used to always see these complete freaks just stroll up, people that you would never see again, who just radiated an aura that a mostly namby pampy group of young guys were a million miles away from. I look back and think how strange that all was. Anything could have happened.

I am not sure, but we made no money. I don't even know if the rental van was paid for. I don't know how on earth you can look at driving endless miles to play in a tin shack to nobody as being a worthwhile and exciting adventure, but decades later, in a weird way, it kind of was.

I moved to the east coast five months later and have been in Raleigh ever since. Scared Straight kept going and turned into Ten Foot Pole, which also led to Pulley. Both bands still play.

The Grim play shows these days as well, after what I imagine was a long break. Jordan is a world renowned drummer who played in a lot of bands in the same universe as well.

I don't know when Entropy disbanded.

I guess everyone knows about NOFX.

All of this seems like several lifetimes ago, and that is pretty much what it is.

Mike Dean

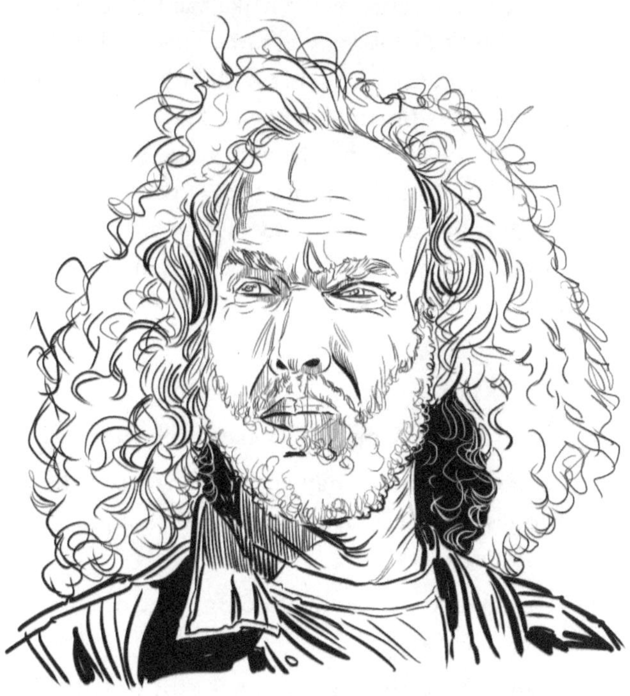

I have known Mike Dean since 1984. I was infatuated with what he was doing musically with Corrosion Of Conformity, whose earlier work was genre-pushing and now legendary. When they came out with their first record they got a lot of instant recognition in both the punk and metal underground scene. Mike wrote the song "Animosity," the heaviest song that ever came out of the state of North Carolina. I was so taken with COC during this time period that, on a whim, I moved to where they were from. That sounds really, well, kind of silly when I look back. I never left. Punk rock mail correspondence also had a lot to do with it, but North Carolina had a great punk scene back then, with COC, No Labels, Stillborn Christians, Ugly Americans, Bloodmobile, and so on and so on.

The period that I was infatuated with for Corrosion Of Conformity didn't last very long, the band had morphed into a different thing, and for a little while Mike had bailed but rejoined in time for the band's *Deliverance* album. The band still goes on to this very day, they still have a big fanbase that will come out wherever they are touring and see them. Playing bass is Mike's job. Along the way he has learned how to record music as well and has worked on a lot of various projects over the years. Mike has always been a great guy and one of my favorite overall musicians. He also knows a thing or two about being self employed and hustling, so take it away Mike.

Brian: Does Corrosion Of Conformity have a manager?

Mike: No. We have tried that maybe twice or three times and it always seemed less than efficient. So we just thought we would try to take it on ourselves.

Brian: You have taken on the role of doing some of that kind of stuff yourself for the band.

Mike: Yeah, I do a lot of the management type of stuff. Woody [Weatherman] does a little bit of it. We just save a bit of that ten or fifteen percent that you would normally give to someone else to do things on your behalf. We have had offers for management, from people with some really sassy offices and you just wonder well, how do they pay for this office? And we have gone the other way with people who are more DIY-based, people doing smaller bands, but they seemed kind of stretched out from doing so many of these bands that maybe they couldn't do much for you. So you have to step up and do this adult stuff on your own behalf, you know.

Brian: You guys have been touring very continually since the band has gotten back together but when you get back from tour I know you have a couple of things that you do to keep stuff going and one of them is that you build stages and set up things for events, concerts and stuff.

Mike: That is one thing I do, I do rigging work. When a giant concert comes through, there is a local crew. You got to rent out a PA, get some carpenters to build the sets, and the riggers get there first, there is lighting and things like that. There is a little bit of climbing. My first stagehand job actually was a one-off in Atlanta when the Cult played the Center Stage Theatre and we really didn't know what we were doing and they were late, and we went into the dressing room and we saw a bunch of food and we ate it, and then a really mean English man arrived and told us that we were off the gig. And that was my first thing and then I sort of forgot about all of that. Then COC were doing some stuff with Metallica and you watch this giant thing get put together every day for sixty or seventy shows, and you see how it works...

So when I went home and things got slow—when Pepper [Keenan] was doing Down and stuff like that—I was like, "well, I don't know what is going on but I could do that." So I started doing that in 2002-2003.

Brian: I know the other thing you do is you have learned how to produce, engineer, and record music. Was it a natural thing to eventually become interested in learning all of that because of all of the time you had spent playing music?

Mike: It is a difficult career to break into, it would kind of like be a dream job but you know, you can chip away at it. My interest in it was because COC was making records for a while and being in a studio is pretty fascinating. When we recorded the first record *Eye For An Eye* with a couple of guys, they had a twenty-four track machine and a giant console in a room of their house, and watching the engineer on that one, David Mahon, that was pretty interesting. He just invited us into that process a little bit more than most people would and I just kind of got the bug at that point.

Later on, COC recorded at places like Electric Lady and all of these famous studios, and even the demo stuff that we would do with John Custer in Raleigh here, I just got fascinated with the process. At the beginning of this millennium you could basically record on a computer and just start chipping away at it, so it has been fun. I have done a lot of engineering on basically every COC record since *In The Arms Of God* and it is kind of a fun experience, and kind of a challenge. All of the three-piece stuff we had mixed ourselves here and on the last record we actually went back to the guy who mixed *Wiseblood*, way back in 1996, Mike Fraser.

Brian: Did he mix AC/DC records or am I just imagining that?

Mike: Oh yeah. We went from this modest place that we work at, to this lavish place in Vancouver. He has worked there a lot. We drove out there for that, me and Custer, because Custer doesn't like to fly.

Brian: That sounds like a David Bowie thing. At least you didn't have to take a boat across the pond. Anyways, you have been in Corrosion of Conformity for a really long time, except for a little sabbatical in early 1997 for a few years. Why did you quit for a while, looking back at it as an adult? You guys were touring a lot and hitting it pretty hard, it was an intense period of time.

Mike: I think we weren't getting the value from our time that we could, people were making money off of us but we weren't making any money. I have seen somewhat profitable or self-sustaining people do good with the DIY ethos but I have also seen foolish, "yeah, everything is just between friends" kind of stuff. What we were doing was like, go out to L.A. and play a Goldenvoice show, and it wasn't managed properly, you know. We didn't have the chops to do that right. It was exhausting after a while, and there were also some personal and creative differences, of course. It could get a little intense. I think I also had a lot of other musical influences and stuff that I kind of wanted to jump into. I think the band ended up catching up and surpassing what we did and realized that there were more things to do musically, so it all ended up working out.

Brian: You ended up in Atlanta afterwards, in the short-lived band you had with William DuVall called The Final Offering. William thought it was the one thing that he did musically that got away from him and that he wished they could have recorded.

Mike: We were kind of finding our way with that, we had this trip of being really into this Sun Ra and the MC5, just creating on-the-spot crazy stuff but at super loud volume. At the time, William was known for being in Neon Christ and I was in COC, so there were some people that were expecting to see an combination of that, with maybe a little bit of Black Flag worship. And they would come and see us and it was actually really loud but somewhat chaotic and there were these kids that were trying to like it, ha ha.

Brian: I thought it was good, man! And you guys never recorded.

Mike: No, not really. No. We had this drummer who was really amazing and gifted, he was in a hardcore band in Atlanta called DDT. He could do all of this crazy Mitch Mitchell or Elvin Jones type of stuff, but he was probably the first junkie that I ever ended up working with and it would be like, "Why is he not showing up?" And we just had to figure out what was going on, his girlfriend had a key to a local hospital, she was a nurse and they were all strung out and shit. He moved to Portland and promptly OD'd. So that kind of put a damper on things.

Brian: Eventually, you were asked to re join COC.

Mike: Yeah, the band I had in Philadelphia called Spore played a few shows with the Karl [Agell], Pepper, and Phil [Swisher] version of COC. And the record they made, it was like "those guys made that? What?" The only problem about rejoining was that it felt a little weird because I was good friends with Karl and Phil, who are now out of the band. So the funny thing about getting back with it and listening to the recordings—the rhythm tracks that were going to be *Deliverance*—was that some of them were kind of finished, and that was pretty impressive but it was a little weird stepping in.

They were looking for a singer. And they had this box full of, this is before the internet, a box full of cassettes and photographs of people that wanted to be in a rock band, and some of them were really silly and most of them were really inappropriate. They had all of these people that wanted to be celebrities, you could tell there were a lot of desperate people that just wanted to be in a band that was getting ready to have a record released on a label. But Pepper wanted us to talk him into being the singer, which is what he came up to do in COC anyways. You know, *Blind* was a great record but probably the best song on it was the one that he sang.

Brian: As long as I have known you, you have kept a pretty cool head throughout some pretty interesting scenarios.

Mike: You never know, today could be the day that I snap. There has always been something there worth doing musically that is fulfilling, and we can make a living, it is kind of a no-brainer.

DALE CROVER

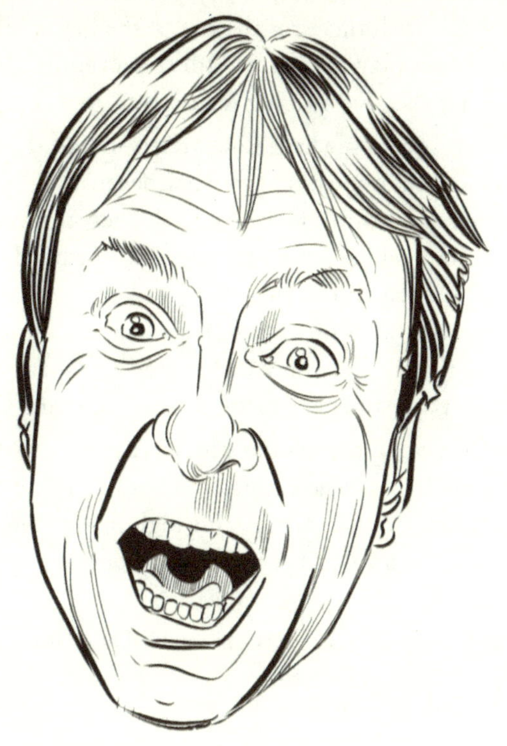

Let me set up the scenario. The year is 1986. I had just relocated to Raleigh, North Carolina, a few months before summer starts. It is hot. It is humid as shit. It pretty much sucks, it's my first exposure to summer in the south, and it blows.

The Melvins come through town to play a show on their first-ever tour of the country. They walk through the door of the house where Reed Mullin of Corrosion Of Conformity lived, which is a block away from where I live. An eighteen- or nineteen-year-old Dale Crover walks in. He is wearing short shorts, has a John Denver type bob haircut, and these really thick coke bottle glasses. He is also wearing a Ted Nugent t-shirt. Like, a then-recent Ted

Nugent shirt, "TNT." I remember thinking to myself, "Man, not even GOOD Ted Nugent." He and the rest of the guys in the Melvins were nice guys, I felt a connection right away. After hanging out with them for the rest of the day, a bunch of us went and saw them play in Chapel Hill that evening. I became a huge fan of what they were doing instantly.

I have known Dale ever since. He is one of the nicest people I know, and with almost no ego whatsoever. There is a quiet confidence though. I think he is one of the best drummers alive, who only seems to get better as time goes on. The band has had the sort of cult audience and appeal that just keeps on going and going. My friendship with Buzz and Dale has been a huge and big deal. It was fortunate that they had played in North Carolina all of those years ago and very fortunate for me that I had met them.

Dale has been a working musician with no other job since towards the end of the eighties. He has a family on top of all of that to balance out. Years ago, his high school guidance counselor encouraged him to quit school and go on tour with the Melvins. So far so good.

So sit back and enjoy this chat with Dale. We did this between tours probably a year ago.

♫

Brian: What was your first job?

Dale: I had a paper route in fifth grade. I saved up enough money to buy my first drum set through that. It was only a hundred and fifty bucks. But I had a paper route after school every day and I would have to collect money from people. I know a lot of people that had done that and I didn't really make that much money because it was hard to get money out of people. Luckily, my mom was on top of me about that, she would go with me to help me collect and made sure that no one would fuck with me.

Thinking about it now, sometimes it was hard to collect money from people going door to door, even though they owed it. And we are talking only about four or five bucks a month. And out of that I got a quarter, or fifty cents, or something and you know... I was also relying on tips.

It was funny, I would go door to door, and I would see that they were home and then I would see them running away inside their houses. (laughter) People didn't want to pay a paperboy a few bucks.

It wasn't everybody, some people were certainly nice. I think I did it for a couple of years. I had a couple different routes. I remember one time playing baseball, I had hit a home run and my mom said something like, "if you hit another home run I will help you with your paper route tomorrow." I think she even said that she would do it for me. So I hit another home run. But my mom didn't even know my paper route anyways so...

Brian: Buzz is usually the one who goes off in interviews about how horrible and depressing the area that you grew up in was, which is a rural part of Washington state. He certainly has quite a bit of contempt for your surroundings.

Dale: Well, Buzz had it a bit tougher growing up.

Brian: You get the sense that he couldn't blend in right away, and I think he has said that the idea of moving into a small town where everyone already knew each other for generations was a pretty shitty thing in general, that breaking into that sort of thing was impossible. But I will also add that every time we get anywhere near your neck of the woods, it looks pretty and very nice to me. But that is just me as an adult looking at it. And I grew up in a nice place and I still hated it and wasn't able to appreciate it.

Dale: Every time we have been up there on tour, it's the summertime when it is actually nice out for a very small portion of the year. But usually it rains a lot and it is really cold and depressing. It will rain for ninety days straight, everything is cold and wet. There was nothing to do, which is why we played music. In the early days, we practiced all of the time and once in awhile we played a gig. And then when we got to California we played gigs all of the time and didn't practice as much anymore.

We spent a lot of time writing music and practicing, learning songs. And as you know, a lot of those songs never ever saw the light of day. We had no means to record them and had no record label, so eventually we just wrote songs that we liked better.

Brian: I remember meeting you for the first time and you had that really bizarre looking, beat to shit drum set that had drum heads that looked like soup bowls and you still got a great sound out of them. This really mismatched drum set. When did you get your first huge drum set, the one with the Hot Wheels sticker on it?

Dale: You saw me for the first time with my first drum set. I think I even recorded the first album with that drum set.

Brian: Really? I love the way the first record sounds, like it was recorded in an airplane hangar or at the bottom of a canyon.

Dale: It was a big studio.

Brian: What about the Hot Wheels drum set? That huge black kit? Those drums were as big as Bill Stevenson's gray kit.

Dale: I was aware of how big Bill's drums were, but by the time I had got in the Melvins, that *Slip It In* record had just come out and I really liked it. I already had missed some school playing with the Melvins, and of course Black Flag were playing in Seattle on a Tuesday night, and my parents wouldn't let me go. And then Bill was out of the band soon after that so I didn't saw him play until later. We played with the Descendents, and I don't remember if I had that drum set then or not. But anyway, we came back from the first tour and our van was pretty much dead at that point. I think it might have been the end of 1986, maybe early 87. We played a show with Green River and we talked them into letting us just use their equipment. I remember that Jeff [Ament] was a little apprehensive about letting Matt [Lukin] use his bass amp. Anyways, we played a show with their gear and the drummer, Alex [Vincent], had a twenty-six inch bass drum, a nice new Tama kit, and I was like, "Wow, that is really cool!" It was like going from driving a Volkswagen to driving a tank. I said I really wanted to get a bass drum like that and Alex said, "good luck, I had to order this from Tama and it took six months for them to get it to me." He just kind of laughed at me.

The music store in Olympia was called Music 6000 and it was where we got a lot of our gear. It was where Buzz got his first Les Paul that he put the Kiss sticker on. Anyways, I went in there and asked if they had a twenty-six inch bass drum and they were like, "well...we don't have any singular bass drums for sale but we do have this Ludwig kit back there for sale that has this twenty-six inch kick drum. As a matter of fact, it has a twenty inch floor tom, too." (laughter) My jaw hit the floor and I was like, "Fuck!" And it also had a eighteen inch extra floor time and a fourteen inch rack tom.

I was working at my first real job, but I hadn't had enough money to get it, so Lukin lent me some money so I could get it.

Brian: I remember that set. You used it for all of your early recordings.

Dale: Definitely. From *Ozma* through to *Houdini*. The was the kit on all of the Nirvana stuff too. But I didn't set it up like Bill Stevenson at first, I had to get rid of a couple of toms and then I had the full Black Flag drum set up. I got a deal with Tama shortly after that.

Brian: I loved that drum set, it was so intimidating. And now Ashton [Bird] from Tweak Bird owns it.

Dale: Yeah, but I told him that he can't get rid of it. If he does, he has to give them back to me. (laughter)

Brian: One of my favorite stories that you have ever told me is your guidance counselor story in high school. It is really funny. Can you repeat that for me here?

Dale: It was the first time that I had ever talked to him. I would see him in the hallways and it turned out that he was a counselor. We played shows on the weekends and sometimes on the weekdays and because of that, I started missing a lot of school. I was much more interested in practicing and playing and I wasn't doing good in most of my classes with the exception, of course, of band. (laughter)

I knew what I wanted to do, I knew even in grade school that I wanted to be a drummer. I loved Kiss, and I didn't want to be in a band like Kiss, I wanted to be in Kiss. I never even thought about going to college. I am sure that my parents would have wanted that, but I knew what I wanted to do. So we started to do little tours and stuff. I am trying to think of when this tour was. I think it was the tour where we met you. (1986), and I remember talking to this guy about the tour and saying, "I want to go on this tour, but I am going to miss school for it. What should I do?" And he said, "This is what you want to do. Obviously you know what you want to do in life. My advice to you is to drop out, quit school, go on this tour, and when you come back—if you want to come back—you just re-register. It will be no big deal." (laughter) And so I said, "Oh. Okay." It made perfect sense. So that is what I did, and I never looked back. I am sure that the guidance counselor might have known, it was the same time when Kurt Cobain went to high school, I am sure he knew who everybody was.

Brian: So when Buzz broke up the band to move to San Francisco it wasn't too much later that you moved down there as well. Eventually the two of you continued the Melvins with Lori Black on bass. What was it about Buzz and playing with him that made you decide to move down there, instead of—and we will get to this part in a sec—ending up being in Nirvana, because you had recorded that first demo with them?

Dale: Playing with Buzz was fun and challenging. We had to start over again completely in a whole new city. With Nirvana, I liked it, I liked playing with those guys. At first they sounded a lot like us but I liked it. At that point I would say that Kurt was my best friend. He spent the night at my house the night before I moved down to San Francisco.

But playing with Kurt… it was at the time when the Melvins

had broken up, or went on a hiatus, whatever you want to call it… in transition. Buzz had told me first that he didn't want to stay here, you know? He wanted to do something else and had a chance to move to San Francisco. He said, "there is nothing here for me." I was like, "there is no reason for me to stay here. I want to come down there and figure out some way to make it work." There certainly wasn't anything going on there.

But anyways, during that time the Nirvana guys, who were good friends with us, had been playing with this local drummer that we knew and for whatever reason, I don't think that they were completely satisfied with him. They had asked me to join because, at the time, I didn't have completely solid plans. But at the same time I was, "Yeah, I want to get out of here and I want to continue with the band with Buzz if we could." Anyways, in between that time, they had asked me to join and I said, "Well…I might not be sticking around. But I would certainly love to play with you guys." And so that was the deal—to stick around, learn their songs, and record a demo.

Brian: With Jack Endino.

Dale: Yeah. He is great.

Brian: He always seemed like a really nice guy too.

Dale: Totally. And I remember that Kurt picked that studio, and part of the reason was because, I think, Soundgarden had recorded there. And at that time Green River broke up, we broke up and so Soundgarden were one of the last bands standing and was starting to do pretty good. They had their first EP out and we listened to it a bunch. Kurt called the studio up and said, "Hey, I am Kurt, blah blah blah… we play with Dale Crover, we want to record a demo." And it was Jack he was talking to and Jack thought that sounded cool. So what he knew about it was that it was a new band that I was in. So then we came and recorded, it was ten songs at the studio. Really quickly, no real overdubs… maybe vocals. It was done in an afternoon and some of the songs you could tell were done quickly. We drank a bunch of coffee and were gulping down chocolate covered espresso beans. Certainly on some of the songs you can tell because the drums take off. (laughter)

And also, we were going to play a show that night in Tacoma, so we kind of had to finish this thing and then go pack up and play this show. Jack really liked it and was kind of impressed and, I think, played it for some Sub Pop people almost immediately because I know that even the next day he had called those guys and said, "Hey, I really liked your stuff and I liked what we did and I already played it for some people and they are kind of interested."

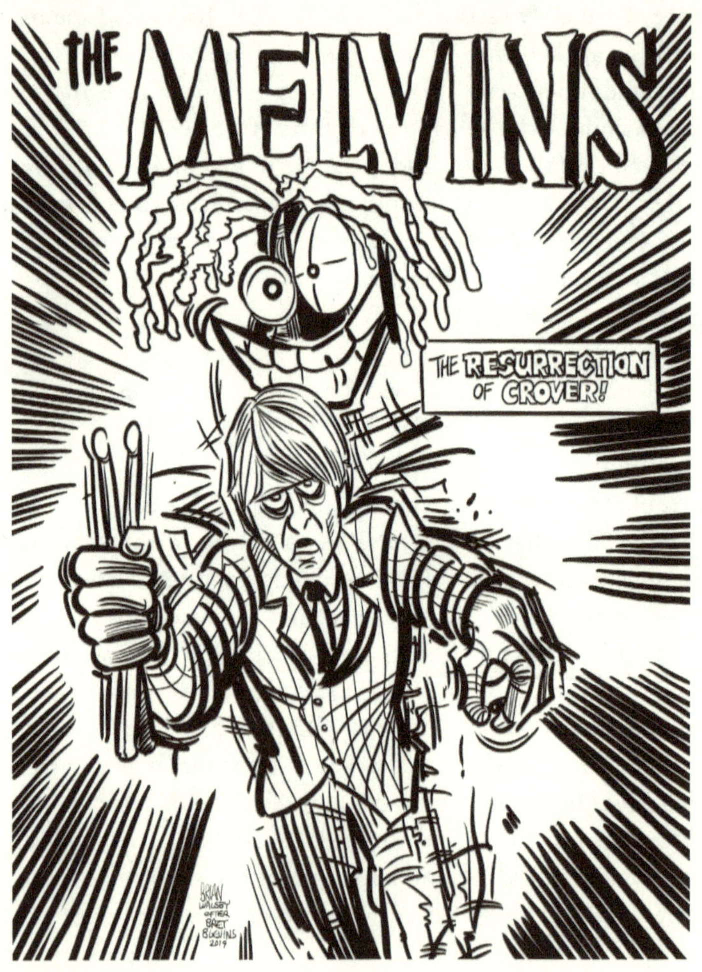

Brian: It is kind of funny how you turned out to be there for this upcoming part of history. But I do think it is even more funny how when people don't understand the history of all of that stuff look at your involvement in it like you are sort of the Pete Best of that story. Like that Howard Stern interview you did where he keeps sort of trying to goad you into admitting…

Dale: How I messed up?

Brian: Yeah. But all along you wanted to stick with Buzz. And no one knew what would end up happening.

Dale: Exactly. And they were heavily influenced by the Melvins for sure. Yeah, I liked their songs and thought that they were great, but I felt that I was already in the Melvins. I didn't want to be in the other Melvins. (laughter) And we already had a record out and were more established. But you know, had I not moved to San Francisco, I am sure I would have ended up playing with them, you know? Oh well. And I almost ended up playing on what would have been the *Nevermind* record. Because they fired Chad [Channing] after doing *Bleach* with him, and then right after they fired him they were offered a tour opening up for Sonic Youth on the west coast so they called me and had me do that.

And while they were discussing that tour, they were going to come down and play, they also said that they had wanted me to play drums on their next record. So I said, "Great. I would love to." But in between the time that we had talked about that and the time that they came down to a San Francisco to rehearse with me, Mudhoney were breaking up and they decided that they would just get Danny Peters to play with them. But I don't think that he was what they were really looking for. And when they came down to rehearse with me, that was when we took those guys to see Scream and that is when they saw Dave Grohl, who was playing with them.

Brian: Right, who is a powerful drummer influenced by a couple people that I can think of…(laughter)

Dale: Oh yeah, exactly. He totally had a similar style, and he definitely liked Reed Mullin and probably definitely liked me a lot, too. So while they were rehearsing with me and then saw Dave play, I think that they probably realized that they had picked the wrong drummer for what they wanted to do. And it just so happened to work out that Scream were stranded on the west coast about three days after that. And so Dave Grohl called up our house and Buzz talked to him and said, "Well…there is this band up in Seattle that is interested in you and interested in your drumming." And so…that was that.

Brian: So it is Buzz's fault.

Dale: Pretty much, but I would say that I am to blame, too. (laughter) I will take the blame too. But whatever, obviously I am joking about all of that.

Brian: But it is funny being at the footsteps of music history.

Dale: Yeah. Exactly. But with the Howard Stern thing I was saying, "I had no idea." And he was saying, "Yes!! Yes you did!!" It was pretty funny.

Brian: Working at Round Table Pizza with Buzz in San Francisco was the last job I think that you had before just playing in a band full time as a living. I think it was 1990 and you had released records with Tom Flynn of Boner Records, like *Ozma* and *Bullhead* had already come out. And Tom Flynn presented you guys with a pretty decent royalty check, maybe your first one ever. And then you guys kind of jumped off the cliff. You told me that you kept your job but for the most part you guys were making waves and planning to do the Melvins full time at that point in time.

Dale: After we did that tour where we met you in 1986, it was so miserable and we were so disliked. And we didn't make any money. And we just thought that we would never do that again. None of us wanted to pay to go on tour and have a miserable time, and that tour was more of a giant learning adventure than anything else, you know? All of our best stories are from that tour just because it was our first time out.

It was tough. It was rough for us. We didn't go on tour until

Ozma came out, and by that time, that's when bands from Seattle were starting to get attention and there were labels like Amphetamine Reptile starting up as well. And we got hooked up with a booking agent, someone who could book us a tour rather than us doing something. So that certainly helped out. That was our first proper U.S. tour where we were actually supposed to be there and everything, where we were advertised. (laughter) As opposed to the first one where we just jumped on somebody else's tour because one of the bands couldn't make it.

Brian: That was Beyond Possession from Calgary. You toured in place of them with Rich Kids On LSD. Which is pretty funny, because I sort of knew them a tiny bit, they weren't from too far away from where I lived and they seemed really experienced in life compared to me. (laughter)

Dale: Right. For sure, they seemed to know a thing or two. You could tell that they had been on the road a few times before. But anyways, the next time that we toured we came home with some money, enough to where I actually bought an electric guitar. And at the time we still had jobs, we were still working at Round Table. I held on to that for as long as I could. I mentioned before that we were pretty good workers, we showed up on time. The boss was kind of a jerk but he liked us enough, he liked me enough to where it was okay that I went on tour and was gone for a month. We went on our first ever European tour, and right before that tour my dad had died. A week later we went on tour, and then we came home and I had decided that I would maybe hang out for a week and not go back to work right away thinking that I would still have my job.

But when I went back to get some hours the boss said that they weren't going to hire me back. So that was it after that. I was let go and I never had another job again. I was just in the band and focused on that.

Brian: There was a very brief time during the Atlantic Records era where you had management. You never had it before and you never had it again. Why is that?

Dale: Yeah, I guess we just thought that we could take care of it and that we didn't want to pay somebody a percentage to do it. The manager that we had was good. Unlike most managers, he didn't take his percentage right off the top, he took his after the bills were paid. Most managers do not do that. We hired him after we signed the Atlantic deal. We oversaw the whole thing, and Atlantic almost insisted that we get a manager because they had never dealt with just the band. It just doesn't happen in that world. So we had to find somebody, and it was weird.

Anyways, after three or four years and during those records on Atlantic, we both decided that there wasn't anything that he was doing that we just couldn't do ourselves. It wasn't like he was going out and finding us a bunch of money, which is what most managers should do. I am sure Buzz has said that. A manager should make money for both you and him, and he did what he could. We just came to a point where we thought that we didn't need anybody. When we had him we really wanted to go to Japan. We had never been to Japan before. And he couldn't find anything.

The one thing he did do for us was he got us a really good booking agent with the William Morris Agency, and we have been with them ever since. After we parted ways with our manager, Buzz called up those guys and asked if we could go to Japan. They said that they would look into it. Then they called us right back and said sure. (laughter)

Brian: The way it always goes with the Melvins is that you guys get all of the accolades and credibility but you are never invited to the party.

Dale: Right. It's like the Grammys and the Rock And Roll Hall of Fame. Who are those people anyways? We have never been a part of that world at all. We are something else.

Brian: The Chris Cornell tribute concert that you guys were invited to play a few weeks ago, I think that was literally the first fucking time that I could think where some of your peers invited you to take part in something, even though it was a sad occasion. It was cool that the rest of Soundgarden thought enough about you guys to invite you.

Dale: I don't know if everybody involved in that concert wanted us at the party. But when this concert was being organized and there was a meeting about what bands did the guys in Soundgarden want to play, Matt Cameron, the first thing he said was, "I want Paul McCartney and the Melvins because Chris' two favorite bands were the Beatles and the Melvins." That is great. I am glad we got to play and I am glad that we got to pay tribute. It was weird. And I think that definitely that is not our world. Ultimately any of that big time rock and roll arena rock and roll stuff is not our world and it never has been. We kind of tried playing shows like that with bigger bands—Kiss and Rush, White Zombie. And Tool. All kinds of bands like that. It was fun and cool but that is just not us.

We called bullshit on a lot of that stuff. And as harsh and cynical as Buzz might seem to be, he is not being harsh or cynical, he is just telling the truth. The truth isn't pretty I guess. It is funny, people seem to think that he is bitter or jealous of our peers' success and that is completely not true at all. That is not how we feel success is at all. We feel happy and successful, we don't have to answer to the man. We ARE the man. (laughter) For whatever reason, we are still around. And when we go and play shows, there is an audience there that aren't a bunch of people our age. Certainly there are some. It is strange, but I am grateful. Even on this last little round we did—we got to play in Santa Barbara, where we haven't played for awhile and I was just looking out at the audience, and we aren't talking huge shows by any means but we are in Santa Barbara on a weekday night and the place is packed and there are kids there that were not there the last time we played. No way. And they are young people.

Brian: Let's talk about having kids. When you are a parent, everyone around you sort of disappears. It is very alienating. Sometimes I think that people that you used to see, I almost get this idea that maybe they think that you wouldn't want to see them. And it's like, this is when you need to see people.

Dale: Oh Totally. This is when I need you the most. I kind of figured that out early on before I had kids because I had some friends that had kids. One of my best friends in particular, Dan Southwick, who I played with in Altamont, I remember when he had his kid and some of his friends that he used to hang out with just never called him anymore. At all. And he would tell me that. And I thought that was pretty crazy. I never abandoned him or felt that we couldn't hang out because he had kids. When we had kids, I saw the same thing happen to Maureen. Like, one of her really really good friends, once she got pregnant, that was it. She never called Maureen again. It was weird. They don't want to be involved for whatever reason.

Brian: The last time I had talked to you, you told me about how you and Maureen had discussed the idea of children and your job as a drummer around that sort of life change.

Dale: Yeah. We certainly had big discussions about it. "Should we have kids? Because I am still going to have to do this." It's not like I am going to settle down and get a straight job, this is what I do for a living and this is what I wanted to do since I was a kid. It wasn't like some surprise. And we were fortunate enough to be able to afford a house before that and had everything in place in our relationship. And so we had Scarlett. And after a year we went on a three month tour. Now she is thirteen.

Brian: I guess that since both of your kids have grown up with it they are used to it.

Dale: Exactly. They don't know anything else. It's hard for me to go away. It is hard for me and it is hard for them. The first week is always the roughest because it's the biggest change but then you kind of get in the swing of things. When they were younger they could come out and visit, but now they are both in school so it doesn't happen. But we tour about three months out of the year and I had figured out that an average parent who would have a nine-to-five, five days a week job, that I was still home more and free to spend more time at home when I didn't have to work. It kind of equals out. It's different. The only other career I could think was similar would be if you are in the military, which in that situation you could be gone for a long time, like being shipped overseas in some place.

TODD KOWALSKI

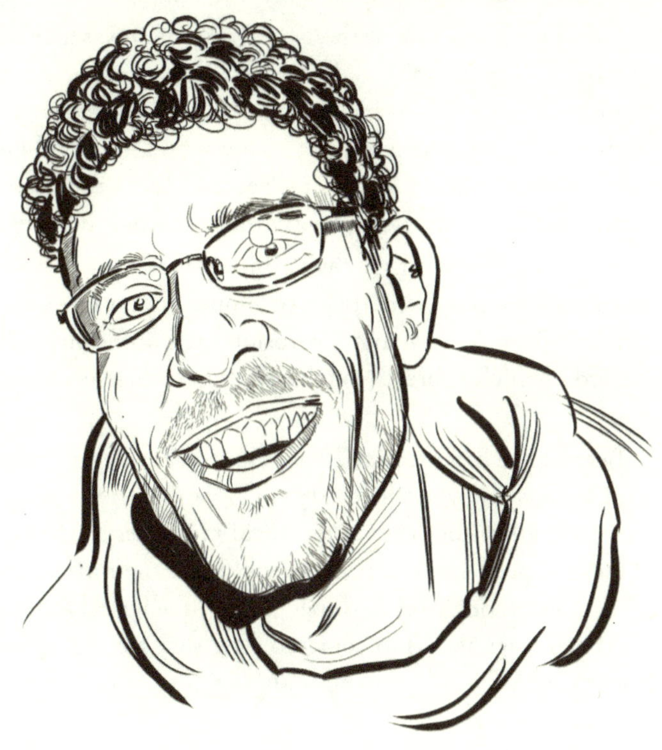

I met Todd Kowalski a couple of years ago when I discovered how much I enjoyed his band Propagandhi and their more recent output and thoughtful and committed stance on what was important to them. I got turned on to the band by Charles Cardello but had already had this funny experience where I hung out with Scott Radinsky. He was playing me some music in his car—Strung Out or Good Riddance or Lagwagon—I had never heard any of that stuff at all, even though all of those bands are basically peers of Scott and his band Pulley. At one point he said, "Well, this is the best band out there right now. They are called

Propagandhi. They are the best. They have the best everything—best musicianship, best songs, best lyrics. They are the best. YOU will like them."

So he played some of their stuff. He was right.

I am sure it was one of their later records. I was a latecomer to the band Propagandhi, as I was never aware of the Epitaph/Fat world so I never would have come across Propagandhi back then anyways. I caught up and went backwards, after Todd joined the band onward, where I seemed to "get it." I think they keep getting better and better the farther away they get from their beginnings.

And it turned out that they all had this heavy metal/eighties punk background where they worshipped things like Celtic Frost, Voivod, Born Against and Corrosion Of Conformity's *Animosity* period—which is pretty much the aggressive music that I liked, too.

Because the band seems very committed to what they sing about, and because they are just very nice people, they have a certain aura that allows both super technical music nerds (the band plays a lot of super technical parts mixed in to their often emotional music) and thoughtful fans (people into the lyrical aspect of what the band sings about) to come up after they are done playing and shoot the shit with the band, hanging out with whomever wants to talk to them.

After we met, we went out for dinner a few times when the Melvins would come through Winnipeg, and became friends.

It also turns out Todd is a very talented painter and artist. I mean, really jaw-dropping talented. And he is working on his art and keeping it on the downlow. Which is very respectable, especially considering how goddamn talented an artist Todd is.

Anyways, I like Todd and respect him and Propagandhi a lot.

♫

Brian: How long have you been playing bass for Propagandhi?

Todd: I guess twenty-two or twenty-three years? Since 1996.

Brian: I was wondering about how the band operates because it seems to be a little different than most bands. It seems like you guys work, record, and play shows when you feel like doing it, and not so much on a schedule or a routine, or a cycle. Is that a correct thing to say about it?

Todd: Pretty much, I guess. If we do have a record, we tour a bit more than if we don't have a record. And we only go for two weeks at a time, so they are kind of spaced out, and by the time our touring cycle has stopped it has been quite a length of time. And the other times we are making new riffs and stuff and then we start working on new songs a little more seriously.

Brian: Was your decision to go out for only two week jaunts something that happened over time? Like a conscious decision?

Todd: Well, we started out doing month-long tours and then it whittled down to two weeks. We are actually at ten shows. We are going as hard as we can because we really do try and put everything we have into every show, so after ten shows we are done. Like, physically done.

Brian: So during all of the time that you are not doing the band, do you do anything on the side to make money, like a job?

Todd: Well I did one year. I had a job working with refugee kids teaching them drawing and stuff like that. I had that for one year, that was after the *Supporting Caste* album.

Brian: So you have been able to not worry about money and get by with a semi-sporadic schedule of the band?

Todd: Yeah, some things worked strangely in our favor, like... Winnipeg is one of the cheapest cities that you could possibly live in, and a long time ago when houses were so cheap, we all bought one, you know? So that eliminated all those expenses. It is not like living in New York and paying a lot of rent. So we kind of lucked into that. Even my property taxes are cheap. And none of us really buy anything. I guess we are thrifty or cheap people.

Brian: Maybe you are just pragmatic.

Todd: Yeah, I guess. Also right now, anywhere that we go, the Canadian dollar is low. So we come home with more than we would if we were an American band. I mean, we have to pay more but...

Brian: It is almost an accidental advantage.

Todd: It kind of works for us and against us because if we ever want to buy anything, if we ever bought as much as we pulled in, then it would work against us, with the dollar being so low. But if we are just playing in the U.S. and not buying anything really, it's fine.

Brian: When the old model for music and selling music went into the toilet, did that affect you guys very much? Because bands

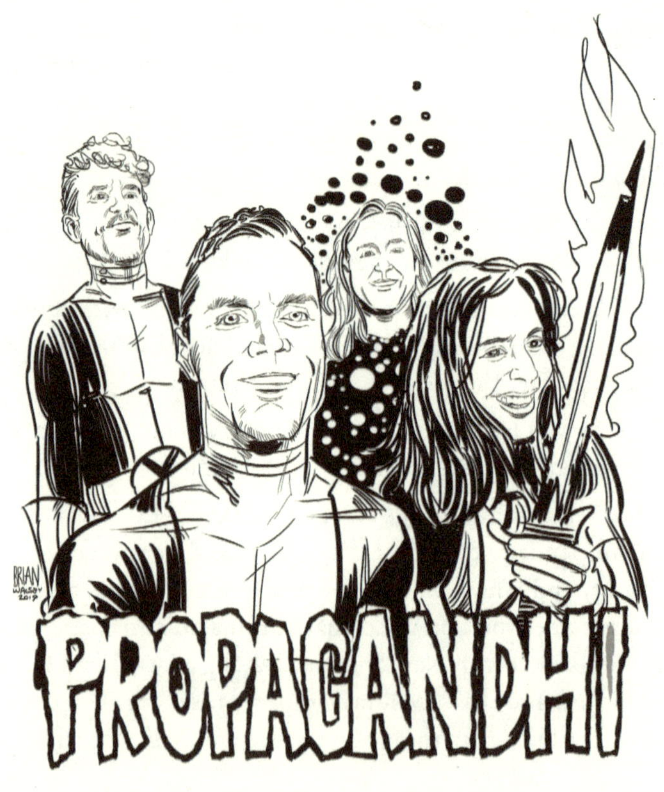

generally don't sell as much, I hate to use this term, physical product. And they have to tour a lot more to make up for it.

It seems like the kind of people that like you guys are probably loyal but also there is a certain type of thoughtfulness that you guys present, in like how you present yourselves and what you believe in. And certainly the lyric writing.

Todd: I think that we are probably at a third of what we used to sell, roughly. Something like that. We actually—because of some of the deals that we kind of negotiated for ourselves and because of the fact that we completely own *Supporting Caste* on our own—our digital download payments are actually pretty high, too. Like, maybe compared to other bands.

It's not like actually selling a bunch of records but it is still a substantial amount, you know? And then the records—I think partially it's because we put so much time into the covers, the songs, the lyrics, you know—I think that when people can feel that it's not just thrown together, they are more likely to buy it.

Brian: Sure. I still consider music to be an important thing to me, but I really don't care too much about the format that people choose to listen to it in.

Todd: The one thing I do like about digital is that it is environmentally, totally. Like, all of the vinyl and stuff, so much petroleum products and paper and printing and ink and shipping and gas and all of that—digital completely eliminates all of that, which I think is kind of cool.

Brian: Has it been hard for you guys to take stands on things that you believe in, in terms of what it might have cost your band as a whole? Or is that something that you guys at this point don't even think about?

Todd: I think that the most obvious way that it has cost us is that all of those festivals with sponsors and all of that, you know? They pay out just huge amounts of money to all of those bands and we don't play any of those Some of those payouts are just humongous. If we didn't care, and wanted to do any old festival to make that money, then we would have at least ten times as much money, you know? I think that is the most obvious.

I guess the setbacks are that there are probably tons of people that don't listen to us because of their interpretation of our lyrics and all of that. But at the same time, I think that the people who know where we are coming from, it endears them because we are just trying to be honest.

Brian: I didn't even realize that you did artwork at all, or that you did anything for your bands inserts and record covers. Did you draw that thing in the *Supporting Caste* record where the band is eating this grisly meal of just meat?

Todd: Yeah. That and the owl, the seven-inch that we did with the band Sacrifice...

Brian: ...Where you guys cover Corrosion of Conformity's "Technocracy"? You drew that?

Todd: Yeah. And the cover for *Failed States*. And some of the shirts, but some of the shirts are just old, you know what I mean.

Brian: Have you done any work for other bands and their records and stuff?

Todd: Uh, yeah, this band Cauldron. And then this band Plague. That was a seven-inch. They offered me eighty bucks and I was like, "Sure, whatever."

Brian: Eighty bucks!

Todd: Ha, ha. Yeah, but they ended up giving me like a hundred and sixty. So that was cool. Usually I wouldn't do that but they are all friends of mine.

Brian: I don't know anything about painting or how to paint but after seeing it, and you know Kristin who you met, and our friend Allison, we were talking and we were like "that guy Todd is really nice but Omigod his painting is fucking incredible." But it seems like you are being kind of protective about what you are doing as a painter. Are you trying to keep that aspect of what you do creatively on the downlow for later? You have obviously drawn and painted since you were really small, right?

Todd: Yeah. But actually, I quit for like ten years, at some point in my late twenties.

Brian: Was that because you were more into playing music?

Todd: Yeah I think so. And I would draw just a little bit here and there. But the painting, I just do it because I just like it so much, you know, and sometimes when you introduce commerce into it, you know like selling it…

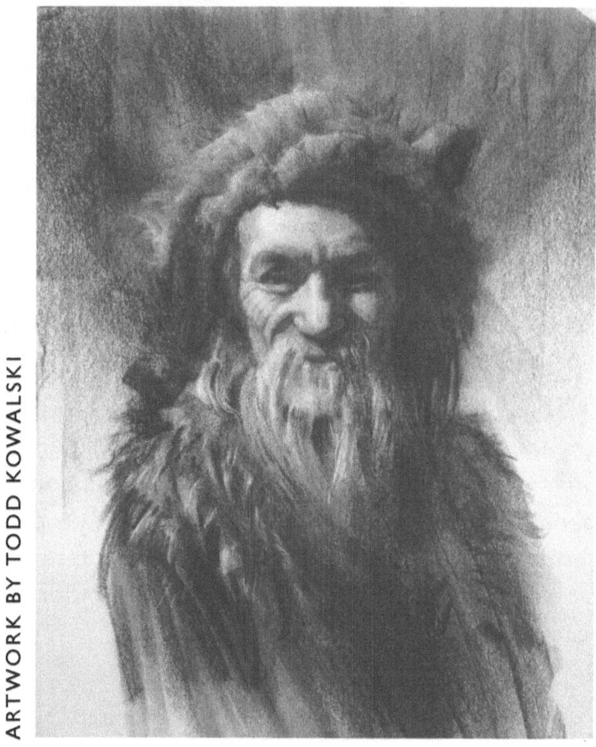

ARTWORK BY TODD KOWALSKI

Brian: It seems kind of wrong?

Todd: Yeah. But a couple of paintings I really like but, for the most part, I just find that it is just not as good as the people whose paintings I really like, you know? With Propagandhi, our band, I feel like we are as good as the bands that I like. When I look at my paintings, I feel like I understand what I want to see in painting—it is clearer than music, I can see my shortcomings—where with music it's usually such an abstract idea. Like, I don't know where it's going but I just know when it feels pretty good, you know?

Brian: Okay, That makes sense. We were all really impressed by your stuff. I really don't know how to judge art at all but I have respect more for actual talent than painting a blue dot in the center of a giant white canvas that sells for fifty million dollars. I don't understand any of that.

Todd: I think that is one other reason why I keep my paintings to myself, I don't want to know anything about that world too much, you know? Or feel let down by it in the same way. When you know the inner workings of music…

Brian: My gut feeling says that the art world is even more full of shit than the music world.

Todd: Oh yeah.

Brian: Plus you are in a position where you don't really have to do that.

Todd: Right. But, you know if I had to, I would. Yeah, I think it is just an honest pursuit of trying to get better without anything attached to it at all. And, if I don't need to do it then I don't have to think about it, right? I guess I am just one of those people who is really just trying our best at stuff and seeing how far you can go without it being influenced by other people. Except for people that you care about, or people that can help you.

John Hopkins

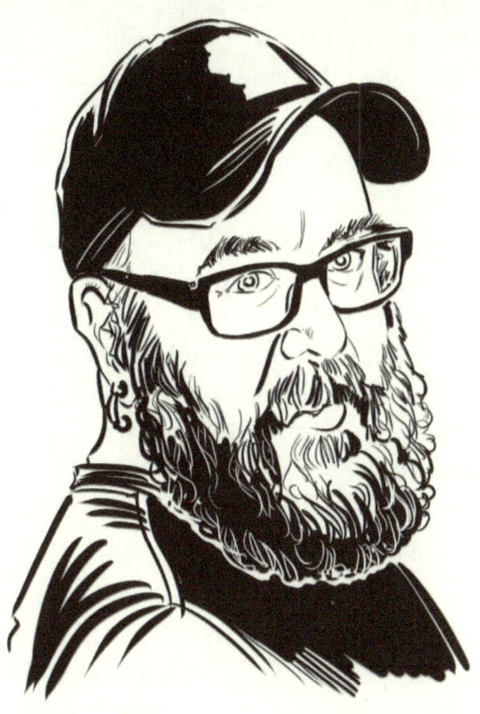

I met John Hopkins a few years ago when he was the tour manager/sound man for Corrosion Of Conformity in a short tour that I was asked to go on with the then trio version of the band. John was gruff but funny, took little shit, and always had something interesting or funny to say about pretty much anything. I went on a couple of recent Melvins tours with him as well.

John is a very much in demand sound engineer/road dog who is constantly on the road and constantly busy. Being on the road as a self-employed person certainly has its ups and downs but John has seemed to make it work for himself, as he has been busy for years.

John: I grew up south of Rock Island, Illinois, about an hour south of there in a town called Oquawka. It is a tiny ass river town. Maybe fifteen hundred people live there. Those were my formative years. And then after high school, the first time that I got out of the house, I moved to Ft. Lauderdale to go to school at an art institute.

Brian: How long did you go to school down there?

John: I was down there about a year and a half. Music and video business was the course that I took. It was sort of a catch-all—they had a little bit of video production, they had a small production studio down there, and they had a pretty decent little recording studio, I recorded my brother's band down there. And then I moved back and almost immediately I started going to Iowa City. That was the closest place where there were shows, really. Within a month of being home I had gone up there with a buddy of mine to see a show. We went to see L7, actually.

Brian: So we are talking mid-nineties?

John: '91, '92. And then the next show that I went to was three local bands. I went with my friend and I was just completely blown away by all three bands. And it was all local. I was just like, "Holy shit! This is happening here?!" And then I thought that I had to move here.

Brian: What kind of jobs did you have when you first moved there, and did what you study in Florida have any bearing on what you did?

John: Not so much. I came home from Florida and started working in kitchens, because that is what I had done before I went down there. I had a boss that was not very understanding of me running around playing shows and going to shows, and that was the big impetus to move to Iowa City. And then once I was there, there was still a lot of kitchen stuff. But I had cool bosses that were like, "Oh yeah, you can take off," because at that point I was still playing in bands. And then I started working at the punk rock bar doing door, and then this guy Jason, who went on to work for Wilco, he found out that I had gone to school to do sound, and he busted my balls for like two weeks every night, telling me that I should be doing sound, and it was stupid that I wasn't. And finally I was like, "Okay, I will do sound!" He moved, and I ended up being the main guy there for a really long time.

My house ended up being sort of a flop house for any cool bands that came through, they would stay with us. And when some of those bands ended up making enough money to take some crew out, I started getting calls to be a sound guy.

Brian: So you are a sound guy first, and then the road manager stuff came later.

John: Yeah, but tour managing stuff came because I had done a couple of tours with Weedeater, and their manager was also the tour manager, and they weren't very happy with the situation. They were like, "You can't be the tour manager anymore, John is the tour manager from now on." And I kind of just got thrown into the fire but quickly figured out that when things are kind of lean with touring, that if you could do two jobs, it is a lot easier to get a lot of work. It kind of snowballed from there.

I am not crazy about tour managing at all but you know, I learned how to do it and I think that I am pretty effective at it. It was something that I did to make a little extra cash on tour.

Brian: You have been doing this for fifteen years?

John: Yeah, pretty much.

Brian: Do you ever miss playing music?

John: Yeah. I miss playing out with my dudes and getting together a couple of times a week and practicing and going and playing shows. That was such a huge part of my life for so long, but I never made any money doing it. When it turned into a situation where I could be more on the technical side of it and turned it into a job I thought, well I could play guitar anytime. One band that I was in, we still get together and try to jam if I am home for awhile. Me and the drummer are the only two guys out of that five that aren't married with a small army of children.

Brian: I hear ya. I enjoyed playing but I never made any money. Who have you worked with?

John: I do stuff with High on Fire, they have a sound guy who has been their man for a long long time who is also, ironically, from Iowa City. And he also worked at Gabe's.

Brian: Did you know him?

John: Oh, yeah. He was in one of those local bands that I saw that made me think that I had to move to Iowa City. I have been friends with him since '92, '93, I saw his old band a million times. My old band toured with them. So when he can't tour with High on Fire, I will go. And then I do front of the house for Sleep. And I do front of the house and am tour manager of Uncle Acid and

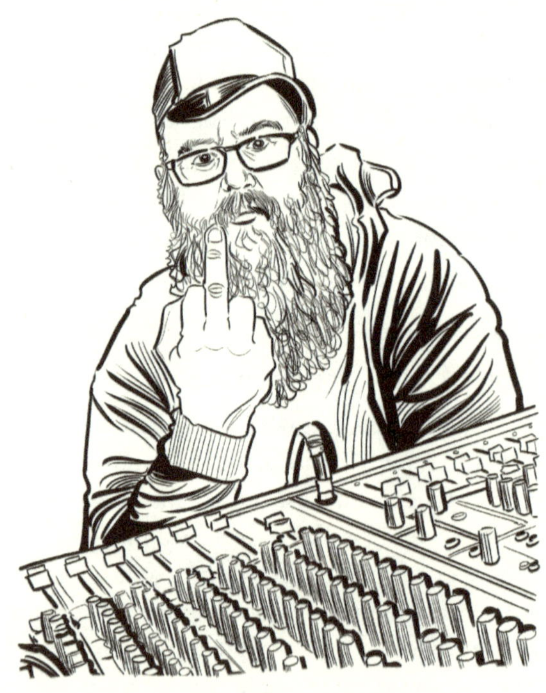

the Deadbeats. And those are kind of the main ones right now. Municipal Waste...I tour managed for Yob, I did a couple of tours for Orange Goblin. I have done a couple tours with Overkill. The metal world is a weird world for me, but those guys are awesome, and it is fun.

Brian: You seem to be really cut out for the tour life, going away from home for long periods of time and embracing the strangeness of it.

John: A lot of my friends in Iowa City have moved away. I still have a lot of friends there. I get home, and I am almost immediately bored out of my mind. If it is summertime—which is rare for me to be home—it is not a big deal because I like to ride my motorcycle and I can do that. But that wouldn't come out of the garage when there is snow on the ground. So if I am home in the winter—which is the majority of the time I am home—then I am going insane usually.

Brian: This is different than being a sound guy. When you are a tour manager, it seems to me that doing that is something that you learn as you go along. What happens when you go out there and get into a difficult situation, like working for people that are problematic, even if they are nice people?

John: I think all of the years working in kitchens and being under that sort of thing, most of the restaurants were pretty high volume. So being able to operate under a lot of pressure and I think that I kind of adapted some of that too. And then as I have gotten older, because I have definitely worked with some really, really difficult people, I have gotten to a point where, if I was in my twenties or in my teens then I definitely would have lashed out and then worried about the consequences later of what I said. Or how I reacted. And now I will take a step back and try and take a calming breath and then try and rationalize the situation. A lot of picking your battles.

I have ended up on tour with some really strange characters that are really difficult to work with sometimes.

Brian: It seems like you can do whatever you want and pick who to work with band-wise because you are really in demand as either a sound man or a tour manager or both. You have a good reputation. Are you happy with how things have gone in your chosen profession?

John: Oh yeah. I mean, it is nothing that I ever have taken for granted. Some of the bands that I get to work for are awesome. There would be times early on working for Corrosion Of Conformity—Woody [Weatherman] would always ride shotgun, and Woody is one of my favorite guitar players. Ever. And he and I would sit and bullshit about music and listen to a bunch of Dwight Yoakam and Scorpions, and sometimes the fourteen-year-old me that still lives inside my brain, trying to wrap my head around that, like, "Oh, I am driving in this van going to this gig, and Woody Weatherman is riding shotgun," you know? Shit like that is kind of mind-blowing.

I have been really fortunate to get to work with a lot of bands that I grew up loving or that I have been a fan of for a really long time, and that I get to think of those guys as peers or friends now is mind-blowing to me. Especially when I think back to the boss I had at the restaurant who wasn't necessarily cool about me taking time off to go on tour and shit like that. I remember her telling me one time that the day would come when music wouldn't matter to me. Like it was just a phase that I was going through. And I knew it wasn't a phase. It has been the be-all, end-all for me since I got my first Kiss record when I was eight.

Rebecca Sevrin

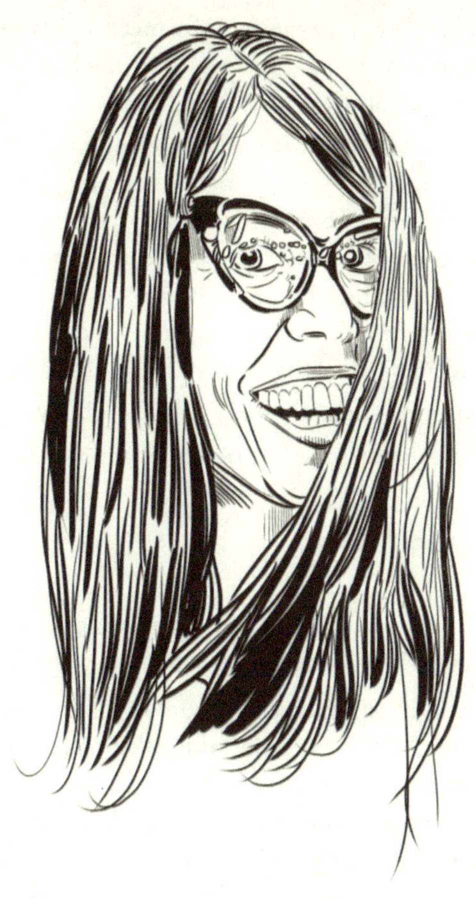

Rebecca Sevrin was one of the first pen pals I had back in the early eighties. I don't even know how we started writing to each other but it happened. She was from Montreal, she played guitar in her own band called No Policy. She built her own guitars. She was artistic. She got a nice write up in *Flipside* magazine talking about her guitar-building adventures. She sure did a lot of cool stuff!

I lost track of Rebecca after a few years, probably when I moved out east. But I knew some stuff. I knew that she had moved to the

U.S. and lived in either San Francisco or Los Angeles. Or both. And lived out there for a long time. She had joined the beloved San Francisco band Frightwig. And that is pretty much all I knew, which had led up to me actually meeting her in person for the first time on a Melvins tour in Montreal where she now lives again. That was about three or so years ago.

I learned a lot more cool stuff that she has either already done or continues to do. She worked for Kiss fitting Gene Simmons' costumes for starters. To me, that is very impressive. I learned that she has always been self-employed and knows the art of "the hustle" very well. Rebecca is a very cool person who really embodies that whole DIY thing completely. She has gone through a lot in recent times, which happens in life eventually, to all of us.

And…it was nice to finally meet her after thirty-plus years.

We talked over the phone in early 2019 and this is how it went down.

♫

Rebecca: Well, I like your book. I was pretty interested in reading the interviews with those other guys. It's cool.

Brian: Yeah. And it was basically the feedback that you left that made me think, "Oh, wait. I should talk to Rebecca," because you are no stranger to hustling and working for yourself and all of those other things. So let's take you back to the year 1983 or 1984 when we were pen pals. All I knew, really, was that you were this creative sort of person who played guitar in your band, No Policy. Which was the only thing I really knew back then about Montreal, to be honest, as far as punk rock goes.

Rebecca: Ha ha. That is all you need to know. No, there were a couple of really good bands but I am glad that you remember No Policy. That is cool.

Brian: Well, you stood out because you were this interesting looking person that played guitar in a band and you did art and you also built your own guitars. So that is a lot going on.

Rebecca: Yeah, I thought that everything would be so fabulous because of that—it sounded like a winning combination—but it turned out that a lot of guys did not want females to touch their guitars. I mean, it was the early eighties, I had been doing the guitars since 1979, 1980. I was a teenager. I was like nineteen or twenty.

Brian: So people were threatened by the fact that you a. could play guitar and b. could actually fucking build guitars and make them?

Rebecca: Yeah. I was too young, you know this is before these super-powered woman like Beyoncé, who has her own line of clothes and makeup and stuff like that. People just want you to do one thing, and they are pretty sensitive about it. Like I would work jobs at music stores and they would say, "well maybe you could sell some strings."

Brian: So you might have just confused people back then.

Rebecca: I think I confused people, yeah.

Brian: I think I even remembered that issue of *Flipside* magazine that had an article about you and how you built guitars.

Rebecca: Oh, I remember that, that was cool. Yeah, I used to talk about that and I used to show people things because it is all math, it is all geometry. And I thought that anybody could do it, you just have to follow this golden rule.

Brian: When was it when you decided to move from Montreal to the United States?

Rebecca: Los Angeles.

Brian: Oh, so you never lived in a San Francisco?

Rebecca: Oh no, I did. But first I went to Los Angeles, because a friend of mine claimed he knew Youth Brigade and claimed that they were looking for a guitar player and that I should go and try out.

Brian: Youth Brigade, Shawn Stern's band?

Rebecca: Yes. And I had a couple of relatives in Los Angeles so I thought, "well if this works, then great." But I want to be in Los Angeles so I kind of used that as a excuse to try and do it. And when I got to town, they wanted to go like U2 and have a keyboard player so I didn't even get to play for them.

Brian: Oh right, that is when they turned into The Brigade.

Rebecca: Yeah. And then when I tried playing in hardcore bands, everything was so far apart—like everything was in Oxnard that was punk rock, or in Orange County, and where I was, it was glam, and Guns N' Roses and Poison were starting, all of those hair bands. And I felt like I was totally out of my atmosphere because I didn't look cool enough and people weren't cool enough and they were kind of jerks. Like, the first batch of people I met were jerks. I tried out for this band and this girl was like, "What color is your hair?" And I said, "It's blonde." And she said, "I'm going to be the only blonde in this band. Would you dye your hair red or black?" "No!"

"What kind of guitar do you have?" "Well, it is zebra wood." "What's that?" "It's exotic wood. I build guitars. And this is wood from Africa and it has stripes in it." "Would you be willing to paint your guitar red and black because we want to be like Mötley Crüe."

Brian: That was a weird time because the hardcore stuff, as great as it was, was over. People forget how big all of that hair metal crap really was, and I was long gone before all of that Bad Religion and NOFX stuff got huge.

Rebecca: It was a hard time, it was really weird. I saw Redd Kross for the first time, and I liked what they were doing instantly. But the hair metal hard rock stuff I just thought, "Wow. This is so what I am not into." And then I played with Gwynne [Kelly]—she was in the Pandoras for a while—in a band called Boo. That lasted a little while but I wasn't into bubblegum, apparently my hands were made out of ham, so it didn't really work out too well.

Brian: Your hands were made out of ham?

Rebecca: Yeah it was the way I played guitar,.I didn't do upstrokes, I just did downstrokes on the guitar like a jackhammer, and they didn't like that.

Brian: Right. Well, what did you end up doing for money when you first got to Los Angeles and you were trying to get in a band and all of that? Were you hustling even then?

Rebecca: I was hustling. I was born hustling. Because when I lived in Montreal, I would recreate whatever album cover people wanted and I would paint it on a t-shirt , or do stuff on the backs of motorcycle jackets, a couple of guitar repairs. And when I moved to Los Angeles, because I knew how to use a drill press from building guitars, I worked for The Gauntlet, a body piercing shop in West Hollywood, making their body piercings and jewelry. And that was a stupid job, too, bending metal—and I would have to look at whatever that magazine was, piercing and body modification stuff.

. They were probably the first people doing that stuff, this is before that book *Modern Primitives* came out, where everyone first started getting pierced everywhere and scarification. That was like the late eighties.

Brian: I remember now, it was one of those RE/Search books?

Rebecca: Exactly. The Gauntlet is in there.

Brian: That was like the weird fringe before the fringe became normal.

Rebecca: Yeah, Exactly. It was weird. I worked there and my eyes got opened to a lot of stuff that I didn't really need to know about. Just because I knew how to use a drill press and power tools I got this job. So I did that for a while, and then I started making clothes and selling them to that store Retail Slut, on Melrose. And that kept me going for a long time. I made skirts, and whatever I felt like, and I always made things for people who wanted something, so my overhead was low but I always made enough to get by.

Brian: I saw that wonderful picture of you dressing Gene Simmons. How did you end up doing that?

Rebecca: Well, I really got excited by making money sewing. And I got more excited making stage wear then actually being onstage, so I started to sew. And then from there I made stuff out of glitter vinyl, and corsets, and I would sell that stuff to Retail Slut and all of the other punk boutiques in the early nineties. And then from that, a guy saw my stuff in the window of a store and said, "How about you start working for me, just me, and start making clothes for my photo shoots? I am a photographer. I like your vibe of doing stuff." And I said, "Okay, let's do it," and it turned out it was for *Penthouse* magazine. I made the clothes before they had to get naked. So from one sleazy job to another. But working two days for him was enough to pay all of my bills. So I did that for a while, but the guy was nuts and I had to quit. I got tired of that adult movie stuff, plus I couldn't really show any of my work or portfolio to anyone, it was pretty much a dead end. That wasn't my world. My world was like art and punk rock, not the adult film business. So I quit all of that and I had to build my portfolio over again.

So I will tell you how I got the Kiss job. I started working for a guy who made armor for the movies, this guy Tony, and he said, "Oh my friend Udo makes clothes for Gene Simmons. What a job." And I said, "Wow. I would kill for that job."

Brian: Were you a Kiss fan?

Rebecca: I wasn't a Kiss fan. Not really. I am a fan of hardware buckles, shiny leather, spikes, and fetishy looking clothes. And that is what they were selling and it turns out that the guy Udo hated the job so much that he punched a cinder block and broke his hand. And he called and said "Rebecca. Tony said you would kill for this job. Do you want it? I quit." So I came over and it was a codpiece and a set of wings, a harness, and all of this stuff was in pieces and he goes, "I hate this. I hate this job, I hate doing this." You know, before this—and I know I am not supposed to say this—I was doing bootleg movie props, like *Blade* stuff, the stuff Wesley Snipes wore, and then I did costumes for the second movie and that had financed everything that led up to doing Kiss.

So I took the job, but he gave the job to me without telling the costume supervisor. And when she found out, she was really pissed when I came to the meeting. She wasn't told any of this beforehand and she looked at me and she didn't like what she saw. She said, "Do you think you could get this together by tomorrow?"

I was like, "Yeah." So then I sewed it up and we went to Gene's house to fit him. And he liked me. You know, apparently he is this big comic book collector. I think I had a Hulk t-shirt on or something stupid like that, and I knew who drew it. So we became friends from that. He is like an encyclopedia on that stuff. I would wear another shirt and he would say, "Name every artist who drew this," and I could. He said, "You are not bad for a girl, you know all of this stuff about comics," and because of that we connected. I also knew how to sew and sometimes I would go out on tour and dress the band because they felt comfortable around me. That was a trip. I was doing that since 2004, along with all of the other jobs.

All you need is one good job, and then everyone else wants to hire you because...when I did Kiss that is when I got Raquel Welch. And because of that, it would lead to something else, I think I did Diahann Carroll. And then I got to do Mötley Crüe and I got to bounce all over the place because all you need is one good referral and then your name goes all over the place. It was cool, I never had to look for a job, I just had to wait for something to be over.

Brian: That is awesome.

Rebecca: And then I got a job working for Mattel, and that was my favorite job of all because I liked toys and I got to look into their archives and look at all of their stuff.

Brian: Man, you are like the poster person for this book. It seems like your entire life is pretty much my book.

Rebecca: Ha ha!

Brian: I have to ask you a little about Frightwig, you were in that band for a long time.

Rebecca: Right until the end. I joined in like 1985 or 1986 and then I left in 2013. They went another year or two without me. It was an enjoyable experience. I was from L.A. and I saw them play and as soon as I heard "Bag of Bondage" I thought that I had to be in this band. I will do anything to be in this band. So I got their album, I learned all of their songs and I moved up to San Francisco and stalked them until I got in the band. Deanna [Ashley] liked me. I stayed at her house—she knew my boyfriend at the time, he was in the band Celebrity Skin and they liked him, and they were interested in his weird girlfriend from Canada who liked the band and played guitar. And I learned all of the stuff and I hung around like a hemorrhoid and then I was in the band. We recorded *Faster Frightwig Kill Kill*, I was in the band for two weeks and then we did a little mini tour, so that was pretty amazing. I loved every second of it, it was really exciting but it wasn't the same as playing in No Policy because it was bigger and better shows and I was always the new girl, I came from somewhere else and it was weird but they made me feel welcome. I liked it but I never felt like it was my band. No Policy was my band. Frightwig were a band that I loved and was in awe of and I was part of it, but I had a hard time relaxing and running with it. But I did my best. It was fun.

Brian: So as I understand, you have moved back to Montreal.

Rebecca: Yeah, I got stressed out and overworked and I had a bunch of tumors grow out of control, and then my husband said he couldn't take care of me. I was married for twenty years. He decided that he was going to tune out, so I closed down my shop and I put everything in storage, and then when I had my surgery I didn't go back to my house in L.A., I stayed at my relatives. And then I got homesick for Montreal and went home for Christmas and thought about if I really wanted to go back to L.A., because there was no love for me there. My family was here, and my sister was sick. And I wanted to hang out with my sister and I hadn't seen my brother in years. So I stayed, and my trip just kept getting longer and longer. Then my sister, who was sick—she had leukemia—she passed away and then I thought I was just going to stay here and help everyone pick up the pieces. We are still going through her stuff and figuring out what we are going to do with it. And now my father isn't doing too well, so I don't really see me going back to the States. I am just starting over again, and at this point of my life, it is just easier to stay here and enjoy everybody's company.

So I have to start working all over again and I have some of my machines out of storage. I have some of my old clients back—I was back working for Kiss last month.

Brian: Awesome!

Rebecca: Oh, my goodness! It's crazy because they had told me that after I left Los Angeles, I wouldn't be able to work for Kiss anymore because apparently they didn't know that the band flies people out to do the job, they just said that I didn't have enough money to fly to Los Angeles. So that was kind of messed up and they said, "We don't want you in Canada," and then they hired another Canadian to make the Kiss outfits. And then he didn't know how to do anything properly and he needed to pick my brain so I got hired back! It is sort of a weird dynamic now but I don't need this to be part of my ego, I just want a little respect for what I did, is all.

Brian: It sounds like a little bit of a bitter pill to swallow, being asked back and working under a new guy even though you made all of the stuff and you have known them longer.

Rebecca: It is. Plus all of those guys are on Facebook and they are all my friends but they are all over Facebook kissing each other's asses and tooting their own horns when I did all of that stuff before them and I keep my mouth shut. I guess I will look for something else to do, because working for a band who is doing their last hurrah is not really something worth bragging about. They are nice guys and I hope they have a nice tour but my problem is more with the underlings, not the band.

Brian: Are you going to do any more music in Montreal? There was the No Policy reunion show and the other band you had [Pig Buddha] that opened for the Melvins and Indian Handcrafts not too long ago.

Rebecca: I have been putting any future musical plans sort of on the back burner so I can concentrate on making money again and sewing because that is what generates my cash. Because playing, you gotta buy equipment, it's a big money pit and I can't really afford to spend any time doing anything that is going to take away from me getting forward financially. I had to declare bankruptcy, I had nothing. My husband divorced me, and I am getting a hundred dollars a month for one year in alimony. Right now, I am at my parents' house like the world's oldest sixteen year old—which is good because I can get grounded, but as far as being a working adult and stuff, you know I still have a way to go.

Milo Aukerman

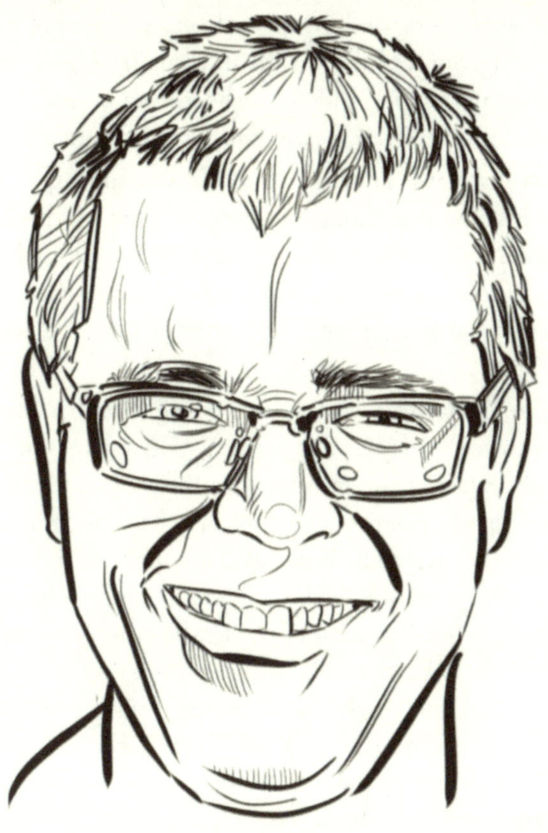

I bought the Descendents debut album *Milo Goes To College* right after it came out. I think it was in the fall of 1982, maybe a little later. I played that record to death and loved everything about it. Right around the same time, an issue of the late and lamented Los Angeles fanzine *Flipside* came out and the bands singer Milo Aukerman graced the cover. There was a big interview done with the band, even though at the time it was printed, the band was pretty much over. Milo, true to the band's album, was in fact in college, somewhere down in San Diego. The band's drummer, Bill Stevenson, had joined Black Flag. Future Descendents guitarist Ray Cooper was brought in to replace Milo and sing a few shows, before he went to second guitar to beef up the sound of Frank Navetta and Tony Lombardo. Milo came back and sang a few shows, making the Descendents a short-lived quintet. But it was pretty much over for the Descendents at that point.

Bill Stevenson was another story. His drumming on that first Descendents album was amazing. And how old was he? Eighteen? Nineteen? It's an album of genre-defined drumming, and as a performance it is nothing short of amazing. His playing in Black Flag, regardless of what he thinks of a lot of it, was always amazing to me.

Milo Goes To College was an interesting cross between poppy, sometimes sweet melodies and aggressive hardcore punk that had lyrics that reflected the mindset of all four members. Some of these lyrics have been dragged through the coals in recent years for the way they lash out. But right or wrong, during the period of time in 1982 a word like "homo" was common language for an adolescent. I was called it all of the time! Other lyrics were about abstract subjects like love, marriage, insisting on having some sort of individuality, fishing on a boat, hating your parents, and so on and so on. Musically, everyone was pretty accomplished. It's one of the classic records of the era, up there with the first Adolescents album or Black Flag's *Damaged*.

In 1983 and for the next year and a half or so, the stature of Milo Goes To College seemed to grow. Everyone knew it was a great album. All of a sudden, Bill is out of Black Flag, the Descendents are put back together, the band's second album *I Don't Want To Grow Up* was released, and a tour was planned. I was on the east coast at the time in the summer of 1985. This was after the Ill Repute/Scared Straight tour I was on fell apart, and I decided to stay on the east coast, basically being a pest to members of Corrosion Of Conformity and their friends in Raleigh, North Carolina. I formally met the Descendents during that time on several occasions. They hit it off with COC. We went and saw them at CBGBs, my first trip to New York City. When I returned to SoCal, I even ended up singing in the place of Milo for one show when he was late coming up for San Diego. I got to sing eight songs until someone tapped me on the shoulder. It was Milo. I handed the mic to him. It was a cool moment.

Milo stuck it out with the Descendents for a while until he left towards the end of the eighties. The rest of the band went on as the outfit All, worked their asses off, put out a bunch of records, went through three singers, and couldn't seem to get a break as time went on. It was weird watching punk rock bands have newfound commercial leanings and actually sell records and make a decent living when the nineties marched on. If I never had moved to the east coast as early as I did, I am sure I would have understood more what some of my old friends and peers were doing in this new world. At the time, all I thought was that I had already heard the Descendents, and liked All.

I checked out every All and Descendents album that Bill Stevenson did with guitarist Stephen Egerton and bassist Karl Alvarez. Even though *Milo* is always going to be the blueprint, the sound of these three guys playing together is uniquely their own thing. And regardless of whoever is singing for them, it's always going to be their own thing. They carved out their own thing. You can't honestly say that about a lot of people.

Milo came back into the Descendents for an initial reunion album called *Everything Sucks*. It was a great album. All of a sudden, the band was back, and were pretty goddamned popular. This lasted for about a year before the band went back to All. But later there would be more Milo activity, and now for the last couple of years the band has been pretty well established again.

Milo Aukerman these days actually makes his living being a singer. This situation is a far cry from what he went to college for all of those years ago. Not only that, the whole thing sounds kind of nerve-racking. How do you go from working for DuPont while raising a family during all of that to playing assorted, well-picked shows across the world, where by a weird trick of fate, the Descendents are now looked upon as legendary, and the band is super popular with young kids who don't mind watching guys in their fifties play fast, quirky music? That was sort of what was on my mind when I talked to Milo over the phone for a little while earlier this year. Besides all of that, Milo has always been a nice guy and it was cool to talk with him about some of these things.

♫

Brian: When you were in high school, what were some of your first jobs? Did you know that you were already thinking about going to college?

Milo: Let me see, what were my jobs...I was a paperboy for a while. I flipped burgers for a little while. I guess my most interesting job was I worked at an environmental health office. I was a senior in high school and then a year after high school. We worked at a hospital and there were a lot of research labs in the hospital. We would go around to all of the labs and do radiation monitoring, or we would do chemical waste pickup, like hazardous chemical waste pickup and disposal.

It was something that I was interested in mainly because, at that point, I had already figured out what I wanted to do, you know—that kind of research, some kind of research, in the field of biomedicine or biochemistry, or some kind of biological research. And so that was a way of experiencing what the labs were like. And getting to wear a lab coat, that was always cool. I am wearing a lab coat, how cool is this? I was playing the part of a scientist even though I wasn't a scientist. I was just a high tech garbage man, or whatever.

Brian: So you had a sense of what you wanted to do with your life really early on.

Milo: Yeah. It was probably senior year of high school, I had to give an oral report in my bio class and I did it on DNA, and for me, that kind of flipped the switch. It was like, "Whoa...this is cool.

I like this stuff, this DNA stuff."

So it was a very focused interest for me. Biology was cool but what was *really* cool was DNA, and that is what kind of set me down that path. I guess I had the philosophy at the time that if you are really interested in something, then you should make that your kind of calling, or just go for it and see what you can do. I suppose that I was kind of fortunate, because I know that a lot of people just go off to college and don't know what they want to do, they are undeclared. Or they think that they will figure it out. I kind of bypassed all of that because I had this intensity with DNA, it was all about DNA to me.

When I finally left the field of biology, it was after a few years with a company when they had taken me off of genetics and put me on to essentially soil science and to me that was like, "Why am I doing this?"

And when they finally laid me off at DuPont, I was like relieved. I was glad that I was done with that, basically.

Brian: When you were in high school, is that the time period when the Descendents were actually getting ready to record the debut album *Milo Goes To College*?

Milo: Yeah, back in high school was when I knew what it was that I wanted to do. I took a year and went to community college. At that point the band was starting to record. We recorded very little except for the *Fat* EP, which was done when I was still in high school. But when we recorded the first album, that was in fact during the year that I was going to a community college, taking some basic courses. It was a place in the South Bay called El Camino. It was a typical community college that was set up to help you transfer into a four year, which is exactly what I had used it for. And it was good because it allowed me to pursue the music thing.

I think it all worked out in the end. Obviously the band wished I would have stayed around at that point, but as history tells, I just kept returning to the band again and again.

Brian: You were straddling two separate things that were fulfilling for you. Looking back, I remember that I had actually met you and Bill during the summer of 1985,which was when the band reformed and you put out *I Don't Want To Grow Up* and you toured the country that summer.

How did you get by during that time? Did you find time to work in between all of that or did you not have to do any of that?

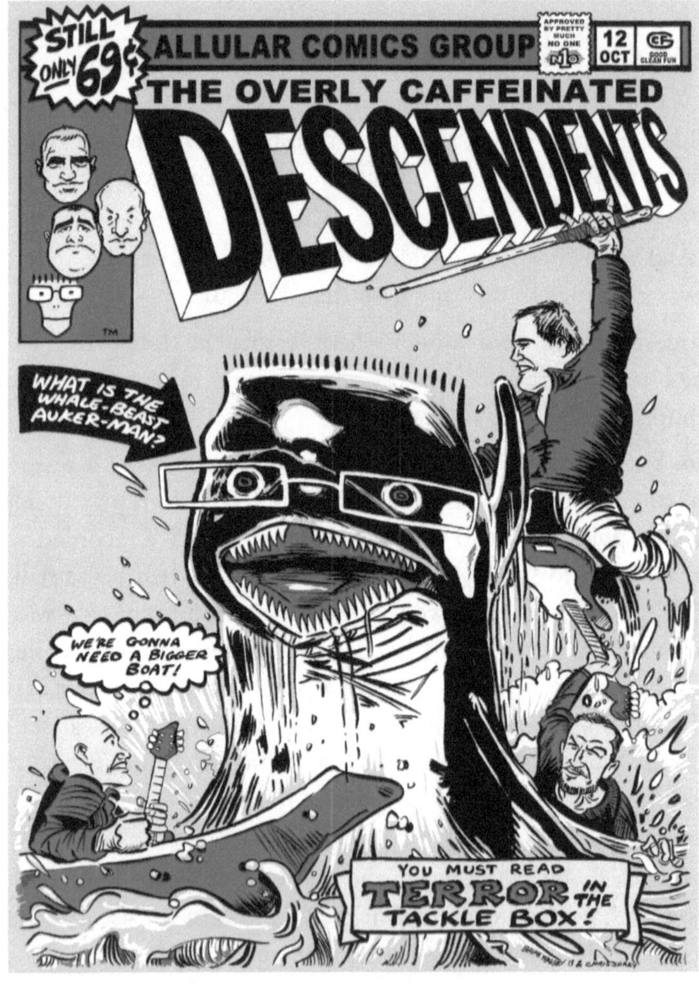

ARTWORK BY CHRIS SHARY AND BRIAN WALSBY

Milo: I think the first couple of years at UC San Diego I had a pretty stellar grade point and then it dropped after that and got less than stellar. I was there for '82 and '83 and '84 and I was totally crushing it. And then in '85, we started touring again and I think I still did quite fine but I think that my studies might have suffered a bit. It wasn't anything that kind of ruined my academic chances but I think the one class that I failed in college was in '86. It was my last quarter there and I just couldn't be bothered. I just got back from tour—I am totally tour damaged, I am a wreck—and I have to study for this test or write this final paper, and I couldn't do it. First I took the incomplete and then it turned into an F. The irony was that it was an opera class!

Brian: After you quit the Descendents, the rest of the band called themselves ALL and got Dave Smalley, the first of many singers to front the band. I am sort of bemused about ALL being eternally the secondary band for those three guys. And I have heard you say sort of the same thing about it. What do you think about that perception? Because Dave, Chad [Price] and Scott [Reynolds] are all fine singers. Plus, even after you had bowed out and the new lineup would come through, I just thought it was a continuation of things.

Milo: That is true but there are people that like ALL better.

Brian: True, but it is still weird. I don't think people are giving everyone involved, including yourself, a fair chance. Cause to me it is the same thing, just with different singers.

Milo: Right. Well, like you said, you were bemused. I was frustrated. Because when they started playing out, first with Dave and then with Scott, they were my favorite band. To me, I thought that it was the obvious next step. They were different in terms of becoming more musically proficient and more musically involved. And I liked it a lot. Stephen is such a great songwriter and player and he kind of raised the bar for them. I thought it was great, I thought it was the next evolution, definitely for the three musicians and whatever singer that came with them.

I was always frustrated for them at the fact that they never hit it big. I thought that they deserved to. You know, I think it is one of these things—I have a couple theories about it—the fact that they had named the first record *Milo Goes To College*, and it is kind of a trivial thing but they put that cartoon up there on the front cover, and a lot of stuff just sort of becomes set in stone to people. And then that is the thing for them.

Brian: A catchphrase, or some kind of hook.

Milo: Exactly. And then, the other thing is that people tend to really romanticize the early, early punk rock. We weren't the earliest but we were one of the bands in L.A. that helped to make it more of a thing that could end up being popular…

Brian: I totally agree. Well you know, first, it is usually romanticized by people who weren't there. And secondly, that first record was, for me, as influential as what Black Flag was, or what Saccharine Trust was, or what the Minutemen were. Or X. You know, everybody sounded different.

Milo: Yeah, it was a great time. And I romanticize it myself because I do think of that period as being such a great period. So if we are lumped in with that—and those other bands and people—a band like All can't have that cache just because of how that band arose, basically. And it is a terrible thing for people to compare the two bands.

If you are going to compare us to them, compare the two bands musically. If you do that, then they come out ahead. They have always been more musically sophisticated then we were. Some people have considered us to being a little bit more Neanderthal or dumb compared to some of the All records.

Brian: What is it like being a singer full time? Especially with Bill getting better from his health scares and everyone else wanting to do it again. I imagine you guys must be doing pretty well these days to have this become your main gig. People are responding to the band in a huge way and the shows are packed full of people. Are you surprised? What do you make of all of this? I mean, you had this serious job and career at DuPont and yet you had this singing thing on the side, now that is your job. How does that feel?

Milo: It definitely felt weird, especially in 2011 when we started doing it again. Because at that point I was well into my career, and the first time we got onstage again was at the Fun Fun Fun Fest. I was wondering how it was going to go, and I was really just flabbergasted and blown away. It seems like the interval of time in between us doing it, I would have thought it would have made people forget us but it was actually the exact opposite. And I think at that point the kernel was set that I could conceive of doing this more full time, you know? Because it is a whole different thing now. This is something I could conceive of doing and not doing biology.

And then it took several years after that when DuPont helped me make that decision, ha ha. I was there for fifteen years. And then they laid me off, they laid a whole bunch of people off at once back in 2016. And I was one of them. Ever since then, I am doing what you do, which is I am self-employed.

To me, music was always a hobby. So to have it convert into a career has actually been something that is really exciting. Because when you make that commitment to that sort of thing, all of these new challenges emerge that I hadn't even considered—like, can I do this day in and day out? can I work on my craft, so to speak? I never worked on my craft, I never worked on being a singer, because it was a hobby and you don't do that if it is a hobby. So I am trying to learn how to sing correctly so I don't blow my voice out, that was something I had to learn.

And then even just songwriting, too. I relied solely on pure inspiration to write a song, almost a random inspiration. I look at what, say, Stephen does—he goes home every day after dropping his kids off at school and then goes home to write some kind of music. He sits down and decides that he is going to write some music.

Brian: Some people have a job-like attitude towards making music. Buzz from the Melvins has a very workmanlike attitude towards writing music and considers that to be his job. He doesn't wait around to be inspired and maybe that is what Stephen does, too.

Milo: Yeah, I think he spends a lot of time noodling around but then he will get some inspiration just from noodling around and then he captures it, because he is in the right environment to capture it. Whereas if I get inspiration, it is just when I am walking around or something. I will think, "Oh, that is cool. I hope I don't forget it!" Mainly because I am walking around, I am not in the right environment. So Stephen has been sort of my role model in terms of that kind of thing. Because when we talk about me being self-employed now, I need to have the correct discipline for being self-employed, which I still struggle with. I still have a challenge in terms of waking up and saying, "I am a musician so I am going to do musician-type things," instead of saying "I am basically unemployed, so I am going to sit around and do nothing," you know. That is kind of a continual struggle.

I mean, I definitely enjoy my leisure time but I need to show some discipline and have some kind of career at what I am doing here.

Brian: Funnily enough, your songs—looking back over the years—have had this push and pull over the two worlds that you have been involved in. Like the song "I Quit," which was sort of about the parts of being in a band that you might not like. And then there is "This Place." Was that based on the job you had?

Milo: That was based on being in Madison, Wisconsin. After San Diego, we moved to Wisconsin and I started up a postdoctoral there. It was a long, excruciating postdoc, mainly on a professional level. I didn't make as much progress as I would have liked in my research and it did not parlay itself into a fantastic career after that. I was not highly employable, I wasn't a high-flying postdoc that could get a job at any university that I wanted. So then we moved out here to Delaware and I kind of languished around for a year, trying to figure out what I was going to do. And then I got this job at DuPont.

It wasn't really my pick, because I would have preferred to go into academia. And it was fun for about ten years but then, like I said, year after year after that, it just started to get more and more of a drag, basically. "This Place" was just me talking about that environment that I was in when we were in Wisconsin. I loved Madison, Wisconsin. I would move back there in a heartbeat, but my professional environment there I found to be not very inspiring, basically.

Being self-employed—I am still trying to figure that part out. It is such a new thing for me to not punch a clock. I used to drop the kids off and then go off to a 9-to-5. And now...

Brian: You are at the mercy of people being consumers and wanting your trade. You are at the mercy of stuff that is beyond your control.

Milo: I think that for the past few years, I have been riding on the enthusiasm of the band and the enthusiasm of the audiences. But, like you said, it is kind of like here today, gone tomorrow. We are now in this situation of wanting to keep playing and having people come, but maybe we should put more records out because we need to give people something new to listen to. There is such a thing as wearing out your welcome, and so that is our current challenge right now. As you are very aware of, the record now is just an advertisement to get people to come and see us. We are not making any money off of our records.

Brian: You make money off of playing shows, merchandise...

Milo: Right. And the recording is just us going, "check it out, we still have something to say, we still have good songs that we can thrust in your face." So that is kind of what we are doing now.

Brian: Look at Dinosaur Jr. They got back together and figured out a way to keep putting out new music afterwards. And the audiences for those guys, the Melvins, and you guys—I saw you in New Jersey and there are always younger kids there. When I saw you, it was like that. Like, you guys figured it out, which keeps you from becoming a novelty act. But it wasn't like you *did* anything.

Milo: You said we figured it out, but I don't know how it happened. It wasn't by choice or by design, it just happened. So I feel very fortunate that it ended up becoming how you described it, because a part of me is thinking, "Why? Why are you guys here?"

So I just think, "thank you, thank you."

TOSHI KASAI

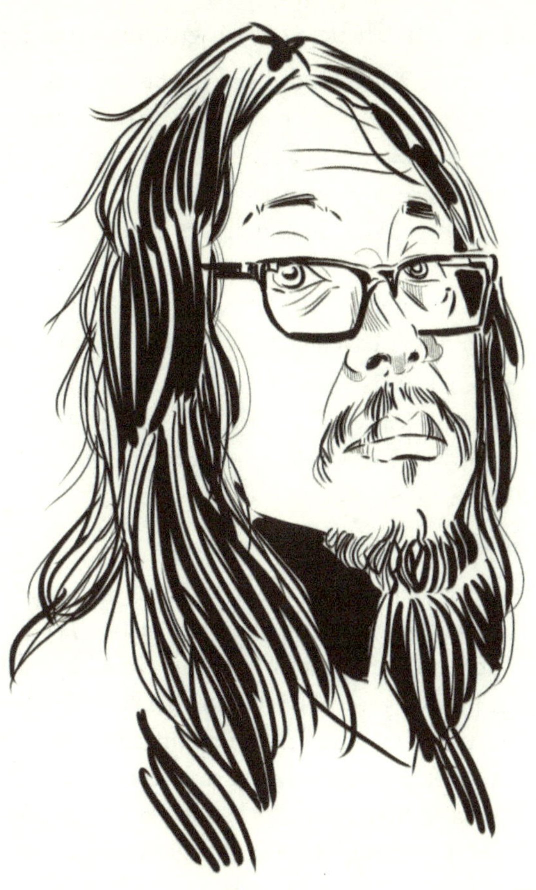

I have toured with recording engineer and sound guy Toshi Kasai extensively on two occasions. I really wish I had a band to record with, because I would travel three thousand miles to record with him. Toshi has been the guy who has recorded everything that the Melvins have done for a long time now. He has worked with bands like Sepultura, the Foo Fighters, and Tool, amongst many others. He played guitar in the band Big Business for a while but recording music is how he survives and is his job.

♫

Brian: Could you talk a little bit about growing up in Japan?

Toshi: I was born in Tokyo, and lived in the suburbs. It is a little like living in Los Angeles—if you drive a little bit, you will see a baseball stadium. Tokyo had a few baseball stadiums. It is really an entertaining place when you are growing up. When I grew up, I was sort of a sports kid, watching lots of sports, watching a lot of TV. When I was in junior high school, my brother introduced me to some bands. All major stuff. That is maybe the one thing that back then Japan didn't have much of, an underground music scene.

When I was a kid, I would hear Michael Jackson all of the time, Blondie, you know, it's all over the place. And then when I heard Queen, I was shocked. Something in my head or in my mind totally changed.

Brian: Which Queen record was it?

Toshi: It was a later one. My buddy from junior high let me borrow a greatest hits collection. And then the record *Jazz*, I think. I didn't like "Bohemian Rhapsody" the first time I heard it—it was a weird song, I didn't get it. But the catchier stuff, I started liking. And I would listen to it again and again and again. Suddenly that "Bohemian Rhapsody" song? I started to like it. Because of Queen, I started to listen to other bands like the Beatles and Led Zeppelin. And if any musicians would show up in Japan I would try and go see them. Mostly at this point, there were only hair metal bands that would come over to Japan because that kind of stuff was huge. Some festivals.

Brian: When did you decide to pursue being involved in music? When did you decide that you wanted to learn how to record and engineer music?

Toshi: When I was thirteen I started to learn how to play guitar, right after I was introduced to English and American rock music by my brother. I formed a band with a few friends. We did mostly covers, maybe had a few songs. I soon realized that I didn't want to play the same music every night, didn't want to be a real musician, in a way. I had listened to so much different music of all types—mainly music outside of Japan, soundtracks—and I decided I didn't want to be in a band playing the same music every night.

I had a friend who went to Los Angeles and learned how to record and engineer and he did it when I was twenty, and he was the same age as me. He told me that I would really like it. I wanted to be a songwriter after I gave up being a musician and then I thought, "Oh, recording and producing!" I was interested in it from checking out who was recording the music I was listening to, like George Martin or whoever. So my buddy suggested it because then I could record all kinds of different music, so that is how I changed my mind. I didn't want to be in a regular band but I didn't want to give up music.

Brian: Did you do any studying in Japan to learn all of that before you came out to Los Angeles?

Toshi: No, my buddy went to engineering school in Los Angeles. He came back and told me the story and told me how I had to go and he kinda pushed me to do the same.

Brian: Wow, So you came all of the way out there to learn it.

Toshi: Yeah, North Hollywood.

Brian: How many years did that take?

Toshi: It was a half-year program. I worked every day. You can pick how long the program is, there were three month programs. I had saved up some money and the most affordable one was an almost half year.

Brian: Was it odd coming here from Japan? Was it kind of a culture shock?

Toshi: I didn't feel that much difference, except for the language, you know. Like I said, Tokyo and Los Angeles kind of felt the same except that Tokyo is way more crowded, Los Angeles is way more widespread but they both are huge. In Los Angeles, you have to spend two hours driving to the other side of the way on the roads. That was about it. I met some students for school right away so I didn't feel the pressure or culture shock too much.

Brian: Did you have to do anything aside from your studies, like for money?

Toshi: I was lucky, I was teaching at this school for foreign students who didn't speak much English. I became friends with a student advisor at the school and he asked if I could teach these students. He helped me out a lot. So I didn't make money when I started, of course, because I was learning but I had saved up some money when I was in Japan so that kind of helped. The first couple of years were tough. I would call my mom and ask to borrow a little money but eventually I got a job in a few studios.

Brian: What were some of the first groups that you did stuff for?

Toshi: The first thing when I was a staff member at this one studio was Sepultura. I think that was my second gig. I was helping and assisting.

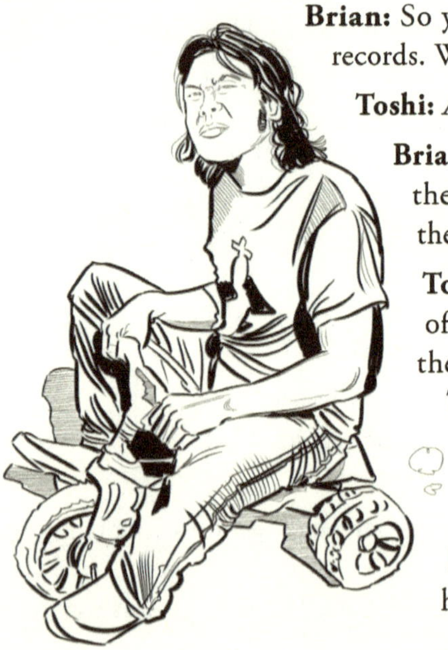

Brian: So you worked on one of their records. Which record was it?

Toshi: *Against.*

Brian: I had that record. That is the first record they did after they switched singers.

Toshi: Yeah, I became friends of the band. They put me on the guest lists for their shows. They are really nice people. The producer was named Howard Benson, he became huge after that. I had some conflict with him, he was kind of mean to me.

Not mean like racial, but he was kind of difficult. And then I worked with the Ventures.

Brian: Funny. Those are two bands are far away from each other as you can get, Sepultura and the Ventures.

Toshi: My job was assistant/interpreter because they were writing songs for the Japanese female bands. Yeah, I met those guys. Sepultura and the Ventures are very different from each other, but as a studio employee, I can pick the bands. And then I became chief engineer at one of the studios after that.

Brian: Other then the Melvins, what are some other things that you have done? I know you worked with The Foo Fighters and Tool.

Toshi: With the Foo Fighters, Dave Grohl used to come into one of the studios where I used to work. Tool came to one of the studios in 2000 and I became friends with Adam Jones right away. I did everything, it was a small studio so I ran everything for them and somehow I became friends with him right away and I would help him set up his studio and record some of his solo stuff. Buzz came to the studio and I met him, Adam would invite me to his house so I started hanging out and I met Kevin and Dale.

Brian: You have recorded on almost every thing that the Melvins have recorded since the early 2000s. The first record was *Hostile Ambient Takeover*?

Toshi: Yeah.

Brian: You guys have a good thing going, and they practice at your studio and stuff. Why do you guys seem to work together so well?

Toshi: It is really hard to say. They came to the studio a couple of times and we didn't hang out right away but maybe Dale and I hung out a couple of times, that was about it. And then Buzz called and said that they wanted to come back. We did *Pigs Of The Roman Empire*. We did the Jello Melvins album [*Never Breathe What You Can't See* by Jello Biafra and The Melvins]. And we all had similar tastes, we listen to the same sort of sixties and seventies music, we kind of clicked.

Brian: My personal favorite Melvins record that you have done with the band, I still have to say it is *(A) Senile Animal*. It sounds really interesting and I love the way Dale and Coady [Willis] are recorded for their drums, with Dale in one speaker and Coady in the other. That is still the one for me.

Toshi: I really like that album. For sure. And also *Hostile Ambient Takeover*. We did some really, really weird shit on that album. They gave me freedom, which I never had before. They would tell me to do some weird shit and I would say okay. (laughter)

That was great. And I agree about *(A) Senile Animal*, it had a huge impact with two drummers. It was challenging too, like, "How am I going to record these two?"

Brian: The other record that was right up there was the one with Jeff Pinkus and Paul Leary, *Hold It In*. Even though I know that the songs that Paul Leary wrote, he recorded too, but do you pretty much oversee the rest of it and put it together with the band?

Toshi: Yes. There are a lot of different sounds all over the place. I really enjoy that one, too. The only thing was that the recording time was kind of limited because they had to go to Austin half of the time. I don't have too many memories of doing the record just because it was really short. But that album came out really good, for sure.

ERROL ENGELBRECHT

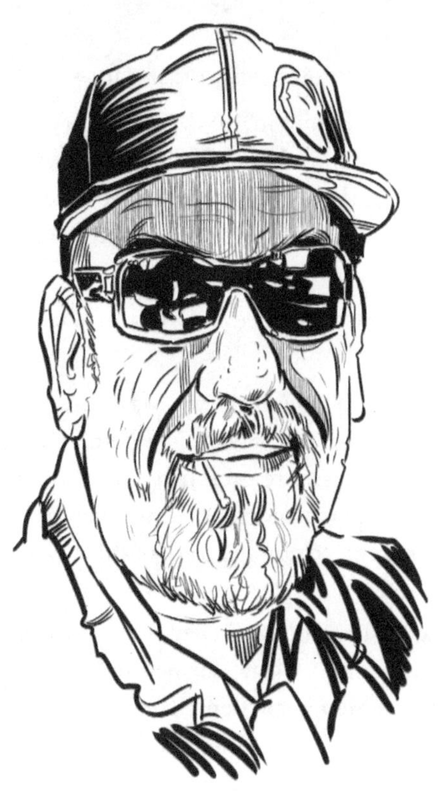

Errol Engelbrecht lives in Raleigh, North Carolina, with his wife and daughter. He is the owner of the Blue Flame Tattoo shop and he is also an artist/painter and self-described "hermit." He drew the infamous Corrosion Of Conformity skull that might be one of the most famous drawings in all of punk rock/hardcore. That was decades ago.

I was first aware of Errol as being Raleigh's resident "punk rocker" when I was introduced to the punk rock scene back then. He looked punk. He drank beer. He was a nice guy. He also drew a lot of flyers, did a bunch of artwork, and eventually got into tattooing. This led several years later to opening his own business, which has thrived ever since.

♬

Brian: How long have you been working for yourself?

Errol: I opened Blue Flame in 1998. So, twenty years, a little over twenty years now. Before I opened the shop I was painting houses and doing some stuff on my own, but that never really lasted very long. It was just little stuff here and there. Opening the shop was a big one.

Brian: How long was that idea brewing in your head before you made it a reality?

Errol: Well, it had been several years. I was working for other people and I was noticing how they were just being able to take off on a whim. The businesses were established and the owners saw that everything was in place and that things were running smoothly, and they were taking advantage of that and I went, "Damn. Well, that must be nice."

I would ask for time off and they would say no. Someone had to stay and work, and it always seemed to be me. I was a little fed up with that. I remember when I first talked about it with the guy I was working for at the time and he was pretty cool about it. He gave me advice and stuff like that. I had worked up to where I was sort of the manager because, of all of the people there, I was the most responsible—which was pretty funny at the time because I certainly wasn't very responsible but I don't know what it says about the other people. One of the things he said was, "Be careful what you wish for, you just might get it."

Brian: Was there a learning curve in opening up your business and learning how to deal with people?

Errol: Yes, there was a big learning curve. One problem that I had, because it was my business, I would just work my ass off. For many years. Way more than anyone else. And I realized that I had a problem micro-managing and I realized that often that ended up biting me in the ass. So there is a fine balance between being in charge and having to be the bad guy at times, and also just sort of picking your battles. You know, just like being a parent—you have to decide whether you want to get into something and make it an issue, or whether you can decide that this is not that big of a deal.

Brian: The idea of picking your battles might also be a good thing to apply to anything.

Errol: I have found that the best thing for me to do is to not react instantly, but to instead take a couple of days to kind of mull it over in my head, eventually cool down, talk to people. There are also some other sides of the story that I never knew or heard, so I could just go off on what I see. There would be more to do it than what I saw so obviously I would learn to take the time to talk about it calmly and rationally, and discuss it.

Brian: When I was interviewing Tom Hazelmyer[1], he said that having a restaurant these days, during the internet age we live in, is sort of like having a record label where all of these critics that think that they are important say a bunch of crap online about his businesses. Does the Blue Flame get that kind of stuff too?

Errol: Oh yeah. Oh yeah. And I just realized that, unfortunately, people are just entitled assholes, and if they don't get what they want, when they want it, they will go write you a bad review. I have learned to not even read them anymore. That is probably the best thing to do, because otherwise I would just lose my mind. I try to tell the people that work at the shop, "Do what you can to make them happy—bend over backwards and do what you can—but if there is no appeasing them, then fuck them." There is something to be said about customer service but the customer is not always right.

Brian: Before I went freelance, I worked at Whole Foods and their

---

1 Tom Hazelmyer: The internet age has changed restaurants into being a record label, where you are dealing with asshole critics who think that they are more important than they actually are.

customer policy basically encouraged people to be assholes to you and take advantage of you. There was just no pleasing or appealing to any of those people in that situation.

Errol: Unfortunately the bad reviews travel faster and they are more likely to write bad reviews than good ones.

Brian: You have been an artist for a long time, way before you ever opened up your tattoo shop. You used to be immersed in punk rock when you were a kid and drew a lot of flyers and things of that nature. And you drew the infamous Corrosion of Conformity skull. Is this something you still hear about?

Errol: It is getting to be more of a rarity for anyone to bring it up, which is fine with me. Time has a way of making things seem less important and I kind of realized that nothing was going to be done about it, and that they were not going to change and go, "Oh yeah, we actually need to make this right," you know? Even though Reed (Mullin, drummer for the band) had talked about it and admitted that he had fucked me over, I realized that nothing was going to happen so I had to let it go and just not be bitter about it because after awhile, it consumes you and it's just not worth it, so I was just like, "Screw it."

Brian: You don't want to go into your fifties being bitter about something that happened thirty five years ago, or whatever.

Errol: Exactly. Karma comes back.

Brian: There must be some degree of satisfaction in having your successful business for as long as you have, and especially coming from such meager beginnings. Do you ever sit back and think about it? Like, "Wow look what I did, that is pretty cool."

Errol: Oh yeah. Oh yeah. I really had no idea how successful it was going to be but I had to do it, I had to find out for myself, if it was going to work or not. I had this idea and I had a plan, a business model of sorts, of how I wanted it. When you work for other people, hopefully you can see the mistakes that they made and you try not to repeat them. Or things that you can do better, you know. I had another business venture and that one just failed pretty miserably. But, you know, you will never really know unless you try, and I had to try. You have to at least try, and if you fail, you just keep going and learn your mistakes from that.

Brian: Well, now I have to ask you what your failed business venture was.

Errol: It was the Gnombies. I made zombie yard gnomes. I had a product—it was a regular gnome with the red pointy hat and overalls but he was just zombied out. Unfortunately, the product was made in China, which I hated doing. I found out that the only way to make things cheap was to make A LOT. And we didn't have the money or storage to do hundreds of thousands of them, we just had enough to do a really small run and we just did the absolute minimum that we could do. And because of that, the cost was high and people didn't want to pay that much money. And there were always things that kept popping up that we weren't expecting, additional expenses and stuff. This was all done during Blue Flame going on and already being established. I had to sell my old Cadillac to finance it, which I wasn't happy about but you know, you gotta do what you gotta do. You have to have that money.

Brian: I know you have had some of your work shown at different places around town. When did the painting stuff started?

Errol: The painting stuff really started after my neck surgery. I had to retire from actual tattooing. I had to do something to be creative, not just because I wouldn't be able to tattoo anymore, I also wasn't going to be able to work any other job.

Brian: You have had a lot of medical stuff go on and you have dealt with a lot of shit.

Errol: Yes. I have had my neck fused and I can't do anything when my head is down. That is how you are when you are tattooing, you are hunched over.

When I started painting I was doing watercolors, but then I realized that I was in the same position again and it was causing issues, so I switched to oils and worked on a canvas where I am looking straight ahead. And that worked. So it was just finding the medium and the way that I could still do something. So I do that.

Brian: Why did you gravitate towards painting cars?

Errol: I have always been a car guy and there is just something about them for me. I love old cars and think that they have a lot of character, especially the old rusty ones. I am not a pretty landscape kind of guy, nor do I want to paint flowers, shit like that.

Brian: I really enjoyed the thing you wrote about getting comments about your work in the art world, about what you should do.

Errol: Oh yeah, that is pretty much what happened. "If you want to be successful, this is what you should do." I got a lot of that. I mean, people could appreciate it, but it's just that no one is going to buy it. But then there is a little thing there where the old punk rock attitude comes from, where it is like, "Fuck you, I am going to do what I want and if you don't like it you can bite me." The art world is pretty much a joke for the most part anyways. It has nothing to do with talent.

Now there are all of these celebrities who paint and they are getting all of this money and acclaim for their paintings and it's just because they are a celebrity.

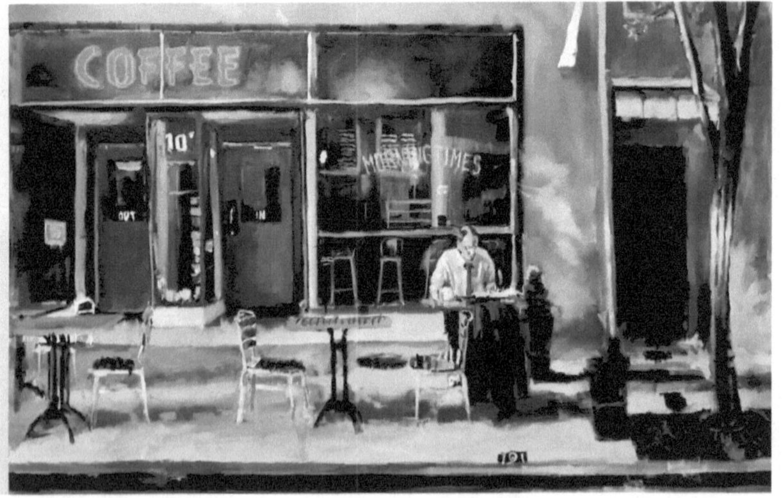

ARTWORK BY ERROL ENGELBRECHT

Brian: Like Paul Stanley of Kiss. He is a painter.

Errol: Jim Carrey, he is a painter. Bob Dylan is a painter. I have seen work from both of them and I just went, "Oooooh." And they will sell because they have a famous name, people will buy it. "Oooh, Jim Carrey did this. I will put it next to my Bob Dylan painting." I buy art and I will buy it because I actually LIKE the art. I don't care if there is a fucking name attached to it, and actually, I prefer buying art that is local from people around here. To me, it has more meaning and it's better than the shit that people will spend millions of dollars for.

Brian: What is the best thing you have gotten from being self-employed?

Errol: The best thing I have gotten from being self-employed and getting my shop to where it is successful—to where it would run by itself—is that I was able to take advantage of certain things. Like, I had worked twelve years straight without a vacation, and then a friend of mine was working in Italy and said, "Why don't you come to Italy for a couple of weeks? You have a free place to stay." And I was like, "Shit it sounds great, I would like to go." Because I hadn't really been anywhere where I wasn't working. I mean, I went to Germany but I was working six days a week so it wasn't a vacation.

So I said screw it and went to Italy. I spent two weeks there and it was the most amazing experience and then I came back and decided that I was going to go to Japan. And I went to Japan, and then I came back and said fuck it, I am going to go to Jamaica.

Brian: So you are saying that because of working for twelve years non-stop, you were able to afford to take a little time off and do all of these things.

Errol: Yeah. And even though I am unable to do that work anymore, the shop still supports me. But you know, all of those years of hard work are also what screwed my neck up. That was the downside. And I paint, but I realized, you know I don't need to sell my paintings to support myself. I can just do these for the enjoyment of doing it. I can paint what I want and don't have to worry about anything else. If people buy them, awesome. If not, I am going to have a house full of my own paintings.

Dale Flattum

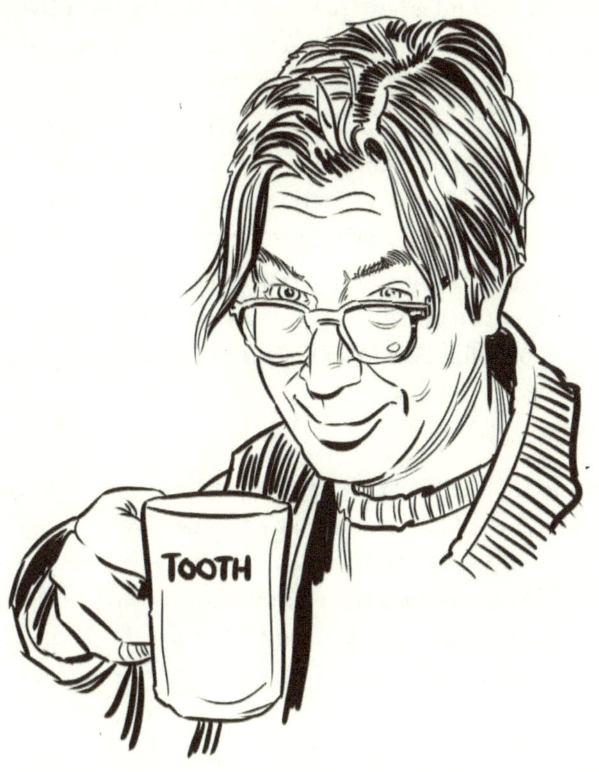

Dale Flattum came across my radar decades ago, initially as the bass player/singer of the band Steel Pole Bath Tub. The band originated in Montana where most of the band was from and then ended up in San Francisco where they put out some terrific records for Tom Flynn's Boner Records. I found out a little later that he was artistic and did a lot of art as well. He was really good, and a wee bit mysterious to me. Or maybe just quiet. I am not sure which.

He was my favorite part of Steel Pole Bath Tub. I liked his bass playing and onstage presence. Buzz Osborne said that they always had their eye on him as a potential bass player for the Melvins. That probably would have been really good! Dale ended up living in North Carolina for awhile. I remember trying to coax him into playing with me and a few friends of mine in a short lived band we tried to do. He might have been smarter than the rest of us, he never returned to that practice space.

He has a lot of really cool artwork under his belt. I have always admired what he does. And he is a nice guy, but still sort of an enigma to me, still sort of mysterious. And quiet. But he was nice enough to send me some writings to share, and share I will.

He has lived in Minnesota in recent years, has a really nice book of his work out, still does his art stuff all of the time, and still plays music. Support whatever Dale Flattum does, because it's good.

Dale Flattum: I joined my first band when I was 15. We knew from reading about the Germs that all you needed was the equipment and a name, so I took my dishwashing money and bought a used bass. Mike [Morasky] bought a guitar and we plugged them both into this little Peavey practice amp. For drums Tom [Darren Mor-X] had a kick drum (no pedal) a floor tom and a cracked ride cymbal. We had a portable cassette deck so we recorded everything. We'd get Tom's dogs to start barking and he'd start kicking his kick drum and we'd just plod away until the tape ran out. Then we'd rewind it and listen, convinced we were geniuses if we stumbled into the same key. (We'd also take the tape deck to school and turn it all the way up and hide it in a locker between classes, convinced this was like the punkest thing ever).

Later, Mike's parents kicked him out and he joined a metal band and started dealing speed to the football team, so we didn't hang out that much until we made a band during our last year of high school. We got a house that summer and wrote a bunch of new wave-type songs. In Montana at the time, if you wanted to play shows you had to play from like 9 to 2, Thursday through Sunday, so we also learned a bunch of covers. For our first show a designer friend of ours came up with this flyer that looked like it might be an ad for a ski movie and we spray painted the edges fluorescent green and put them on all the cars at the ski hill, so the show was packed with all these confused tourists and ski bums asking when the movie started. We went over ok. It was partly the novelty of watching a bunch of 17-year-old kids playing Pretenders covers but we were pretty good, and the only other live music options were these awful old country rock bands. So at 17, I guess I became a "working" musician.

Since we were all under age we used to have to sit in the kitchen between sets but eventually the owners got bored keeping an eye on us and we were allowed to just hang out. We played around town for about a year before everyone got sick of us. We attracted all the weirdos in town who wanted to scream along to Bowie songs and most of the regulars at these bars hated that "queer shit" so the gigs and the money dried up. Then someone told us that "there are only 6 bands in Seattle" so we bought a crappy van and convinced our parents to let us move there. We got like 4 flat tires on the way, which was kind of an omen.

It turns out there were more than 6 bands in Seattle and we had no idea how to get shows so we ended up playing these weird gigs like 3 nights at a Naval base on Widbey Island, or a homecoming dance at some awful frat. I don't know how we got booked at the Naval base, but about 25 sailors would show up each night to drink and yell nasty shit at us. It was intimidating at first but between sets they would sneak us beers since we still weren't old enough to drink. I think they were all just bored and didn't have passes to leave the base. They were really friendly until we started to play, and then it was like; "FAGGOTS!" But I think they just thought that's how you were supposed to react.

Our next big break was when we won a New Wave Battle of the Bands in Tacoma. (No other bands showed up.) The prize was a RECORDING CONTRACT, which actually just meant we got to record 2 songs at this studio above a bowling alley that you couldn't make noise in until after midnight. We also met this guy who wanted to be our MANAGER. His big idea was that we should all wear the same color tennis shoes. I remember asking "like Blondie?" and he got mad and said that "they wouldn't be the same KIND of shoes as Blondie." Plus he had a beard, which seemed really weird at the time. Our drummer's reaction to this meeting was, "Are you ready to compromise a little and make a bunch of money?!"

I think we broke up the next day. Or maybe we broke up after I freaked out at him for spending our last $2 on chocolate Pop Tarts. I mean who buys CHOCOLATE Pop Tarts? We were on our way home from our Tacoma-recording-adventure, changing (another) flat tire and he walked up with this dopey grin and a box of CHOCOLATE POP TARTS. For some reason that was the final straw and I completely lost my mind, screaming and

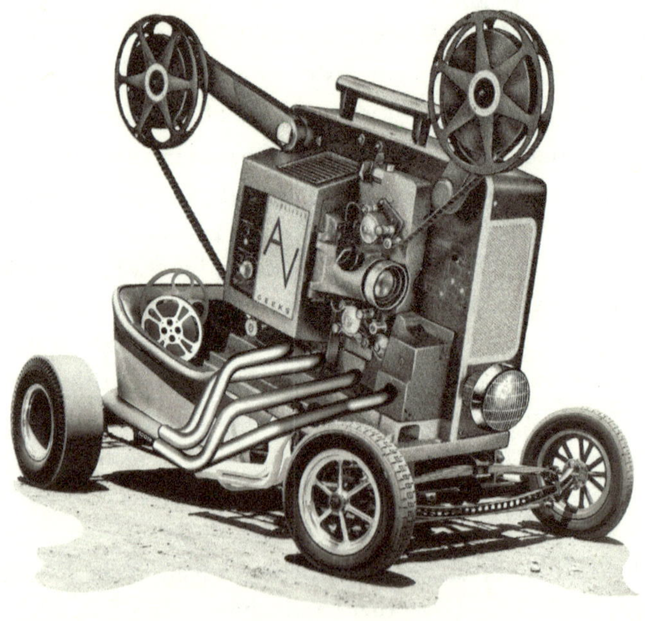

ARTWORK BY DALE FLATTUM

throwing things. The kids were not united. The recording though, actually turned out great! As much as our whole Seattle adventure was a complete financial and emotional disaster, artistically we ended up with some really cool songs. I think the weather just broke us down, and we went from being this feisty little new wave band to this bleak and dark and bummed-out drone. After we broke up, I just moped around Seattle for a while in a thrift store trench coat trying to learn to smoke cigarettes. I decided I was done with music and started hanging out at these weird art galleries downtown where some punk rock bands lived. I got to see some really cool art shows while bands like PMA, the U-Men, and DOA played. Then I moved back to Montana, got a job stocking shelves at Pay 'n Save and decided to be a painter.

Our high school had a really great art department so I had gotten to take all sorts of drawing and painting classes, plus we had an amazing film and television teacher that would show us Laurie Anderson videos and weird foreign art films, so college was a bit of a disappointment. Reagan was president and I was convinced he was going to blow up the world, so drawing a bowl of fruit seemed like a waste of time. Growing up, my brother was always good at drawing and he'd have us do these projects like "you can only use straight lines" or "you can only use curved lines" and he also had this huge stack of *Mad* magazines that I was obsessed with, so I was forever trying to draw one of those droopy Don Martin shoes. It turns out I didn't really want to go to college, I just wanted to go to the library and check out records, so I failed out after two semesters, moved back to Seattle and got my old dishwashing job back.

That was the summer that I met Dorothy. Our roommates were obsessed with the E-Street Band and it was during a party when they were blasting a Clarence Clemons SOLO record that I heard all this noise coming from her room so I knocked and was like "HELP! WHAT IS THIS?" She was about to go out and just said "Here, these are all VU records, start with this one. See ya!" After that we became fast friends. She gave me a 45 of her old band Mr.

Epp and showed me a video of their last show where they made up these fake political chants ("U.S. EL SALVADOR! WHY NOT YOU?!") and then dumped a bag of hair on the audience. This was a revelation to me, that you could just have fun and not really care what the audience thought and so we made a vague pact to "start a band someday." Then I moved back to Montana and tried to go to college (again).

A few months later Mike came back to Bozeman from Japan and we started hanging out again. He got us this weird job in Colorado making new age music for his rich uncle who had had a spiritual awakening and was hanging out with healers and psychics and wanted us to make these trippy meditation tapes. We convinced him we needed to have an expensive ribbon mic and a new 4 track to record "nature sounds" but mostly we ended up stealing bird sounds from library records and using the mic to record demos. (It turns out it is surprisingly difficult to record nature sounds in the middle of a city!) We once recorded a "soothing forest stream" behind a 7-Eleven where a culvert emptied out, and it sounded really relaxing even with the trucks driving by.

Eventually we had to finish these tapes and get real jobs. I saved money by moving into the kitchen pantry and living off of pancakes and coffee. (It took me a decade to be able to eat pancakes again.) In Seattle I had existed that first summer on oatmeal and blackberries you could pick in the field next door. (It took about another decade to ever eat oatmeal). Later in San Francisco, I lived above a restaurant in the Mission that got huge bags of potatoes and onions delivered regularly. The trick was to carefully open the bags, fill a pan, and then tie the bags shut and run back upstairs before anyone saw you. "Baked potato?" Uhh, no thanks.

Dorothy had been living in Paris and I'd gotten a letter saying she'd be back in Seattle soon so I played Mike the Mr. Epp single "Mohawk Man" and we decided she should be our drummer. We didn't think to ask her or anything, we just loaded everything in the trunk of this big 70's Bonneville with crappy brakes and drove there. Miraculously, I ran into her on the street the day we arrived and said "Hey, do you want to join our band?"

We only played one show in Seattle that summer but a friend of ours in Montana had realized he could book pretty much any SST band for a hundred bucks since most of them just drove straight from Seattle to Denver or Minneapolis. He'd call us and say "Do you want to open for the Meat Puppets?" and so we'd drive to Bozeman and open for the Meat Puppets. "Firehose? Slovenly?" Sure! And finally we got a call asking if we'd open for Sonic Youth! So with the guarantee of one show in Montana opening for Sonic Youth we all quit our jobs, sold our stuff, made some shirts and cassettes and stickers and went on "tour."

A few weeks later we ended up completely broke in California. Mike had a friend living in a warehouse in East Oakland so we drove there and decided to stay. I had a long series of weird jobs that first year. The warehouse had a secret room under a staircase where they grew weed and I would occasionally help trim plants and bag up shake that they'd boil down into oil. You had to be really careful what you ate there because they tended to use pot oil in everything. Another friend was a contractor and he got us all jobs painting apartments, but the hang up was the people were still living in them. So you'd find yourself stoned out of your mind from mistakenly eating pot toast, painting the kitchen of a retired cop who was not at all happy with a bunch of giggling punk rockers painting his cabinets.

Eventually I got a job at an art supply store in San Francisco that I kept for years. We had made a record by then and started actually touring but the manager liked me so I was able to keep the job, although he would make me officially quit every time we left town and then he'd hire me back when we got home. That way I never worked long enough to qualify for health insurance and he never had to give me a raise. I did work one stretch long enough to get dental insurance that I used to get a GOLD CROWN. It promptly fell off, got re-attached wrong, got infected and then required emergency dental surgery in Iowa City, Iowa. I don't recommend it, but it's good to know you can stumble into a random dental office with a swollen jaw and sixty bucks and they'll pull your tooth and send you on your way. Recovering in the coffin loft of a punk rock van in the middle of summer is another story though.

Considering all the times I tried going to college, I learned very little there that would apply to what I do now as a graphic designer. For some reason I never took a printmaking class so I learned the basics of screen printing by printing the backs of Beck shirts. As for the rest of it, it turns out, making flyers and stickers and album covers for your noisy little rock band is a great way to learn the basics of design and production. An art director once looked through my book and told me I was good at establishing a "hierarchy of information," which I guess translates to "your band name should be larger than the price." (He didn't hire me). But you quickly learn making crappy Xerox flyers how to make something that can grab someone's attention long enough for the who-when-where to sink in. How to do it fast and cheap. How to make separations, calling out the colors etc. Super basic knowledge but knowledge that I still use every day. As for the technical side of it, there are plenty of books that if you can stay awake through, will teach you the ins and outs of all the graphics programs.

I feel lucky to have played in bands that got to tour and make records. Travelling taught me more than college ever could have and although no one hands me drink tickets when I show up at my current job, I didn't wake up next to an ashtray on some stranger's floor either. Realizing that no one is going to "discover" you or pluck you from obscurity and make you "famous" is probably the most empowering thing you can know. Once you accept that it's all up to you, YOU are suddenly in control, and then it's just a question of deciding WHAT you want to do.

MONTY COLVIN

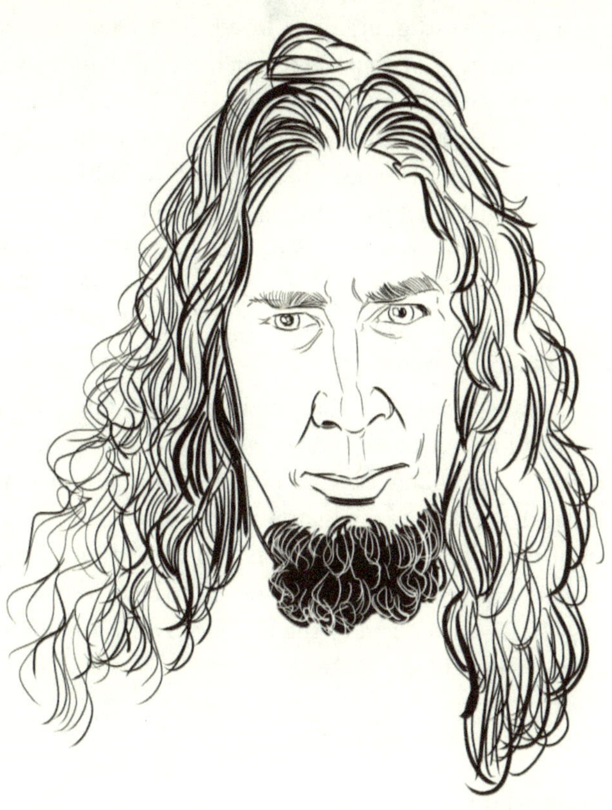

Monty Colvin was the bassist of a band called the Galactic Cowboys. They came out of Houston, had ties to Kings X, and had the unfortunate experience of being signed to the same record label as Nirvana when their *Nevermind* album came out. Both albums dropped around the same time. Obviously, you can figure out what happened afterwards.

To say they fell between the cracks is a fair assessment. These things happen. The other thing, however, is that the first two releases by the band are really odd. I mean that in a good way.

They combined the heavy thrash riffing of what was good about Metallica and Anthrax with three-part harmony vocals that made the overall effect really strange. And even after that, there was all of this ear candy stuff going on. I loved those records, especially the second one, *Space In Your Face*, which sort of sounds like Slayer covering the Beatles in places. When you listen to it now, you know there is no way in hell mass popularity could happen. Or could it? Maybe people would like it now? We will never know. The band were dropped by Geffen and found life on Metal Blade Records, where they put out some good records that failed to catch on. Eventually they disbanded. I still hold those first two Galactic Cowboys albums in very high regard. The band has a small but fanatical following.

Monty also has had a parallel life as an artist and painter. He is really good at both and that is what he is doing these days, even with a recent Galactic Cowboys reunion album available. It is not an unrealistic conclusion to decide that sticking with art in a post-rock band world maybe isn't a bad idea—You can do it alone, you are the boss, and you don't have to compromise anything. Being the cousin of the late Dee Dee Ramone is also a pretty interesting thing

♫ .

Brian: Where did you grow up?

Monty: I was raised in Phoenix, Arizona. We lived there till I was about twelve or thirteen years old and then we moved to Oregon for a little bit. The thing that started me getting into art was actually because my folks were really religious and we had to go to church constantly, every Sunday, sometimes Monday night and Wednesday night, just church all of the time. And it got to where I was just bored most of the time, and they had these little envelopes where you would put your money in for,you know, the offering plate. And before the service would start I would go around and collect these little envelopes and then I would sit there and draw during church. So that is where I started and I just kind of kept doing it. It's weird, because when I was like twelve years old or so, I decided one day that I wanted a set of paints. I really liked to paint and so that is what I did, I bought a set of paints and canvas and started doing some stuff and I kept doing it. I did a lot of stuff, a lot of my early stuff were athletes. I was really into sports because my dad was into sports. I made up little stories about imaginary players and all of that, and that is kind of how it all started.

I took art all through high school and had a really cool high school art teacher who was just so into it, you know? He just loved art so much and I think I drew off of that as far as being inspired. And then I went to college and got a degree in drawing and painting and I kept doing it, all of these years.

Brian: Did music enter your life a little bit later?

Monty: Yeah. It kind of intertwined, though, because these guys in my art class were musicians. I got the bug to play from them. One day I was running around the high school auditorium in basketball practice and I heard this music coming from the auditorium and I walked in there and it was these friends in art class and they had a band. And I saw them in there playing and I was like, "I have to do this."

I bought a guitar and it took me a while to learn, but I just kind of got the fever for music, all through high school and college. That is kind of where all of that started.

Brian: Did playing music professionally happen after college? And after that happened, did the art stuff sort of take a backseat?

Monty: Kind of. I mean, I always kept doing it, I made paintings and had a lot of paintings in my house. A lot of people didn't even know that I did it for a long time, unless you were close to me. And when the Galactic Cowboys formed I started to do artwork and did the backdrops and people started to notice that I did art.

Brian: Your artwork is all over the band's stuff, from album covers to t-shirt designs and stuff like that.

Monty: Yeah. I wanted to do album covers early on, but when we were with Geffen, they were like, "No, we are going to hire a photographer and bring him in from New York," and all of this kind of stuff. And I was like, "Yeah, but I got this really cool painting we can use for *Space In Your Face*." And they were like, "Yeah, maybe a B-side or something." So when we left Geffen and were picked up by Metal Blade, I asked if I could do the artwork and they said it was no problem. And so, from that point on, I did the album covers and that was a great thing for exposure and that kind of thing.

Brian: Were you able to generate freelance work from that exposure as the albums were coming out?

Monty: Yeah. It really did. It came more from people that I had met on the road, I got a few hook-ups with two or three magazines who put my stuff in there, and I have always done quite a few commissions for people who wanted paintings of their kids or their pets, stuff like that. So I always did a lot of stuff like that over the years. And once I got on Facebook, it helped even more to kind of expose people.

Brian: It is a double-edged sword. So I have to ask you—it is not every day that I can talk to someone who is the cousin of the late Dee Dee Ramone. (laughter)

Monty: Yeah. (laughter)

Brian: I knew that he grew up in Europe, but did you spend any time with him—did you actually know him—or did you just pick up rock magazines and go, "whoa, there is my cousin?"

Monty: Yeah, it was like that because he wasn't anywhere around where I was but I heard stories…I lived in this place in Missouri and some of my cousins were like, "Yeah, Dee Dee came through a few weeks ago and stayed and hung out with Grandma for a few weeks," and all of this kind of stuff, which I thought was cool and yeah, I was buying magazines when I was in high school in the seventies when the whole punk rock thing was happening and I was like, "Man, this is so cool. My cousin is in a band."

I just followed him for years. I didn't actually meet him until sometime in the eighties. They were playing a show in Houston and I think it was right around the time that I was in The Awful Truth. And I got to go backstage and hang out with him and talk a little bit. That was really the only time that I met him, but I was a big fan and I loved the Ramones. It was such a cool thing to think that my cousin, you know, basically invented punk rock. He was one of the originators of that genre. It has always been something where I think, "Wow. Did that really happen?" (laughter) It is weird to think that I am that guy's cousin, but I actually know his mom a lot more than I ever knew him, but I was a big fan of his.

Brian: Awesome. I am curious about how the Galactic Cowboys signed to Geffen. I like all of the Galactic Cowboys records to varying degrees, but later on, besides those first two Geffen albums, I really liked *The Horse That Bud Bought* the most.

Monty: (sounding shocked) Yeah? Wow.

Brian: I imagined I would be in the minority there. I like the songs and how it sounds.

Monty: Really? That is cool.

Brian: But the first two records, there is so much going on. I was just listening to the second record and it still sounds great—the vocals, the arrangements, and the production. It is a really cool record. And it just seems really interesting that it was thrown out there on Geffen Records.

Monty: Well, like I said before, I was previously in a band called The Awful Truth and when I quit the band, I didn't know what I was going to do. I thought that my career was over.

Brian: How old were you?

Monty: I was getting close to thirty. I just thought that nobody would get signed after they were thirty, I thought that it was over. But then I thought that I would start another band and give it one more shot. So I started the Galactic Cowboys and within six months we were signed to one of the biggest labels out there. I think that they had heard of us through our manager, Sam Taylor. And he gave them our demos, and at first they didn't really get it. But then they came to see us play and practice and he said, "Oh, okay. I get it." He just loved it and he signed us to a big deal and told us that we were going to be huge.

But unfortunately right at the same time, right before our album came out, Nirvana hit. And it was the same guy who signed us. And so everyone there just sort of turned their attention towards Nirvana. So it was kind of over for us.

Brian: Right. So the band was kind of lost in the shuffle.

Monty: Yeah. But I think that we were just a little too far out there for the mainstream.

Brian: Oh I totally think so. Without a doubt. And I definitely don't mean that in a bad way or anything like that, that's partly why I liked it.

Monty: Sure.

Brian: The Nirvana thing is funny because no one around really thought what ended up happening was going to happen at all. I thought that they were okay but it was just timing mostly. They were in the right place at the right time and I certainly can understand the influence that they had.

Monty: I totally agree with all of that, I feel the same way, too. When we were making the first record, the guy who signed us, Gary Gersh, was listening to what we were recording and everything. And we went out to dinner one day and we were asking him if he had signed anybody new lately and he said, "Yeah, I signed this band from Seattle called Nirvana. We don't expect them to do much but they are a cool band. I am going to give them a shot." And so that was like first hand stuff, and we were like, "Okay, we don't have to worry about that." (laughter)

And I remember at our record release party, Gary was there and he said, "Check this out," and he played us "Smells Like Teen

Spirit" out of this little jam box. We were like, "Oh, wow. That is really good." And a few months later it was all anyone wanted to talk about.

Brian: That must have been incredibly frustrating too.

Monty: Oh, it was.

Brian: There is so much going on on the first record—such a spread of influences. Funnily enough on the song "Sea Of Tranquility," the way it starts off with your bass, that's almost a Melvins thing but it's on bass instead of a guitar. And all of the vocals and stuff, the layered vocals all over everything... I know that you always get the Beatles but what else was out there that influenced the band vocally?

Monty: Strangely enough, I grew up listening to gospel records because it was all that my parents would let me listen to when I was a kid. And it was all four part harmony gospel quartet stuff. And my folks both sang and they were always like, "Hey, harmonize with us on this." And we would sit around and we would harmonize. So I got a lot of inspiration from that, and then later stuff like the Beatles. Alan (Doss, drummer) was really into the Beatles too. And at the same time that we were working on that stuff, I was really into the whole thrash metal movement. You know, early Metallica, Anthrax, Megadeth. So I wanted to sort of blend the two, and that was what we did with the Galactic Cowboys.

Brian: What was the reaction when people heard the vocals over the music at first? I loved the contrast, I just wish more people would try stuff like that.

Monty: Yeah. We just wanted to add harmonies to more metallic sort of music.

Brian: You guys are friends with Kings X, and were often compared to them, but I never really thought the two bands sounded the same except for maybe some of the vocal influences both bands shared.

Monty: Yeah, I never thought we did either. We were getting that comparison all of the time but we were a lot weirder, we were a lot heavier, and were a lot more metal and punk and all of this stuff. A lot of people, they either loved us or they didn't. We went out on a tour with Overkill and their fans just flipped us off and threw shit at us every night. We weren't metal enough. So we had a hard time on that tour. And we didn't fit in with a lot of bands, we didn't fit in with certain genres. It was kind of tough in that way.

Brian: You brought up your parents being religious and I know the guys in Kings X had a Christian sort of background initially. Was that something that you guys were a part of as well?

Monty: The only connection with that at all was because Alan and I had played with a Christian artist for about a year. We were his backup band and we went through that whole thing. They called it contemporary Christian music and by the end of that year, I wanted no part of it. It was pretty fake and cheesy and it wasn't for me. We just wanted to be looked at as just a band. We were Christians and stuff, but I didn't care if Christian people liked it or not. I think we got tagged with that a little bit.

Brian: And Kings X obviously did, too. So, *Space In Your Face*, the second Geffen record, came out. What happened after that?

Monty: We did a tour with Dream Theater that was excellent. We gained a lot of fans from it. A afterwards, we were out on another tour and we literally got a phone call from our manager and he said that Geffen had just dropped us. He told us to quit and go home. (laughter) Yeah, so we just loaded our stuff and just went home. And that was it. We kind of regrouped after actually breaking up for a little bit. But Metal Blade came to the rescue. So we were able to do the rest of our records with Metal Blade, they sustained our career for probably another seven years.

Brian: Being in a band takes up a lot of time. Where were you as far as doing art during these times? I know you also have kids and stuff like that. Was it kind of hard, balancing all of this stuff out?

Monty: I always did stuff just for myself, just for fun. I did portraits for people just to make a little extra money on the side. I always had hoped that I could get something going where I could make enough money to live on with the art, but I could never come up with anything that could do that. But I had the band and that was also a source of income. I always had them both and somehow I was just able to juggle it, whether it was writing a song or doing a painting.

Brian: And then it got to the point where it was time to take a break from the band and do something else.

Monty: Yeah. We really were against the wall for about ten years and it just wasn't going anywhere. We were making what we thought were good albums but it just felt like I was more frustrated more than anything, I think we all were. In fact, Alan didn't even play drums on our last album. And I had decided that I wanted to do a solo album and try a little different style of music. So I've done three solo records now. Crunchy is my solo thing.

But it's tough. It's hard to make any money at it unless you are playing cover tunes or are already really big. There is nothing in between anymore, everyone is basically broke. So…

Brian: I was thirty years into a bunch of not very successful musical endeavors. I have no idea what a young band would do today to get noticed. I don't know how anyone really gets noticed anymore. Most people don't even care about owning physical product of music, or a book, or whatever.

Monty: It boggles my mind because music was always so important to me. Just going out and buying that new album by whomever it was that you liked. Now, no one even cares. My stepson is a really cool kid but he doesn't have a favorite band, you know? He doesn't own a CD, I think. He has other interests. It is really so sad to me. (laughter)

Brian: During all of the years I played music and hoped for the best, there were always these really shitty bands that got insanely popular, so there was also that sort of professional jealousy I had.

And I decided that the only thing worse than being in a shitty band where nothing happened was being in a pretty good band where nothing happened and no one cared about. (laughter) That was the story of a lot of the music I played. I am just speaking for me.

Monty: Right!

Brian: I noticed that you are putting your art out there a lot more, as far as freelancing. Is that something you are trying to concentrate on a bit more these days?

Monty: Yeah. You know, for years I just wanted to find something, a niche or something that I could do so I could make a decent living. Even if it was small, you know? But I just couldn't come up with anything. And then a few years ago I got hired to do all of these murals for *The School Of Rock*. And doing that was like the greatest, funnest job ever. And about a year ago, I woke up one day and thought about how those murals were so much fun, I wish I could do something like that. But maybe I could do small paintings of those murals and sell them. I made a couple of them and they sold instantly. And I thought, "Oh. Okay."

And so I started doing more of them and I made a website where I sell paintings off of it now. And once people saw those paintings, people started to get in touch more. So I started to get commissions from people. And so it has started to blossom to where I think it is really going somewhere now. And that's kind of where I am putting most of my focus these days. I am still in the Galactic Cowboys—we are doing a couple of shows in September—but that is not really my burning desire anymore. I gave it fifteen or twenty years, I gave it everything I had. I still enjoy it—we made an album, I enjoyed that. But I am more focused on my art now. I really love it and that is where I am at these days.

Brian: That is great. Do you still hear from people that were big fans of the music you made in the Galactic Cowboys? I imagine you hear stuff from people, mostly on the internet, probably?

Monty: I actually get messages almost every day. About songs and albums that meant so much to these people. More than anything, I am just kind of surprised that people still remember us and liked it. It means a lot because then I think, "Okay, it wasn't all a waste of time."

We had kind of a rough career, we never got to where we had wanted to be, you know? But we still got to do a lot of cool things. We were on the *Headbangers Ball* on MTV. We got to tour with Anthrax. There were a lot of cool things, we got to make a living, at least for a little while, doing it and I will always be thankful for that opportunity we had to do those things.

CHRIS SHARY AND LORI HERBST

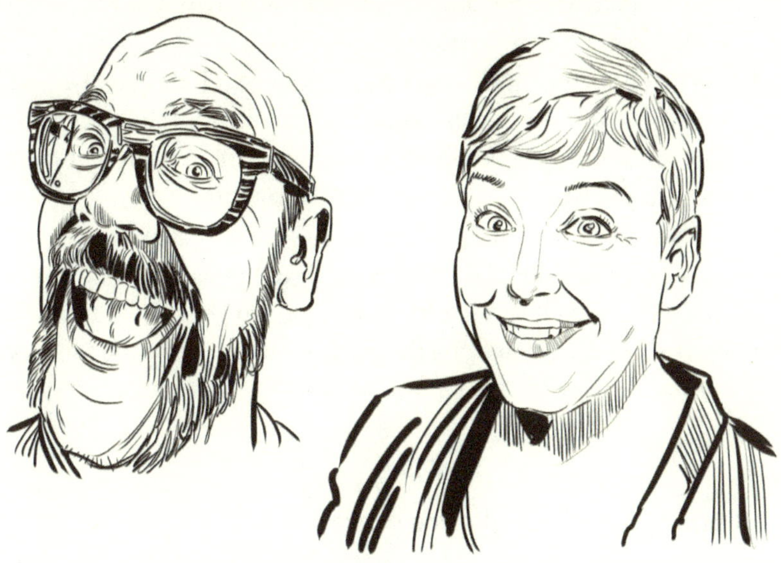

Chris Shary and Lori Herbst live in Stockton, California, with their son, Sam.

Lori lays out new information on what kind of art you can do with a sewing machine. She does great stuff, and she is super prolific, she puts amazing new stuff out there in the world every day. Her work is unique, and really great.

Chris called me out of the blue in the early nineties and asked what had happened to me because I had stopped drawing and faded away for a bit. That might have been the first time that anyone ever reached out and wondered what had happened to me.

He has sort of a similar experience with punk rock and drawing, just like me. But Chris is a way happier, upbeat, and outgoing kind of guy than me. And definitely a little less cynical. I always had joked that we were almost like art brothers somehow, along with Voivod's Michel Langevin. He wanted me to draw some art that was meant to go inside of a CD version of the Big Boys' *Wreck Collection* release that he oversaw, and I was more than happy to do that for him. We became friends after that. I had to wait a few years to meet him in person. That took place in Sacramento, I believe, on a Melvins tour. It was like meeting someone that you had already known your entire life.

Chris has done numerous crazy things and his artwork is all over the place. He is also tightly associated with the Descendents and has done almost everything that people have seen that has to do with the band in the last twenty or so years.

I owe Chris a lot, because he was one of the first guys to contact me and get me out of my wilderness years, to pave the way for me to reapply myself to my artistic abilities, to get better, and to do more stuff. So for that, I will always have some gratitude towards him, and his friendship means a lot.

♫

Brian: How long ago did you two meet?

Chris: It was the spring of 1998 and we had a couple of good friends, one of mine and one of Lori's, they were brother and sister, and we all decided let's get the brother and sisters groups of friends together and go out dancing.

Lori: And so we all went, and I saw Chris and I was, "Yeah, that is somebody I would like to get to know." And he was an excellent dancer and that helps too. So we really hit it off.

Chris: Yeah. We were making fun of drunk people that were grinding on each other all night and it was pretty fun. And I was like, "Wow, she was kind of cool." And then I went on the Warped Tour with All that summer and kind of disappeared. I get back, and I am on a date with this girl, and it wasn't going very well, and I randomly ran into some friends of mine. She went to the bathroom and they said, "Well, how is the date going?" And I said, "Well, not that great actually," and they said, "Aw, I wouldn't worry about it. Do you remember that girl, Lori? She was asking about you and wondering what you have been up to." And I said, "Okay. Hold on a second."

So the girl that I was on a date with gets out of the bathroom and I say, "Well, it has been a fun night but I think it is time to take you home." So I took her home immediately, and came right back and said, "Alright. What is Lori's telephone number, tell me more about her." I called her up, we went on a date and here we are, twenty years later.

Lori: Just like all of the great romances, we met at a bar.

Chris: I am not even a drinker, it was so awesome.

Brian: Making fun of drunk people is a great way to bond! I don't drink, Kristin doesn't drink, we made fun of drunk people, but I think that maybe you guys like people in general more than we do.

Chris: That is probably true!

Lori: It depends on the week.

Chris: The state of California pays me to like people.

Brian : I think your outgoing nature is probably quite an asset. I mean, I am probably a little less good about networking and befriending other people at flea markets and stuff like that. You seem like you have an easier time doing that kind of stuff because you are less introverted. I have seen a half dozen times around you where I can see that has already helped you.

Chris: Yeah, that is definitely for sure. You know, it's funny, talking about Lori and I meeting, I was very socially awkward with girls and relationships, but I had no problem with a band, and going up to them after they were done playing and going, "Hey you guys were really great. I do artwork. Want me to do some artwork for you?" I have never had any problem with that and I have always gone after those sort of things that I was interested in.

I think I am relatively easy to work with and I really, truly do love the bands that I do work with and for me, I am persistent and if I hit it off well with the people who are in the band, they are more inclined to want to work with me in the first place, because they aren't going, "This guy is really annoying. Why would we do anything with him in the first place?" So I think it has been very helpful for me, and being able to maintain good relationships with those bands and some other people, maybe tour managers or whatever. That is the world that I wanted to be in, so I think that has been very, very helpful to me. Lori tends to be more introverted, but when we do go to art conventions and stuff, she turns it on and is the focus of the room.

Lori: I think anti-anxiety medicine helps. Ha ha.

Brian: I hear ya. I have turned to that sort of thing, and it has really helped me. I am a little bit more on the introverted side, too. Did you both have similar backgrounds as far as art goes? Did you know that you were sort of the weird, arty, misfit kid growing up?

Lori: Yeah, I came from a real creative family. My dad is a scientist and he has all kinds of patterns and my mom sewed all of my clothes through high school and taught me how to sew and that kind of thing, so I was always around creative people and I was always making up stories in my head and doing stupid stuff.

Chris: My mom and my dad did draw some, even before I was born, and my mom is definitely the reason that I am doing what I am doing today. I knew really early on that I wanted to be an artist, that was very apparent. We were living in Germany and I think I was three and my mom didn't speak German and she was at home with me. My brother was just starting kindergarten so he was gone and it was just me and my mom who were home, and so she would get coloring books and paper and we would just sit and color and draw all day. And she always encouraged me, and then I had gotten a little bit older and I saw all of these drawings that she had done as a kid and they were really cool. I just remember going, "Whoa, my parents can do that." And then my dad had *CARtoons* magazines and *Mad* magazines and would draw some of the monsters from those, and I remember seeing some of that and thinking that if they could do that then I could do that.

I think when I was in junior high, when we moved to New

Jersey, I was in a new school and I was just drawing something—probably something stupid like a barbarian or some monster—and there were these kids that I didn't know looking at my stuff going, "Wow, you are really good." I don't remember actually hearing that from other people until then, probably. And then I kind of went, "Oh I might have some talent here."

Brian: I had the exact same experience in sixth or seventh grade. I had copied something that looked sort of like what it was and went, "Oh, I can draw. Cool."

Chris: You don't really notice that when you are little because everybody draws. And there is a certain point where people stop or certain people will just start getting naturally better at it. And when you start getting better and better, you keep doing it. And people like you and I, that was the case. We just kept at it and people were like, that's pretty good and that was all I needed to hear.

Brian: Same here. Another thing was always having music around. It was always there. So I was always interested in drawing and listening to music. And then, when I discovered punk rock, it was the background for whatever sort of creativity that I thought I had. So when I discovered that stuff it just seemed to go hand in hand with it, and I also discovered that you could draw for people and write to people. That was what sent me on my way. It was like tapping into the counterculture of those times, or our version of that thing.

Chris: For me, when my buddies in the Stupids put out a record, it was like, "Holy crap! You guys actually for real did this. You are my friends, let's go skate." And then it was, "Oh, you are playing. Oh, you are on the cover of *Sounds* magazine now. You are touring Australia and Japan. That's weird."

And having that connection and doing artwork for them was great. Because, you can do it. I think when you know people on a personal level, it makes all of the difference in the world.

Brian: Sure. I was very immersed in that, and when we first met—

when you had called me out of the blue—I hadn't been drawing for a while. I took a break. And it was your phone call, you going, "Hey dude. What happened to you?" And I think the reason for that, looking back, everything that I did was so tied into that scene that when I kind of got tired of it and stopped, I wasn't ambitious or smart enough to think that maybe I should just try to paint, or maybe I should try and draw some other stuff.

Chris: You didn't realize that you could have just tried some different stuff or whatever.

Brian: It was your phone call that made me want to get back into it and get better, and eventually that happened.

Chris: And it is great that you did, because when I first started, you showed up in everything. You know, I couldn't pick up a issue of *Maximum Rock N Roll* and get more then two or three pages and see something that you did—whether it was for a scene report or whether it was for BCT Tapes, or flyers that you had done that were reprinted or whatever—I couldn't escape it and I thought, "I would like to do that kind of thing, I would like to be able to be as out there and as prolific," so it certainly gave me the kick to try and just put my artwork more out there. So then when I was thinking about what did happen to you, I was so happy to finally get in touch with you and get you to do that piece for the Big Boys *Wreck Collection* album insert, and then you have this kind of re-birth. I am very, very happy about that.

Brian: Oh yeah, me too. So another question I have is about what you guys do, besides art. Chris is a high school drama teacher. Have you ever considered trying to do art full time?

Chris: No, not really. First of all, the health care and the security and everything that I have by having my job is so valuable. And the truth of the matter is that I do really love doing that job. I love being a teacher, I love working with kids and I get a tremendous amount of satisfaction from that. Also, I would really hate to have thrown away what I really worked so long and hard for because, you know, there's an eventual retirement and all of that really pays off at that point.

The other thing is, I always think back to this interview with Chuck Dukowski. It was probably 1981 or '82 and the person that was interviewing Chuck had said, "Well do you guys have other jobs that you work?" and he was like, "Yeah, we do because I don't ever want to look at doing my music as being something that I have to do to pay bills." In that regard there are a lot of times you will have to make big concessions and do things that you wouldn't normally want to do artistically just to get the bills paid. Or it might not become enjoyable to you anymore because it is a job.

Lori: The other thing is, working at that environment—I was working in the drama department too—I was teaching costuming and teaching kids how to sew and how to act and build sets, so it was still a creative job that didn't feel like I was going to go and do something for work to get it over with, and then do something that you really wanted to do.

Chris: I am sure we have both daydreamed about it, like, "Boy wouldn't it be cool if we both just did this?" and it will be, because eventually I will be retiring.

Lori: Eight years.

Chris: Yeah, eight years. That will be thirty years for me teaching, and at that point I will be looking at retiring because I can then say that I put in all of this time and now I can focus on just doing artwork.

Lori: And we will have the house paid off.

Chris: We will have a retirement plan and all of that stuff, so I think that has always been very important in the back of our minds. You need to have some sort of stability. Lori homeschools Sam and I would hate for her to go, "Okay, we are just going to throw him in a public school and then I am going to get a job to have to pay for it," and she is doing something just to support that, and that just seems stupid to me.

Lori: Well, you have seen our house. We live in a modest neighborhood and we have one car and we are careful with money.

Chris: And we have never lived beyond our needs, we are not extravagant people or anything which I think most people in our world just aren't. Living smart like that helps because you are not working to support this consumer lifestyle. To me, that just seems stupid.

Brian: I was going to ask how you guys balance your family with your son Sam, but after talking to you this far it seems like you have everything figured out, where art is just part of life.

Lori: We are really fortunate because Sam has friends down in L.A., so when we are going down to art shows we just swing by and pick up one of his friends and he is always willing to help. We really hit the jackpot with Sam.

Chris: What we do is who we are, so it's not like I come home and I am putting on a different hat to do something I. It's like, I was maybe working on artwork at school and I come home and I am doing that, and, "Oh, we are going out tonight to go and see such-and-such band? Oh, I did stuff for them." So it is all connected back to that. Or we are planning the next big art show or whatever, and Sam is helping us pick up artwork and take stuff down. It is all a part of what we do.

Brian: You do a lot of art shows, both of you it seems.

Chris: Lori is asked to do a lot of art shows, all of the time. We will be at shows where people are inviting her to other ones and things like that, and I love it because I think her work is wonderful. And between the two of us, I have come to the realization that my "gallery" is, like, at a concert. Seeing my shirts walking around, to me, that is my gallery thing. Or going to a record store and flipping through the bins and seeing some of my work, that is my gallery.

Lori's is on the wall in a gallery. Because you have to see her original pieces to truly appreciate them, whereas I am doing drawings that are being reproduced on record covers or t-shirts or whatever. I will do stuff at shows and I certainly enjoy doing them and they are great but I am not striving to do that; that is Lori. I want Lori to be in more shows because that is how you can see her original pieces. You can't go to an online catalog like Bifocal Media and order fifty of Lori's pieces and have them be twenty bucks, you can't do that. She is constantly having new galleries get in touch with her.

Lori: You know, you have to go to the galleries to build a persona around your art. It's not like you can just send stuff around and say, "Hey, look at this. Isn't it great?" You really have to work the whole thing.

Chris: Lori gets a lot of questions about how she makes things.

Brian: And there is so much of it. It's like every day there is something new.

Lori: I know! What is wrong with me?

Brian: And there is a huge variety of subject matter, from the band X to seeing a really nice thing of Rowland S. Howard from the Birthday Party.

Lori: Yeah, that was cool. I luckily get a lot of commission work so I get to do a lot of stuff that maybe I wouldn't think about on my own. I really enjoy that, and anything that I do, I am kind of a researcher type, I really like to look at the time period and the history of everything that goes behind the image that I am working on at that moment. I really enjoy that.

Brian: Chris, tell me about your friendship with the Descendents. You have done all of their recent album covers and the band has set up this huge, wonderful thing where they play all of these shows in various cities and then they print up a certain amount of shirts that all feature your artwork on them. They keep you very busy. How did that friendship start?

Chris: So, when I first heard *Milo Goes To College*, they were my instant favorite band—from that very beginning of "Myage" it was like, "Okay, here we go, that is my band." I was living in England at the time and there was no chance that they were ever going to tour, so when I finally moved back to the States, they had broken up as the Descendents and had formed All. I was, okay well, I loved Dag Nasty and now Dave Smalley is singing with them, and now this is my favorite band. So All is happening and Karl [Alvarez] is doing their artwork and Karl is great. Why would I be able to do anything artistically for them? It would be really fun. I had done some artwork after seeing them in 1989, I did a flyer for them. I think it was '90 or '91 and Bill [Stevenson] had seen the flyer and was really pretty excited about it and asked if I wanted to do something for them. I said of course I would, so I just started doing drawings like you do, and just started sending them to him. I really didn't stop, I just kept going with it. And the more that I did it, and the more that they were on tour, the more I saw them and the more we hung out and the more we became friends. I was working with my favorite band, this is all I really want to do artistically. Any time that they need something, I pretty much drop the other art that I am working on because it was always a priority for me.

Here we are now, like twenty seven years later. We are close as friends, so now it is just kind of a given. We all do a lot of different things, and because of that we have done fun things—like the Descendents ugly Christmas sweater thing. We really kicked that off, we were the first ones who were doing that. That was us.

Lori: Chris is to blame for that.

Brian: So it is your fault.

Steve Shelton

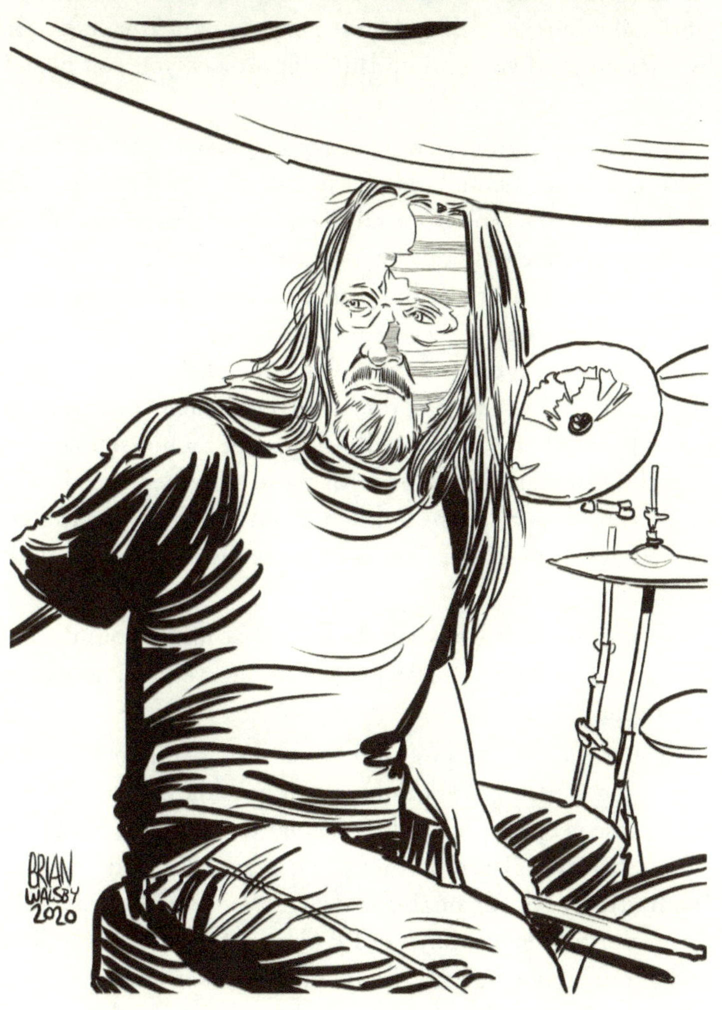

Steve is the drummer for the long-standing off and on (but usually on these days) heavy metal band Confessor. Sure, there are eight thousand sub genres for heavy metal these days, but back around 1987 here in North Carolina, Confessor were this enormously popular local metal band who packed in the clubs with tons of kids who enjoyed their waaaaay ahead of their time music. Mostly thanks to the drumming of Steve, Confessor were an incredible early example of technical heavy metal minus that label and minus the stiff and boring end result of after a few songs by a lesser band you end up thinking, "okay, you can play. It's still boring. Next."

The riffs in Confessor were heavy and menacing in a Trouble circa their debut album kind of way. But when you add the precise confusion of Shelton's drumming on top of those riffs and then add the completely at odds high-pitched singing of Scott Jeffreys, you have an unbeatable band that held their own completely against anyone else, either than or now. You have early Trouble, you have Celtic Frost, you have Voivod, and then you can easily put Confessor in there no problem. Even though you might have never heard them. Admittedly they aren't a household name in eighties metal. But along with those aforementioned bands, especially Voivod, at the time they were the future. And they still are, even in 2020. Confessor were pioneers. Some people know this.

A lot of bands these days do stuff that might sound a little similar to Confessor. But no one still to this very day sounds like Confessor.

Steve is the kind of guy who has at least two people in every city in the United States thinking that he is the best drummer on earth. The people who like his playing REALLY like his playing. What Steve has played on that you can actually go out and find is admittedly sort of small for such a long period of time (Two Confessor full lengths and an EP plus three demos, two albums and a four song single by the recently defunct Loincloth, a self released CD album by Fly Machine) but what is out there is great. Remember: quality, not quantity.

My angle for Steve is that he has maintained his passion for music and drumming for decades and doesn't push any of it, it's almost like it will come when it's supposed to come. He never tried to rely on his art for financial gain and has had landscaping jobs since day one. So he is not self employed and doesn't want to be. But to be so driven at his craft since 198whatever as well as being so original and so good made me have to shoehorn him into my project, and maybe offer it elsewhere to others to read some cool stuff about an absolute legend on the drums.

Not surprisingly, Steve Shelton is a laid-back affable smart and humble man. I thank Steve for giving me this chance to interview him."

♫

Brian: You started out playing drums in high school, right?

Steve: Yeah, since the end of high school, which was in 1984.

Brian: And you were really into Neil Peart…

Steve: Oh yeah, absolutely. The first time I heard "Limelight," with the little flatulent drum roll at the beginning, I knew I wanted to be a drummer.

My best friend in high school was Phil Swisher, who played on Corrosion Of Conformity's *Blind* album. He was the one who convinced me to get a drum set and to be in a band. So I got a drum set with the intention of playing with people, but it took a little while to get to the point where I could play with anybody. It took a while to get to the point of even playing with anyone in the house because I was really timid and self conscious.

So I started to play with Phil. He was my introduction into punk rock and he was my introduction to the local punk rock scene in Raleigh. Otherwise I would have been listening to what I like to call "smoking court Metal" at the time, back when schools had smoking courts.

Brian: So like….the *Blizzard of Ozz* album?

Steve: I was a little late for that, it was actually the *Diary Of A Madman* album. So I was listening to that kind of stuff, and the first punk rock show I went to was the Battle Of The Bands at Dorton Arena when COC were playing. Within thirty seconds the power was cut and the stagehands got into some fights with some of the hardcore kids. And then two or three weeks later,

COC played at that infamous church in Durham.

Brian: Oh, that show where… oh wait, Eric Eycke was still in the band…

Steve: Yeah, it wasn't the time that they got stabbed if that is what you were going to say.

Brian: That was a year later.

Steve: Yeah, at the same place. But the energy of it was totally captivating to me so I started to get more and more into punk rock. And that spell lasted maybe only for a year and a half. Or maybe two years. Long enough for me to dye my hair black. (laughter)

Brian: Always a good look for a redhead.

Steve: Yeah, considering you can't see my eyebrows. It wasn't the smartest decision. But around that time the first Slayer album had come out, and the first Trouble album had come out. And those records hit me in a more impactful, even emotive way than punk rock ever did. To me, punk rock, the energy of it I liked, the aggression of it I liked. But the jangly nature of punk rock, it's not in all bands but I had a hard time with it.

So when the Slayer and Trouble albums came out, the energy level was the same but it was meaner, the musicianship was a lot more precise and they were trying to do more things with their music than the punk bands. And as I was just beginning to get comfortable with playing the drums, those records were a much more natural outlet for me so that is how the evolution started. I never turned back. There were a couple of punk rock bands that I still enjoy but I never listen to.

Brian: Like what?

Steve: Like Discharge. The Crucifix album.

Brian: I love both of those. But I can't say that I go home and put them on a lot. It's not the first thing I would reach for, but it still sounds good to me.

Steve: It's like a once in every five years thing for me.

Brian: The first Trouble record. To this day, is one of the top five metal releases of the eighties, which is sort of our era. The record doesn't seem to be held with the same regard that a lot of their peers, which is totally bizarre to me. People talk about how bad it sounds but I don't care how it sounds, you know?

Steve: Right. We came from punk rock! There are a lot of records that sound worse than that. (laughter)

Brian: So Slayer and Trouble paved the way towards you discovering other things. Did you do anything band wise between your short-lived band Bloodbath and when you met Confessor?

Steve: No. I guess there was a two year lull where I didn't play with anybody but I just practiced drums. And I was getting more into the more complicated metal that really was pretty new at the time.

Brian: So, a lot of people in the punk rock scene at the time, we had already seen Confessor's earliest shows, like at the Fallout Shelter in North Carolina. I remember seeing them and thinking that they were really good and also sounded like they were influenced by Trouble. Meanwhile outside of that, you had formed a friendship with Graham, and you started to play music with him. Would you say that you and him working on things together led to the kind of music that Confessor would do in the future?

Steve: Oh yeah. Absolutely. I liked them too, I had seen the band several times. And Graham was somebody…we went to the same high school, my senior year. I knew who he was, he always struck me as being the most accessible and probably most down-to-earth, humble person. He was always someone that I wanted to meet. And when I was still living at home, Scott (Jeffreys, Confessor vocalist) approached me originally. His girlfriend apparently lived in the same neighborhood as my parents and he heard me playing drums as he was driving down the street one day. And he was interested in finding another drummer for Confessor.

So he knocked on the door not knowing who was living there. I opened the door and it was, "Hey! I know who you are." but we had never met. So he gave me their tape and I really liked it but

I felt like if they had a more interesting drummer that this music could be more interesting. So I ended up meeting Graham and we hit it off right away. In fact, the very same day we ate at either four or five places together. (laughter) So, brothers in food, brothers in music. But it took about a year of poking him every now and then to ask him to bring over his stuff and play. He was reluctant, but eventually he did. We played some Trouble stuff and some Black Sabbath stuff. Not long after that, he invited the other guys in Confessor to come over to my place, just to watch the two of us play.

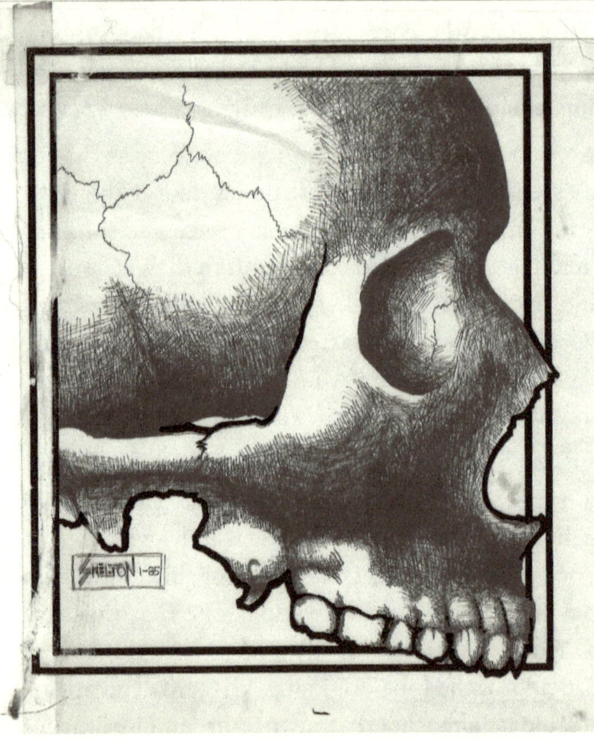

ARTWORK BY STEVE SHELTON

They decided to give Jim (Shoaf, original drummer) a chance to do what he wanted to do. He could either just put a little more effort into the band, or not. Or whatever. He decided that he wasn't interested enough to put in whatever it was going to take to stay in the band, so I filled his spot. And we learned things together. I had the freedom to play around with drums as we were learning things and I just did whatever I wanted. And every time that I did something on drums that made the rhythm feel like a completely different rhythm, by highlighting this or highlighting that, they loved it as much as I did.

So I was able to learn in a really abstract way. I never sat down and read books or anything. I never took lessons. I just played what was fun to play.

Brian: It almost sounds like everyone learned how to be in Confessor together. And to me, that early era was documented by those three demos coming out, one after another. "*The Secret*" was the first one, right? With the blue cover?

Steve: Yes, with the blue cover and that really busy design that became what people called our "rebel flag" shirt. (laughter) So there was that and then *Uncontrolled* and then *Collapse Into Despair*. I think all three of them came out within a two year time frame.

Brian: Meanwhile, as those demos are coming out, the band is playing out locally a lot more and even are beginning to play out of town. I seem to remember some shows where you opened for Corrosion Of Conformity. They wanted to help the band.

Steve: Yeah, we went out of town with them at least a couple of times. Our first out of town show was in New Orleans with them, during COC's Simon Bob [Sinister] era. We were definitely not the kind of band that a lot of these people were interested in seeing, but we have had some life-long fans based on that one show. People have even come up fifteen or twenty years later, making a trip up here to see us when we play. I wish I could remember where the other shows were, but I don't. COC, I already had a friendly relationship with them just from being around. I traveled with them when they went out west to record what would have been *Technocracy*. So I already knew those guys and we got along great and they were very helpful and encouraging, especially way back then.

Brian: Confessor has a lot of fanatical fans that love the band but a lot of them probably weren't around back at this time. So any time over the years where I have talked to people about the band, they seem to have a hard time imagining that Confessor wasn't a band playing this crazy music to small audiences, that they were actually an enormously popular local band packing in the clubs here in Raleigh. Scott's vocals were the deal breaker for some people, but to me, I always loved it. It almost made the band art rock even though it was heavy. When you look back on that time period, do you have any explanation on why Confessor was so popular even with playing this pioneering weird sort of heavy metal?

Steve: Back then, underground heavy metal was still underground. Metallica hadn't burst out of the underground and brought everyone else into the sunlight yet. So I always felt like some of it was because we were a small enough town where everyone knew each other. But I also think that things were new enough—and we were different enough—that a lot of people felt this type of ownership, that they were a part of what was going on. It was more of a communal thing back then. Plus, metal had not been commercialized yet. People hadn't figured out how to make a lot of money from it yet, it was just a lot of people having a lot of fun. And I think we had tapped into the high school that we had all went to, that Scott and Graham's band went to. There were a lot of Millbrook High kids that went to the shows, and we were the only clubbing band that they had an outlet for. There might have been a newness to it, too, because I had plenty of conversations with people, who as individuals we were friends with and who might have not liked our recordings but loved seeing us live. So I think that played into it too. Plenty of people who didn't even like heavy metal seemed to like us and would come and see us.

Brian: I remember that there were definitely some non-metal people checking out the shows.

Steve: Yeah. And I have to be honest, I still haven't heard very many bands that remind me of us. So I think we probably stood out even more back then.

Brian: I don't know what you listen to these days, and even though I still love the form of heavy metal, it's not what I actually like in that world these days.

Steve: I go back to the same five bands I liked thirty years ago.

Brian: Me too, more or less. And all of the stuff that I hear that gets compared to Confessor or the other music that you drummed on, ends up being stuff that I just don't seem to like very much. There are a handful of acts that work a little bit of the same territory, but it's almost nothing but technical for the sake of being technical and there is no emotion in it at all.

Steve: Oh, I know exactly what you are talking about. It becomes very lifeless. Confessor's number one objective was that it was always meant to be heavy, no matter what. We just happened to like being weird, too. It was the same in Loincloth, too. Loincloth, more than Confessor, could have been more technical then we were, but that is not what we were trying to do. We were trying to honor the bands that had inspired us a long time ago and playing within our limits.

As a busy drummer, it was a hard lesson to learn. Yeah, I can sprinkle an entire album with sorts of detail but it gets to the point where it is detracting from the music.

Brian: After Graham quit, he was replaced with Ivan Colon. Did Ivan play on the album *Condemned*?

Steve: He did.

Brian: Graham quit because he wasn't feeling it anymore.

Steve: Yeah. That was it. I knew, because of how well I knew him, when he started listening to things like John McLaughlin and Mahavishnu Orchestra, I thought, "okay, his days are numbered." (laughter) Metal is not going to cut it for him anymore. It took maybe a year or a year and a half at practice, but you could feel it. It was the first experience of having someone in the band longer than they should have stuck around. So we have recognized that when it has happened since. Graham was just interested in other things. There were no hard feelings. He quit six months before we recorded our first album so he quit just in time to miss the record and to miss out on the subsequent touring and all of the fun stuff that we had worked so hard for.

Brian: You toured Europe in 1992?

Steve: Yeah, we went over there twice. Once with Carcass and then we came back and did another tour with Nocturnus, still supporting *Condemned*. The first tour, the Earache Records sponsored one, that was top shelf, all the way around. When we got to mainland Europe, there was a catering company that followed the tour. We had cooked meals at every show. That was our first experience beyond just renting a van and seeing what you could do for one weekend. So that was great. And when we came back to do the second tour a few months later, it was considerably less than great. Some of us were fine with it, some of us pretty disillusioned with it and members started dropping off after that.

Ivan was the first to go, so he could go back to school, and once we found a replacement in Chris (Nolan, current guitarist), his first show was the show where Scott announced that he was leaving the band. It took us two years to find a replacement singer for Scott.

Brian: Was that the reason why Confessor was shelved and Fly Machine began?

Steve: Yeah. We realized that with different members we weren't writing the same kind of music. When you are in a band you are compromising with everyone else in the band. And anyone who has ever played in a band knows that when you replace people, it is going to sound different, suddenly everything is different. Unless you have a dictator who forces things. We had little chips on our shoulders, we were sort of a little resentful on how things had worked out. Resentful maybe isn't the word.

Brian: Disappointed?

Steve: We didn't want to have to live up to what people had thought Confessor was supposed to be. We weren't even going in that direction.

Brian: What was the reaction to Fly Machine?

Steve: With diehard Confessor fans there was enough of a connection to keep up with it but we were definitely not having any momentum. Plus there was a two year gap where we didn't do anything. And at that point metal had changed. It had become commercialized. So there were ways—there were tried and true ways—to make lots of money on it. Record labels weren't interested in taking a chance on some weird, quirky little band who had a name a few years earlier but not anymore.

Brian: I liked the second Confessor album. It is definitely different but there are some great songs on it and Scott did a great job.

Steve: I have to say, that was a different experience and a perfect example of how different members write different music. Graham was the one who wrote a good deal of Confessor material. Brian Shoaf (other original guitarist) also wrote a good deal of material, but me and Graham were the driving force. Brian was very comfortable with having Graham show him what to play but once Graham was gone, Brian's "rock side" came out more. Brian and I would write some songs. And then the other guitarist we had at the time, we would write some songs together, too. And the resulting songs from each guitarist resulted in songs that didn't sound like they belonged on the same record. So there was some butting of heads and personalities that didn't get along too well. So instead of a unifying thing it became a thing where they were writing against each other. I was trying to get everyone to get along. So for years when I listen to *Unraveled*, that is what I heard. The butting of heads, and I just couldn't do it.

Brian: Do you like the record now?

Steve: I do, but it took a really long time. I always felt like Scott's vocal performance was the thing that made the album work, and I still think that's true. I had to put the experience of that time behind me before I could really appreciate the subtlety of *Unraveled* for what it was. There are some really solid ideas on that album.

Brian: Now moving on to Loincloth, who were very enjoyable but it was frustrating because so little seemed to get done. Pen Rollings was second guitarist on the first four song seven-inch that Southern Lord Records put out. It was a great record. But I know that the band members all lived in different places and no one was in any real hurry to do anything. (laughter) How many years did Loincloth actually exist?

Steve: Our first album, *Iron Balls Of Steel* came out in 2012. Our first practice was in 2000. (laughter) But there were times where—since Tannon [Penland] and Pen lived in Richmond—we would agree to get together for certain weekends, they were supposed to come down here Friday night. And I would get a call Sunday morning from them saying, "Hey, by the way, we aren't coming down this weekend." And yeah I had kind of figured it out by Saturday morning. There would be these six month spells where we didn't do anything. That happened a couple of times.

Brian: So after the album comes out, you actually find guys that could play in Loincloth, Craig [Hilton] and Tomas [Phillips]. You played a handful of shows, went out west, and then you finished the second album and disbanded, shifting everything back to Confessor again.

Steve: Yeah. Chris is still in the band on guitar, and Brian quit. We found Marcus [Williams] who, I get a kick out of this, was born after my first show with Confessor. (laughter) Cary (Rowells, bass player), Scott and me remain. And we have the two other guys, Chris and Marcus. We just recorded with Greg Elkins, we have some rough stuff down. We have to add the vocals and fluffy guitar parts.

Brian: The year is now 2020.

Steve: Yes, I have noticed that.

Brian: You have never tried to make a living playing music. It's not a job for you, and instead you have a day job doing landscaping.

Steve: Right. And I have always done that. Landscaping, particularly when Confessor first started doing things, was an easy industry to go in and out of. If I needed to break away to travel for a little bit, I could always come back and find a landscaping job that paid pretty well. So it just worked out well with what Confessor were trying to do. And it wasn't a career that I had to devote all of my time to so I could still do music. Eventually I came to like it, I love working outdoors. And I definitely appreciate the exercise benefits.

Brian: You thought that you were going to be an artist or an illustrator before you bought a drum set. What kind of stuff did you draw?

Steve: I always doodled when I was really young. It was the same kinds of silly things lots of people do in their notebooks. My best friend in the 8th grade drew his own comic book heroes and I started to do the same thing. It was really pretty bad. After a while though, I realized I could emulate things pretty well and I started drawing more detailed things. I did roughs in pencil and would then ink over them. It was mostly single illustrations. I did draw a comic book or two but it was sooooo bad! Fun, but embarrassing. I got much better when I stopped with the comic book stuff and started ripping off better artists. I spent most of my time drawing in my room when I lived at home. I was very introverted as a kid. Buying a drumset changed all of that and I stopped drawing almost entirely.

Brian: How long did it take to draw the Confessor skull? It's an infamous piece of work.

Steve: Most everything I drew took days, if not weeks. The skull was one of the only things I ever cranked out in a few hours. I still remember drawing it in our living room when I was 17. Shading was what I spent so much time on, and the skull was an exercise, really. I was drawing a skull from *Grey's Anatomy* and got lucky. It seemed a natural fit when I came up with our Confessor logo a few years later.

Brian: Do you still do any artwork or other types of creative stuff outside of playing drums at all?

Steve: I got way into abstract photography for a few years. I was just trying to photograph things to have different screensavers on the computer and eventually decided to try and sell them. I did several markets and have given them as gifts but I had to back off once Tannon moved down to finish the Loincloth album. Practices were taking up a lot of time and my photo adventures ate up my Sunday afternoons. I was beginning to feel like I was never home and it didn't seem fair to leave my wife home alone for me to pursue all my creative outlets. The autonomy of photography, combined with the ease and convenience of digital photo editing made it really rewarding, especially after years of having your creative energy slowed down by a group process, like being in a band. Photography allowed me to see my ideas flushed out without others' input. I have to say, not feeling like every step was a compromise or that every idea was watered down somehow was a very nice change.

Brian: You have been pretty unwavering in keeping on drumming and have never tried to push the careerist angle of what you could have done. Was that always deliberate?

Steve: No, it just sort of evolved that way. A lot of that is really just a reflection of the personalities in the band. We get along so well that we are hanging out at practice almost as much as we are working. There have been no screaming matches or fights. But that laid back approach has its flip side. Where more people might be more driven and more motivated for financial gain in the music, no one in Confessor has every been uncomfortable with their lifestyle choices. Everyone has enjoyed their jobs and couldn't afford to lose them. So that certainly has had something to do with it. The starving artist thing just never appealed to me too much. You know, there is so much uncertainty there. I have seen the pitfalls that happened with other people and I tried to avoid that.

I never have to worry about where that paycheck is coming from. When I actually had thought about going out on my own, I thought about all of the other guys that I had worked for and how their extra time was spent chasing down checks that they should have gotten two months ago. And I just couldn't do that, particularly when I got married and had someone else to be responsible for, there was just no way on earth I was going to jeopardize anything. So that boat has to stay afloat, and as long as I still have the time to explore what I want to do, than everything is fine.

When I look back and think about what could have happened playing music, I am thankful that nothing happened that could have changed where I am right now. I am so happily married and I wouldn't do anything to disrupt that.

Brian: Has anyone ever asked you to play with them over the years?

Steve: Not too many people, no. I spoke briefly with the guys from Trouble about filling in but nothing ever came out of that. That was years and years ago and back then, I definitely would have considered it.

Brian: How long ago was that?

Steve: When the first bassist was still in the band. He was the one who got in touch.

Brian: So it was the first two records version of Trouble.

Steve: Yes. Jeff Olson had quit. It was before the third record. And then a few years ago I was asked again but then something had happened to the people in the band and they formed two Trouble tribute bands.

Brian: I always wondered why they couldn't get along and formed two versions of Trouble. The first two albums were the best ones, by far. By far.

Steve: I am the same way. I loved the first two. The third one had some good leftover riffs and then they were a rock band afterwards.

Brian: The Rick Rubin stuff is okay, but...

Steve: "Okay" is being diplomatic. (laughter) Plain rock has never done anything for me, and that is what they became. With some interesting riffs now and then. It's like they had no idea what made them cool in the first place.

Brian: Ha Ha! So, what you have done as a musician has not resulted in you becoming a household name, but you have achieved a bit of respect with that *Modern Drummer* interview a while back. And then there is this obvious status that you have as a musician within certain circles as being a legendary drummer, which you are very humble about. In every town in this country, there are probably two people that think that you are the greatest drummer to have ever existed. Do you know what I mean?

Steve: You know, it is funny because I can relate to that and I know exactly what you are talking about. For those two or three people in every city, I think about how I had first discovered Terry Bozzio, or any of the musicians that I loved. I pored over the liner notes and everything with all of the records that I was so inspired by, his inspiring it was and how it made me want to go and do stuff. So when I meet people who tell me that I have been an inspiration to them, it is incredibly humbling. I can relate to that a thousand percent as that feeling that I had. And in my wildest dreams how I had hoped that I could do that for just one person, to have inspired them I some way,

So when I have these conversations now and then, it is completely satisfying and fulfilling. I wouldn't say vindicating but it's that spark. That spark of inspiration. And communication. I love it. That's exactly why I play music.

CATHAY DE GRANDE

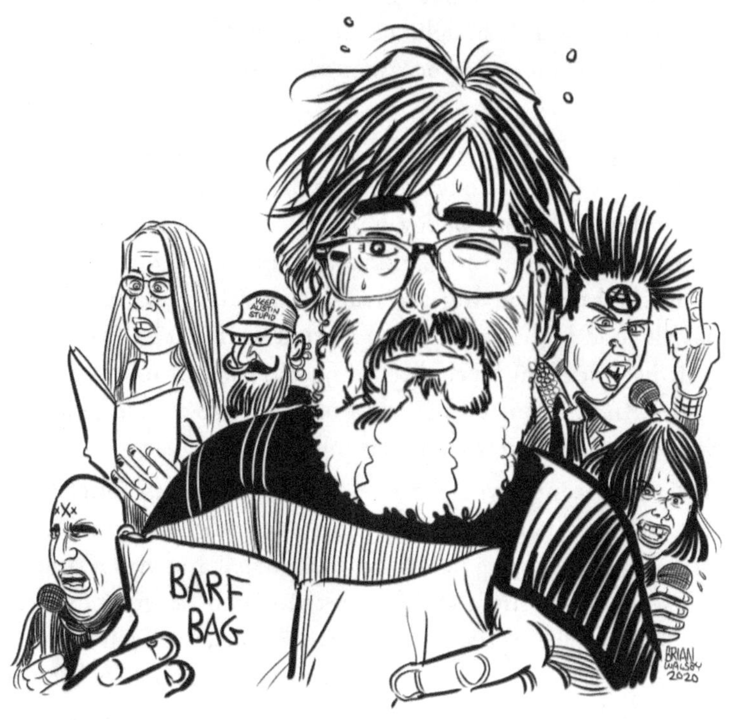

The Cathay de Grande was this seedy basement club a block or so away from Hollywood Blvd. in Hollywood. It was on a street called Selma Ave. and Mystic Records was a block away. I think I spent the bulk of 1984 going to this club to see a variety of cool bands. I was sort of making up for lost time; at this point I was already a published cartoon scribbler and started to get mail, but I still hadn't gone to a real show until December of 1983. I didn't drive, so I waited till some of the friends I had made as pen pals would actually go out of their way to come get me for some shows—even if I did live in Ventura County, seemingly a million miles from anything cool or exciting.

By this time, I had also met the guys in Scared Straight. Scott Radinsky drove a blue pick up truck. We'd make the trek into Hollywood a lot to see shows, and for whatever the reason, most of them were at the Cathay de Grande. It was exciting. Finally I was able to see all of this cool shit. And there was a dangerous vibe to it as well. I thought anything could happen at any time, and there was rarely any occasion that made us feel that it wasn't worth the trek.

Looking back, I am struck by what a naïve and undeniable dork I was, definitely not one of the tough and scary kinds of punk rocker. I was a slightly pudgy, long-haired, Jewish kid with glasses. I was just totally into the music and lived to find out more about what I had been buying and reading in this subculture. And it was all good at that point. Even when it wasn't, it still was. It was exciting just being in that room far, far away from my parent's house. And of course I met a lot of other like-minded kids that were also really into the same things.

Die Kreuzen played there on their first album tour. To say they were good and ahead of their time would be a great understatement. They were perhaps the ultimate band at the time but still seemed so weird and different than almost everybody else at the time. I have a picture somewhere of me and Ryan Hoffman (of Justice League) sitting on a monitor on the nonexistent stage watching bassist Keith Brammer play. And we are both sitting there, looking at him with our eyes and mouths wide open like we are watching the second coming of Jesus, or at least Marc Bolan. I mean, he really had good hair.

7 Seconds and Uniform Choice played a great show there as well. It was like a nonstop sing along, one would be hit after another, the bulk of *The Crew* and *Committed For Life* unfurled. There was another show where I saw this band called Condemned To Death. They were from San Francisco and they were an amazing band. A lot of people don't really remember these guys but they were great.

Another show that I remember there was during the summer of 1984. Some of you might remember that the Olympics were being held in Los Angeles, so the city appeared to have looked a little cleaned up. The previous night was a big Goldenvoice show at the infamous Olympic Auditorium where Dead Kennedys, Raw Power, Reagan Youth, and BGK played. We had heard that a quickie show was being held the next night at the Cathay and that some of the same bands would be playing. The bill ended up being Cause For Alarm, Adrenalin O.D., and BGK. It was a great show but I remember BGK totally stole the show. At the time they were one of the most precise hardcore bands I had ever seen. It was hot as shit down there that night. Good times.

The club also had this once a week thing called DUNKER NIGHT. For the price of one dollar, you could get in and watch up to eleven bands in one night! And a lot of them were real good. There was one band that seemed to play that night all the time called Incest Cattle. They were this amazing trio that had all of these weird songs that ran the gamut from post-punk screeching noise to furious hardcore to overt metal songs and everything in between. The weird looking short bassist with the Human League haircut turned out to be Doug Carrion who joined the Descendents when they reformed a year or so later. I remember seeing a band called MADMEN that featured people that looked (gasp!) old. What were these people doing here? Remember how it was when you were eighteen and when you met someone who was not even thirty, and you couldn't believe it? Well, these guys were older than that, I bet. The singer was this furious front person who really had presence. They also seemed to have more command of their instruments; unlike some of the other fellow youngsters I had seen playing music. Dunker Night was always really cool for me. I wonder if anyone else remembers that.

I met all kinds of people there. I remember hanging out with Tim Kerr and Randy "Biscuit" Turner of the Big Boys in the stairwell one night. I was struck by how nice and friendly they were, which is what everyone said. It left a big impression on me. Almost every single living punk rock "celeb" that I knew of seemed to drop by there at least once. Sometimes I would bother these people but most of the time I would just admire them from afar, too nervous to actually engage in conversation. I met the legendary El Duce of the Mentors, who was everything you would think he would be; a total laugh riot. Of course he was shitfaced. Hanging out with Al and Hud from the legendary *Flipside* magazine was also a big deal. And it was really cool to find out that almost all of the people that I had admired, known about, and looked up to were all personable and nice. I wasn't sure why I expected anything else, but there you go.

Speaking of shitfaced, the funniest thing about all of the times I went to the Cathay de Grande was how I was this dumb little kid who didn't do anything but religiously watch these bands and the fact that I usually was surrounded by all of these fucked up and drunk people. I never drank or smoked pot or anything like that—not at that time anyways—so it meant nothing to me but I had no problems with it. Actually, it was kind of exciting to be around. It made things scarier. And for every time I saw a show there like 7 Seconds where there were more young people that didn't necessarily want to get fucked up, there were plenty of drug addicts, speed freaks, and alcoholics at various other, slightly more "adult" shows, that catered to those damn punk rockers.

I can't seem to recall when and why the club closed down, but I think it happened right before I moved to the East Coast. So I am guessing that it was the end of 1985 or so. I haven't been to a club that had that kind of vibe since. It was disgusting and seedy and falling apart but for a while it was like a second home to me. There have probably been at least a thousand photos that people took of bands playing at the Cathay de Grande, and some of those photos have made it into fanzines and the back covers and inserts of rare records that some of you reading this right now probably own.

Eugene Robinson

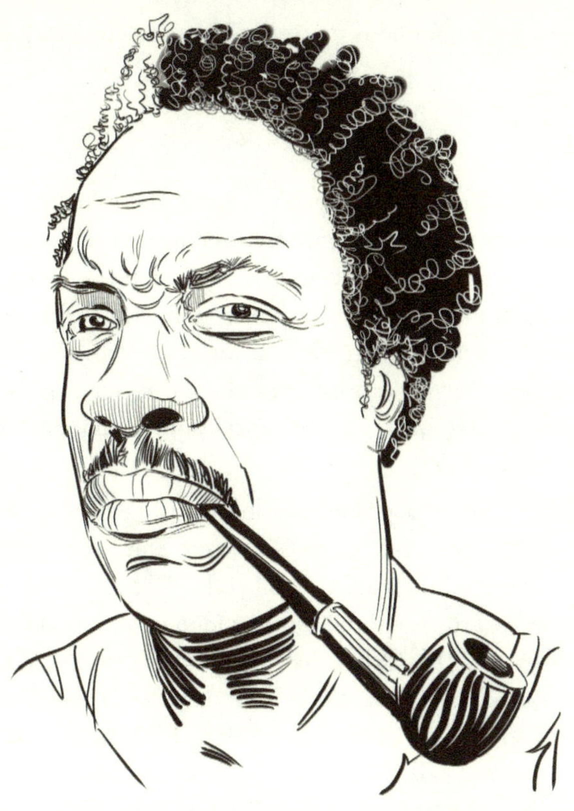

Eugene Robinson is a super interesting guy to me. He is really smart, very intelligent, and a little scary looking up there on stage, singing with duct tape on his ears in various stages of dress/undress with his long-term band Oxbow. He is a published book author, who has done various pieces and writings for publications and websites all over the world. He has a lot of kids. In short, Eugene is a very busy guy.

I just sort of assumed that he was a self-employed, hustling kind of person, but I was wrong. That doesn't mean that I am almost more impressed: he does all of this cool stuff AFTER work? How do you do that?

Eugene reveals that he is not super big on sleeping. I guess that is one way.

♫

Brian: I thought initially that you're would be perfect for being in a book where the theme is about freelancing and self employment but you let it be known to me that you have a "real job" in between all of your other activities, which vary from singing in your band Oxbow to begin the author of a handful of books to writing articles for various online websites. What exactly is your day job these days, and what have you done in the past as far as having a job like that?

Eugene: I'm editor-at-large and employee number one at the international digital news magazine OZY.com. Have done everything on the staff outside of finance and tech. Won one OJA [Online Journalism Award] for some online video commentary I did on politics back in 2014. Other than that and the three OZYfests in New York's Central Park, the new podcast *OZY Confidential* is consuming all of my time and my mind. I just hated what other podcasts—what I called Nodcasts—had been doing, so I'm lucky enough to be at a place where they listen to good ideas, and doing one that doesn't suck was definitely a good idea. They're essentially conversations with people who pique my curiosity and ideally end up making you feel for a little bit like I feel all of the time.

But I've been a journalist forever. Since high school. The funny thing is, as a big weightlifting, fist-fighting guy, no one ever took me seriously and even by the time I was writing for *GQ*, people—at least in the fight world—thought all of my stuff was ghost written. But that's OK. Like Pacino as The Devil once said, "Never let them see you coming." Works well in this job. And I've done it both at real magazines/publishing venues AND in-house at corporations like Intel, Nikon, Apple, Adobe and so on.

Brian: You have three children and are married. How do you balance all of that along with work and then your artistic pursuits on top of all of that? What is the secret?

Eugene: Well, I have remarried but I'm the father of three daughters with my ex-wife. A large part of how what happened could happen was her willingness to make it possible instead of applying any pressure to get me to stop. I mean, most people who know me have never known me to do anything else, or be any other way. Maybe people I went to high school with remember when I didn't do music, but I've been doing something onstage since I was 2. So music was just a new stage wrinkle back in 1980. Oxbow's longest tour was about 8 weeks, and that happened well before some of us were married and well before kids. After that, the tours dropped to a more manageable 2 weeks—which is the kind of vacation time most people in corporations get.

But being with my kids was one of the true and clear-cut joys of my life, so there was nothing to balance. I have pictures of me in the studio with my oldest when we were working on *Serenade in Red*. My kids are not so impressed with all of this stuff, though at this point, they recognize that some of it is actually cool.

Oh, one noteworthy thing I think people should do if they want to be really productive—forget about sleeping. And I'm not joking. At my most ridiculous I was sleeping 3 hours a night. Put the kids through dinner, bath, and bed, then hit the gym, then run, then get home and work on stuff. And this was on nights when there was no band practice. My ex-wife would say that I was more cranky with less sleep, but recent DNA advances and some testing I've had has shown that I have a genetic disposition for needing LESS sleep, so there's that.

Brian: It seems like perhaps you had some cool people on your side to encourage you. Plus you did go to Stanford University in the early eighties where you eventually formed the band Whipping Boy with guitarist Steve Ballinger. The first thing I heard by the band was the song on the *MRR* compilation album, which was the first punk comp album I ever got! How did Whipping Boy get together, and what was it like touring the country off of it? That is quite an experience for so long ago, really uncharted territory.

Eugene: I didn't like Stanford. In 1980 it was like Reagan Revolution Central and I was a New York kid. All of that hokum shit Reagan was spewing just stunk to me so to go to school with kids who were excited about it was tough And, of course, the race politic in California was—probably still is—weird, at least for a New York kid. So I got back after my last summer in New York, working a shit job after my freshman year, wanting to do two things: start a magazine AND band. The magazine was *The Birth of Tragedy.* The band was Whipping Boy.

We toured for the first time in 1982 and then again in 1983 with the old line up. I remember telling everyone I could that I wanted to start a band. With a mohawk and a black leather and tattoos, I was easy to spot in 1981. So when I heard that there was this "big football player" who could play guitar, I started looking all over for him. Saw him one day just walking down the street and pulled over my moped, introduced myself, and that was that. Steve had already played a little bit in some Oxnard bands, I mean outside of football and getting into Stanford. But he had gotten hurt his senior year, so music was a great thing for him. It saved my life which ordinarily wouldn't have seen me stay in California and Stanford, I hated it that much.

But the scene was not that big then. Ian MacKaye was a great help with our second tour. So was Tesco Vee. Have to give credit where credit is due. And, little known story, I had met Klaus Flouride's ex-wife at The Mudd Club and she told me when I got to California I should look him up, and so I did. Just went to a show, busted into the backstage, and introduced myself. This is how I think Biafra came to know about us and probably got Tim Yohannan aboard. Plus, we were always hanging around KPFA and I wrote for a lot of the first few *MRRs*, as well as *Ripper,* another big punkzine at the time.

Touring back then was crazy. I mean, before we went all uni-culture you could actually pull into Nebraska and feel like you were on another planet entirely, not to mention when you show up all leathered out, with mohawks and chains and boots and so on. If we hadn't been so big, physically, I sense it would have been a lot more miserable than it was. But people generally steered clear of us, so no bad scenes. And lots of good ones. Hanging with Minor Threat, being there when Stigma started talking about forming Agnostic Front, seeing John Brannon being John Brannon. The Necros. And Bad Brains, Bad Brains, Bad Brains. My favorite scene and place to hang was, and remains, NYHC.

Brian: Did school get in the way of the band? Was there anything you picked up on after that period that you were able to apply to your life as it is now, as a parent and a Renaissance man?

Eugene: The band made it possible for me to stay in school. It kept me interested. It also made me a little money so I could eat. My father disowned me when I was 19 so he paid for zero of my college. My mother helped however she could my freshmen year, but was also going through a divorce so couldn't. The school got me some student loans so I knew I had to finish. I took off one quarter to put together a tour, so I graduated one quarter after everyone else, so my degree actually says January 1985 on it. For 17 months after I graduated, I freelanced and moved furniture and painted houses and hung drywall. Then I was a bouncer on and off. Finally got a job at a defense magazine. My junior year of school it was the worst—I lived in my van for a bit. The year before that, I got arrested for false information to a police officer! But getting that first job changed a lot. I moved into a garage and Whipping Boy put out a third record and I started getting more pro about *The Birth of Tragedy* magazine.

Being a good parent begins and ends with being a good person and on top of that, not being an asshole. Sounds simple, but when I see other people with their kids it clearly isn't.

Brian: Outside of the your family, your job, and your band, how do you decide which project is the one for you to take on at any given moment. What was your experience like for *Everything You Ever Want To Know About Ass Kicking* and *A Long Slow Screw* in general? How were your books received and is there anything coming in the future in the form of another book?

Eugene: I just say YES to everything. The writing time is really the least of it. Total elapsed time for the writing of *Fight: Everything You Ever Wanted To Know About Ass Kicking But Were Afraid You'd Get Your Ass Kicked For Asking* (Harper Collins), *A Long Slow Screw* (Robotic Boot) and *The Inimitable Sounds of Love: A Threesome in Four Acts* (Southern) was less than 2 years. A friend of mine from high school was working at Random House and he just asked me if I had anything I wanted to publish. He moved to Harper Collins and showed his boss at the time, Judith Regan, something I had written for the *LA Weekly* on fighting. She called me to New York, we met, and the deal was done.

I have a new book called *LOVE? LOVE!* that I've been fucking around with not so seriously for a few years now. Not so seriously because *A Long Slow Screw* has been translated into French and now, soon, Italian, which has kept me busy. But it's a lot of work for not much return, so I keep hoping something will happen that will make it both easier to have lots of people get your book, and also to have lots of people BUY your stuff. In the interim, I write my ass off for OZY.

The books were amazingly well received. I sold about 10,000 of the *Fight* book, about half of that for the novel. No idea on the play. But these are all great books. Diamanda Galás read the *Fight* book and wrote me saying that she thought I was just one of those rock guys "writing" a book but figured out I'm really just a book guy making music.

Brian: Oxbow seems to operate as a band that does stuff when it's the right time and when the band members can get it together, and less about keeping a rigid schedule. Is this how the band has been able to survive for as long as it has? Was there a time in the band's past where you could have made it more than what it is?

Eugene: No, it happened as it has happened. Between the four of us we have 8 kids, 4 wives, 2 ex-wives, 4 jobs, 8 cats, 8 cars, and 5 houses. It's a lot to manage and it has been. I mean, Dan was the first one of us to get married so we've NEVER had careerist notions about music. It just wouldn't pay enough and none of us was willing to spend 8 months of the year on the road trying to make it pay.

Brian: I am curious about the short-lived band you had with Chuck Dukowski, Black Face. I read the interviews, I heard the seven-inch, and I thought it seemed like a really good project. Then it seemed like maybe someone got cold feet and the project was shelved. Soon afterwards, Flag appeared. What happened? It looked like it could have been a cool thing!

Eugene: Very much so, but you're too kind in your characterization of what happened later. Yes, Flag appeared but then there was a swelter of legal recriminations, infighting between and betwixt Chuck, Greg, Keith, and totally legacy-destroying ridiculousness that it was absolutely wonderful to not be a part of. But the project ended because Chuck ended it for reasons he tried to explain to me but, you know, I've never been one of those "let's have a heart-to-heart talk" guys, so when he started telling me that he wasn't feeling like it was something he could do, I stopped him and said that it was like fucking and no one should ever have to explain why they don't want to fuck, so that was that.

Brian: I like the fact that you are a very intelligent and thoughtful guy with a vast knowledge of music, art, and literature yet you can get onstage, duct tape your ears, strip down to your speedos, and boast a lot of threatening looking tattoos while doing your thing. You present quite an aura onstage. Were there any other folks that you were inspired by in terms of how to present yourself?

Eugene: Little Richard. There's some live concert footage from France and he's absolutely captivating. I'd love to play him in the biopic but I think I am too large. All of early hardcore framed my understanding of stagecraft so while not a direct influence, the Bad Brains were mesmerizing. As were The Birthday Party, Black Flag, Negative Approach, SSD, Minor Threat, Reagan Youth. What should be noted about the bands I mentioned is how absolutely electric what they did on stage was. 100 percent committed. We've also played with a lot of those bands, excepting The Birthday Party and Black Flag, so this is firsthand witness stuff.

But influenced? Nah. I remember talking to Biafra about what I wanted to do with a project that became Oxbow. I told him I just wanted to capture the sounds in my head. His response was, "Don't we all?" But that became my mission. I had initially planned to pull a Prince and play all of the instruments on *Fuck Fest* myself, but outside of brief dalliances with violin, banjo, sax and keyboards, I couldn't do it. What I could do is give Niko [Wenner] lyrics and notes about how I heard the songs sounding and, musical genius that he is, he could make it live, really and truly.

So it's that that informed what we did/said. The song drives the sounding of the song, if that makes sense. We're working on our first record after *Thin Black Duke* now and it's how we're doing it. The whole record, least as I can tell now, is all about love because where we are in life now coheres with great joy around love—for our children, our wives, and indeed how our lives are playing out. So if *Fuck Fest* started as a suicide note, this new record will continue as something they can play at our funerals, something whose essential message is "We Love You All. Dangerously, completely, eternally."

RYAN CASE

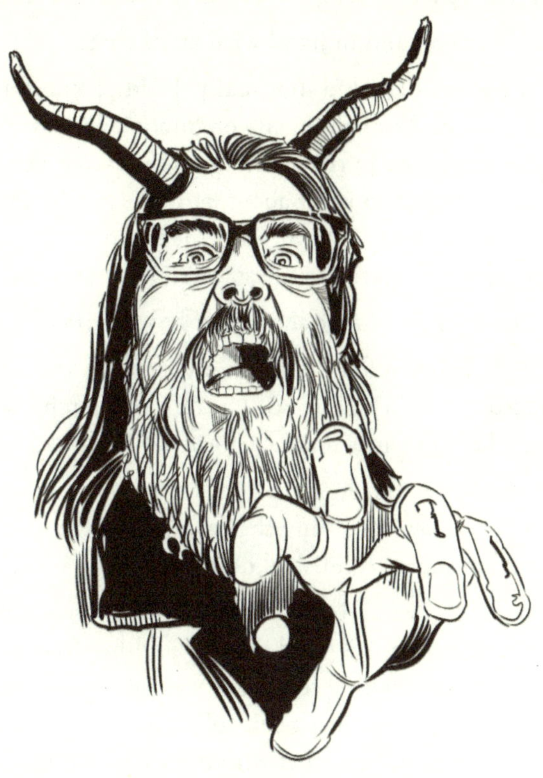

Ryan Case is a very talented self-employed artist who lives with his family in Louisville Kentucky. Check out his masterful artwork.

♫

Ryan: I was always a really nervous and anxious little kid, so I always had a sketchbook with me. So anytime I was drawing I could not pay attention to being nervous. I was shy as a kid, really shy.

Brian: And drawing is a way of getting attention…but not too much attention.

Ryan: Right. Although it was also a way of blocking out the entire world and just concentrating on whatever the fuck I wanted.

Brian: Did music go hand in hand with all of that?

Ryan: When I was a little kid, not really. I didn't know anything about music, my dad brought me up on Simon and Garfunkel and shit like that, and then in the eighth grade I started hanging out with some older kids who knew about hardcore music. They asked if I knew about it and I said no. They then said, "Well, come on out with us to Cincinnati and see some shows," and that was it.

Brian: Did you ever go to school to learn how to draw?

Ryan: No. Well, I took a few classes in high school and I took like half a semester of college but no, I am pretty much self-taught and I just picked up stuff from other artists that I had liked here and there.

Brian: Was freelancing something that you had in the back of your mind as you got more established doing art?

Ryan: No, it didn't even cross my mind until someone was like, "Hey, how much for this?" And when I sold my first painting I just paid half of my fucking rent, so it was just like let's see what else I can do. And it has just been full force ever since then. It was when I had first got together with my wife, so it was probably like twelve years ago.

Brian: Do you do a lot of the selling of your art online and go to flea markets and stuff like that?

Ryan: Yeah. I do a lot of the prints sales online and then original sales, private commissions, those are done when people contact me. We have been to little art fairs around town. Louisville is an artist's dream, really. There is such a cool art scene here. I grew up about two hours away from here in a small podunk town.

Brian: How are you with the ups and downs of freelancing in general? It's ultimately worth doing but there are incredible highs, and I don't want to really give the lows much attention...

Ryan: Oh yeah. Right. It is definitely a rollercoaster. When shit is not going your way, as long as you keep on holding on to that feeling of when it was really good, it gets you through those low times. It's weird. If I get low on cash, I will just scroll through Facebook and see what people are into and I think that I have to find something out of pop culture to make that I just know people will just grab on to. And if I do that and think about only making something with the purpose of selling it right off, it never sells.

But if it is something like, "I want to make this weird looking, fucking nasty demon with twenty eyes and fifteen arms, no one is ever going to want this," and I will post an "in the works" photo and somebody will ask me, "How much is it?"

Brian: What kind of medium do you like to work in?

Ryan: I like quick-drying mediums like inks and acrylics. I like to layer a lot of shit on top of each other. It's really fun to like mix the inks with the acrylics and then spray it with water and just let it fucking make a mess, and then once it dries, fine tune it and then turn it into something else.

Brian: How are you in terms of inspiration? And holding on to it? Because you have two daughters.

Ryan: Right, one is nine, one is eleven.

Brian: Obviously you are no stranger to being inspired, but having to wait several hours before you can work? Do you have a scheduled method to how you work around being a husband and a father?

Ryan: Well, I homeschool the kids while my wife works during the day. So I am with them from the second they wake up till bedtime. And we do a lot of artwork during the day. My art studio is right across the hall from their bedroom, and their bedroom is also their mini little art studio, because they both want to be artists as well. So it's really fucking amazing the way that they latch on to it. They just go for it. And it's like we bounce ideas off of each other. Because you know that when you are a kid, you will come up with the craziest fucking ideas out of nowhere, and you are just going to make this. And then when you are an adult, you are sitting there trying to think of shit and you are like, "Okay what do I need to do? How am I going to get inspired?"

And you have the whole fucking adult world on your mind. The kids don't have that. They are just pure inspiration, twenty-four seven. I always think that it is great to get feedback from them.

Brian: Are they fans of your art?

Ryan: Yeah, they love it. And I started teaching monster art classes to kids. And I have an adult class, too. There is a wine and canvas place in town that kept sending me emails to teach a class but I didn't want to do landscapes, I don't want to do a fucking cardinal or anything like that. My wife was like, "A friend of yours owns a bar. You can just have your own wine and canvas there. Just start your own class."

So I started one for the adults and a couple of days after that, a few of them said, "You have kids. Did you ever think about teaching a kid's class?"

So I found a venue for that and that has been fucking amazing.

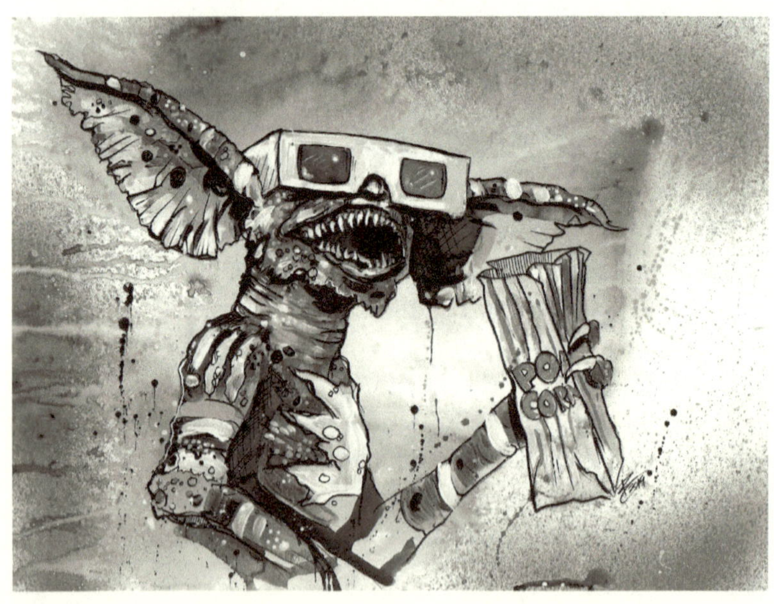

ARTWORK BY RYAN CASE

The way I have taught the kids and the adults—and this goes back to when I was a nervous, anxious little kid—is, "We are going to start off with a blob, just a straight up blob. It has no real definition, don't know what it is yet. But whatever you are afraid of, whatever you are anxious about, whatever stress has you worried that day, just focus it on that blob. And then we are going to build layers on top of it and build eyeballs and teeth and tails and horns. And just make it so fucking ridiculous that it's nothing to be worried about."

That always helped me to get over my shit. And it's really taken off and it's really helped a lot of people, from the feedback I have gotten from it. If you are going to be creative you have to learn to adapt and find other ways to bring any income in.

Brian: Are you one of those people where, if you don't draw anything in a couple days, you start to get antsy?

Ryan: Oh, yeah. I turn into a total spazz if I can't get some creativity out. I was a body-piercer for about ten years and I managed a buddy of mine's tattoo shop. It didn't make me happy. I made decent money at it but I was surrounded by miserable, egotistical people who just wanted people to kiss their ass. It was probably just a small percent of people in that industry but It wasn't me and it wasn't what I wanted to do anymore. My wife said, "Well, what if I went out and worked and you stayed home with the kids?" And I said, "Yes." (laughter)

TYLER WOLF

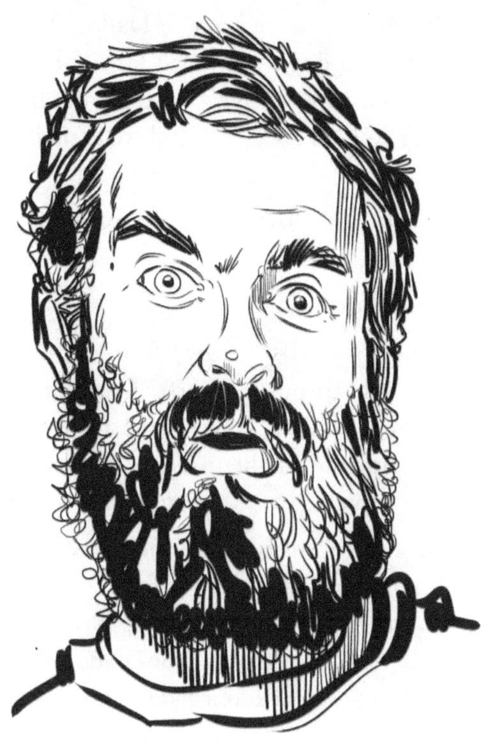

Tyler Wolf is/was the bassist of the band Valient Thorr and a working artist and painter. He lives in Wilmington, North Carolina, with his wife and two children. He is a cool dude that still plays a little music here and there in between his life work.

Tyler: I am back in North Carolina. In Wilmington.

Brian: Oh, no way.

Tyler: Yeah we moved back here in time for all of the hurricanes.

Brian: Congratulations. You were living in, I am not sure...I want to say Texas?

Tyler: Yeah, you are right. I moved out to Dallas, Texas. My wife is from there, we moved down there for family reasons and we ended up moving back here. I have a huge family here in North Carolina, we have two kids and stuff and we actually moved her mother out here, too.

Brian: Yeah, it helps to live close to family so that they can help out and stuff.

Tyler: Yeah, you know how it is.

Brian: I don't actually really know that much about your background. I met you through Charles Cardello because you were the bass player of Valient Thorr. And from what I understand, your band came out of the middle of North Carolina in Greenville, because some of you went to school there?

Tyler: Yeah. Herbie and I went to art school at ECU. We were in school there, kind of going through the first couple of years and had another band together. We met Jason [Aylward] through his other bands, met Benny through his other bands. We all kind of came out of this Greenville Backdoor Skate Shop, DIY punk rock scene, kind of. So Heriberto and I graduated from school, Jason moved to Raleigh, that was where he sort of finished school. All of our bands went their separate ways but then Valient Thorr kind of came out of nowhere. On a whim, we put this new project together and we kept rolling with it. Herbie still had to finish graduate school.

Brian: So it almost started out as a school band.

Tyler: Yeah. Yeah it was. Big time. There was definitely a performance art element to it, and if we needed to build anything or create any kind of crazy stuff in the very early days we would take it down to the Backdoor Skate Shop and just see what worked. Twelve foot robots... Anyways, the band started to become sort of heavy rock influenced, we were way into the MC5 and that kind of stuff at that point. When CD Alley in Greenville was open and you could dig and find all of this cool stuff.

Brian: Did you guys have any kind of jobs and stuff when the band was starting to jell and do stuff?

Tyler: We all got out of school around 2001 to 2002. And then we moved to Chapel Hill because we thought Chapel Hill was the place to be, but I think that was more of the nineties or late eighties. So when we got there it was still fun, it was still a great scene and everyone was awesome. We all worked at restaurants and stuff during that time. Me and Herbie were on our way to try and become teachers. I have come full circle because that is what I am trying to do now.

So we were there for a couple of years and that is when we met up with a good record label and then just went on for about between 2005 to about 2012, and it was really just band stuff.

Brian: You guys worked really hard for a really long time. You guys did so much stuff—a lot of records and tours, Charles did that movie for Bifocal Media[1]...

Tyler: We were lucky. We always just stuck to our guns as far as what we wrote and the kind of music that we made, and we had a few people along the way who were really supportive of us with the record label. It was the kind of deal where if we wanted to stay on the road then we could do it. It was an interesting time because it was around the time when the internet really exploded big time. That is a whole other conversation you know, but we were kind of in the mix of all of that and still putting out CDs. It was just a really fun, interesting time and we really had free reign over the music. We had an awesome time. I try to not take any of that for granted and try to just be like, "when we had it, it was pretty amazing that we could do this."

---

1 *The Actuality of Thought*, 1998 https://bifocalmedia.com/Bifocal_Media/The_Actuality_of_Thought_VHS.html

Brian: I remember running into you at the Pour House in Raleigh, I was selling merch for Corrosion of Conformity one night when they first got back together as a three piece and you were telling me that you had bowed out of the band, started a family, getting back into art, and moving away.

Tyler: For all of the Valient Thorr stuff and the fun stuff that we got to go do—More than fun, fun is sort of the wrong word—it was amazing. But at the end of the day, there is no finance in it; it paid for itself and that was killer. And when you are single and living out of a backpack, you can pull it off. But then personally—and this is just my end of it, I am only speaking for me personally—I just burned out on it, and I met my wife. I think she was pregnant at the time when I was talking to you. And all along, during all of the tours, I always had my art going and the shift was starting to happen creatively to where my mind was more focused on art. And it was just a perfect time to kind of bow out and say to the guys, "Go for it, I don't want to bring anything down but if I was going to start a family then there would be no way to do it while I was going out on the road."

My last couple of years on the road I always had my art with me, it could have been small paintings at first and I would show it at the merch table, and I started to bring out my own shirts with my artwork on them and started to sell those, too. And the guys didn't mind, it was different you know? It is a different purchase when someone is buying art. I always did the merch until we could afford to bring somebody on the road to do that for us. And also, by bringing and working on my art on the road and trying to sell it, it kept me away from reaching for a six pack of beer or whatever.

Brian: People don't seem to realize how boring being on tour can be and why so many people are alcoholics on the road. There is a lot of time to fill.

Tyler: People get the wrong idea. But there were some really killer times on the road with the band. When we would fly into a country and were close to a certain museum, I would make sure that I was able to go and do that. That was my thing, I would always make sure I went to any museums, if I could, no matter where we were, whether it was New York or Madrid, Spain. Those were highlights for me. But at that point what was happened was that the family was starting to come into the picture for me. I was starting to weigh my time, there wasn't enough time.

Brian: And when you introduce children, it is just a whole new game. I sort of made that choice a long time ago, even way before I stopped playing in bands. I mean, I never had a situation with a working band like you but it was obvious after a while that I enjoyed doing art more and it was something I was more successful at, plus it was something I could do by myself.

Tyler: I am sort of like that in my situation too, it was something I could just do by myself. The collaboration of music, it is fun but it's also really hard at times and after so long it was a trying thing. But going back to concentrating on art wasn't a trying thing. I did go to school. I do have training for this. In painting and drawing, that is what I got my degree in. And it wasn't trying to go back into painting because I just get consumed by it.

Brian: I love that feeling of doing stuff and suddenly you hit this groove and it is one of the best feelings imaginable.

Tyler: Right. And that was what was happening with my brain, just deciding that the art was what I needed to focus on. Doing art also gives me the same high as doing the music, plus the art world and the music world are very similar in a lot of ways, it is all sort of connected somehow. That whole DIY aesthetic, from the music days and the punk rock days, I try to apply that to my traditional art training and just mash it all together.

And it is almost like I have to do this because I have mouths to feed, you know? Doing art instead, I think I have a better way to stay creative and make things work for my family. I feel like I can provide better being in the art world. I mean, I love playing. We just got back together and did a couple of shows and it was fun. A benefit show with The Avett Brothers and Future Islands, we all came out of the same scene and we might do some more.

Brian: What else do you do to bring in money?

Tyler: I work in a kitchen at a restaurant, with this beautiful view of the beach from my station. And I am working on becoming a full time art teacher I am in the system, as much as I can. And then I work on my commissions and my own stuff. Stuff that I sell online.

Brian: How do you balance things at home with family and your art? I always find that to be really tough.

Tyler: It can be stressful but for me I have to put this out there, my wife is very understanding about being in a relationship with an artist. 'Cause I keep my studio in the house, too. For now. And so, trying to balance it, it is tough because we try to come up with a schedule and stuff and I will get my studio schedule hours, and I know that I have to work that into our other jobs, and then we have kids, too.

For me, I have to get into the mood for doing stuff, it takes me usually forty five minutes just getting into the head frame of making something.

Brian: I bet this has happened to you, then—It sucks when all of a sudden you have an idea and then you have to wait eight hours because of, you know, children or whatever. And that is the way it is, kids come first. And then at the end of the day afterwards, you might not have that drive or desire to do anything.

Tyler: Oh yeah. Today was sort of one of our normal days, and one of the kids took a nap and I thought, "oh man I can get a little bit of work done." And so I set my other daughter up on the table with some paints. And I am working on this painting for a friend of mine. And I turn around and she has blue paint all over her jaw and hands and she says, "daddy, I have decided to paint with my hands!" So it was like okay, that is it.

So what I try to do is do a lot of my work at night when they are asleep.

Tom Hazelmyer

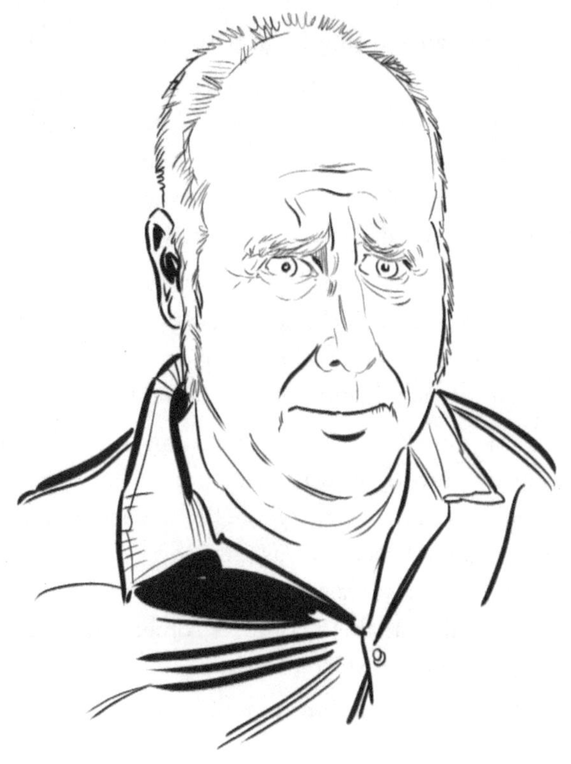

Tom Hazelmyer lives in Minneapolis, Minnesota with his wife and two children. He was the owner of Amphetamine Reptile Records in the eighties and nineties before opening up a series of bars/restaurants named Grumpy's. He has also played music off and on over the years with his band, Halo of Flies.

He is an entrepreneur of sorts, a talented artist and a really nice guy on top of all of that. I met him through the Melvins a long time ago but I always knew who he was. Tom is a real straight shooter and a real smart guy to talk with. I respect Tom a lot.

♫

Brian: You have been working for yourself for a long time.

Tom: Yeah, since I was about twenty three years old. When I got out of the service I got a security guard job for six or nine months. And then I got a job at a factory for another six or nine months and then from that point I was like, "fuck all of this shit. I think I got it." Then I revved up to go on my own.

Brian: So was that when you decided to concentrate on making Amphetamine Reptile more of a real label and work for yourself, and did you have other things going on at that time as well, something else to help bring some extra money in?

Tom: There was never a laser sharp focus on what I was going to do. I was ready to work on stuff that I found interesting. I mean, I was a huge music fanatic my whole life, especially when I was a kid. And putting out records was amazing because I was able to do stuff that no one else was going to bother with at that point in time. But becoming a label was never something that I thought to myself, "I'm going to start a record label."

It was literally, at that point, something I did by default. It was just pursuing things and music that was available to me, because I had figured out how to do records and other bands had started to come to me. Like the Thrown Ups going, "hey you are doing these records. Why won't you do one for us?" The U-Men were doing the same thing, they were bouncing around various labels, so in the meantime, why not do a single for us? And so it just kind of evolved, it was a natural progression.

And at a certain point, that became the focus. I literally shoved aside my interest in doing music myself, personally, to focus more on doing stuff for the label.

Brian: You had your own band for a while, Halo of Flies. And you guys did some touring.

Tom: Yeah. And it pretty much got shelved because the label became a bigger concern. The band was doing really well for the size that we were at, we got a bit of attention and it was actually going quite well for the little bit of touring that we did. Good crowds and turnouts—the door was definitely open there—but it became me thinking, "Well, I like doing this label stuff more." Like generating the graphics, putting together the records… I actually enjoyed myself more doing stuff like that than I did, like…, climbing in the van.

Brian: So you were able to just focus on building the label and not have to worry about generating any money outside of all of that?

Tom: It was a weird, bizarre mix of things. I know it is probably not politically correct to say that you didn't care about money, but at that age, I didn't give a shit about money. I just wanted to pursue this music thing really intensely. And then opportunities arose, like for instance, Twin Tone Records, the Minneapolis record label that put out the Replacements, Soul Asylum, and a bunch of other stuff, was looking for small, up-and-coming record labels to bring on board and to work with, and for a large part, that afforded me the stepping stone from going from working as a security guard and stuffing singles in my trunk to actually being able to get up and go into an office and do it.

Yeah, it was like a manufacturing and distribution deal. Like, "we will make all of your records for you and pay you for them." They put me on the payroll, they let me do all sorts of crazy things, and because of that, I was able to walk out of my day job and say that I was done.

Brian: Can you tell the story about signing the band Helmet and what had happened when they became super popular?

Tom: Yeah, it was not exactly the best deal in the world, because I was like twenty something years old and didn't know fuck all about that end of the business. I mean, I am certainly a quick learner when I am focused on something but…

It wasn't like they had taken me to the cleaners or anything by the stretch of that imagination, but at the same time, it was one of those things where we realized that there were three of us doing the entire label at that point—I had two employees—and we couldn't handle it, you know. The amount of calls we were getting, the amount of demands… we were willing to work with the band to place them somewhere else because we couldn't do it. We knew it. It was obvious as hell that they were blowing up so fast. We didn't want to be the Helmet label. As much as we loved those guys and as much as we were working with them, we just got to this point where we had this whole roster of other bands that needed attention.

Brian: What made you decide to wind things down with the record label? I always thought that at some point it would just have to be a pain in the ass to do a record label, an inevitable time where you say that you are done.

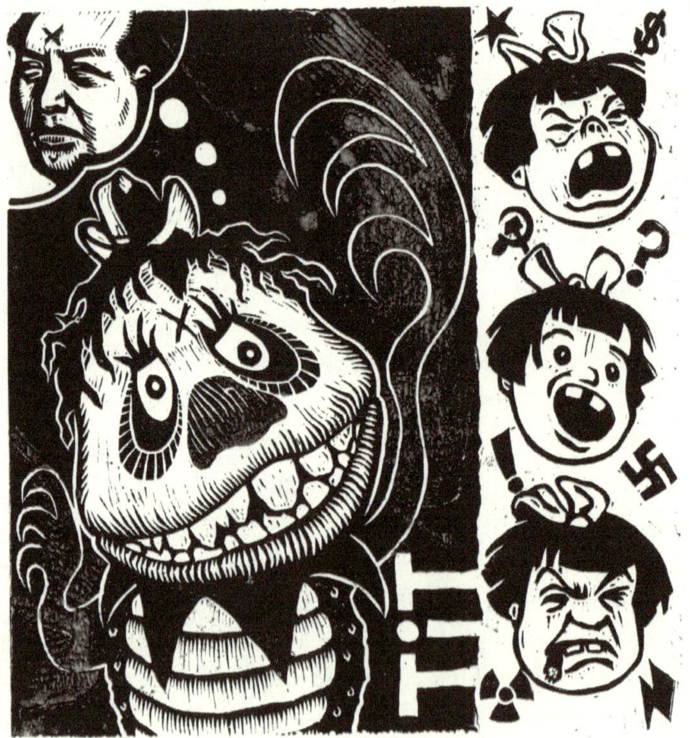

ARTWORK BY TOM HAZELMYER

Tom: There was a burnout factor for sure. And the writing on the wall was at some point around '97, '98, I have always been kind of jumpy and the writing was on the wall that it was over for the music business as it was. I mean, at first I had thought that everyone had had their fifteen minutes and that my fifteen minutes were over, but I am watching sales just trail off, it is not making sense, it is not in the way that would be organic. It was like there was a bigger thing going on here. My first inclination was to blame myself. Like, what did I do wrong? What did we do wrong? What can we fix?

But when you analyze it, it was like, no, this whole industry is fucking collapsing. And combined with working insanely for twelve years straight, you are just like, "I don't want to do this anymore," you know? And it just worked out like that, there was a point where I said that I just really wanted to put this to rest for awhile and be done with it. One of my biggest fears while doing a label was that every band would just break up at once. And that was what happened. The cherry on top was The Cows calling up and saying, "Yup, we just cancelled the rest of the tour. We are done." And that was, like, that is it. Shut the doors. This was my opportunity to get out without fucking over a bunch of bands.

It was like one of those rays of opportunity—you sometimes roll with the punches and then something happens that just totally works in your favor. Like the thing that you fear is actually your blessing. And at the end of that, Nashville Pussy was doing really great and we signed them over to another label and so there was a little bit of a payday there but that payday was big enough to pay off any royalties that I had owned to anybody, and the electric bill, and then I could slam the door shut.

Brian: So it was like, "Hallelujah, that chapter is over."

Tom: Yeah, totally. Totally.

Brian: And Grumpy's, your bars and restaurants... Was that something that you had decided that you wanted to do during the time of the record label, or did that come afterwards?

Tom: It started happening during the label. One of the reasons that I was able to switch from one thing to the other was because that had been started in '95. And that was a weird one because, once again, I had no interest in doing that. I wasn't thinking, "I want to own a bar when I grow up." There was an opportunity sitting there. The short of it was that my father had wanted to go into a semi-retirement and he figured that he wanted to do a bar. And the bar that he wanted to do, he couldn't afford to do by himself. So he just dragged me along and asked if I wanted to do this. We crunched it all and looked at it and I said sure. I was up for trying something different. And mind you this was three years before Am Rep ended.

So I started to do that with my dad and I actually enjoyed it. It was like a nice alternative, sort of a polar opposite to record label stuff. You are dealing with critics in a different way, it's kind of like, "this is what we are. If you like it, welcome. If you don't, there is the fucking door."

I liked that aspect of it more versus the whole having to sweet talk the press and fucking walk them by and kumbaya and try to get them on your side. That whole game got kind of old.

Brian: It is also hard to argue over the merits of a good sandwich. Either the sandwich and fries are good or they are not. It is a little different than taste in music.

Tom: Exactly. Yeah, the high level politics of music had definitely worn out. And the baser, more grounded, restaurant thing, at the end of the day you are still dealing with fucking humans, who are a pain in the ass. But just in a different way. Now, twenty years later, it is caused by the internet age. "My french fries were four short on the order! One star!"

Brian: The internet age has changed everything.

Tom: The internet age has changed restaurants into being a record label, where you are dealing with asshole critics who think that they are more important than they actually are.

Brian: Because everyone has a voice now, everyone's thoughts are all super important, no matter how fucking stupid they really are.

Tom: Oh, it is the most insane shit. I mean, seriously, it is the most insane shit. And that is part of when you are working for yourself, when you say you just can't shrug off those punches and just walk away because you are, at the end of it, you are the one that is just standing there.

Brian: When I first met you I was really impressed with what you had accomplished and that it was totally worthy of respect. A few times I remember Buzz saying that no, Tom actually gets a good deal of crap from people. And I was kind of surprised, because I thought it was great that you were able to do a record label, how that changed into owning these restaurants where you helped give people jobs, and that sort of thing. Any time I had ever met you, you seem down-to-earth and a straight shooter. So, you know, I was just kind of shocked that you had received any kind of shit from people for being an entrepreneur.

Tom: Well, some of it is kind of a mixed bag. Definitely some of it is my own fault for just being me. You know, just sort of crass, saying stuff that other people wouldn't say at times… you know that stuff just doesn't win any popularity contests!

Brian: How do you balance all of this stuff? You are married, you are a father, you do a lot of projects with Buzz and some other people, and you do a lot of art. How do you balance that? Because I have a hard time balancing anything, and I haven't had a job in, like, eight years. It's a non-stop struggle and I am always trying to connect the dots and it never ends. What is your secret?

Tom: Oh, I have never hunkered down and thought about it in those terms. I mean, it's not a big deal but when you are younger, but when you get older, there aren't as many nights out socializing and fucking off and doing the fun shit. I can't get this done because I gotta get that done. And a lot of people around me at that time were partying first. When I say "party," I mean have a good time, go to that show, go hang out at this thing, run off to dinner with so-and-so when they are in town… And now that I am in my fifties, it is not even a consideration, you know?

Brian: Oh sure. I never go to shows these days. Hardly at all, ever. And besides that, the only time I ever seem to feel really comfortable is when I am working on my shit and doing something creative. That is like the only time I feel normal, whatever that means.

Tom: Yeah. I get that way, too. It is definitely the perfect Xanax, the perfect Valium, the perfect, you know... You are moving forward, you get this great sense of satisfaction and all sorts of good shit comes from it. But that, too, you could go overboard with that and spend twelve hours a day ignoring the world around you that is falling apart. I have always worked from the gut on a certain level, but that is part of the balance too, just figuring out when it's time to sit down and think about something instead of just reacting to shit, it's just a mix of both. Too much of one or the other, not to be analytical, but both extremes aren't good.

Brian: I want to ask about your friendship with Buzz Osborne and why do you think the both of you work so well together?

Tom: I think that, first and foremost is the fact that the both of us have a tendency, in our lives and in our business and our work and pleasure, to recognize that, you know, you don't stand there and tell a plumber what to do. I am not going to tell Buzz what to do with the Melvins. Like, when you read these stories involved in rock and roll—like George Martin with the Beatles telling them to do this or do that—that is not going to fucking work. Like, I can't do that. He is the expert, I am not. And vice versa, on a certain level. He lets me do what I am going to do. When we are working together it is just like that. Mutual respect. And trust.

Sometimes you go to someone else who is talented but they are micromanaging you and second guessing you and slowing you down and you are like, "Motherfucker, I will get it done. Trust me." And then you realize that the trust isn't there, I am going to call you four times that day, where did you get the master at, did you bake the tapes, did you do this, you know—second-guessing my job and it's like, "Bitch, I'll make the records. You just sit back."

So first and foremost, it is just recognizing each other's talents and letting them go. I mean, you watch Buzz do that all of the time.

Brian: Sometimes he will ask me what I think. If I am asked something, I will say something. That is the way it should be for any situation like that. Because if there is one thing that I have hated during these last eight years of freelancing, it is the phrase that starts with, "Here is what you should do." I hate being told that. Because usually, it is never based in reality. But, you know, I have done that too, of course.

Tom: Nine out of ten times, it is from somebody who has never done that. Maybe it is just a part of western society right now, but everyone thinks that they know everything all of the time. And I have to stop myself from doing that, I am not above that. "Well, you know what you should do…" and hopefully it might come down to the wisdom of age where you say to yourself, "I don't know fuck all about that, why am I trying to tell somebody else what to do?"

Brian: I was wondering about your recent art. As I understand it, you were really sick at one point and in a coma, and then you got better and then suddenly… and I am not sure if I have gotten this right but you got this ability to do this certain style of artwork that you are doing now for the last couple of years? Is that even close?

Tom: Ehh… kind of. I mean, it is a weird…the way that the story goes was, like, I came out of this coma and that I could speak German. And that is not the case.

It's been a weird thing watching it, but I could always draw. Literally since I was a child. I could always draw and I painted for a long time. I just gave it up when I started doing the record label because I found that doing graphics was way more to my speed and liking because…I am not patient enough to be a real painter, you know?

So I had the ability, but once I was sitting there [after the coma] and they are trying to get me to go to rehab and they are telling me to do… what are they called, these Japanese puzzles and that kind of shit. And I was like are you fucking kidding me? So I started to do these. My daughter had to go out and get this linoleum for her class and I was doing collage stuff as my own personal rehab thing, to get the brain going, because I literally had brain damage. And I was doing these record covers where I was doing a hundred sleeves, these collages. Sort of a factory style.

So my daughter had this thing and I did it, and the first one I thought came out really good. It was a picture of a grenade that said, "pull the pin pussy," and I really liked it. And I taught myself how to print a hundred of them and glued them on to these record sleeves. But where the skill came in was because I was brain damaged. I was thinking about how to do a lot of shit anyhow, so thinking backwards and thinking in reverse were not as tough as it would be for a forty something year old person starting something cold. Like writing a sentence backward. I mean, you get stuck in these ruts that all humans get stuck in, but since I am an empty slate—I am teaching myself how to write anyways—so I slid into it really easily. So, it wasn't like a magic pill. I have had people come back at me and say, "so you came out of this and knew how to linocut?" And I say nah. I am not saying that is what you said but I have had people say that to me a couple of times.

Kristin Smith DeBockler

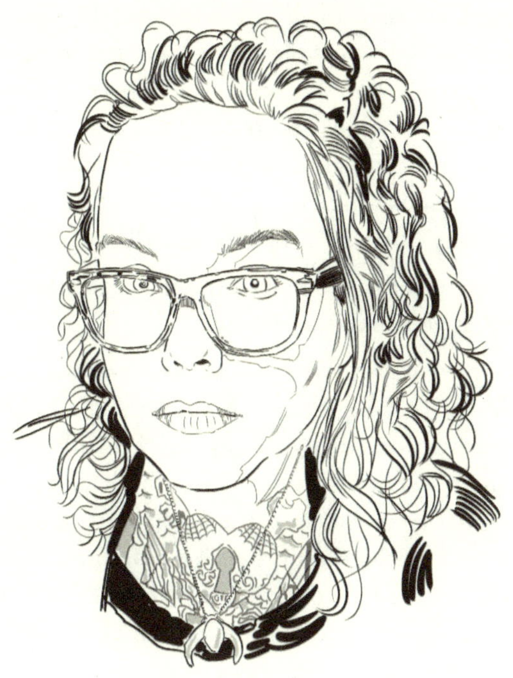

Kristin is a jack of all trades kind of person and her artistic talent is pretty wide reaching. She can seemingly do anything. It is pretty impressive. From painting to illustration to sewing to photoshopped creations, she can do it all. And she is one of the smartest people I have met.

And yeah, she is my partner. I was lucky to meet her when I did. So here I am asking her some silly questions. Check out Kristin's work!

♫

Brian: You also grew up in a pretty isolated part of this country, Vermont. What did you think happened to you that put you on the path you are on now?

Kristin: Well, I didn't have a lot of friends when I was growing up, mostly because I was living out in the middle of nowhere. And even before all of that, I had just been drawing since I was really little—three or four years old. So it was kind of out of necessity of amusing myself, but also because I enjoyed it. Growing up in the middle of nowhere where there is not a lot of people and no real scene of any kind, and not a whole lot to do out there—and to top it off, not only was it a small town where I grew up, but I lived in a really isolated part of that small town, too.

Brian: So there wasn't any raging, straight-edge metalcore scene in Vermont that you could tap into?

Kristin: No, there wasn't. Well, maybe there was but I had no access to it, aside from getting things through the mail. But there were no venues or anything that were any closer than Burlington, which was two and a half hours away and I didn't have a car I spent a lot of time wandering outside because my parents would kick me out of the house. And the rest of the time I would usually send it up in my room just drawing or downstairs drawing. My mom used to buy me pads of paper and pens instead of getting toys and stuff.

Brian: So you were easy to shop for.

Kristin: Yes, pretty much.

Brian: What was your first job? How old were you and what did you do?

Kristin: I was fourteen and I worked as a dishwasher for an Inn, in Weathersfield, Vermont, to varying degrees of success. It was kind of nice because I had my own little corner and didn't have to talk to too many people, aside from some of the waiters and everything. There was a cook I remember, the head chef was absolutely insane and used to throw knives and cleavers across the room next to my dishwashing station, so that was pretty interesting. And then

I had a short stint there as a waitress too but I ended up spilling wine on a politician and that pretty much ended any hope of a waitressing career.

That whole job was just weird anyways. It was a four star Inn with a piano player. He would take food from the plates of the customers after they had left and would put it in his pockets. So that was my first job.

Brian: When you got older you ended up doing a lot of other artistic things aside from art, like music. Playing in a school band and learning how to play a small arsenal of instruments.

Kristin: I had been singing for a really long time, as little kids do. I didn't really seriously start playing music until I was in the fifth grade. I started playing a clarinet that I got from my cousin, and it was the time where you were encouraged to start a band, regardless of whether you wanted to or not. While other people's families were encouraging their kids to do whatever they wanted, I was told, "Hey this is the family clarinet and this what you are going to play." So that is what I did. It actually turned out to be really fun and I enjoyed playing music and took to it really quickly. To the point where I learned how to read music and sight read music and was even writing my own stuff when I was in middle school.

I think I kind of just liked the attention of playing music, too. Especially living out in the middle of nowhere, it was a good way of meeting new people who might have had similar interests and actually wanting to do something. It was enticing because playing in a school band was doing something constructive with a bunch of other people, and it was really fun.

My parents bought me a keyboard at some point, a little Casio keyboard. It was super small and I think it had a demo that played a Billy Joel song. I used to noodle around on that a lot, and eventually I got a guitar, and then I learned to play a bunch of different woodwind instruments over the years—like saxophone. I played the bass clarinet for a really long time and kind of was in that whole band nerd scene. I was going to competitions and playing in the marching band for football games. I didn't really enjoy being at the games but I got to play Edgar Winter's "Frankenstein" on this big wind synthesizer.

A wind synthesizer is set up like a clarinet but it was plugged into a giant bass cabinet that they hauled around in the back of a big pickup truck. And they would drive me over to the football field and I got to pick one of the songs that we got to play one time and so I picked "Frankenstein." I think I was like fourteen. There weren't a lot of fourteen year old girls that were excited about "Frankenstein" but it was the greatest. I was so excited.

Brian: Is there a picture of you doing this somewhere?

Kristin: Yeah, there has to be. I was super into it. If one exists, I am sure I would be the only person in the picture looking excited.

I didn't even care, it was just really fun. And that song has a really good bass line, too. And with all of the synth stuff that goes on in the song anyways, I got to play all of it and it was great.

As far as what I listened to outside of that, I started to buy my own tapes and records at thrift stores, I ended up getting some David Bowie and Queen. I really liked both of them. There wasn't really a whole lot of stuff out there so you would get really influenced by just a cover of a record, like the cover of David Bowie's *Low* album—just that weird picture of his profile and the font on it. I took it home and listened to it and it was just totally bizarre, I loved it.

I ended up picking up a magazine at the library—it had a bunch of metal bands in it—and I found some names that I ended up writing to. Nothing super extensive, but I would get tapes in the mail, pen pal-type stuff. I didn't really have anything to give them but, through that, I figured out that Napalm Death was something that I enjoyed.

I never succumbed to anything—it was just whatever I thought was interesting to listen to. I like The Beach Boys a lot, I like Napalm Death, I like prog rock, weird stuff, like Rush. My cousins were listening to Hootie and the Blowfish. (laughter) Meanwhile,

I was listening to this weird stuff and getting into classical music, getting into these bands where you would have to travel around New England, and getting into band competitions.

Brian: Working at these punk rock flea markets up in New Jersey where you used to live, you built a name for yourself, and you were doing a whole bunch of work and selling stuff online, and doing mail order. And you did that while taking care of your daughter during a difficult situation, with very little sleep, which is very impressive. In a weird way it is kind of like art and your daughter saved your life.

Kristin: I went to school to study classical music, and after a year and a half into that, I decided that it was something that I really didn't want to do. I graduated when I was seventeen and left Vermont, moved out of my parents house as soon as I could, and went off and did my own thing. So, after I dropped out of school, I ended up working a bunch of shitty retail jobs which were completely miserable—just enough to live off of, but not enough to where you had to think about things a lot. I would go home and do my thing, and I kind of got out of art.

For whatever reason, I had decided in my head that music and art had to be mutually exclusive. Like, if I was doing one then I couldn't really focus on the other. Even though I had done a bunch of art in high school, it never stuck with me so I just focused on music more. At one of the retail jobs, I was an accountant for an arts and crafts store. It was intensely boring and the store ended up closing, so I decided that I was going to go back to school and study something that was going to be a sure bet making a living with it, and that visual animation was it. It was kind of interesting, so I went back to school for that. And there were a bunch of fine art courses that I had to take to get that degree, and as I was taking those, I realized that I really intensely enjoyed making art and that I missed it. And because I wasn't making music anymore I just threw myself into it. I had a really prolific period of about three years. And people started to actually buy my art while I was there—pieces that I was doing for class, people were basically buying the homework that I was doing—so I thought, "Well, I could probably make a living doing something like this."

In going to school, they basically give you this false hope that you are going to get a job and have a career. If you were going to be a doctor or a lawyer, I suppose you would have a better chance to having a career. But as an artist… how many artists actually get out of school and find a job in the arts that is substantial enough to be able to pay back all of that debt that you have?

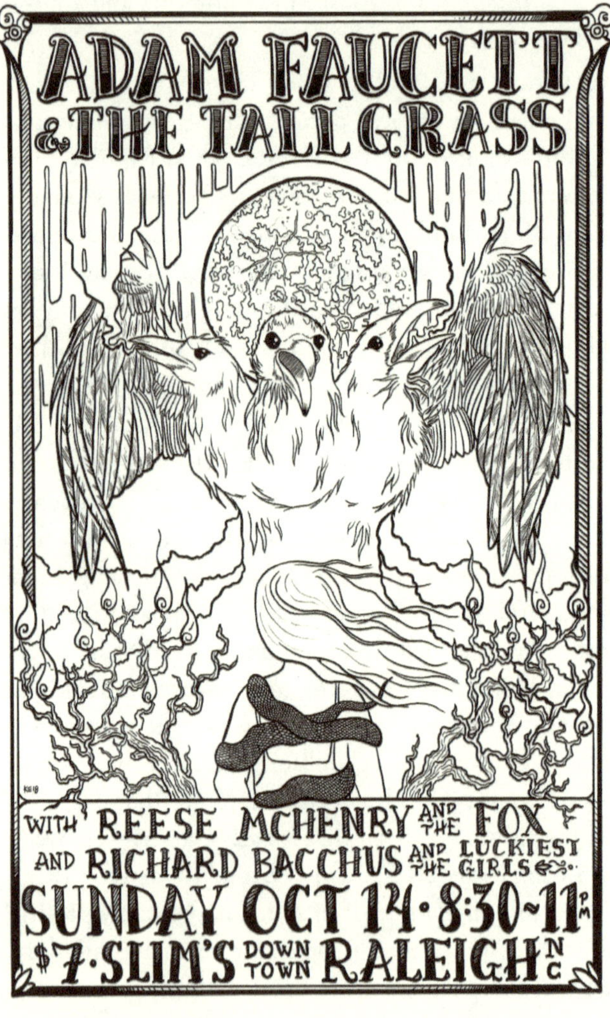

ARTWORK BY KRISTIN SMITH DEBOCKLER

Brian: I am going to say that that is probably very, very rare.

Kristin: Oh, it absolutely is. I can tell you this, I kept up with some of the people that I went to school with and most of them are not artists now. They will do it as a hobby, but they have jobs doing something completely different.

Brian: Do you think being self-employed as an artist is kind of a trade off?

Kristin: Yeah, I think so. I mean, I would prefer not to be in debt but I did learn a lot of valuable stuff in school. I didn't really meet a lot of people to make connections with, but that wasn't my intent going into it. I don't want to say that it wasn't worth it to go to school, because I know that some people find it really valuable. It is just a lot of the stuff that we were learning was stuff that I already really had a handle on. It was a good backdrop for being focused and making sure that I was really working on art all of the time, but at the same time, I remember that they actually made up some classes for me to take as independent studies because I was already beyond where I should have been at that point.

Another thing that was kind of iffy about going to school was that you don't really get any guidance about how to market yourself as an artist. After you are done I mean. They give you techniques and tools to be able to make things, but they don't really ever focus on the business side of things. They don't really tell you how you could go forth and actually make money doing it, which is actually kind of difficult. Like, those documentaries that we watched about the art world, the fine art world. It is all sort of a game that, if you don't know how to play it, then you might as well not bother.

Brian: That stuff is like looking through a telescope at Mars. There is no point of even thinking that you are going to visit there. (laughter) You no longer live in New Jersey, now you live in North Carolina. What kind of stuff are you doing now that you are here?

Kristin: Well, I moved down here last April, almost a year. And I have had to pretty much start over, aside from the online sales that

I have done. I kind of established myself in New Jersey and New York and the Philadelphia areas and then I picked up everything and moved. So I have been doing some small shows down here and I have been traveling back and forth, up north for shows to be able to sell stuff. I have some pieces in some galleries across the country, but basically I have been meeting people down here who are in the art community and trying to re establish myself. Which has gone pretty well for less than a year, I think.

I run a paint studio in New Jersey from here, administrative stuff. I kind of run a gallery here with a woman who is very supportive of my artistic endeavors. That has been really great. I am about to get started on a book with a local illustrator which should be pretty interesting. And then just a lot of freelance stuff—making prints and other stuff. I hit the ground running, I think, and things seem to be expanding at a pretty quick rate, which is pretty cool.

I had an opportunity to do some stuff in California with some of Jim Henson's people. I ended up moving to New Jersey instead, which was a pretty big difference. And so I just kept making art, and I was invited to do a show by someone that I had met who was also an artist. I had sold some things online with platforms like Etsy, but I had never sold anything in person at something like a Punk Rock flea market—making a bunch of things in one location to sell to an audience of people walking through. So I gave it a shot and actually did pretty well.

And at that show, that is where I met Joseph [Kuzemka], who is the organizer and creator of the Trenton Punk Rock flea market. It started off as a really small show with maybe thirty or so vendors, and then has evolved since then into this massive goliath of art and music. It's two days and happens a few times a year and thousands of people come through now. And getting in on the ground floor of that was really great. I just started selling with them, and as the shows got bigger, I figured out how to market myself a little bit better.

Brian: So being a freelance artist is it for you.

Kristin: Yeah. There's a big difference between being a fine artist, I suppose, and being a commercial artist. I guess as a fine artist you could also say that you are a commercial artist—there is a certain amount of pandering that you will do if you take on some projects that maybe you aren't super excited about but you know that it will pay the bills. It's really hard to find a balance there.

Brian: I usually just look at it like, "Well, someone wants to hire me to draw something and pay me," so I really don't have a problem with that.

Kristin: I totally get that, too. Some of the best clients will just give you a general idea and then just let you do it. Those are always fun because you really do have a chance to add your creativity to it. But no matter what, it is great to be able to make a living doing something creative that you enjoy do.

Brian: We talked about people who make art and do stuff like music and writing, and then get grouped into these categories—a big one seems to be about being a woman. What do you think about the tendency some people have to group people into these things based on their gender or something else?

Kristin: Well, it's kind of a difficult topic because I want to preface this by saying that I do respect people who are prominent female artists and are proud to be recognized for being female. To each their own. For me—and this is because I have never experienced any discrimination or felt belittled for being a woman—but I have worked too hard with what I have done to have it be categorized as something that a woman has done. That doesn't make a whole lot of sense.

I don't want someone to come up and buy a piece of art from me just because I am a woman. I want them to come up and buy a piece of art from me because they like what I have done, or they find some kind of beauty or meaning in something I have done, or even if they just like the way something looks.

I don't want to be placated or supported just because I am female. I am not saying that there aren't some woman out there who haven't had some type of struggle based on, you know, being in a male-dominated field or anything like that—I respect the people that have risen above that—it's just that I don't think of myself and go, "Well, I am a female artist." I am just an artist.

Sam McPheeters

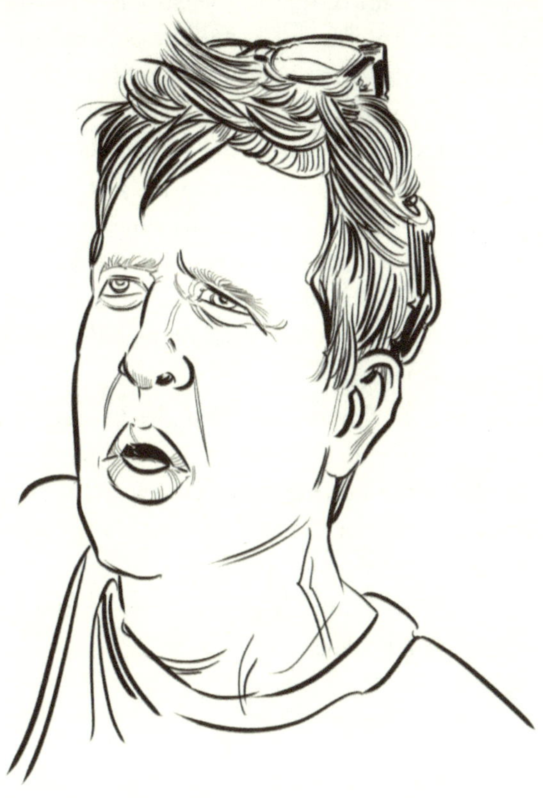

I have been a fan of Sam McPheeters' for a long time. First as a member of the band Born Against and subsequent future musical acts, and secondly, as someone who just sort of makes me laugh. He has become a writer and has released a few books, with a third one to come in the near future. The third book is about his involvement in the punk rock hardcore world, and I cannot wait to read it. He had sent me a chapter about the band 7 Seconds, and it was not only super relatable with my own experience in that eighties punk rock world, it was also downright hilarious.

Based on that alone, I think it is going to be great.

His writing is something I always thought was entertaining, and you can see some of that in the early fanzines he used to do. He has a pretty unique voice. And he is funny! Born Against were also one of the small handful of bands in the early nineties (hell, let's just say after the eighties) that did stuff that I felt had ANYTHING to do with what I liked about punk rock and hardcore in the early eighties. They were also smart-assed nerds, which I also liked, because a lot of the time that was pretty much what I was. A lot of what the band did, I think, was looked back upon by a few of the band members as being kind of pointless—like being outraged about bar codes on records, for instance—but it was enjoyable nonetheless.

After the relatively short-lived Wrangler Brutes, he said goodbye to screaming into a microphone forever and moved to California to be with his wife and write. It took a few attempts to re-establish some contact with him to see if he would be game to talk to me about a bunch of stuff and luckily he said yes.

Sam is one of the funniest guys out there. Buy his books and support anything he does.

Brian: I watched a few online interviews with you and I gather that you are not very sentimental about the musical end of things that you did. That totally echoes the feelings I have had about that stuff, too. But I kept playing in bands and I am 53 now. The last band I was in broke up a year ago.

Sam: But you are a musician, though. That is a huge difference. I am not, and so there was always this feeling of what I could do. And also physically, I don't think that I could be in a reunion show even if I wanted to, because I don't think that I could yell like that, you know? I was getting weird headaches towards the end.

Brian: Have you been offered that kind of stuff off and on over the years?

Sam: Yeah, a little bit. Not much. And it is interesting to me that every reunion offer, the attention gets lower and lower. We got offered to do a show at CBGB's, one of their last shows which was ridiculous in many ways. One reason was, the scene that Born Against was associated with was grown out of disdain for that CBGB's world. We had nothing to do with that world. Even though before that I had gone to a lot of matinees there.

Brian: Are you talking about the New York Hardcore thing? When I think of that stuff, the only stuff I think of that I liked was the Urban Waste seven-inch. I wasn't into Sick Of It All or even Agnostic Front or that stuff.

Sam: Yeah. We had this weird public rivalry with Sick Of It All. A lot of that was based out of how violent and awful those CBGB's shows got, so it was definitely ironic that we were offered… ironic isn't the right word, it was just a dumb offer like we shouldn't have been offered that. And I think there was some money involved in that, not a massive amount. The amounts got lower and lower. There was some festival and they said, "well, you won't get paid but it would be really cool to see you guys."

Brian: As if you could really exist in a world without money, especially after punk rock.

Sam: Yeah, it was ridiculous. The offers, as well as the enthusiasm, got lower and lower. The implication was that I had been sitting around thinking, "somebody offer me this, I just want to get back on that stage!" (laughter)

Brian: You made enough money the first time, you can just sit back and retire and wait for that call.

Sam: Yeah. But you are a musician, and you have very different… it is literally a different part of your brain, you know?

Brian: Yeah, but I managed to find a way to alienate myself away from even that, ha ha.

Sam: It's also… you are operating against the tide just culturally. There is just a glut of fucking everything now. I guess because of the internet, but it doesn't seem entirely because of the internet. My wife was in bands and it was hard for them to get traction, you know?

Brian: These days I have no idea what people would do or what a young person would do to even get noticed. I still think the best advertisement is someone you trust telling you that you might like this thing. Word of mouth. To this very day. And also, even though I still love music, it doesn't mean as much to me to look for stuff anymore. I don't have the time to waste and be indulgent looking for three good bands out of five thousand.

Sam: Yeah. So, here is a question for you, I am curious. Does it get weird for you, that music doesn't maintain that central role that it once did, as it did for me? Does that concern you?

Brian: No, it's more compartmentalized. But I still love and am obsessed with music, it's just not as important for me to keep up these days.

Sam: That makes sense.

Brian: It's put on a shelf. My girlfriend is also an artistic weirdo who likes music, too. But other than that, I really don't have a posse of people where I can go over to their houses and play old records with. It's not really weird, but it is kind of amazing to me the legs that this punk rock stuff still has.

Sam: Yeah. So, I should tell you at this point in the conversation that I have a new book[1] out about hardcore punk and it sounds like some of the same questions that you are discussing, I definitely explored. I don't think that there is much overlap here but there were several times where I really wanted to look into this subject of motives, especially the motives of people around my age. I am only a few years younger than you. It's a weird fucking thing. I know a lot of people who are still in hardcore bands, well into their fifties, and it's clear that this is a thing that works for them

---

1 *Mutations: Twenty Years Embedded in Hardcore Punk* https://www.rarebirdbooks.com/collections/frontpage/products/mutations-twenty-years-embedded-in-hardcore-punk

and they are not giving up. So if you factor out whatever my opinions are about doing that music, it's interesting to me because I wonder about the motives behind doing that. Because there is not money involved a lot of the time. It's just to have that feeling of working at full capacity.

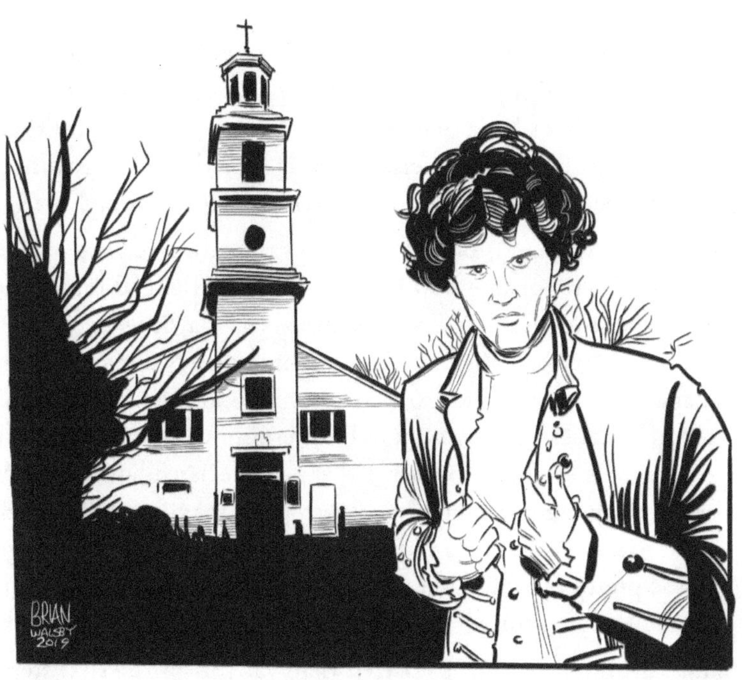

I have no interest in video games—I feel like I was locked into the Pac-Man era—I read this book by Jane McGonigal called *Reality Is Broken*, and she discusses the neurochemical stuff behind what the brain does when you play video games, and it finally started to make sense to me. Why the fuck do people waste their time playing video games, spending hundreds of hours doing it? Part of the reason is because people are using their brains to its fullest capacity only when they are playing video games. And that really makes sense to me, it's like oh I have that headspace now when I am writing. I had that experience when I was in bands, that was me working at full capacity. And it's a thing that humans really need, almost everyone doesn't get that opportunity at their job. You go to a job and you are underused, maybe you are humiliated, or you have office politics, there are a million other things that could be going on but one of the big things that happens to your brain is that your brain is being used the way it wants to be used.

And when I read that in the book, I recognized it. And I think that happens with people in bands who just continue. They need that, and I don't fault that at all, but I guess I am grateful that I have that with something else. I clearly have that when I work on writing regardless of whether the writing is good or bad.

Brian: Your writing is one of the things that attracted me to Born Against. I am not sure how long you have lived in California with your wife, but I feel like I was writing to you maybe when you were still in Richmond, Virginia, You sent me these little fanzines and magazines that you did. And to get that kind of stuff in the mid to late nineties that were actually entertaining and interesting to read, that is kind of a lost art. I always appreciated how you wrote about things and even how you wrote about the dismantling of the band that you were in, and you figuring all of that out. So to me, it was pretty obvious that writing was something that was kind of the next step for whatever it was you wanted to do creatively.

Sam: Yeah, well I think I realized that was sort of the first step. I think we started writing when I moved to a California in 1999. Once I was out of bands, in 2004, I kind of remembered that I wanted to be a writer all along and that maybe I should focus on that and not be in bands any more. But I have done a lot of bad writing also, I have a lot of writing that I just don't show people and things that didn't work. I consider this a process that continues you know, like, I aspire to be a better writer.

There was no room for that in hardcore. I couldn't aspire to be a better hardcore singer. I mean... what would that be? (laughter) I don't even know what that would look like.

Brian: I gravitated towards Born Against because it was one of the few bands that I heard after I was done with that stuff that reminded me of what I liked about that music in the first place.

Sam: That is interesting, so first of all, thanks for that compliment. I have heard that before from some other people and it was always a strange thing to me because I don't have any perspective on that band, I have no way of formulating an opinion on it. I have heard that from other people and that is probably the best and highest compliment, the version of me that was in that band, that is the highest compliment that that person could have gotten. (laughter) So,thanks.

Brian: Of course. You have also had a lot of your writing showcased in both online and actual, real-life publications as well as two novels and a split book with another person, and so I was wondering if the books did well enough for you. I noticed that you went on a book tour—which is kind of a fantasy of mine—instead of touring in a band, just going out and going to whatever different place that would have you, and just talk. Was that arranged by you, or did someone else do it for you?

Sam: The first book, *The Loom Of Ruin,* was self published in a really sneaky way. A friend of mine, Anthony, and I set up a publishing company called Mugger and we decided that I would be the silent partner in this and I would handle a lot of the production because I had a record label and I sort of knew how to do these things, and I also knew how to ask the right questions of other people, and this friend of mine was mostly responsible for getting the money together. We got loans from friends who we knew had money. We pushed it for awhile as his project, because he is—still is—a really interesting charismatic person who taught high school in Compton for awhile and played in some weird bands, so he was a good guy to be a front man for this publishing company that we had aspirations for for awhile.

But we barely had enough money to get that book out and we haven't even sold out of the first printing yet. I think I still have five hundred copies in my garage. So when I did the book tour, it all had to be self-financed and there was no way that I had the money to do that myself so I did it in a way that was way more labor intensive but plausible for me to make money at. I would do two shows a day—I would do a reading during the day at a bookstore, which is almost always zero money because book stores get really fucking weird about you selling your own merchandise, which I discovered on the road—and then at night I would do some other event. There were a few actual band shows but I tried to stay away from those, it was mainly just weird events. Like a spoken word show. I did one in maybe Cleveland with a magician. There were some where I did stuff with movies. Just events.

So at those I would bring merchandise and I would just make sure that I was really well-armed with weird little screenprints to sell. And even then it costs so much money because I wasn't staying at people's houses. I really hated that part of touring, staying at people's houses, and also I had so much work to do each night that I really couldn't stay at someone's house, so I would stay at a cheap hotel. But even those, at a hundred dollars a night, sort of adds up. And I had to cancel the last two weeks of a seven week tour because I just ran out of money. I couldn't afford to have my friend roadie with me, and I had medical problems with my eyes and I couldn't drive.

So I don't know if I would do that again but I will have to do something like that again when the next book comes out. I didn't do any promo for the second novel. At all. I only did one reading for it and consequently the book didn't sell much but... the election happened two weeks after the book came out so that was a nice excuse for the book failing, which I think I am kind of fine with. (laughter)

Brian: Even with what didn't work out, was the experience of doing a book tour still more fulfilling than getting on a stage and singing in a band?

Sam: Oh yeah. I enjoyed it instantly more than a band tour. And it was interesting because I remembered a lot of the things about a band touring that I had forgotten in the eight years since I played shows. Like about how demoralizing it was playing a show and how demoralizing it was afterwards, drenched in sweat and my voice is hoarse, and I would get these weird headaches during those last couple of tours. Yeah, there was none of that. I mean, I had some book readings that I did to four or five people, but it was FUN. And I didn't feel depleted afterwards, I would just go do something else. I didn't realize on the book tour—and one thing that you should realize if you are going to do it—is that you are really going to have to do everything on your own, and it seems almost beyond one person. I just ran out of time.

And then also dealing with bookstores. Bookstores are kind of a shitty culture, which I really hadn't expected. My conclusion was there are a lot of people in the bookstore industry who are bitter because their industry got really destroyed by Amazon, and probably some other factors. And they are really looking for people to take it out on and I became that person. I had multiple bookstore owners and managers just be shitty towards me for no reason, and that was really creepy. I don't want to be on bad terms with someone at a bookstore—I don't need that, you know—so if I ever do it again, as I will in the fall, then I have to figure something else out, some way to bypass bookstores. So it was a good learning experience and I was very keen on being observant and making notes about things that did and didn't work, so I learned a lot. But I don't know that I would recommend it. And it definitely wasn't a substitute for this thing that we are talking about, the feeling of having been important playing in bands, and then you wake up one day and you are just a middle-aged person.

Brian: Do you freelance, have a regular job, or some combination of all of that stuff?

Sam: Yeah, I have been doing combinations for a long time. I did a lot of freelance writing from 2009 to maybe 2015. I don't feel like I really cracked the code on that. I mean, I had some good experiences at *Vice*, they sent me to the Middle East and into Africa, which was great. And they also paid me to get agoraphobia therapy and I wrote about that. So those were all really good experiences, but they didn't really equal a living. And it got really hard to make that work and I finally stopped. I had a discussion a couple of days ago about trying to get back into freelancing and I sort of realized what an uphill road it's going to be because I don't even have those relationships with those writers anymore.

Brian: I am still hanging in there but it's like I have to remind people that I am still alive every day and that I could sell them some artwork.

Sam: And you are working in a huge marketplace where the bottom keeps dropping out. There seems to be new trap doors.

Brian: It's sort of a dying thing, in a way.

Sam: I don't know that it is completely dying, it's not totally impossible. You know, there is this really crazy Steve Martin quote that I read last week where he was asked about his advice to young people in any artistic medium and it was, "be so good that they can't ignore you" and I thought that is really great advice for the twentieth century but it doesn't apply to the twenty-first century. I mean, I am on Instagram and I see these artists who are great, but there's just too many of them, you know? There are too many talented people, and trying to break through on that level is almost impossible. I would think because there's too many people period, and too many talented people.

Brian: I have a few more band questions. The *Normal Man* record that Men's Recovery Project did is one of my favorite records of all time. I had thought that it would have been great to put together some sort of blazing hardcore kind of record that was … I don't want to say funny, or tongue in cheek, but something along those lines. So when I got that record I was like, "Son of a fucking bitch! This is brilliant!" It was perfect. It was a perfect little record.

Sam: Ha ha. Before Born Against broke up, we had all moved to Richmond, Virginia, from Jersey City but essentially we were still a New York band, just on the other side of the Hudson (laughter). And we moved to Virginia, it was pretty self-consciously like, "we are no longer a part of the New York scene, a lot of our former friends hate us, let's just start our lives over again." Everything just kind of fell apart in New York. Many of our friends in the ABC Rio crowd turned on us, for reasons that I understand. Doing a band like Born Against... there was no good way to end it. If you attract that into your life, if you are that belligerently obnoxious, you are going to have other people be that belligerently obnoxious towards you. It hurt, and it was a shitty part of my life but it kind of made sense. And moving to Richmond, we had a reset. I mean, my rent was ninety five dollars a month. I learned how to ride a bike at age twenty four and did nothing for a year (laughter).

Brian: Of all places, why did you pick Richmond, Virginia? Did you know people there?

Sam: We were on tour a lot. Yeah, we knew people there. I mean, I am not a huge fan of the city now...

So, we moved down there and played one show and broke up. So Men's Recovery Project was started with kind of an attitude on wanting to alienate Born Against fans.

It's interesting... in this new book that I wrote, I really tried to retrace some of my reason for being in Men's Recovery Project and it took me awhile to figure out that I was really not comfortable with the lack of innovation in that whole scene, the world that Born Against travelled in and the period of time that we covered, from 89 to 93, there was a lot of change in that. When we started, you could still play shows that had a semblance of eighties hardcore shows. And also it was a really crazy time in New York, where CBGB's closed for matinees and people would do these really bizarre shows, it was like there was a truce. It was people from very different scenes showing up—from really weird crusty punk bands with straight edge hardcore bands with performance artists.

Brian: Ha ha...a truce?

Sam: Yeah, it was kind of like the movie *The Warriors*. (laughter)

There was one show where there were all of those bands, and then Allen Ginsberg got onstage and did a poetry reading, and it morphed into what the nineties were, which was just...something different. Music that wasn't as good and people who were very serious and earnest, endless discussions about sexism and racism. Stuff that needed to happen but also wasn't simultaneously artistically fun.

Brian: It's like reading the letters section of *Maximum Rock N Roll* for like the last thirty five years.

Sam: Exactly. And so it was good for us to do a band that would be unrecognizable to all of those people. And in the middle of it, I think we thought, "hey wouldn't it be funny if we did a hardcore record?" And so it was all of the people from Born Against, different versions of Born Against, playing on that.

Brian: Adam [Nathanson] was in it obviously. Wasn't Brooks [Headley] on it?

Sam: Yeah, Brooks played drums on it. We were all living together in this house, but there wasn't much more thought that went into it then that. I think at some point we were going to try and do a couple of different genres. Neil [Burke] worked with this gospel choir and he really wanted to do a gospel record. (laughter) I said, "I don't know what that would look like and I don't think that would be a good idea." We never actually did it but we started off thinking well, we will start off with doing a hardcore record.

Brian: Was the reaction good to the record?

Sam: I guess. Yeah. I read reviews in fanzines where they would say, "Oh, this is what Sam should be doing, I don't know why he is doing that other garbage." The point, for me, was to alienate the people who liked my other stuff. That was far more fun than preaching in a hardcore band. Later, when I was in the Wrangler Brutes, the idea there was not to be exactly what we turned into; we turned into sort of a hardcore revival band and that was a shame. That wasn't exactly what I wanted to do but I don't think I was able to articulate what I did want to do to the other members, and also like I already said I am not a musician.

Brian: I agree with what you said about hardcore and all of the navel gazing and lack of innovation, but I took Born Against, even if it was a hardcore band, as a bunch of introspective intelligent and nerdy people who were smartasses, and that is exactly how I thought of myself as a young person. But of course, years later with the benefit of real life experience, that was not how I was going to be for the rest of my life.

Sam: It is not sustainable.

Brian: Right, it is not sustainable. And during that time period when you guys were a band, you had things like Fugazi and that culture. And even though I liked that band to some degree and what was going on musically, it seemed very serious and humorless. I wanted to joke around and be an idiot and have fun.

Sam: Now didn't you get in "trouble" with the scene for doing that Monobrow Jones and The Spring cartoon? (laughter) I remember that.

Brian: If you look at it now, you would think that it was the most inoffensive, stupid, juvenile, and dumb thing. Maybe a five percent shred of being clever.

Sam: Why would anyone get upset at that? Yeah, it is totally ridiculous.

Brian: I think people took themselves very seriously.

Sam: In that scene, yeah.

Brian: All those people are really nice. So when I look back I think, did that really happen? And it is really interesting that you are going to be doing another project that might have a little echo of what I am trying to do. Because of your attitude about all of that stuff I am already looking forward to it.

Sam: When I started it, it was just going to be a collection of existing music essays I had written and two that had never been published. One was about that book *LOUD 3D*[2]? I am assuming you probably have a copy of that. I tracked down the guys who made that and I wrote this thing for the *Believer* and then they killed it under shitty circumstances. Then I wrote another piece about Born Against and some specific band experience that Born Against had but it was sort of my vehicle for writing about Born Against. But when I started working on it, I realized that there was this potential for it to be something really good and not just a collection of half-assed essays I wrote. So I think I turned them into something that is a really good book. But it was hands down the most unpleasant experience I had maybe since my parents' divorce when I was ten. It was just fucking awful, it just turned into therapy. Just the actual act of writing honestly about my experiences playing music and also my experiences as a fan.

To really figure out these things and to acknowledge how important it had been to me at the time, was just too much head resting. I feel like it would be irresponsible of me to say to you not to fall into that trap with your project—because there are so many good valuable threads that you will be able to follow—just don't let it kill you because I got really really fucked up writing this book. Physically and mentally.

Brian: Yeah, well, the only thing that has happened so far is I had to step away from it a few times because I was thinking, "what the fuck am I doing? How am I going to put this together?"

Sam: Going back to what people get out of being in bands and working creatively and using their brains at peak level, I could see how bleak things could be without it. And that is most of the human experience. You know, the stuff that we had, it's hard to keep in mind how rare it was, how most people don't have anything like this in their lives, and that it leaves such an impact that it leaves you feeling kind of hollowed out afterwards if you don't find something to replace it. I definitely struggled with that

---

2 One of the only early books on hardcore, and published in the heyday of the movement. 3-D glasses included. https://www.goodreads.com/book/show/1717130.Loud_3D

and I know everyone who has been in bands has struggled with that at one point or another.

Brian: Totally. But I had dual identities all along. Quite awhile ago the artist identity sort of won out. Punk rock provided a really great temporary home for a lot of people. But when that ended, you had to take what you learned and do something else. The other big thing about punk rock was just the ability to connect with people.

But sometimes weird stuff happens. A few years ago I had a chance to reconnect for a minute with Kevin Seconds. I drew some stuff for his band, 7 Seconds. I just gave them that artwork because I was a big fan and then got resentful later. It went on for years and years and then I thought, "you know, I don't want to be bitter going into my fifties still thinking about 7 Seconds artwork from over thirty years ago," you know? So I wrote him and he was cool about it, which lead to actually doing a few shirts on my own, to close the book on all of that.

And his band broke up and real life happens. Nothing stays the same. So the idea of any of us giving our lives to punk rock decades ago, and him ending up wanting to do his acoustic music and draw, but also having to be tied to singing songs he wrote when he was 20 years old—expected to sing "Young Till I Die" forever—that must be a weird thing to deal with. Can you imagine being forever tied to this moment in your life, as great as it was, and no one wants to pay as much attention to what you are doing since? Tons of people that were punk rockers are in that situation.

Sam: Totally. It would be very hard to be Kevin Seconds. One of the chapters that I wrote in my book is on 7 Seconds, cause I had always been curious about why they kind of vanished. There was a lot of weird stuff in there and also I had some weird experiences with them over the years. I got the Better Business Bureau on them because they didn't send me my record for a year. (laughter) And then there was a big show that they were going to play in Albany that I booked in 1987, and they just blew off the show, which was weird. Anyways, there was a chapter's worth of weird stuff. But if you are really going to discuss this world honestly, then actually do it. The thing that I find really distasteful is all of the biographies that have come out and just all of the little online social media groups; glory, the word GLORY keeps coming up.

Brian: Which is all bullshit.

Sam: It is just gross, you know?

Brian: Have you seen that Straight Edge book written by Tony Rettman[3]?

Sam: Yeah, he has written a couple of books, that and the New York Hardcore book.

Brian: He is a nice guy, I met him and drew a little bit of stuff for that book too. But all of that stuff, especially the first part of it, there is this stuff where all of these L.A. guys are talking about wading through all of the gangs at these early shows like, "you had to fight your way through the crowd." I went to those shows and I never had any problems, or trouble. I am not saying it wasn't there but it seems trumped up.

Sam: It's very dishonest, all of that mythology stuff. People that want to document the mythology, that is not interesting, you know? Whereas, I am very interested in the ability of hardcore to attract people with mental illness, or the effect that the scene had on me and my depression, or how there are not many good honest songs about depression—even though there are like a lot of songs called "Depression." (laughter)

---

3 *Straight Edge A Clear-Headed Hardcore Punk History* https://www.goodreads.com/book/show/36574809-straight-edge-a-clear-headed-hardcore-punk-history

WILLIAM DUVALL

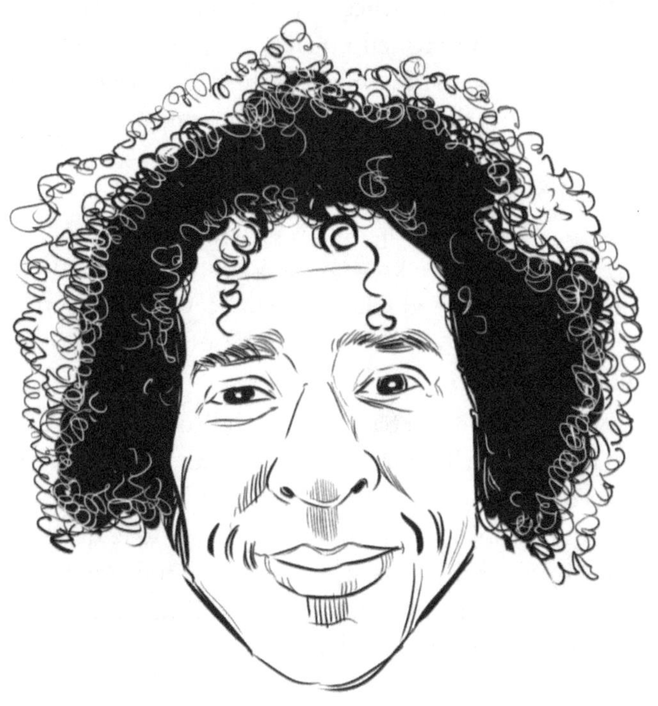

William DuVall came on my radar in 1983 or so when I was busy being immersed in punk rock letter-writing pen pal apprenticeship.

I was corresponding with his friend and bandmate, Jimmy Demer. Jimmy and William (then known as Jimi and Kip) played in the band Neon Christ, who were from the Atlanta area. Sometime in early 1984, Jimmy sent me their debut seven-inch. Lo and behold, it was a great record. Plus there was some pretty accomplished guitar playing all over that fast hardcore type of record. Listen to the solos, breaks, intros and outros. This kid Kip knew what he was doing.

Flash forward a year or so, I found myself in Atlanta when Corrosion of Conformity played with Neon Christ one hot and steamy night in 1985. The band had a bunch of newer songs that were all a step away from hardcore punk and were just great songs. Kip was very influenced by Greg Ginn of Black Flag and was a highly accomplished musician. It seemed like he could play anything. Bassist Danny Lankford confirmed this to me years later, saying that William was quite taken by the hardcore scene but was already very talented for being as young as he was. He formed Neon Christ and picked the band members based on friendship. That night Kip sang a very good version of "Got To Choose" by Kiss, so he knew what a good song was already. In less than a year, the band was finished. A few of those unrecorded songs that he wrote are still top notch, missing-in-action songs from that era.

He briefly joined the Santa Cruz California band BL'AST!, whose first album/lineup was and is some heavy duty music. He played in a short-lived band with COC's Mike Dean called Final Offering. Neither of those lasted very long despite being quite good. After this period, I sort of lost touch with what he was doing musically but after recently filling in the holes, here it goes: He played experimental music not too unlike someone like Jeff Buckley, but before his time, in a band called No Walls. Afterwards he was in another Atlanta band called Madfly, then the trio Comes With The Fall in Los Angeles. They self-released all of their music and did all of that work themselves.

While that was going on, Jerry Cantrell of Alice In Chains becomes a friend and fan of the band. Comes With The Fall went on tour opening for Cantrell and became his backup band afterwards. This paved the way for William to eventually join Alice In Chains later. This might be when most people become aware of him. It is a big deal and sort of a breakthrough for William. Undoubtedly, a lot of people are not aware of his long and lengthy history.

Also, it should be noted that William is a really nice guy who loves music of all kinds. I remember a really nice evening on Buzz Osborne's acoustic tour when he and Jimmy showed up at the gig in Atlanta and the four of us stood in the parking lot after the show for like forty minutes talking and shooting the shit. The four members of Neon Christ remain tight to this day. That is pretty cool.

His new acoustic guitar and voice only solo record is also, not surprisingly, really good. He has worked very hard and devoted himself to music for decades, so I was glad to have William wanting to take part in this.

♫

Brian: I noticed that you had an extremely early start as far as being interested in music and had a very diverse group of musical acts that you found interesting. Did you have a supportive family growing up? What turned you on to music, and also when did you first start playing guitar?

William: I have to credit my home town of Washington, D.C. There was such a rich musical heritage there and so much great music in the air all the time, especially from the late sixties through the early eighties. It was a renaissance for virtually every genre. I feel very fortunate to have come from there.

I started playing guitar at eight years old. Mine is the typical story of the first guitar being a beat-up old nylon-string acoustic with the strings stretched a mile high off the fret board. I found it in my grandparent's basement. It had belonged to my uncle, Kenneth.

The big catalyst was my cousin, Donald, moving in with my mother and me. He was having a rough time at home and my mother was always trying to help people. Donald was 18, ten years older than me, and he brought his beat-up record collection with him—amazing albums by Weather Report, Santana, Roy Ayers, Jaco Pastorius's first solo album, etc. He would play these records on my little Show 'N Tell turntable. The album that really knocked me out was Hendrix: *Band of Gypsys*—"Who Knows," "Machine Gun," etc. That started EVERYTHING. Donald's copy of the record was warped and scratched beyond belief. And it was missing the cover so, at first, I didn't even know what Hendrix looked like. The sounds I was hearing were so fascinating that I started bombarding Donald with all these questions. I was trying to understand what was going on: "You mean he's doing ALL THAT with a guitar??" Donald would try to explain feedback and Fender Stratocasters and Marshall stacks and all these amazing things. But we had no pictures. This is 1976, decades before the Internet. So Donald eventually went to the public library and photocopied some pictures of Hendrix from old issues of *Rolling Stone* magazine. I was already captivated by the sound. But once I saw what the dude looked like, I was DONE. That was it. My life was mapped out. I had the whole thing visualized.

That was also when I started record collecting in earnest. Donald and I would go to these cool used record stores and head shops that were around D.C. at that time, places like Bread & Roses, and we would pick up things like *Cosmic Slop* by Funkadelic for three dollars. Donald really taught me how to listen to music. We'd be listening to Weather Report and [Joe] Zawinul would play some interesting phrase on the piano or make some weird noise on his synthesizer and Donald would say, "Wow, man! Did you hear THAT? We gotta run that back." And he would move the needle back on the record to play the phrase again. He actually took me to see Weather Report at the Warner Theater in D.C. on their '77 tour supporting the *Heavy Weather* album—Jaco at his absolute peak. It was unforgettable. This is what we did nearly every minute of every day for almost two years. We played music and we made art: gigantic psychedelic collages on enormous slabs of cork board; tripped out comic books chronicling the adventures of our superhero alter-egos; perfectly balanced mobiles made out of wire hangers, fishing line, and sea shells that we'd hang from the ceiling—all while the best soundtrack in the world would be filling the room. We played that *Band Of Gypsys* album so much

I learned to scat sing every note of it—all the solos, everything. I can still do it to this day.

Eventually, reality stepped in and Donald had to figure out some sort of career. So he joined the military specializing in electronics. By then, I had acquired enough ability on that beat-up old acoustic that it was time for a better instrument. So, with his first paycheck from the military, Donald bought me my first real guitar: a brand-new 1977 Fender Mustang from Chuck Levin's Music Store in Wheaton, Maryland. I used that guitar right up through my first professional gigs as a teenager in Atlanta.

Looking back, I can hardly believe my luck to have been born when I was, where I was, and to have someone like Donald walk into the picture when he did. My biological father was not around very much. And, to the extent that he was, he brought a lot of chaos and danger with him. So having Donald as a cool older brother figure during that time in my life was very important.

Nobody in my immediate family played music by the time I came along. But I later found out that my grandmother on my father's side (where I found my first guitar) had wanted to be a songwriter in her youth. The story goes that she even wrote a successful tune that had gotten stolen from her. Anyhow, she ended up abandoning that dream. As I grew up and got more and more serious, she kind of relived her dream vicariously through me. Both she and my grandfather were very supportive. My grandfather bought me my first real amp: a little Ampeg solid state combo. My grandparents were both huge music fans. They'd tell me about all the amazing shows they saw at the Howard Theater in the 1930s—Duke Ellington, Fletcher Henderson, Chick Webb when Ella Fitzgerald was his singer, and my grandmother's favorite, Billie Holiday. Nana (as I called my grandmother) would always sing Billie's version of "These Foolish Things" as she cleaned the house. That was one of the first melodies I learned to pick on the guitar. But it wasn't like we sat around jamming in the living room. Playing guitar was mostly something I did alone for myself.

The rest of my family tried to be supportive or at least tolerant but it was challenging at times. When I get into something, I go at it pretty hard. There is no let-up. It's not always an easy thing to be around. My mom and my step-dad had no reference point for that level of intensity, especially around something like music, let alone coming from this little kid. It must have seemed insane, even dangerous. My whole family is really big on education. My mother was a schoolteacher who then became a lawyer. She wanted me to be a lawyer or an academic. In hindsight, knowing what I know now about the music business and the way the world works, I can totally understand where she was coming from. Despite all her reservations, I would beg my Mom to bring me to gigs I was too young to attend alone and, whenever she could, she would do it: shows like The Ramones or PiL at the Agora, Blood Ulmer at 688, and others. Mom sat through some craziness.

Except for the first couple of years when Donald was around, my first seven years of playing guitar, from ages eight to fifteen, was a very solitary pursuit. I jammed with the records my cousin and I collected, which I continued to expand after he left. By the time I was twelve, I had everything from the Stooges to Ornette Coleman to King Crimson to Prince down cold. I could imitate James Williamson, James "Blood" Ulmer, AND James Marshall Hendrix. So, at thirteen, when hardcore punk happened and a guy like Greg Ginn came across my radar, I was more than ready. It was like I was born to that music. I intuitively understood what he was doing because I had already absorbed many of the same influences he was referencing.

In summer 1982, when I was fourteen, we moved from D.C. to Atlanta (just before I found out about the whole Dischord scene—yes, tragic, I know). In Atlanta, there was no hardcore scene at all. We had to create it out of nothing. From that point on, I learned by forming bands, writing my own songs, and being onstage.

Brian: To this day, along with the DDT album, Neon Christ is what I thought of when I thought of Atlanta. I thought the seven-inch was fucking great and that it was obvious that you were a talented guitarist and writer, throwing in some odd ideas in the context of a hardcore seven-inch. The guitar work sort of sounded a little like *Jealous Again*-era Black Flag with some more speed and a few abrupt departures from the world of 1984 hardcore. How did the band self-release the record and when and where was it recorded?

William: The first Neon Christ EP was recorded in March '84 at the Avondale Towne Cinema, this old movie theater in Atlanta that was converted into a studio. There was a stage and the control room, if memory serves, was down on the floor where the rows of theater seats would have been. We set up on the stage, thrashed through our set, and that was it. The whole thing was done in an afternoon. We were very well-rehearsed because we practiced religiously every single day since forming the band. I don't remember how we paid for the studio time. For the pressing, we borrowed the money from Jimmy Demer's dad. I believe it was $600.00 to press a thousand seven-inch 45s. We got ten songs on there because they were so short. There's actually quite a few out-takes—other songs we were playing in our set during that time that were recorded but never came out. Maybe those will see the light of day at some point.

The record was released in June. Reception was good. *Maximum Rock-n-Roll* gave it a positive review. Pushead gave it one of his adjective-packed reviews in *Thrasher* magazine (I believe "rapid-fire pistol-packed bolts of hauling mayhem" was the opening phrase). Things like that meant a lot to us because, again, the scene in Atlanta was in its infancy. You could count on your fingers the number of people who would consistently show up to gigs (we knew them all by name). So we felt pretty isolated most of the time. DDT were the only other band remotely related to us and we loved those guys. They were older and we looked up to them. But our two bands were very different from one another, as it should be.

The biggest thing was the EP being embraced by the *Maximum Rock-n-Roll* crowd directly led to Jello Biafra asking us to be on the "P.E.A.C.E." compilation album. By then, we'd gone back into the studio and cut four new songs. So we gave them "Ashes

To Ashes" for the compilation. That record got us all over the world. That's when we started receiving a steady stream of letters in broken English from dozens of countries stuffed with their local currency asking us to send them the Neon Christ EP. Very cool indeed.

Brian: What was it like hitting the road in that era of punk rock?

William: Innocent is the main word that comes to mind, particularly on that Summer 1984 tour Neon Christ did right after the EP came out. We were just kids. Jimmy Demer and I couldn't legally drive a car yet. I'm not sure either of us even had our learner's permits. The entire hardcore punk culture was still pretty innocent as well, at least in most of America. The only towns that sometimes had bigger things going on were New York, L.A., the San Francisco Bay Area, perhaps D.C., Boston, and maybe Chicago (which is not to say it was easy in those places). But for most everywhere else, it was like hacking through the wilderness with a butter knife. Our innocence is what saved us. All we wanted to do was play. That's all we cared about. So, for that '84 tour, we piled into Jimmy Demer's parents' station wagon with a plywood trailer that we built ourselves for the gear and we did the best we could. You never knew where you were going to sleep. In one town, we slept outside on a skate ramp. Of course, it started raining. In another town, maybe Richmond, we pulled up to find the show was cancelled. So the local kids banded together and, within a couple of hours, they got us another venue, three opening bands, and a nice little crowd, which gave us enough money to fuel up the station wagon and get to the next town (remember, this is pre-cell phone, pre-Internet). In New York City, we had another cancellation (happened a lot in those days). We were stuck in the city with nowhere to stay and no money. So Chris Charucki (RIP) and the guys from Cause For Alarm put us up in their apartment in Alphabet City, which at that time was Heroin-Prostitution Central. Nevertheless, I remember walking—by myself—from Charucki's apartment all the way to Katz's Delicatessen (again, the innocence). Back then, as you walked in the door, the guy behind the counter would hack off a hunk of pastrami and give it out as a sample. I was so hungry (and probably looked pretty forlorn) that, when the guy saw how fast I scarfed down the sample, he hacked off another one and slid it to me. But all was not lost in the northeast. We played a really good show with Adrenalin O.D. in New Brunswick, NJ. The next day, our trailer fell apart on the Jersey Turnpike. End of tour.

Brian: To this day, it is sort of a bummer that the band's second wave of songs that you wrote for them were never properly recorded and released. I was even told that Bob Durkee of Fartblossom Records was poised to actually release this future album, but I don't know if that was true or not. Was it? And why exactly did the band dissolve?

William: I agree it's a shame that we never properly recorded those latter-day Neon Christ songs. We made a start by recording a basic track and a lead vocal for "Drawn In" on December 26, 1985. But we didn't get any farther and now, tragically, that master tape is lost. That group of songs—"Crush," "Drawn In," etc.—was our best material. We got so into it playing those songs live. To me, those songs symbolize the peak of the band and the peak of the early Atlanta hardcore scene.

I recall some talk about Bob Durkee wanting to do something with us. I remember personally not being in favor and felt that, if we were going to work with an outside label, I wanted it to be SST or perhaps even crossover to a Metal Blade like COC did. Otherwise, I just wanted to put it out ourselves like we'd done before.

The band dissolved for a number of reasons, some of them typical—getting older, growing apart, wanting to pursue different things musically—but we also had the skinhead situation. By late-1985 going into early '86, things were getting pretty intense in Atlanta. Neon Christ was a target. I, personally, was a target. It was no joke. The violence those guys were perpetrating—the beatings, the assaults, the rapes—was rampant and unrelenting.

And with some of the skins in Atlanta, we're talking about guys who were wanted for attempted murder, guys who would end up in prison or jump bail and go on the run. They were being financed by groups like John Metzger's White Aryan Resistance to travel, set up headquarters, and recruit in cities throughout the country. I suppose the fact that the Atlanta scene was growing made our town a desirable recruiting ground. So they moved in, got themselves a warehouse right across the street from the Metroplex (or main club), and started doing their typical "What the fuck, fuck shit up" routine. But beneath all the "rabble-rouser" nonsense was a very real agenda. I took what those guys were doing quite seriously. Yet, even with everything that was going on, all the awful things they were routinely doing to people all over town, I remember a lot of downplaying and rationalizing from many people in our scene: "They're not that bad." "Boys will be boys." Or my favorite: "They're nice to ME." Needless to say, I had a huge problem with those responses. There were even divisions within my band about how to deal with it all. This was pretty heady stuff for some kids who just wanted to play music. Then again, Neon Christ was never lightweight party rock. Our music addressed systemic problems in this country (which still persist today). And we were politically active outside of music. So some opposing reaction was inevitable. But by February '86, between the cops, the skinheads, the musical and personal differences, etc, it became too much and I disbanded the group. I was 18 years old.

Brian: During this time period, what kind of jobs did you have and how did you support yourself?

William: I had typical teenage jobs. I worked at Kinko's. I worked at Mellow Mushroom. Things like that.

I worked at this Ethiopian restaurant for a little while. The boss was from Ethiopia, ex-military from what I was told, expatriated to the U.S. to escape war crimes committed abroad. Whatever the real story, he was a pretty angry guy. His management style was yelling and screaming at people. The day I started working there, the cook quit because of all the verbal abuse. He left right as we were opening for the dinner shift. I'd been hired as a dishwasher. All of a sudden, I was drafted to be the cook AND the dishwasher. Although I'm now a huge fan of Ethiopian cuisine, at that point, I knew absolutely nothing about it. So it was a crash course, to say the least. But the true heartbeat of that kitchen—and the entire restaurant—was this woman, Sali. A lot of Ethiopian dishes—the stews, the sauces—require a tremendous amount of care and time. In this particular restaurant, the "cook" merely did all the short order and finishing work. But Sali did all the really hard work preparing those more involved dishes that took all day. She also did the majority of the gnarly cleaning jobs. She worked insane hours. I don't remember one moment when she wasn't there. She was an illegal immigrant from South America. The boss reserved his worst verbal abuse for her, just tore into her every chance he got, called her all sorts of awful names to her face and behind her back. Sali was a very quiet, shy, incredibly sweet person. I absolutely hated the way this man treated her. I asked Sali why she took it—that place literally could not have functioned without her. But she was so afraid. She needed the money to send home to her family. Because of her illegal status, she had no leverage. The boss would always threaten to throw her out and have her deported. I started taking the blame for "infractions" that neither Sali nor I was guilty of just to deflect some of the screaming away from her. Eventually, it got to be too much for me. It was the middle of a packed dinner shift. We were totally in the weeds. The boss flipped out on me for some needless reason, something in my mind snapped, and I just looked at him and walked out—right through the crowded restaurant and out the front door, with him still screaming behind me. A few days later, I snuck back there solely to visit Sali and apologize because I felt so terrible for leaving her there. The Neon Christ song, "Crush," is about her and the situation at that restaurant (and millions just like it). I imagined a scenario where one day Sali finally gets fed up and resorts to extreme measures.

Brian: In early 1986 you were asked to replace Steve Borek in

BL'AST!, whose first album to this very day I think is terrific. The record was sort of Steve's baby for the most part. What did you like about the band that made you decide to take a risk and go out to Santa Cruz at a very young age so soon after Neon Christ disbanded?

William: As I said, Atlanta was getting a little dangerous. I needed to get out of there. California seemed like the obvious place to go. By that point, I was friendly with Greg Ginn. We spoke on the phone regularly. Whenever Black Flag came through Atlanta, he and I would hang out or jam. One time I had Greg, Sim Cain (drummer for Gone and later the Rollins Band), and Cel Revuelta (the last bassist for Black Flag) over to the Neon Christ practice space and the four of us just jammed all afternoon (I still have a cassette of it somewhere). As you know, late-period Black Flag and the sound Ginn was exploring with his instrumental band, Gone, was quite different than the earlier Black Flag music for which the band was best known. We shared a lot of the same funk and jazz influences and a love of instrumental music and improvisation. In 1986, SST was where it was at. No-one could touch them in

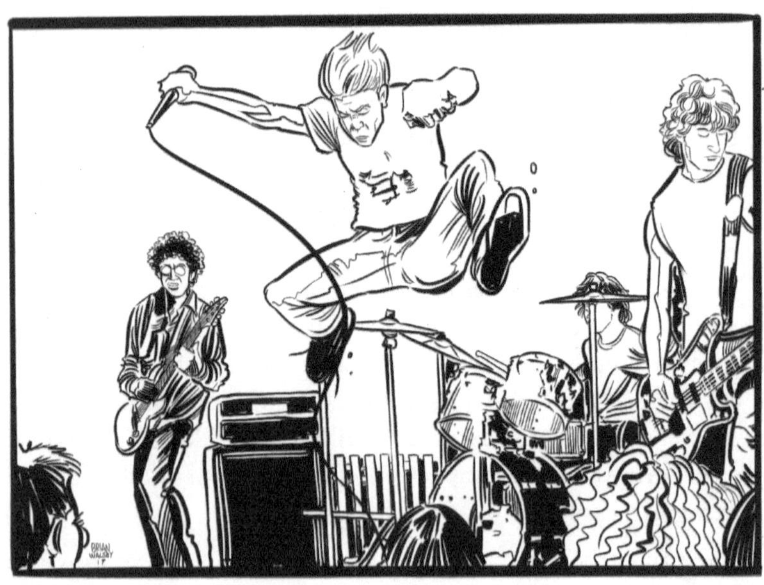

terms of musical or cultural relevance. I wanted to be involved with them in any way I could.

At the same time, I'd gotten the first BL'AST! album and really dug the sound of it. Whereas Greg Ginn had kind of moved on from the Black Flag sound of 1981-82, the BL'AST! guys really took that ball and ran with it. A lot of bands were "influenced by Black Flag," especially that period from *Damaged* to *My War*. But Steve Borek, Mike Neider, and those guys really distilled that whole aesthetic like no-one else at the time—except maybe for me. We all even played Dan Armstrong guitars. Plus they dug SSD and Sabbath. There's a certain distinct brand of heavy-osity. Those guys had it going on out west. I had a similar thing going on in Atlanta.

I got that first BL'AST! album right around the time Neon Christ broke up. I wrote to BL'AST! just to say I understood what they were doing and, if there was ever an opening, maybe we could do something. Steve Borek actually wrote me back. He basically said: That's awesome and thank you but the five guys in BL'AST! had been together since grade school and it wasn't likely that anything was going to change on their end anytime soon. A month or two later, Steve left the band.

Right around then, Reed Mullin (COC) drove down to Atlanta from Raleigh to hang out with me. We went to go see Run-DMC at the Omni. COC and BL'AST! had become friends when COC toured out west in '85. I'm not sure if the four remaining BL'AST! guys reached out to Reed about me or vice versa. But I remember riding with Reed in the old COC van back to my parents' house after the Run-DMC gig and him telling me that Steve Borek had left BL'AST! and those guys wanted me to join.

Brian: I had read that you were initially surprised that you replaced Steve, since Steve is the one who contacted you and that, although it was fun, that you were too young to be undertaking such a move and maybe you weren't the best fit for the rest of the band. I saw the band with Steve a lot and they were always great. The one time that I had seen you in the band, it was great. They were never as good again for me. What made you decide to go back home in the middle of them recording that second album? And what are your thoughts on the recently released album with your guitar tracks included?

William: I was very committed to the music we made in BL'AST! But there were a number of challenges. I had never joined a band before. I was used to forming bands and doing pretty much all of the writing—music and lyrics. The BL'AST! situation was different. Clifford [Dinsmore] wrote his own lyrics. Steve Borek had written all of the music for their first album. Now, in his absence, Mike Neider was stepping up to write a lot of music for their new material. Those guys had a very defined, long-standing camaraderie. Like Borek said in the letter he wrote me, they'd been together since grade school. So they were a tight-knit club. And, though it was never openly discussed, I think they were deeply affected by Steve suddenly leaving.

At the same time, I had been very tight with Neon Christ and all my friends back in Atlanta. I had never lived away from home. I missed everyone there very much. And I was younger than the other guys in BL'AST! I was 18 just turning 19 when I joined. Those guys were all 21-plus. At that age, those few years really make a difference.

Plus the living wasn't exactly easy. Money was always tight. I worked various jobs: at the Santa Cruz skateboard factory, at a pizza place, etc. I lived with Clifford and his roommate in this little apartment that was part of a larger house. They'd taken some thin plastic fake wood paneling and sectioned off a portion of the living room just big enough for a sleeping bag and boom box and that was my "room." That was fine. I didn't care about creature comforts. But it symbolized the whole situation. I was just sort of wedged into this scenario. We shared a love for some of the same punk bands, particularly Black Flag and the Germs. We shared a belief in putting across maximum energy onstage. But everything else was a bit ill-fitting.

Nevertheless, I remain VERY proud of the work we did. It was amazing for me to play shows in California. The scale of some of those gigs was incredible—thousands of kids in these huge halls to see a punk show. Bodies flying all over the place. Multiple pits going on simultaneously. I'd heard and read about the California scene for years. To actually experience it firsthand was awesome. Several of the shows I played with BL'AST! remain among the most memorable I've ever played anywhere to this day. It was also a tremendous honor getting signed to SST and recording the *It's In My Blood* album. I wrote the music for the song "Sequel" and most of the lyrics to the song "Poison." I actually didn't leave in the middle of recording. I did the entire album, plus the covers of the Germs ("The Slave") and Alice Cooper ("School's Out"). As I recall, all of that music was recorded in a single day. We set up in the studio just like we did live and ran it all down. But then I left the group and Mike Neider went back and re-recorded most of my tracks. He couldn't re-do my parts on "Sequel," though because there were too many starts, stops, and weird pauses that I controlled. You had to be in the same room looking at one another to get those right.

I love *Blood*, the reissue of the album that Dave Grohl remixed and Southern Lord released in 2013. I think it rights a great wrong in restoring all my guitar tracks. That version of BL'AST! was awesome and *Blood* more closely captures how we actually sounded. I think it's a miracle that the original master tape was found. I had dinner with Clifford a few years ago in San Francisco when Alice In Chains was playing the Shoreline Amphitheater. He told me the tape was found in a storage unit. It had been sitting there for 30 years. Incredible.

Brian: When you went back to Atlanta you formed the short-lived band The Final Offering. I interviewed fellow band member Mike Dean about it. He said that he thought looking back that you just sort of confused the kids who might have had expectations with your punk rock pedigrees. You always said that you were bummed that this was the project that sort of got away from you for various reasons. I also understand that your late drummer struggled with drugs, which sort of puts things out of anyone's control. What are your thoughts on that short-lived band looking back?

William: I absolutely loved The Final Offering. I just wish we could have done more. There's no doubt in my mind that we would have made a major impact had we been able to work more. Mike Dean on the bass was the Geezer Butler of our generation. Greg Psomas (ex-DDT) was a total savage on the drums. He was our Keith Moon or Chuck Biscuits. And, like both of those guys, Greg had major problems with substance abuse. We would book a tour and, on the eve of departure, Greg would disappear. Mike and I would have to call the venues and cancel. It was tough. We could never establish any real momentum. We never got into the studio. Beyond how hard it was on the band, on a personal level, it broke my heart. I loved Greg Psomas. He was a local hero of mine since I was fifteen years old. And now he was in my band! It was like a dream-come-true. But it soon became a nightmare. I hated seeing Greg struggle like that. I tried to let him know how loved and important he was. I begged him to get help. But he genuinely felt trapped. I know he felt ashamed. He didn't want to let us down. He just didn't see a way out. I'll never forget the night I spotted him through the crowd in a club and started walking toward him to say hello. He looked up and saw me, a terrible sadness came over his face, and he just turned and slinked away. It was the last time I ever saw him.

Brian: I don't know too much about what you did musically or otherwise, until you decided to bring the band Comes With The Fall out to Los Angeles years later. I think we are talking a pretty lengthy amount of time. What were the bands that you had in this time period, and also what were you doing between bands? How did you support yourself? I also understand you started to write songs that ended up being given to a woman who had a hit with it, which might be your brush with bigger (for a lack of better words) things.

William: The Final Offering was so named because I knew going in, regardless of however long the band lasted or however much it succeeded or failed, it would be the last thing I would do that was firmly rooted in the hardcore scene. I needed to stretch out further. So, in late-1988, after the Final Offering imploded, I placed an ad in the Creative Loafing (local Atlanta weekly paper) looking for my Elvin Jones. I got a call that eventually led me to Matthew Cowley, a genuine jazz dynamo, a real-deal red-headed Elvin Jones. I went to meet Matt in the rehearsal room he used on the Georgia Tech campus (he was a member of the school's jazz band) and a bass player named Hank Schroy was there. Hank played like a combination of Jaco Pastorius and a young Charles Mingus. It was like magic. Just like that, I had my next band. We immediately started jamming. I named the group No Walls because, musically speaking, there was nowhere we couldn't go.

The chemistry was immediate and indescribable. Our improv jams were transcendent. And my songwriting really blossomed because, for the first time, I had no restrictions. No Walls pulled together ALL of my influences. It was like Hendrix, Ornette, Prince, Sonic Youth, Nusrat Fateh Ali Khan, and more all thrown into a blender. Hank Schroy used his bass to respond to my vocal lines the way Jaco did with Joni Mitchell on albums like *Hejira* and *Don Juan's Reckless Daughter*. Right from the start, we somehow effortlessly combined rock, jazz, punk, and world music in a really singular way.

I gave a cassette of some of our songs to Vernon Reid of Living Colour. At that time, late 1989, Living Colour were one of the hottest bands in the world—platinum album sales, heavy radio and MTV rotation, stadium tours with the Stones, critical acclaim—the whole package. Vernon had the ears of a lot of influential people. So, in 1990, he brought No Walls to New York City with the express intent of showcasing us to every record label possible. We played all over town—CBGB's, the Bitter End, Woody's (Ron Wood's club), the Cat Club, etc. He also took us to Electric Lady (the studio Hendrix built) to record a new tape to shop around. When Living Colour made the cover of Rolling Stone, No Walls even got favorably mentioned in the article. David Fricke said we were like "a psychedelicized Prince in a Mahavishnu-Minutemen mode."

It was a great time in many ways and Vernon could not have been more supportive. But, at the end of the day, all the labels passed. They just didn't see it. They said we had "no songs," meaning that, in their opinion, I wasn't writing obvious hit singles. I now understand that "no songs" is a widely-deployed industry dismissal that's been used against nearly every artist in my record collection. But, at the time, it really devastated me. I took my songwriting extremely personally. I WAS my songs. As for "obvious hit singles," I knew I wasn't writing those, nor was I trying to. No Walls songs were more like poetry sung over jazzy rock music. The lyrics were often free-associative. The whole atmosphere was meant to be open, leaving a lot of room for improvisation. Onstage, Matt Cowley would keep his eyes trained on me the entire time from behind his drums, looking for subtle signals and dynamic shifts, his long red hair hanging straight down, arms flying like Shiva around a torso that was perfectly straight and unmoving. No Walls never played a song the same way twice.

Again, I was thinking of Hendrix, The Doors, Joni, etc. Some of the more in-the-know musos who'd come to see us would liken No Walls to Tim Buckley. I hadn't heard Tim's music at first but would soon come to regard him as another kindred spirit. Given those precedents from the sixties, I figured surely there was more than enough room for an updating of that approach in the nineties. Are "obvious hit singles" really the only barometer of success? And what does that even mean? Is "Purple Haze" an obvious hit single? Is "Kashmir" by Led Zeppelin? Is anything off of Joni Mitchell's *Hejira*? I was 23 years old and very much at a loss for how to deal with such assessments of my work. No Walls was coming from such a pure place. We wholeheartedly believed in what we were doing. We had some important tastemakers in New York on our side who felt like we were the "way forward" for contemporary rock music. The fact that none of that was enough made the rejection extremely painful, to the point that it threw me into a tailspin for quite a few years. But it was a powerful lesson. It was my first confrontation with the vagaries of the music industry. Coming from punk rock, I'd had no interest in, let alone contact with, any aspect of the commercial music world. So, naïve as it may sound, I actually found it surprising that the gate-keepers often don't know what they want or why they want it. It's all just a game. I truly did not understand how arbitrary it all was until I was directly faced with it.

I knew then that there was no way I could let my life be wholly governed by the machinations of people whose tastes and motivations I did not respect. I had to figure out a way to exist as a musician on multiple levels at once. I would have to develop my craft as well as my knowledge of history and business to the point that I could walk into any musical situation and contribute something meaningful. I had to forge myself into something that could not be destroyed no matter what.

After putting out one record on a local Atlanta indie label, No Walls disbanded in 1992. By 1995, I was the co-writer of the most played song on American pop radio for that year. "I Know" by Dionne Farris got to Number 4 on the Billboard Hot 100 and was an airplay juggernaut all over the world. So much for "no songs."

Dionne had just left the successful rap group Arrested Development and was looking for a solo deal as a singer. She sought out my friend David Harris, leader of the noted Atlanta funk-rock band, Follow For Now. David told her that, if he was going to be attached to her project, he also wanted his favorite writer, William DuVall, onboard. Milton Davis, a talented writer from Birmingham, Alabama, also joined the fold and the three of us began knocking around song ideas a la Holland-Dozier-Holland in the mid-sixties at Motown. "I Know" was something Milton and I put together. We recorded Dionne singing that and a few other tunes into David Harris's 4- track cassette recorder and that tape got Dionne signed to Columbia Records. The album, *Wild Seed, Wild Flower* came out in late-1994. "I Know" became the first single and that was that. Suddenly, she's performing it on

Letterman, Leno, *Saturday Night Live*, etc. The song is zooming up the charts. It's everywhere on pop radio. Then, one day, I got a check. And then another. And then another. Finally, I had some significant tangible success to show my family. When the song took off, I was working as a barista/waiter in a local coffee shop. I quit that job and have never had a "normal" job since. I was 27 years old.

I would be remiss if I didn't mention my biological father dying in February 1994. His passing had a profound effect on me. As stated before, he always traveled in an aura of chaos and danger and (likely for the better) was rarely around when I was little. But he and I had begun reconnecting in the early nineties. I came to understand a lot about him, why he'd made some of his mistakes. Suffice it to say, along with his flaws, he was also a tough, sensitive, extremely well-read and knowledgeable guy who suffered many trials and tribulations and who went to his grave with a lot of regrets. His life would make a pretty epic book. It was good getting to know him during the time we had. And it was really sad that it got cut off so abruptly. But talk about a motivational force: watching your dad go into the ground prematurely with a ton of regrets, seeing your own name on his gravestone (we share first, middle, and last names) at the age of 26, and seeing your grandparents lose BOTH their sons within six years (they lost my uncle Kenneth in 1988). If all that doesn't motivate you to move the ball down the field and put some points on the board, then I don't know what will.

One last thing to note is that right around the time Columbia Records was promoting the Dionne Farris album, they were also giving a huge promotional push to another artist by the name of Jeff Buckley. Jeff was the son of Tim Buckley, the singer-songwriter to whom the hipster musos would sometimes compare No Walls. Jeff was a singer/guitarist combining rock, jazz, and world music in his own way. His style of writing and performing was very free, open, and improvisational. When he performed with his full band, his drummer, also named Matt, would keep his eyes fixed on Jeff awaiting any signals or dynamic shifts, long brown hair hanging straight down amid flailing arms and a straight unmoving torso. Jeff had moved to New York City in the very early nineties and developed his reputation as a solo performer around Manhattan. I would later learn that we had some mutual acquaintances in the city. Jared Nickerson, who helped promote No Walls shows at CBGB's, was Jeff's first bass player in town. Is it possible that Jeff could have even seen No Walls play and perhaps been inspired? I still don't know. I met Jeff a couple of times but I never asked him. In any event, his rise being virtually concurrent with No Walls's demise around such a very specific and unusual musical approach just goes to show how things transpire in this crazy music business. That said, make no mistake, I absolutely loved Jeff Buckley's work and was heartbroken over his untimely passing.

Tim also died early so there was an element of romantic tragedy and unsettled scores. Then Jeff comes along twenty years later looking a lot like his dad. He's handsome, plays a mean guitar, and he's an unbelievable singer. He had it all. And he got the bounce. Deservedly so. He was incredible. But, because of what I had been through with No Walls just a few years before, there were moments that were admittedly tough for me to watch.

Brian: Did you meet him or anything?

William: Oh, sure. Yeah. When he first came to Atlanta, he played a place called Eddie's Attic in Decatur. There were five people in the audience and I brought one of them with me (it was Jimmy Demer). I think Jeff had that EP out, *Live At Sin-é*. He was playing solo—no band. He went up with just a bottle of Guinness, a Telecaster, and a tiny Fender amp. And he fucking destroyed. I soon found out that Jeff and I had mutual friends in New York and it's possible that he knew of No Walls. I never found out for sure but it was just eerie, all of the things that we had in common. The point is he came along and did his thing. He got his band together, did the *Grace* album, and I loved it.

Like all serious musicians, he had his own struggles with art and commerce. He was trying to figure out a lot very quickly under pressure. It was probably even more of a struggle because his tastes were more exotic and esoteric than a lot of the "rock" rock bands, you know? He was into so many different kinds of music. He was fluent in a variety of styles. Had his only goal been fame and money, he could have easily done the "blue eyed soul" thing to death. But he was after something more interesting. Plus there was this punk rock thing of, "I don't want to get too big too fast." I think all of us from that generation were processing our ideas about what "success" means in our own way. It was especially challenging for musicians who came out of the early eighties underground scene. Many of us struggled with how we should (or shouldn't) appeal to more mainstream audiences. It was an interesting time.

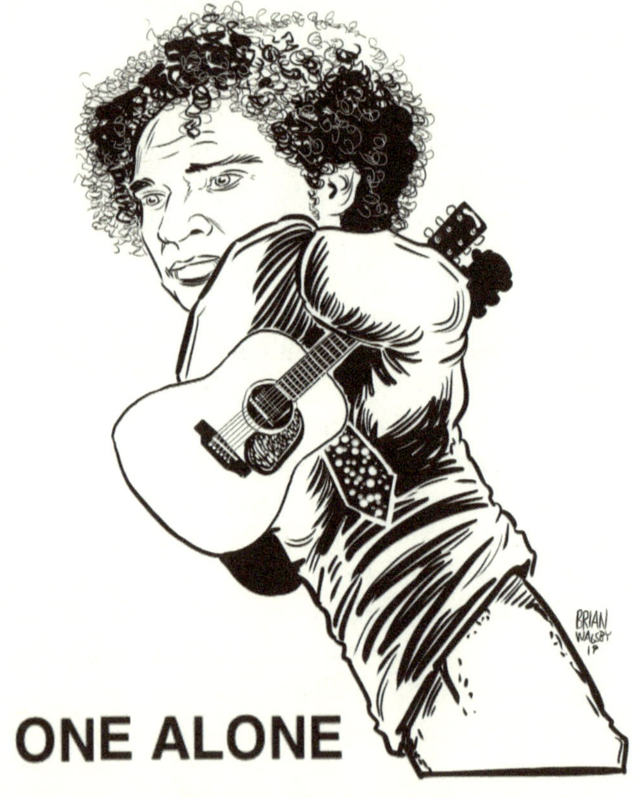

He had the full backing of Columbia Records behind him while playing music that was very progressive. He got the bounce. It was gratifying to see but it was tough at points for me. I was still just a kid, man. I was twenty, twenty-one years old when No Walls started. So when we were going through our whole hassle with the music industry, when those people rejected us the way that they did... You have to understand the idealism that I had at that age. Looking back on my own struggles, I guess it all worked out for the best. I'm still here. And I'm still doing work that I believe in very strongly.

Brian: What made you decide to be a singer after being a guitarist songwriter for so long?

William: No Walls made me a singer. I was writing things that I couldn't imagine handing off to anyone else to sing. So, with the encouragement of Hank and Matt, I gave it a shot.

Brian: What made you decide to relocate to Los Angeles with your band? That is quite a move. It can be sort of a weird place at times, and this comes from someone who grew up there. How did you meet Jerry Cantrell and how did he decide that he wanted you and the rest of your band to back him for his touring activity?

William: By the time Comes With The Fall came along in 1999, I was out of the tailspin that the No Walls experience had put me into at the beginning of the decade. I had taken a lot of the money earned from "I Know" and invested it by putting myself through a kind of record production grad school with Madfly, the band I formed from late-1995 to 1998. Madfly put out two albums, both of which I produced, and both of which tackled a pretty wide variety of musical styles. For our second album, I started DVL Recordings in order to do a worldwide distribution deal with Mercury Records through Joan Jett's Blackheart label. By this point, I was long past any illusions that someone was going to come along and "discover" us. And I wanted to own my work. We had a manager who was a radio promo man by trade. And he actually got a couple of our songs to chart in several territories. So

Madfly was an important step forward for me in terms of record production and business knowledge. But the overall presentation and the actual music, while there certainly were some good tunes there, still wasn't right. I still cared too much about being liked. By late-summer '99, however, I finally stopped caring. Something snapped back into place and I found the 16-year-old me again who didn't give a flying fuck. Only now, I was imbued with all this experience, all this musical knowledge and craft that I didn't have before. The new music I was writing reflected ALL of that and I realized that this was yet another renaissance. It needed a new name. So out with Madfly, in with Comes With The Fall.

As soon as Comes With The Fall recorded our first album in Autumn of 1999, we realized that we needed a change of scenery. By that point, I had done just about all one could do as part of the Atlanta music scene—hardcore punk, avant garde, jazz-rock, chart-topping pop success. Who else in the city had a career that varied? Yet there we were still scrounging for gigs at the local bar like a bunch of beginners. My bandmate, Nico Constantine, put it bluntly: "If we don't get you out of here, you'll die an unsung hero." I've never forgotten that and I really owe him for getting me to leave. I never would have done it on my own.

We chose Los Angeles because it seemed like more of a car city and a band city. Comes With The Fall had stacks of amps and big drums. We could never be a hop-on-the-subway New York City band. Plus L.A. had the weather. So in February 2000, we made the move, arriving on Valentine's Day.

As soon as we got there, literally the second we got out of our vehicles, it was like we'd been running uphill with ankle weights on for years and suddenly the weights fell off and the ground leveled out. It was unbelievable. We hit the ground running immediately, playing every club in Hollywood. We also seemed to have no trouble getting invited to a lot of parties and exclusive hangs, whether they were at bars or people's houses. Within the first six months alone, we'd accumulated memorable hang-out experiences with everyone from David Lee Roth to George

Clooney to Benicio del Toro. It was surreal and hilarious. Looking back, I suppose we had an aura about us. Most so-called bands around L.A. at that time were "projects." They didn't play gigs, they played "showcases." Comes With The Fall was a BAND in every sense of the word. We landed in L.A. like a gang. We'd been through everything and we didn't give a fuck. That's attractive to people, especially in a place like Hollywood. So we had a good time.

One of the first people we met during our first couple of months in L.A. was Jerry Cantrell. Our drummer's ex-girlfriend from Atlanta had moved to L.A. about a year before us and she hooked up with Cantrell. She was a true-believer in what we were doing and pestered him to listen to the first Comes With The Fall album. When he finally did, he was blown away and asked to meet me. We met at this club called the Dragonfly and from that day forward became pretty inseparable. Cantrell was over at our apartment all the time. Eventually, he ended up renting a place downstairs from us in the same building. And he started appearing with us at all our gigs around Hollywood. He'd asked me to teach him a couple of songs from our first album—"We Come Undone" and "The 3 Wishes"—and he would jump onstage to jam those with us at whatever club we were playing. One time, our bass player got locked up in Atlanta and couldn't make this gig we had booked at the Cat Club on Sunset. We were about to call and cancel when Cantrell said, "I'll play bass." And he did. He learned our full set on bass and played that gig with us.

People thought he was joining our band. But he was finishing up his *Degradation Trip* album, which he hadn't found a label to put out yet. By early 2001, the album was done and he wanted to play shows despite not having a label or a new release. He didn't have a band either. Mike Bordin and Robert Trujillo, with whom he'd recorded his album, were both busy with Ozzy Osbourne. There CWTF were, a self-contained badass band right under Cantrell's nose. So he asked if we would help him out. We toured all of 2001 around the States and Canada. Then, in 2002, Cantrell signed a deal with Roadrunner Records to release *Degradation Trip*. So Roadrunner put us back out on the road and we spent all of 2002 revisiting the States and Canada and also touring through the UK.

From my perspective, this was fantastic because all I wanted was for CWTF to reach people directly without answering to any corporate middlemen. This was a dream scenario and we rose to the occasion, remaining prolific the entire time. During that first year of hectic touring, we recorded and released our second album, *The Year Is One*, in October 2001. It got some great press, including another stellar review from David Fricke in Rolling Stone, some good college radio airplay in America, and some good airplay in England on prominent specialty programs like the Rock Show on BBC One. Then, when the crazy touring schedule in 2002 didn't allow enough time to write and record another studio record, I decided to make a live album. *Live 2002* was recorded over three consecutive nights on the road in May and released in October 2002.

In the two years since our arrival in L.A. and the release of *Live 2002*, we'd seen nearly a dozen of those "showcase" bands we knew from around L.A. who'd signed major label deals (often for insane amounts of money) completely evaporate into thin air. Some got to put out their records and tour a little bit. Others didn't even make it that far. Meanwhile, we were selling truckloads of ALL THREE of our albums directly to fans after shows. It was abundantly clear to me which path to keep forging. I still get fans to this day coming up or writing me to share their memories of those tours. It was an extraordinary time. And it obviously completely paved the way for what ended up happening with Alice.

Brian: I wasn't a super fan of Alice In Chains, but I really liked *Dirt* a lot and to this day maintain that the band has a unique sound, with the metallic well-written songwriting and melancholy sound of the twin lead vocals approach. It is a unique sound that is the band's own and they maintain it with you as seamlessly as they did with their late lead singer, Layne Staley. What was it like to slot yourself in there musically with Jerry?

William: The harmonizing was always pretty easy from the start. All you have to do is listen. I will say that on our records a lot of attention is given to phrasing and pronunciation. Whichever one of us writes the lyric usually sings it first in the studio. Then the other guy has to match the phrasing EXACTLY, even down to the slightest variation of vowel sounds. That can be time- consuming but when you layer that precise approach multiple times, it creates this feeling that we're one person. Even we can't always tell who sang what on some of our tracks.

Brian: I think it took a lot of courage to replace such a loved figure. How did you deal with the scrutiny you faced initially? Because now with the three albums under your belt, there is little anyone can say other than they just don't like it if they don't like it. You have proven yourself and the rest of the band has your back all of the time. Any thoughts on any of that?

William: I just do my thing, same as always. The external circumstances and surroundings may have changed but the essential motivation from the time I was eight years old has remained exactly the same. When I let that carry the day, I tend to do alright.

Brian: It is kind of heartwarming to me that to this very day, you are very tight with the ex-Neon Christ band members Jimmy, Randy and Danny. Why is it so important that you remained friends after all of this time? Also, you had reformed the band over ten years ago and did a few shows to help spearhead that movie project that has seemingly been put on hold. Is there ever going to be a chance where that project is finished and also, is there any chance that the mission Neon Christ will ever be re recorded for the hell of it?

William: We are all still close and it's very gratifying. I'm actually seeing Jimmy Demer tonight for dinner. There's a lot of water under the bridge but there are also lots of exciting things happening right now. Some of us have kids who are now the same age as we were when we first got together. So we have our memories but what's really nice is to have people with whom you share that amount of history that can help you process the present day.

We definitely want to do something with all the material gathered for the film. It got "bogged down in committee," as the saying goes. There were some changes in the production personnel. But it's such a worthwhile endeavor. I have faith that we'll see it through. As for recording those latter-day Neon Christ songs that were never properly documented back in the day, it's something we've talked about. I don't spend a lot of time looking back but I must admit, when I do take the occasional glance over the shoulder, there are a few things that nag me a bit. One of them is that Neon Christ never made that album we talked about back in '85. The main thing is that, in our opinion, the songs still hold up. So, if we do it, it would be for that reason.

Brian: "Drawn In" is still one of my all time favorite "missing in action" songs from the eighties. What is that song about anyways?

William: It's about the sense of loss and betrayal I felt over the scene that I'd relied on as my one safe haven suddenly no longer being safe. And I don't just mean because of cops or skinheads. "Drawn In" is about the people whom I regarded as friends who rationalized and excused what the Nazi skinheads were doing. I was always a misfit toy. I still am. Punk rock saved my life. Of course, the music was tremendously important and I still listen to some of those records. But the friendships, that sense of not being alone anymore, not feeling like I was "wrong" or insane all the time, was what really did it for me. And then to form a band and write songs that spoke to people and watch an entire scene build itself, in part, around what I was doing was, for a kid like me who'd felt alone most of my life, absolutely unbelievable. So to witness it all start falling apart over these major divisions—not just between the newcomers in our growing scene but between myself and the people I'd regarded as my core group of friends—was tough to take, especially at that age.

Brian: Is there anything that you have learned in your background of being involved in the world of the DIY culture that eighties hardcore punk introduced to you that you use to this very day in the year 2019?

William: I was absolutely shaped by the DIY culture I came up in as a teenager. The fact that we turned out to be right and our little grassroots thing ended up transforming the entire world is still a trip to me. But the basic lessons still apply: If something is important to you, SAY IT. Trumpet it from every rooftop you can find. And, if you can't find a rooftop, build one. Just the fact that you say something is cool, that alone makes it cool. That is its own validation. And, if you sit around waiting for the world-at-large to agree with you, you will miss your moment. Every great moment that I ever had as a musician, whether it was Neon Christ or Comes With The Fall or things that are going to take place in the near future, it was because I created the moment and documented it. My only regrets in my career are those occasions when, for whatever reason, I wasn't able to properly document the moment (as in the case of latter-day Neon Christ and The Final Offering).

Brian: You have a record label that you've started to release the new album.

William: That's right. I started DVL Recordings over twenty years ago. It was originally started to put out the second album by my band from the late nineties, Madfly. Throughout the 2000s, the label released all of the albums by Comes With The Fall, as well as a record by Jimmy Demer's band, Accidents. But only within the last ten years has it been officially incorporated and operated as a registered business entity. So DVL Recordings put out my debut solo album, *One Alone*, in October 4, 2019. And the label could release whatever I do in the future. It operates both as a vehicle for any new music that I want to do and also as a curator and custodian for the catalogue of things that I've done.

It has been a lot of work. I'm making a real attempt at a solo career that can coexist with whatever else I do. So I started a merchandise company to handle the merch element. And I started a touring company to handle my touring business. Managing all of that is a tremendous amount of work indeed.

Brian: Have you encountered any snags that you weren't really expecting along the way?

William: Nothing too major. It's definitely a learning curve. But I've always worked hard. I still have the self-starter DIY mindset that goes back to the early eighties hardcore days and what I witnessed first-hand with some of the people that I admired back then, especially the SST guys. But it's still a learning curve because I'm operating from a different vantage point now. I'm no longer a kid. And I'm no longer a complete unknown to the wider world like I was for years.

I'm sort of on a dual mission. The primary mission is to keep pushing forward with new music and get that out to the widest audience possible through whatever means makes the most sense. And then there's this other mission to continue nurturing an audience for my past work. For instance, DVL Recordings could end up being a vehicle for Neon Christ reissues. We've even discussed recording some of the material that never got properly recorded during our latter days as a band. So, even though I'm mainly all about pushing forward, there is all of this history. The label can serve both of those interests.

Brian: How has the reaction been to your new record so far?

William: It's been great. Being solo acoustic, this album seems to cast a wider net than some of the electric rock music I've done. My Mom likes this record. My ten-year-old son likes this record. Alice and CWTF fans like it. Fans of folk and even religious music, who hadn't previously heard of me at all, like it. Not all the music I do has that sort of range. So it's an interesting time and an interesting record to put out at this point in my career. I'm just trying to see where it goes. I've been touring on this album and that's been a trip in itself. I'd never performed solo before and it's really challenging. There's nothing to hide behind. You either got it or you don't. And touring is different as well. Just one guy. There are no other guys. No band. And no gear, except two acoustics. There's just me, a tour manager that doubles as my sound man, and my tour manager's wife selling the merch. That's it.

My mindset at the moment is very minimalist, very survivalist. In many ways, what I'm doing now hearkens back to the early punk days.

It's me on the phone with the merch manufacturers. It's me phoning and emailing the record pressing plants. I'm personally picking up and hauling the boxes of shirts and records. At the moment, I'm doing all the packing and shipping for all orders at my U.S. online store. I personally packed and shipped nearly a thousand pre-orders in the week leading up to my October 4 release day. I handle all the invoicing and billing for all of my companies. I run my own social media, including every ad that goes out. I created my business account with Facebook. I create all my own ads. That's me logging into the Facebook Ad Manager, creating my target audiences all over the world, and launching my ads to those audiences. I try to stay informed on how these algorithms work and how they change. I do all my own data analysis. I set up my Facebook pixels and Google Analytics accounts. I built my U.S. online store. I build my own landing pages. I create and manage all my web domains and branded URLs. I create and maintain my company accounts with GS1. I create my own UPCs and ISRCs.

It's a lot, but I feel it's important to know how to navigate these systems myself. That way, if I ever delegate any of this to someone else down the road, I'll never be asking them to do something I haven't actually done myself. And if they ever leave, I'm won't be completely lost.

Who knows how all of this will work out in the long run? I'm at a new place with this album, both in terms of art and business. It's an interesting crossroads because I'm well-known in certain quarters but I still have this DIY mindset. I'm willing to do a lot of nitty-gritty tasks that perhaps some people in my position likely wouldn't do.

Brian: Everything that you have done has led you to this point now, where you are becoming your own boss. So that is pretty cool.

William: Yeah. At least I'm making an honest effort. God knows, it's a lot of juggling—as an artist, as a business person, and as a parent. In the last twenty four hours alone, I took my son to the skate park. Then we went to his friend's birthday party, the second of two kid's parties this weekend. I don't do the drop-off-and-leave thing. I stay on the premises, partly because "you never know" and also because I like to see him interacting with his friends. He's not going to be ten forever. Before I know it, he'll be driving himself places. So I stay at these things and enjoy it while I can. So the skate park and the party took up the entire morning and afternoon. Then we got home, I made his dinner, got him through bath time and bedtime. And then I went to work. I filmed fourteen shout-out videos for fourteen of the cities on my upcoming tour—these will be used for Facebook ads. Then I autographed twelve hundred limited edition stickers that are going on the front cover of the European and UK editions of the *One Alone* LP, which are being pressed in England and Germany right now. All of that kept me up until 5:00 a.m. I laid down for an hour, got back up at 6:00 a.m. to take my son to school, drove back home, and got right back to work. I was on the phone to my U.K. merch manufacturer. I was on the phone to my European merch manufacturer. Then I called the vinyl pressing plant in Berlin… And that's just this morning. I still have about six or seven calls to make to the west coast.

Brian: I think people just don't realize how much work really goes into things if you are doing it for yourself. Especially music. They think it's just some big party all of the time. It's work.

William: Writing and recording a record, as challenging as that can be, is nothing compared to coordinating a worldwide promotional campaign that creates some impact. That's where the real work begins. I learned from the No Walls experience that I had to start thinking long-term about playing music. That was when I truly began understanding what the term "lifer" meant. I always knew that I was going to do nothing else with my life but play music. But to realize what "lifer" meant on a visceral level was humbling, especially coming into adulthood with all those practical-life responsibilities encroaching on my reality. You know, like family members looking at me and tapping their fingers on their watches… like, "Okaaaay! Time's a-wastin! What's the plan?"

Brian: Until you get old enough to the point where all they want out of you is to just be happy. (laughter)

William: My family certainly wanted me to be happy. But they were also worried, justifiably so. They had valid questions and I had no answers. There were a lot of dark moments, especially since I didn't get the lucky bounce early on. After No Walls, I was 24 years old with no tangible success to show for any of the work that I had done. I had a small taste of validation when punk rock broke big: Nirvana comes along and blows up the whole world and they're literally doing it on the shoulders of you and me, all of our friends, and all of the bands that we knew. So I could say to my Mom, "See? We were right!" But that's all it was—a tiny drop of personal validation. It meant nothing in terms of paying the rent.

I haven't had a regular job since I was 27. That's the age that Hendrix, Cobain, and so many others I admire were when they died. Yet, in many ways, that's the age when my professional life truly began. It hasn't been an easy ride by any stretch. There have been a lot of twists and turns, a lot of craziness. The only thing that's gotten me through was an absolute kamikaze level of determination. I have all of these experiences. Some of them are cool. Some of them are heartbreaking. But the end result is that I can walk into pretty much any situation and not get faded. I can walk into anything and be myself. That's not to say that everybody's always going to love what I'm doing. It just means I have a stronger core of self-assurance to withstand whatever happens.

Brian: You have carved out a very lengthy career as a musician and a songwriter. Was there ever a time where you felt close to taking a break and doing something else?

William: There have been some dark days. There were even times when I WISHED I could just "be normal" and do something else. But there is nothing else for me. This is it. The fact that I had no choice is what got me through the tough times. Sometimes it was pure anger, pure grief, pure sorrow, or pure stubbornness—just not wanting to give any of those naysaying fucks the satisfaction. But mostly it's been my love for this thing and the demands that I put on myself—to keep chasing, to dive deeper, to keep learning, and to get better. And, of course, I am my own final arbiter as to what all of that means.

Dennis Jagard

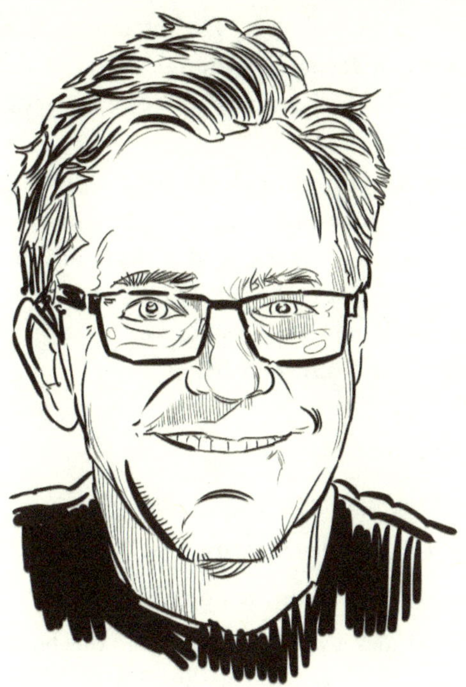

I met Dennis Jagard the same night I met Scott Radinsky, when both of them were playing in the short-lived band S.O.F. at a battle of the bands event in Simi Valley at the infamous Holiday Roller Rink. It was hilarious. But I desperately wanted to be friends with these guys, and I drew cartoons. That was my way in. It was a long time ago.

I joined their next band Scared Straight at the end of 1984 and spent a lot of time with Dennis in that year or so, which seemed like five years.

Then I moved away in the spring of 1986. I hadn't talked to Dennis since then, until this year when I sent him an email about interviewing him for this project.

I knew about his dual career, I knew he was a sound engineer and had worked for a lot of different people over the years.

I also knew that Dennis' band activity sort of fizzled out as his professional career took over. The interesting thing about talking to Dennis was it seemed as though thirty years didn't seem to fly by at all, we fell right into a nice conversation that is represented here.

I was also interested in the struggle Dennis offers as far as wanting to keep his band going when he could, and in sacrificing those creative outlets for the good of his family and hunting down steady work. As anyone knows, it isn't easy to be self-employed, and it is certainly not easy keeping a band going either. But trying to do both. That is a little different.

♫

Brian: How long have you lived in Idaho?

Dennis: A little over eleven years now.

Brian: Were you in California up until that point?

Dennis: Yeah. I met a woman from Idaho on the road, brought her to California, got married, then lived in California for ten years. While visiting her family often in Boise, one of my favorite past times was looking at housing listings. At the time I moved here, in California the smallest shack was about half million dollars. And in Idaho the smallest shack was fifty thousand dollars—I could buy a whole house for under 100k.

There are some downsides, of course, like a lot fewer opportunities here and lower pay. But if I am getting work out of town my money goes a lot further. It is funny, my mortgage isn't much less than what I would have paid to rent in L.A., but at the end of the day, I am owning a house instead of renting. I am currently living off of a second mortgage, which is based on the collateral of the home I have been living in that I have been paying on in the last eleven years. It's almost like a little saving fund that I am spending now because I am unemployed at the moment.

Brian: I have ties to you going back to the early eighties back to Simi Valley, California, where we met and grew up. I met both you and Scott Radinsky when you were both in the band S.O.F. I don't remember the year exactly but you played guitar and Scott played drums and you were playing at the roller rink battle of the bands in town.

Dennis: I don't remember when you took over with the drums.

Brian: It was in the fall of 1984.

Dennis: So we met a few years before.

Brian: You guys played a bunch of covers.

Dennis: Yes, some covers and some originals. We played up against local bands that were much older than us. We were about thirteen? We won the first week, we were up against guys who were much older and had much more professional bands. We did have a little advantage—my dad had a sound and stage company and we had a little sound system, two-foot risers, a real stage. The first week we did really well, we had a good set. The second week the bass player got in a fight with his brother in the parking lot, got drunk and came up and played the songs all wrong.

Brian: A drunk thirteen year old messing up the songs.

Dennis: Yeah. Which was kind of sad, because this was the finals and we just sucked. It was pretty punk.

Brian: You guys played against Lizzy Borden and you beat them! (laughter)

Dennis: We played with one band, called Day One, that was very professional—they had fog machines and a light show, all these guys that looked like they were in Journey—they were really serious. The first week, the other bands were PISSED because these little kids came in and won it.

Brian: No one really knew about punk rock so it was kind of exciting. I ended up joining your band, and it was in all reality a really short amount of time but it seemed like it went on forever, probably because we were all so young. What was also really interesting, and I brought this up with Scott Radinsky, is that our parents fucking let us go on tour across the country. That seems utterly crazy now.

Dennis: Yeah, we were in a generation where parents didn't do that helicopter parenting vibe, for the most part. As long as you were home at a reasonable time, it was generally pretty relaxed and there wasn't this fear that you were going to get abducted that is prevalent now. We were aware that bad things happened—there was this scoutmaster that molested some kids that were friends of ours—there was gnarly stuff going on, but for whatever reason our parents let us go. My parents didn't put up any resistance. I was kind of a model student. I got good grades and was responsible and helped my dad out with his business and worked pretty hard. I did a pretty good job setting up sound equipment and stages for events.

Brian: When did you start doing audio?

Dennis: I was about ten years old. My dad was a defense contractor, he had worked for NASA and then Litton, building inertial navigation systems for cruise missiles and things like that. So he was really into the electronic side of jet fighters and stuff. But on the side he also did films and sound, so for him it was a side gig, almost like a hobby. My first paying job was to work 100 hours for him, to reimburse him for the $90 he paid to send me to Boy Scout camp. And it grew from there.

I turned 17 on our first tour in the summer of 1985, that first tour where our equipment got stolen. I missed the first day of the tour because it was right at the Fourth of July, our biggest sound day of the year. I was working at a football stadium in Northridge, like a ten thousand person show. So we had a huge stage and sound system, and I couldn't leave town during that. As far as my parents were concerned, I think as long as I got good grades and didn't miss work, I was okay to tour.

Brian: You have no idea how much I have heard about Scared Straight over the years. Partially because of the historical aspect and partially because of the internet. Was working for your dad what you did for a while?

Dennis: Yeah. I had other jobs here and there. I went to school at UC Berkeley for about four and a half years. And when I was there, I had some odd jobs like working in a library, because sound gigs were hard to get and didn't pay that well. When I graduated from Berkeley I didn't plan on doing sound. I was a rhetoric major; I was thinking that I was going to go to law school. It is kind of an odd major.

Brian: Was the band still playing shows when you could get down there, while you were in school?

Dennis: We did occasional stuff. It definitely wasn't very serious or frequent because Scott was off playing baseball and was really focused. But there were a couple of things we did during the baseball off-season. And then the Mystic Records album thing. I remember we met Mystic folks at a restaurant in Simi Valley and talked about doing a recording. I remember going to San Diego and recording. We only spent one day and they said we'd finish later. I'm not sure what really happened, but from my perspective, we halfway recorded some songs. I didn't hear anything for a long time and then all of a sudden there was a record in a store in Berkeley called *You Drink, You Drive, You Die.* (laughter)

It was a drag having the straight edge fascist album cover. "You drink, we will kill you!" vibe.

Brian: When did you graduate from college?

Dennis: 1990. The winter of 1990 I graduated. I started looking for jobs and everything looked like abstract, real work and stuff I was unqualified for—job ads that expected years of experience. At the end of the day, the only thing that I had real experience in was being a sound engineer. While I was up there floundering, looking for work, my dad made me an offer to come back to Los Angeles and manage the sound company. So when I did that, that sort of facilitated doing stuff when Scott was back in town from baseball. It was pretty easy for us to get together. And when

Scott went back to playing baseball, I was helping keep a band together so that when Scott came home we were basically ready. So we worked together to make the record *Swill*, and that ended up leading to us making the record *Rev*.

Brian: Why did you change the name of the band from Scared Straight to Ten Foot Pole?

Dennis: We were talking to Fat Wreck Chords and Epitaph, trying to get distribution for *Swill*. Fat Mike said "You shouldn't have the name Scared Straight because you aren't a straight edge band. It's false advertising." The other thing he said was that he would only put out the best 4 songs from *Swill* as an EP, that the album wasn't good enough. At first, we were a little bit offended, we had spent all of this time on it and were proud of it but eventually we realized that he was right on both counts. So we'd decided to change our name. Meanwhile, Epitaph had called and asked if they could put it out, but since Mike convinced us it wasn't worthy, we asked Epitaph if we could make a whole new record. That was a pretty good call because *Rev* is head and shoulders above what *Swill* was.

Brian: It is weird to think that NOFX turned into what they are now and that Mike has turned into this really successful businessman. I never would have guessed that back in 1985. (laughter)

Dennis: Yeah. When we saw them on that tour in 1985, I wouldn't have expected that. I would have thought Entropy would have gone farther than NOFX.

Brian: I thought that Entropy were the best band on that whole tour.

Dennis: Yeah, they rocked.

Brian: I didn't know about any of the world that you guys were in. But I know enough to know that your *Rev* record was pretty well regarded. It was a way different time than when Doug Moody put out the Scared Straight record. You actually sold records and went on tours. You guys did pretty well.

Dennis: Oh yeah. It was good timing and it was well received and it was well supported by the label. For us, it was huge. *Rev* ended up selling around ninety thousand or a hundred thousand. For a punk album with no radio hits, that was big. We opened for NOFX and Face To Face, and being on that tour was huge. So it kind of put us on the map in a bunch of places. We were offered a European tour with the Offspring that we couldn't do and that is when we had to make a hard decision about what we wanted to do. Because when Scott went back to playing baseball, we were looking at ten or eleven months of just sitting around.

Brian: I know about the situation. You wanted to have a band that operated more of the time.

Dennis: Yeah. For kids who wanted to be musicians, it was a dream come true—playing in front of hundreds or even thousands of people. But we knew at the most we could only play a month or two of each year. Without going into detail, it came down to wanting to commit to doing at least one tour per year that we could look forward to, making it worth keeping things together the rest of the year. And when he said no to that, we decided to look into getting a different singer. We approached Epitaph and said we wanted to get a new singer so we could tour all of the time but wondered if—as a way of being respectful and smoothing it over with Scott—Epitaph would agree to do another project where Scott would be the singer and we could be the backup band, and have a different name. Brett [Gurewitz] at Epitaph agreed.

So that is how we tried to do it in a diplomatic way. But Scott didn't accept it that way. He accepted the idea of having a project with Epitaph but he didn't have any interest in us being the backing band. So his new project became Pulley and we kept going as Ten Foot Pole. In hindsight, maybe that was a bad call. Maybe we would have been a huge band now if we had kept it together. But at the time, with our taste of glory, I didn't think I could keep a band together without being sure we had some shows to look forward to each year. And we never were mad at Scott, I mean, he had a great thing going in his life with baseball. But for us, the greatest thing in our lives was the band so we wanted to run with it.

Brian: There was never a climate back when we were kids where there was suddenly an industry invented for punk rock, where people could make a living playing in a band.

Dennis: I didn't know if we could, but I wanted to try. So at first, I was looking for possible singers. I thought that since I was the main songwriter, maybe it would make sense for me to be the singer and not have to rely on someone else. I spent a few months learning how to sing, then auditioned and convinced the other guys. We had two more records on Epitaph and both of those did pretty well and then Epitaph went through some changes. Brett was in rehab and this other guy was running the label and I butted heads with him one day when he kind of tried to strong-arm me into signing a recording contract extension right when I was heading to the studio to sing on *Insider*. I was just trying to postpone the discussion, but I don't know, maybe I wasn't diplomatic enough, and that was it. We didn't even talk about it for awhile. We went out and played over a hundred shows and the album was doing really well and then all of a sudden I got the notice that they weren't going to extend the contract. And so that was it with Epitaph.

Brian: Was that during the time when the recording industry started to take a big shit?

Dennis: Yeah, That was kind of at the beginning of that time, I think. I don't think I saw that coming, at least not at that point. We went over to Victory Records and it was kind of a whole different audience over there. The owner was an interesting character who said he wanted to be the Al Capone of the music industry. He was super aggressive. He was ready to fight all of the time, and it was cool when he was fighting on your side but all of a sudden, when he wanted to fight us, it wasn't so cool. We got into an argument about the cover of the second release. He had this idea on a napkin and we hesitated. And then he said that we were outta there—after two or three minutes talking about a scribble on a napkin. We went to Go-Kart Records for the *Subliminal Messages* record.

Brian: So as band activity dropped off, did that open the doors for more work being a sound engineer?

Dennis: I was always a sound person in my spare time. Before I had a family, before I didn't have as many money pressures, I sometimes made the band the highest priority and in my spare time did sound jobs. So it wasn't like I went back to it—I was doing it all of the time—but I did change priorities. When I got the job with Prince, I was a guest engineer in a club he went to and he was really impressed.

When I got the call to work for him, I said that I was totally available except for this three week tour of Japan with my band in March, and they understood. But right before I was going to go to Japan, I got this call and it was like, "Prince booked these shows in Milwaukee and Chicago, etc. He really wants you to be there. Is there any way that you could cancel your trip to Japan and do these shows for your employer? Who happens to be Prince?" And I said no. It was a tough call, but I was committed.

Brian: You said no to Prince! Did that cost you anything?

Dennis: Luckily he took me back, but it just as easily could have gone the other way. He was known to fire people for looking at him the wrong way. So for a while I didn't book any TFP shows. And when I started again, I lost other gigs in similar situations—like an Alice In Chains tour in 2015 due to two TFP shows that conflicted with their schedule. That, to me, is the hardest part of my life right now—deciding whether to book things because I know there is a chance that it could block big audio gigs.

Brian: Who else have you worked for?

Dennis: I did a whole tour cycle as a monitor engineer for AFI, about a hundred and fifty shows. And monitors for Return to Forever. I did about five hundred shows for Jimmy Eat World, front of house. That was amazing and great. And the last couple of years, I have done a couple of Weird Al Yankovic tours. Each one was around eighty or so shows.

Brian: Wow, no shit.

Dennis: He did two shows at the Hollywood Bowl with over ten thousand people!

Brian: He is still enormously popular. And now the music climate is totally different.

Dennis: Yeah. I think it is kind of like going to Las Vegas—if you win once, you keep thinking that you might be able to do it again. You spend the rest of your life going back and trying. But the thing is, it is fun. It is fun to play, it is fun to write new songs, it is fun to have people singing my lyrics. There are parts that are hard, it is up and down. Honestly there are ups and downs with the band and with my independent audio career. For example, I had a couple of great years recently, and more work lined up through a third year, which is rare. And with a great new album about to come out, I decided to plan 3 months of touring and bought a touring van. I had all of this audio work lined up after the 3 months of tours that was going to pay for everything. About halfway through my tours, I found out that I lost all of the work.

Brian: Oh no.

Dennis: Yep, I thought it was a big touring vacation between jobs, and I invested heavily in the band. But once the work fell through, I cancelled all future band plans because I had to make myself available for a new audio job. The work that fell through was kind of the guarantee that my family was going to eat, you know?

Brian: That sucks. Even with the ups and downs, I am sure you are proud of what you have done with your life professionally speaking.

Dennis: Oh yeah. When you back it up and look at it, I have had some amazing successes but that is part of the thing. That also gave me a little overconfidence in terms of my own band, like paying for my own record and buying a tour van.

But that is another big challenge of being an independent contractor, deciding what level of investment is prudent.

BILL STEVENSON

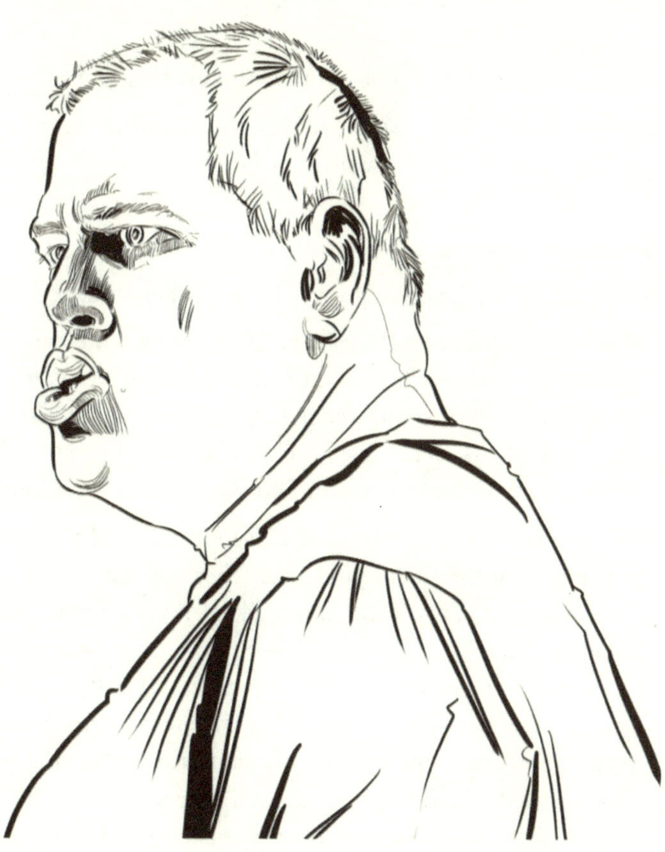

Bill is well known as a producer and songwriter these days, seeing that he has produced a ton of other bands. He has had a lot of health scares in recent times, and has beat them all. We are talking about a lot of scary shit, stuff that will no doubt change how you view life. A lifetime workaholic, he has now settled into a different phase of his life. When we talked, he gave me a really really good interview and wanted me to definitely withhold most of it for the actual book, which as you can tell is kind of a difficult thing for me to do. A lot of what he had to say was really great, especially in the context of working for yourself and making things happen.

♫

Brian: What was the first job that you ever had a kid?

Bill: It was building fishing rods. I would sell them to the fishing tackle store that Keith Morris' father owned. Keith from my area, from Black Flag, etc..

Brian: How old were you?

Bill: I think maybe eleven or twelve was when I started doing that.

Brian: I remember reading in *Flipside* a long time ago that when you were in high school, you had a fishing buddy and you guys would take a boat out of the harbor in Los Angeles, fish and go to Catalina Island, hence the song. And to me, that seems like some pretty brave crazy shit to do. Did you do that for a long time?

Bill: Let's see, the progression of jobage in terms of fishing… first it was building the fishing rods, and then I loved to fish, and I was catching so much fish that it was like, "Well, what are we going to do with these? Oh I know, let's sell them to the fish market." And so that slowly became us being commercial fishermen without a goal, per se. We liked the idea that we could make money, but we really never made much money because things like the equipment that we used would break, or the vehicle would break from hauling too much fish—you know, the suspension would break. So it was not ever really super profitable, but as far as being a teenager and having a hobby that could give him a little bit of pocket cash, it served that purpose.

Then there was another period when I was about sixteen. There was a point where I was working in the tackle store with Keith in the back, running the shrink wrap machine for shrink wrapping hooks and lures, and I had this big rig in there that could hold twelve fishing rods and to where I could put the finish on twelve of them at a time. At this point I was building them for the tackle store. I was kind of a contractor or whatever you want to call it, I guess. So I build them at my house with the threadwork and all of that, and I would bring them all down to the tackle store and put the finish on them. Keith would be doing the shrink wrap.

That was a time back there when Keith really exposed me to a lot of really cool music. He was constantly telling me about bands and stuff, and he is a bit older than me. He knew a lot of cool bands and that really helped me find my footing in terms of discovering a lot of great rock and roll and punk and all of that. It wasn't really a heavy income situation but it was something I enjoyed and I enjoyed hanging out with the guys in the store and listening to them tell stories. So I did that.

And those were the only really conventional jobs that I ever had, with the one exception maybe being in 1983, when I worked in the law office of the lawyer that was helping us (Black Flag) in our court case against a record label. We didn't have enough money to pay them and so we would work in the law office doing grunt work. It could be anything from me tape recording a court case and then typing it up back at the office or filling.

I remember one day finding all of these files about Steven Spielberg's court cases, people that were suing him or people that he was suing. So I would do whatever I could do help the lawyers out. Those are really the only jobs I have ever had in terms of working for someone else.

Brian: So basically the only jobs you had were building fishing rods, fishing, and then working in a lawyer's office. Your last job was in 1983 with the lawsuit thing. I remember Chuck and Greg went to jail.

Bill: Yeah. I had to make a habeas corpus to get them out of jail, and I didn't know how to do it, really, but I figured it out.

But then audio engineering—that is a job, and there is a person hiring me to record them, but since I have done the majority of it as an independent contractor and work at my own studio, I don't think it really qualifies as a typical job.

Brian: Definitely not a typical job, you are self-employed for sure. And you had jumped off the cliff with music and being in a band so long ago on top of all of that.

Bill: There wasn't even an idea that we were going to make a living at this, that wasn't even an option. It was more like, "Okay, this is what I am going to do. I am going to be in my band, period." And we would just sleep on the floor of our practice room. A lot of times there was no shower, a lot of times there was no hot water. I did that for almost fifteen years. Just without even thinking about things like, "Oh, how are we going to get ahead," or whatever. We didn't care. We were going to play in the band, period. And it's not like, "I believe in myself, and one day things are going to happen." No. This is what I want to do and I am going to do it. I don't care, I can get by on two dollars a day. I can get by on ramen noodles, I don't care.

Brian: Right. When did the drumming come into the picture? And while we are at it, the first fucking drum set you had, the grey one? Where did you find that?

Bill: Okay. Well let's start with the drums. I was always a fidgeter. And a tapper. When I was a really little kid I would get underneath the stove where all of the pots and pans were stored, and I would get those out and get some spatulas out and I would get those pots and pans going. I was doing this when I was three or four. It was a compulsion for me, I had to tap on shit all day long. (laughter) So eventually I got a snare drum. And not long after that, my dad bought me a very, very cheap entry level drum set from a friend of his at work. It was made by a company named Stewart, which I have never heard of before or since then. It was just my little first drum set, and I had it for, I don't know, probably not even six months. The guy that sold it to me showed me a rock drum beat, like you know, Pat Boone, Debby Boone… kick snare kick kick snare. He showed me how to do that. And being Mexican, he showed me how to do kind of a Latin beat. He showed me those two beats and it's funny because I still use that Latin beat on a lot of All songs. I have always joked that I had a little bit of Mexican or Latin in my playing, I think I come by it naturally. Somehow I have always enjoyed that kind of stuff.

And then I bought a used Slingerland drum set from the paper. Someone was selling it. And then I got the third drum kit, the one that everybody knows, the great big huge ones. I wanted to get drums bigger than the ones that Robo had. 26 inch bass, 16 inch rack tom, and a 20 inch floor tom. And I still have those, but they don't really work. You can't get them to be in tune. I think the wood is just all laminated, or whatever. They weren't taken care of. I never had cases for them and when we went out on tour, I would literally be sleeping on top of them all stacked into one another because they were concert drums, they didn't have bottom heads. So I would stack all of them and put the snare on top of it and then lay a piece of foam on top of that. And the foam would also lay over the guitar cabinets and I could sleep on that in the van. So these drums weren't taken care of, so they don't sound too good now. I have tried to get them out and use them but they just don't make a good tone.

Brian: Was that kit the one you used to record the first Descendents album?

Bill: Yeah. But when I got them, they weren't grey. It was supposed to be grey, but when they arrived, it was kind of an off-white, pearly white sort of thing. Eventually I had to spray paint them grey and black because I just couldn't handle it. I recorded who knows how many records with that drum set, yeah. I don't even know how many.

Brian: So how old were you when the first album was recorded?

Bill: When the first album was recorded, I believe I was eighteen.

Brian: That is crazy.

Bill: The *Fat* EP, I was seventeen or eighteen and then *Milo Goes to College*, I was either eighteen, or barely nineteen.

Brian: How did it turn out that *Milo Goes to College* was released by Mike Watt on his record label New Alliance?

Bill: He was the person who showed the most interest in it, and so we were really good friends with him and the Minutemen and Black Flag, we used to always share practice rooms together and stuff. We slept on a lot of the same floors together. And he just said that he wanted to put it out and that sounded great to us.

Brian: A lot has been written about the world of SST Records and the characters around it, not just the people in it but even folks like Redd Kross. And bands like the Minutemen and Saccharine Trust. Did observing the work ethic of some of those people influence you as a young man? Was it inspirational, like when you decided you wanted to reform the Descendents in 1985?

Bill: It is interesting because your questions keep covering all the things I would cover and more than what I would cover. I have always been a perfectionist, or OCD, or whatever you want to call those sort of things—I like things to be right. What I did learn from some of the older guys— you know, Chuck and Greg

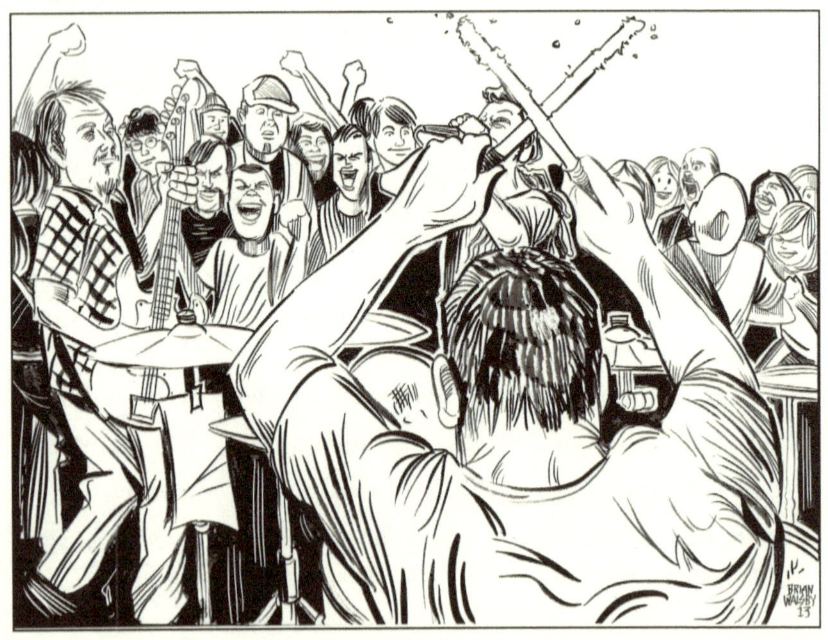

or even some of the not older guys, like Mugger [Steve Corbin]—was I learned that you could apply perfectionism or work ethic to the arts.

In my head, before that, I thought that you could be a workaholic or you could be an artist but I think that the Black Flag and SST kind of vibe was more like, "No, you have to do both. You have to be super creative *and* you have to hustle." So yeah, it was good to be around a lot of those people. They were older enough than me and I often looked up to them—if they were worthy enough to be looked up to at the time, yeah. (laughter)

Brian: The first Black Flag stuff that you played on—the two songs on side two of the *TV Party* single—I really love those songs and the way the band sounds on those two songs but, for some reason, a lot of people don't talk about them.

Bill: Yeah, if we had done an album like that, it would have bridged the gap a bit between *Damaged* and *My War*. Because on that, you hear some of the stalls and pauses that we were getting into. But the music was still pretty fast, and from a drumming perspective, I was still doing the Robo beat. With the sets of three hi hats.

In my opinion, it still sounded like Black Flag. Later, Greg encouraged me to play quarter notes on the hi hat and do more of a conventional rock beat on those sorts of songs. To me, that was kind of when Black Flag quit sounding like Black Flag. Nobody really realized that it was Robo's strange beats that really made it that sound.

Brian: Totally. Like you said, for every hit on the snare it was three hits on the hi hat. A non-stop pattern of threes.

Bill: No, I like that stuff. I was really nervous when we recorded it. When I listen to it, I can hear how nervous I was—like my kick drums are rushing and weird things like that. It wasn't my best performance but it was good enough to where you could tell what we were trying to do.

Brian: I love those two songs and those versions of them. And to this day, some people don't even know that they exist.

Bill: I think it is because that seven-inch, that version of "TV Party," it is just so… I don't know why it ever needed to exist. (laughter) I am not saying that it is really good or bad, it is not my place but…why?

Brian: The hard rock version of "TV Party?"

Bill: I don't know *what* it is. And it is funny because I love Emil [Johnson]'s drumming so much, he is an incredible drummer. He sounded a little bit like a fish out of water, and in that context, I also sometimes felt like a fish out of water on say the *Loose Nut* album and that kind of stuff.

Brian: You have said more than once that you aren't too keen on your drumming in Black Flag. Which to me, as a fan of your drumming in Black Flag, is crazy. I love your drumming on *My War* and *Slip It In*. I understand why you might feel that way since you are the one who played on those records, but having said that, is there an album that you are happy with looking back on things?

Bill: To not divide it up by albums…I love "Nothing Left Inside" so much, and I love "My War" so much and I love "Swinging Man" so much, I think those are strong and I am very proud of them. And then moving to *Slip It In,* I like "My Ghetto"… I mean, I like *Slip It In* but the things I like about *Slip It In* aren't the drumming really. The parts of the drumming that I do like on *Slip It In*, I inherited them from Chuck Biscuits. But I do like it. And then there is some stuff on *In My Head* that I like. I only remember the songs because when I recorded them they were all working titles and had no vocals. But I actually think that a lot of the drumming on *In My Head* is pretty cool. I think *In My Head* is one of the better of those latter-day Black Flag records. I don't really care for the sound of it—all of that gated reverb and the weird flanger on the guitars that those guys got into—I don't like the way that sounds. A little bit of that polluted (the Descendents album) *I Don't Want To Grow Up,* too, and I don't like the way that sounds either. The engineer we were using came out of the L.A. metal scene with all of the gated reverb and that kind of sound, but it's funny because it's the same guy who had eight years prior engineered the *Nervous Breakdown* seven-inch. We weren't smart enough to dig ourselves out of that.

Brian: When you quit Black Flag and decided to reform the Descendents, I remember that, to me and my very small group of friends, it was a really big deal that you guys were getting back together and releasing a new record. It was the summer of 1985, and all of a sudden, you guys were on tour. That is when I formally met you guys—when you came to Raleigh. It was the first actual tour of the Descendents. How was that experience for you guys?

Bill: Well, we were borrowing money from my dad and that first van, we got that for like fifteen hundred bucks. We were just barely surviving. We got five dollars a day and there wasn't any money. We were just trying to get from city to city. Some shows would have a couple hundred people and some shows would have like eight people.

Brian: Right, but it is also exciting. You have your band and you are taking it out there.

Bill: Oh, it was great fun. All of those memories from back then, I wouldn't trade any of that stuff for the world.

Brian: Learning how to record, produce, and engineer music led to a career for you. When did that become something that you started taking an interest in? I think that since you brought up not liking the sound of *I Don't Want To Grow Up,* did all of the interest start afterwards?

Bill: Well, my interest in recordings was probably when I was real young, maybe when I was ten years old. The first thing I remember was that I had bought this album that was called the Beatles *Rarities*. And there is an outtake on there of "Love Me Do" and I remember it was the first time I had heard that song so it was the version for me, I didn't know there was another version. But I would always listen to it and think that there was something wrong, and I would try and break it apart in my mind. I wanted to fix it, and I could never figure out how to fix it. And years later, I gained the wisdom of realizing that it's because the bass guitar on that version is probably fifty or sixty percent sharp E, almost like he is playing the song one half-step higher than the rest of the band.

My brain was drawn towards trying to dissect this stuff. And I always had that interest in trying to hear things and figure it out. Like on Kiss records: what is Ace playing and what is Gene playing and what is Paul playing? That kind of thing. And then I guess it came to a head for me during the *I Don't Want To Grow Up* sessions. The engineer was coming to the sessions drunk and then drinking during the sessions. And one time he actually passed out in his chair while recording. I think he was recording Ray (Cooper, guitarist of that album), and I just kind of slid his chair out of the way and slid my chair in, without knowing hardly anything about any of it—except for twiddling a few knobs here and there on *Milo Goes To College* or *Slip It In*. Spot did all of that, of course. But without really knowing what I was doing, there I was. And from that point on, I decided that this was something that I could be good at if I got more experience, so then I started to look for more opportunities to get more experience.

Brian: When I watched the movie *Filmage*[1], it was kind of interesting to me to see how the whole story behind All had turned out. Because to me, being a fan of the Descendents and all of that, I just considered the new name and new singer just being a continuation. You and Karl and Stephen have played together for so long that you three created your own thing, regardless of whether Milo is singing or not. And I remember seeing you guys during all of those earlier dates in Raleigh and the shows were always packed and everybody liked All. So it was weird to see the movie paint this story of how people lost interest in the band. You guys were self-reliant and self-managed and toured your asses off during those years—putting out all of those records on Cruz Records—so I always assumed the reaction to the band was how

1 *Filmage: The Story of Descendents/All* (2013) https://filmagemovie.com/

it was everywhere, not just Raleigh. I interviewed Milo and he said he thought it was just because of the dumb cartoon of him on the cover of the first album. He thought it was just something that people could identify.

Bill: Well, I will just say that Raleigh, North Carolina, was very kind to any and every incarnation of any and every band that I have ever been in. So, you know, your perception on it is a little different than most of the rest of the United States. We had pockets where All did really well but… I never really questioned it, because from where I come from, I already felt extremely fortunate to have started one band that anyone would care about, at all. And for me to expect them to care about every single thing I lay my hands on, I think that's not realistic. In your lifetime, if you are fortunate enough to have one band that people care about, you shouldn't expect people to do a backflip over every little thing that you do.

And also, I wasn't playing music for popularity, or to be rich, I play it because I love it, and I love playing in All, no matter how many people are there, even if there are only seven people. I mean, the Descendents used to play to seven people too, and it didn't matter. One of my very favorite things to do is to play in my band Only Crime because the arrangements are so challenging for me physically, I almost have a heart attack trying to play a song and I love it so much, and Only Crime doesn't draw anybody. A good show for Only Crime is like sixty people. But it doesn't matter, those things don't matter to me. If I need to make money than I can go get a job and make money. I don't think about that when I play music.

There is some truth to what Milo said. That little cartoon thing, that really gave us something. It is possibly the most recognized logo in all of punk rock, it's either that or the bars. I think it helped to get the band this identity and the nerd thing and all of that. At the same time, Milo is just being humble because people connected with his voice, they connected with what we were saying, and what our songs said. They felt that we were sincere, that we were genuine. And then people that love All think the same way about All, or they only like Scott or they only like Chad or Dave. Art is such a subjective thing.

Brian: You can't really choose how people are going to react to the art you make.

Bill: Right. You just said it better than I would.

Brian: You tend to be pretty busy—you have a family, you have up to three bands that you can choose to play in, you have your studio The Blasting Room for recording projects, and you also have maneuvered through a bunch of health issues and come out on the other side from that. How do you balance all of that, especially with what you have been through?

Bill: I could preface this by saying that I don't seem to be able to manage my time in a way that makes me happy. There are a few things that work, one of which is this kind of fear. I guess this is really just good old-fashioned insecurity. I wake up most mornings—I have done so for thirty five years—and the first thing I think of is, "Okay, what do I have to do today to survive and how do I not end up sleeping under a park bench when I am old"? (laughter) And then the next thought is, "Is today the day that the bottom falls out from this sort of half-assed career that I have put together for myself that we call punk rock? Is today going to be the day where there isn't any more music with guitar in it, that it is now all made today on someone's Macintosh?" So, I spend the first thirty minutes of my waking hours going through all of these fears. It is completely counterproductive, but that is how most of my mornings start.

So then I just figure out what I can do that will help make me survive. And I don't mean survive today, or even next year. I mean, if I became disabled, I would say that I could probably get by with my family, maybe scrape by for three or four years. So when I say survive, I mean that in the long-term sense of it. Because one day I won't be able to play and one day I won't be able to make records and so I just try and figure out what I am going to need to do to survive. And what I do then is I never say no to work. And so this is where the poor management of time comes in. I will have a big handful of bands that I am producing records with, and I will think that I better do this because I won't be booked for concerts when I am seventy years old. So I better do this now.

And with the concerts, I better do those now and just do everything I can. And I end up overextending myself.

But I have spent more time with my family, and even with myself. Like, with my own thoughts. So this is something that I have struggled with all of my life. But I have changed as a person to where I am no longer a workaholic. I am no longer the cliché overachiever guy, I don't care about any of that. I am not trying to prove anything to anyone, I am only trying to survive. Whatever I was trying to prove to the world, I proved it. I have changed a little bit obviously since all of my near death stuff with the brain tumor, that changed me to a degree, I am definitely prioritizing my personal time a little better. And even my happiness. Just figuring out what makes me happy and what things don't make me sad.

Three years ago, I had two other very invasive surgeries. They are not out there on the radar, but I had a triple bypass and I had an open lung surgery where they actually had to flatline me dead after cooling me way down. And they do the surgery when you are dead, and they bring you back to life. They had to get the blood clots out of my lungs because I was getting more and more unable to breathe. So each of these major life events have kind of rectified me to a degree, and I think nowadays I am trying to have a balanced thing. I am trying to take time each day to appreciate the things that are important to me. Whenever my dogs come into my office, when they would come in and flank themselves behind me, the old thing would have been to reach down and pet them a little bit. But really I was just working. And now when they come into the office, I get out of my chair and I get on the ground with them. And I play with them until they are good—until they have been played with and they are happy. And I get up and go back to my chair and finish my work. These little things, in my opinion, are the meaning of life. The things that mean something to you and mean something to me are things like taking a minute to stop and talk to my son when he has a question, or when he has something on his mind and not just going, "Oh, I am busy. I am working." These moments are the meaning of life to me. So I am learning the meaning of life, the meaning of my life.

Brian: Something I can relate to is that I am motivated by fear. I agree with Buzz when he says, "I operate like I am going to be out of business in six months."

Bill: Right.

Brian: The only reason that I haven't had to get a job in nine years is because of working for Buzz of the Melvins, basically. You know, exchanging money for entertainment and art, that is asking a lot of people. So that is sort of what I have done, and it's fortunate that I can do it, even with the fear behind it.

Bill: I wanted to do more this year. I guess I overextended myself already. I seemed to have gone from having not a lot this year but then all at once I started recording a new Descendents record and then Fat Mike called me to produce NOFX and then Russ

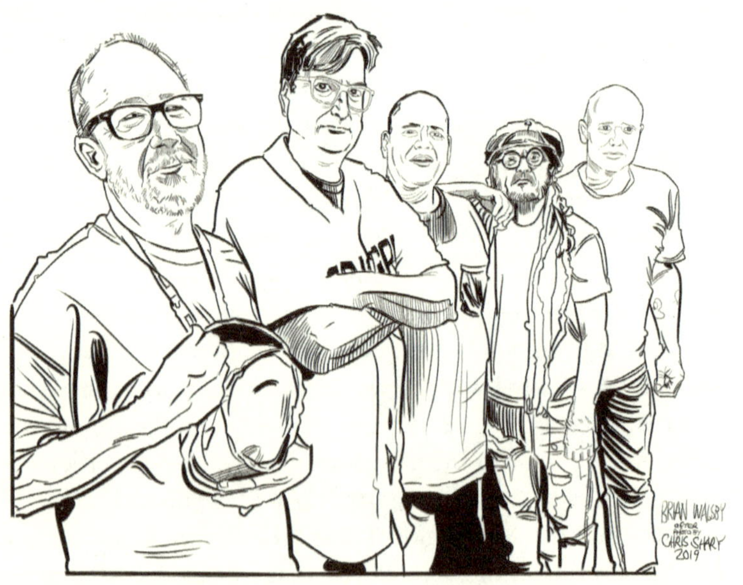

[Rankin] called me to produce Good Riddance and then Rise Against called me. So it was like, "Whoa, I just had a pretty casual year and now..." There is so much work, and I don't see any more room to fit in any more Flag shows this year, but I definitely want to do some more. Yeah, it's so much fun to do that. It's such a good feeling to be around really, really long time long term friends like that.

Brian: Even though you have already explained how you operate as a songwriter, I still have this little fantasy of you recording all of your songs and playing all of the instruments yourself. Like that Rikk Agnew solo record. Remember that? I always thought it would be cool to hear something like that from you.

Bill: When I do demos of my songs for the other guys, I play everything on those demos. But if I was in some weird moment where I thought it would be fun to do something like that, it wouldn't be some rock thing. It wouldn't really be through Marshalls. I have a very gentle voice when I sing, so I would want to sing over softer music. If I did something out of my head, it would be like Cole Porter meeting the band Luna.

Brian: Okay. Could there be any *After The Gold Rush*-era Neil Young thrown in there?

Bill: Oh, there sure could. My voice is kind of like his, kind of high and shaky. Why did you mention Neil Young? You know he is one of my favorites.

Brian: I am kind of cursed with this weird selective memory where everything kind of stupid, that you don't need to remember, you do, but anything important, like your mom's birthday or whatever, is something you can't seem to remember at all.

Bill: I think I have that same kind of thing. Maybe we had talked about Neil Young some time?

Brian: No, I knew you liked Neil Young only because I saw a video of you singing one of his songs seriously in karaoke style.

Bill: Oh, I am singing "Heart Of Gold." That was such a huge, poppy AM radio hit, but those lyrics are so dark.

Brian: Depressing. I remember hearing that song as a real little kid and how depressed it made me feel just by hearing it.

Bill: Yeah, a lot of people just dismiss Neil Young because they don't like the way his singing voice sounds. So, my thing might sound like Cole Porter meets Neil Young meets Luna. (laughter)

Brian: Awesome! One of the interesting things of talking to a lot of the people is figuring out what success means to everybody. Like, the perception of it. Every day, for me, is just up and down all of the time. On the other hand, a good example of someone else might be Steven McDonald. He was explaining that he felt like a bit of a failure at times, which is just crazy to me, because he is such a good guy and I like a lot of what he has done. So it's weird, the perception of success in the eyes of the people who don't make creative stuff is either you are a multi-billionaire or you are a total failure.

Bill: You know, I was just going to say that. You are either Van Halen or you are a piece of gum on the bottom of someone's shoe. That is how America thinks of the arts. We are all victims of that mentality. Steven should know that he is an asset to any situation that he puts himself into, like with OFF! or the Melvins or even those bass tracks that he put up on MySpace of the White Stripes. Remember?

He is just great, you know? He is really a very special person. I admire him tremendously.

AN ESSAY ON DRUMS
BY BRIAN WALSBY

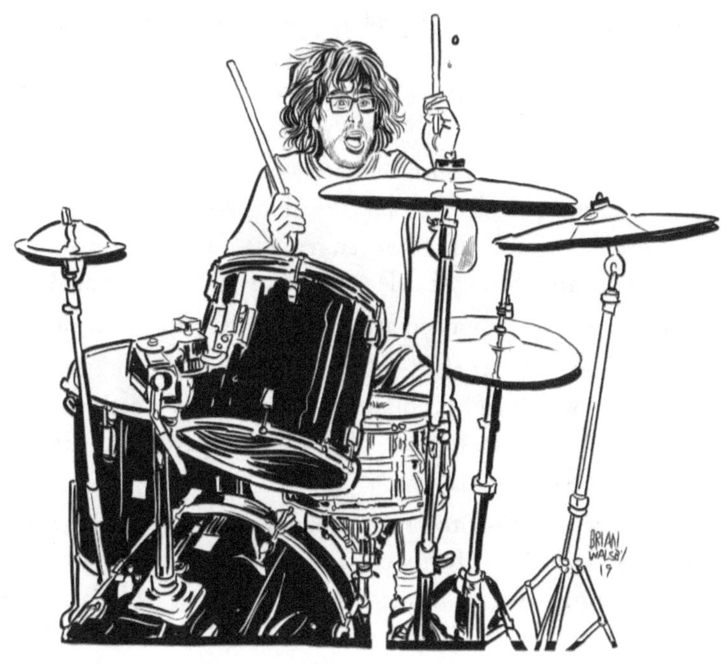

I loved music so much that I always fantasized about playing in a real band when I was a kid. I drew pictures of myself in junior high school playing in bands that I made up in my head. My pals would be in the bands. In the bands, I was one of two lead guitar players and I had three pickups on my guitars because that is what I thought made a lead guitar player, thanks to Ace Frehley on the cover of *Kiss Alive!* I drew elaborate stages and the drummers always had massive drum sets and gongs and stuff like that.

In real life I never had the patience to learn guitar but I was always hitting pots and pans and singing and taping my own songs. I really wish I had those now. I fucked around with bongos and did silly recordings. Then one day in tenth grade I sat behind a drum set and, lo and behold, it seemed to make sense. I could keep a beat. I could even use my foot to hit the bass drum, which was something I thought I would never ever do in a million years.

When punk rock was discovered, I realized I didn't have to wait to play in a band. Even if I wasn't good enough to play Judas Priest's "Exciter," I could probably play Black Flag's "Nervous Breakdown" or whatever. So I ordered a Remo PTS series four piece kit. They were these drums which had drum heads that locked into the shells. As shitty as that sounds, they always sounded pretty good! I immediately covered my kit with punk rock stickers. I practiced by playing along with records. I tried to meet people. I finally did meet some kids, most of which were in the band Scared Straight. I let it be known that I played drums.

So here is what happened after that, to the best of my memory.

Positive Action was the first band. It was after punk rock, like early 1984. We had a bass player one day. We recorded four songs at the Mystic Records studios. We played one party in Chatsworth. It was very short-lived.

Scared Straight invited me to join their band. In many ways, Scared Straight is really historically the only band worth talking about. Mainly because it was the first real band, with real shows and real tours and even a real seven-inch record. We did our band in a climate that was radically different and more exciting than anything that has happened to me personally since. We weren't the greatest band in the world, but looking back I think a lot of my best memories center around the innocence of the time.

Wwax was the first band I was in when I moved to Raleigh. We were around for a year. We played with everyone from Honor Role to COC to Fugazi. We all knew more famous people in bands, so we got some good bills. We were for sure a post-hardcore band. Members of Wwax formed Superchunk and founded Merge Records, both of which still exist to this day. The other member ran for mayor in Raleigh.

Willard was a pretty popular band with no actual records

released in the bands lifetime. We released a cassette. A single came out posthumously. We all got along and dug playing. Comparable to bands like Treepeople and Swervedriver. At least that is what I was told at the time. We all liked cover songs and covered everyone from Gray Matter to the Buzzcocks to Tales Of Terror to Saint Vitus. We got pretty good before we disbanded. It was the period of long hair and shorts.

Snake Nation was a COC offshoot that featured Woody Weatherman and Mike Dean with me playing drums. We released an album on Caroline Records. We played three shows and that was it. No one cared at the time. I have heard a lot about this record since from various people. Next to Scared Straight, Snake Nation is who I hear about the most. It was okay, I wish it came out better, but oh well.

Shiny Beast was formed with David Sullivan, who was in Willard with me. We made the mistake of recording our best recording first, which was partially released by Tom Flynn's Boner Records. Nothing else we did compared. We switched bass players early on. We recorded a split album with Raleigh's Regraped. We toured twice on the east coast, once with Erectus Monotone and once with Polvo. We got the tiniest bit of attention. We stayed a band for far too long. All of the music came out on a posthumous CD years and years later. David plays guitar in Red Fang now.

Patty Duke Syndrome was a short-lived band with the late Jere Mcilwean and the now missing-in-action Ryan Adams. We recorded an album-length demo that is still really good and has some of my favorite drumming. The three of us had both a great musical connection as well as some petty drama going for us. This recording will never come out due to Adams. It was always too bad, people would have liked it. As it has turned out, perhaps it's ultimately for the best not to be associated with him. RIP Jere, he was a good guy.

The Shames was a trio that was centered around Clay Merritt's formidable songwriting and guitar playing. We couldn't get anyone interested in the band and eventually fell apart. Some good music though.

Refrigerator Heaven was four people trying to make a band good and failing in the end. Most of the people in the band were dealing with other things in their lives, which didn't help things much. I think we did one or two shows before the band was cancelled due to a lack of interest, and the fact that we didn't have any good songs. You need good songs, usually. We tried to get Dale Flattum to join once. He wasn't having any of it.

Joining Polvo was great. I knew them and liked the band. They were the only band with ties to Chapel Hill that I actually enjoyed. They had a very laid back attitude to their band, which was bemusing at times. I played on most of the record *Shapes*. I wish I liked the record better in hindsight. Bob Weston recorded the record in a few different places, one of which was Mitch Easter's house in Kernersville. Instead of the great drum sound that Bob got for original drummer Eddie Watkins, I got something else. Some people really loved the record. We did a month long tour across the country that was very successful. Some of the shows were sold out— like Texas, New York, Seattle. The only show that was bad was one in South Carolina where friends of ours showed up and watched us play a shit gig. The band played two goodbye shows at the Cat's Cradle when we got back which was also the day that Carl Wilson of The Beach Boys passed away. Polvo reformed with my one-time roommate Brian Quast and did their best overall record ten years later.

Siberian was another band that played what I thought was pretty good music that no one really cared about. We were a quartet. The concept was people that usually played and liked heavy metal doing something else, which was actually pretty good. Mike Dean recorded us once, Greg Elkins recorded us a second time. I liked our stuff. We also covered an Echo and the Bunnymen song.

Night Moose existed around the same time as Siberian, till I picked one over the other. Quirky SST sounding trio, some good songs. Not a lot of interest. Played out a handful of times.

Daddy was a hateful, ugly sounding band that was a lot of

fun for a long time, until it wasn't. We recorded twice with two different lineups. Band was cancelled due to a lack of interest. The band was fueled by hatred and smoking pot, which can only go so far.

Double Negative was the latter day band that did the most. Imagine a band like OFF! minus the famous ex-members' pedigree and you have an idea of the band, except we came way before those guys and were weirder. Older people playing eighties hardcore kind of stuff. Initially it went very well, people liked it and we had a well-recorded debut album. We eventually started to spin our wheels by the time the second record came out. We toured a few times and played some big shows. We did a lot of house parties too.

A good deal of the time there seemed to be a whole lot of weird interpersonal issues over things that you would expect young adults to get caught up in, not guys in their forties. A lot of it centered around our guitarist. Even though we had been friends for years, we had an abrasive relationship, like being friends with someone who hated your guts some of the time. It was weird.

After my daughter was born, life was changing and I quit/was kicked out of Double Negative. My last show was opening for OFF!, oddly enough. Double Negative was actually a good band and I am proud of what we did. We made some original raging hardcore punk rock. I just can't listen to it because it was the most drama-filled band I was ever in, even more than playing with Ryan Adams in the Patty Duke Syndrome.

Davidians was formed after Double Negative, three ex-DN members with Colin Swanson White, a talented guitarist. Post-punk, post-hardcore music. Two singles and an eight song mini album. We toured twice, did some shows but couldn't get any momentum. Touring at this point in the Davidians, especially after being spoiled for years working for the Melvins, was kind of difficult. After spinning our wheels, we broke up on good terms after playing yet another "final show."

I think almost everything I was lucky enough to do musically was actually pretty decent, but I realized that I had a love/hate relationship with playing music. I sort of cultivated it over time, probably because it seemed like an obligation I was putting on myself, a part of my identity that I needed. But it wasn't just that, a lot of it was born out of being let down by nothing happening with some of these bands. A few times I had "professional jealousy" towards a small handful of other bands, even though I had no desire to do whatever it was that they were doing. I was just jealous for the usual reasons—they were succeeding, and what I was a part of, wasn't. It was lame but almost inevitable to have a little of that creep in.

When I started to get older and got a little squirrelly about forming yet another band, I would question what I was doing a lot. The payoffs were getting less and less. It certainly was a case of diminished returns. When the last band I drummed in (Davidians) broke up, our singer, Cameron, said that we were a good band and it wasn't our fault when no one seemed to really care about the band in a way that would allow us to do more stuff. I decided that was the best attitude to have in the face of failure and disappointment.

I think what happened was that the "creating art" side of me sort of won out. My wilderness years were when I hardly seemed to draw, or had anything to show for it creatively. As I got back into drawing and things started to happen for me again, the music stuff faded. I was older. I hadn't succeeded the way I had hoped. But drawing was different—it was way easier, and cheaper too. I was getting better and improving. Plus, I was finally doing enough art to see that it was becoming way more successful ultimately, and then it finally turned into a half-assed living.

Funnily enough, I still love music as much as I always have, but the "playing music" side has seriously diminished. I don't even like going to shows anymore. I seem to have a lot more social anxiety these days. And I will only go and see music if I really want to see it. I have my hands busy with life and my daughter, and that certainly weeds out a lot of stuff.

I think about it a lot these days because it was a huge and

important part of my life and I am proud of having done it. And even though it was mostly done without a lot of attention or reward, it was still worth it to a point. I loved playing drums and playing music. But I don't feel like I *have* to do it anymore, which is the distinction. I am also not a youngster anymore. The drummer is always the first to go, due to the physicality of the instrument. Maybe this is just a good time and place to leave it.

ADAM FAUCETT

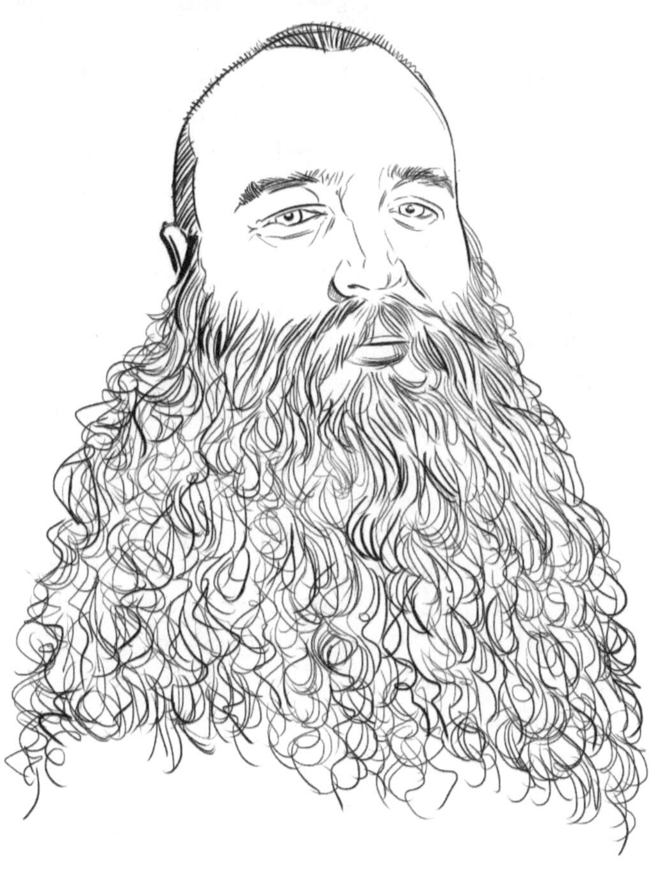

Adam Faucett is one of my favorite people, and has been my favorite singer-songwriter out there for a few years. I crossed paths with him when he was picked to open a week's worth of shows for Buzz Osborne when he put out his solo acoustic record. Adam floored me within a minute—he created this amazing atmosphere. He had it all: a great singing voice, a cool picking style of echoey, swampy guitar playing, and most importantly, he had great songs. He also chose to play Tim Buckley's "Song To A

Siren" that night in Montana. "Holy shit...how did I not know of this guy," is what I thought (which is what everyone thinks when they hear something good that they didn't know about previously.) We became friends during that week and I bought all of his records. They are all good. In fact, his last one, *It Took The Shape Of A Bird,* was my favorite record from a couple years ago, beating the Lemon Twigs and Voivod. I have been pushing Adam on people ever since.

He is an interesting guy, too. From Arkansas. Legally blind (although he can still see, just not drive). Smart. Funny. Artistic. He recently went through some crazy throat problems and made it to the other side and is ready to get back out there and play. He is a lifer who figures this is pretty much what he is going to do, that being a self-employed musician is the path he has to be on, and that he is going to see it through to the very end. From talking with him, this is simply what he does. I had brought Adam here to Raleigh on two occasions. I am definitely not a show promoter and both were low turnout affairs, but you know what? Most of those people came up and thanked me afterwards for bringing him out. The second time was in front of twenty people, including Kristin, Charles Cardello, Erik Sugg, and a few others. There was a hushed intimacy in the room and it was perfect.

♫

Brian: You seem to be one of those people where it is the journey rather than the destination. I think you also said that there is nothing else that you can do besides being a musician and write songs. But you went to art school though, right?

Adam: That is it. I just went to a university and got a BFA in fine arts but I am legally blind. I graduated at the top of my class.

I have ocular albinism, I am an albino so my vision is different from many other people that need corrective lenses and stuff like that. I am literally an albino, there are two different types of albinos and I am the type...

Brian: That doesn't look like Johnny or Edgar Winter?

Adam: Right. Exactly. But I have brown hair.

Brian: Alright, So you were born and raised in Arkansas. Were you always artistically minded as a kid?

Adam: Absolutely. I was just doing drawing, I think that is just a natural sort of kid thing to do— your mom gives you some crayons and a piece of paper and says, "have at it kid" And I was into comic books. What I thought I was going to do going back to the first grade was, I wanted to make horror movies. Because that was my favorite shit as a little kid, and a lot of that was just drawing your stories. I used to make comic books and write stories. And also, I had a reed organ in the back room where my grandma lived, and not that I knew how to play it, but those things, you know those chord buttons on it? So I would just sit there and do stuff on those buttons, they are chords, it is just perfect for kids. It had a spooky sound to it so in my mind I was scoring these horror movies that I had planned out in my head. So it was a big production.

Brian: Taught The Rabbits was your high school band?

Adam: Right. Why anyone would choose to do this as a path, for me—no joke—I had a case worker from a school for the deaf and blind when I was eighteen. Actually, I could have had one into my twenties. They were really wanting me to go to their school, as you could imagine, and I didn't want to, I wanted to be a normal kid. I remember being in Kindergarten and crying to my mom. I remember her asking me, "What do you want to do when you grow up?" I remember saying, "I am going to drive a big truck." And she said, "they ain't going to let you drive a big truck, son." And I was like, "Fuck! Okay, I am going to go into the army," and she said, "They aren't going to let you go into the army."

"Cop?"

"No."

Most parents tell their kids that they can be anything that they want, and my mom being my mom, God love her, was just straight up about it, you know, thankfully.

Anyways, I was at this age where it was very apparent that a normal path was just not going to be something on the horizon. And people could look at me and tell that there is something wrong. It brought on all of the things that you could imagine it would bring on in a school scenario, being excluded and whatnot. So, when I was in high school I was going to play guitar one way or another. I wasn't good looking or cool, and this is before anyone could put their shit up on Bandcamp, so I just decided I was going to be a street performer or some shit. I was good at art and I was good at playing guitar, and that was it. And my mom made me fill out all of the applications for going to college for free and I got to go to college for free because, basically, my parents' combined income...they were poor and all I had to do was keep up a three point average, they would pay for all of it. Yeah, I went to college to start a band, I didn't want to go at all.

Brian: Do you still do any art, or is any of that stuff on your record sleeves or whatever?

Adam: Not on my records. I designed all of the records and then I had my printmaking teacher make woodcuts of them, so those are collaborations but those aren't my artwork. I have done record covers for other people, but not as much anymore. I have moved six times in the last four years and what I did was painting on canvas. I have to have really good lighting, I can just sit and have it in my lap, I have to have be on it, you know? So it is one of those physical pains in the ass these days to get any of that stuff done the way it used to be, and it's no longer my first love. I would rather have someone else do it, and just have me come up with the idea.

Brian: You went to Chicago to live. Did you go there to go to another school?

Adam: No. I graduated college and saved up money and got a job at a bong shop and was working there like four or five days a week and on two days I was a substitute teacher, which was hilarious. Me and my friends ran the only DIY place in town at the time and we also formed this disgusting metal band. I moved to Chicago in June of 2006. And I went to Chicago to be a musician. I didn't know how to be a touring musician or anything like that. I went to Chicago to basically play any open mic I possibly could, and got my ass kicked good, and got some type of mental breakdown, lost my job, and the drummer I had stole a bunch of money from me and ran off with some girl to India. She was from Michigan. She was this hippie girl who got it into her that she had to go to India so that is what she did.

Brian: Okay I am piecing this all together. So you went back to Arkansas obviously.

Adam: Well, I was working—stocking art supplies—and I got fired from there. I got fired in March and my lease was up in June. Me and a friend were just sitting in a Taco Bell one day, he said that maybe we could go back to Arkansas and play at the White Water Tavern and go see some old friends and clear your mind. And I thought that sounded good but why don't we just never go back? Why don't we just record some CDs and go on the road and drink beer and sleep in the van and not give a shout about anything anymore because we were twenty-five years old, we can do that.

Brian: So is all of the stuff from the first album *The Great Basking Shark*, is that from that period?

Adam: Yeah. I wrote that whole record in Chicago. I recorded that record in July when I got back to Arkansas. The song "Lipgloss" is about the same thing, about not giving a shit anymore, we will go up to Portland—I have never been to Portland before, I have never seen the Salton Sea, you know? I had never been out to the West Coast at that point. I had wanderlust so bad.

Brian: So you just put all of that into those songs. Man, I was obsessed with the Salton Sea for quite awhile there, still never have gone.

Adam: I saw this documentary about it, *Plagues and Perils on the Salton Sea*[1]. I did go out there though. That movie doesn't lie!

---

1 *Plagues and Perils on the Salton Sea*, narrated by John Waters https://www.imdb.com/title/tt0438327/

Brian: So this is what started you on the path that you are on now, this is what you have been doing ever since—putting out records and touring—you have five records out.

Adam: Yup. It started out like a "fuck the world" sort of thing, it really was a mental breakdown sort of moment. I didn't move to Chicago to leave it in one year but it only took me one year to realize what I needed to do and that came after a bunch of misfortune. And I never thought that I would make another CD—it wasn't like there were these people telling me that I was good, you know what I am saying? I didn't know that I was good enough to make a CD and then maybe go around making enough money to keep eating and drinking beer, I mean, that was the only thing I cared about. I am not going to work for other people anymore that make me feel like a piece of shit, you know?

Brian: So you haven't had another job since then?

Adam: Not really. Well, after I was on the road for nine months, after putting out *Basking Shark,* I took another job at a smaller art supplies store here, stocking the shelves, and ringing people up, that kind of thing. I even told them that I wasn't going to be here for six months. I was sleeping on my drummer's floor and that is when I wrote and recorded the second record. So I haven't had a job since September of 2008.

Brian: All right!

Adam: But I have been really fucking poor, man!

Brian: I jumped off the cliff eight years ago myself. You must have some reserves of determination to do that. I am sort in the same boat, like "Well, this is just what I am going to continue to do. I can't do anything else, man."

Adam: That is where I am coming from, man. People are always saying, "you should do this, you should do that" I think I told you about the whole *The Voice* thing…

Brian: Oh yeah, that is a great story.

Adam: Yeah. So, they got a hold of me twice and I never responded to them, because it's like you said, the journey—there is no destination. And for me, I feel helpless without this. I don't have the option of being like, "Well, I am dried up. I don't feel like living in a car anymore." That doesn't exist for me. To do that is to give up on life completely.

But it was a really big show when they got a hold of me. It is like *America's Got Talent*, it is the same fucking thing. And the main reason that I didn't do it, I would be a joke. After a while I would have been Adam Faucett from *The Voice*, not Adam Faucett from the van, you know what I am saying? For me, I had lived my entire life looking up to hang next to artists. Very few people that I could sit and talk to and to lose their respect, or to lose credibility over a hopeful desperate cash grab—like "look at me, I am on TV"—it is like, "Fuck that shit! I have worked my entire life to be here."

Brian: How did they even hear about you in the first place?

Adam: They got a hold of my then booking agent. He is still a friend of mine. I don't know where they heard me or how they got a hold of it but yeah, two different occasions.

Brian: You put out my favorite record of the year.

Adam: Thank you.

Brian: What I have read from the press was all super positive. Has anything got better or been noticeable since?

Adam: No, not really. Ha ha. I mean, actually in a lot of times it works against me. I mean, I can get booked a little easier because I have press, and recent press. But then they want us to headline and we are like, "No, we aren't headliners, nobody knows who the fuck we are.

I would say that, with every year, things do get a little better. But it's never been a spike. There has never been a "holy shit!" type of moment. So yeah, a little bit more attention than the last record. So it might be the next step up, I guess. I hope. I don't know.

I always tell my younger buddies—the ones that look up to me because I have been doing it for a long time, the ones that say, "Wow, you are almost forty and you keep touring around on a shoestring all the time."—if you go into this expecting anything, then you are not going to last long. You know what I am saying? Because you are going to become so frustrated and become so jaded, you will talk yourself into thinking that you aren't good enough to do it. Which I have come so close to doing so many fucking times, because it is really easy to lose perspective.

It is kind of a rock and roll joke, and I like the dark jokes.

BOB HANNAM

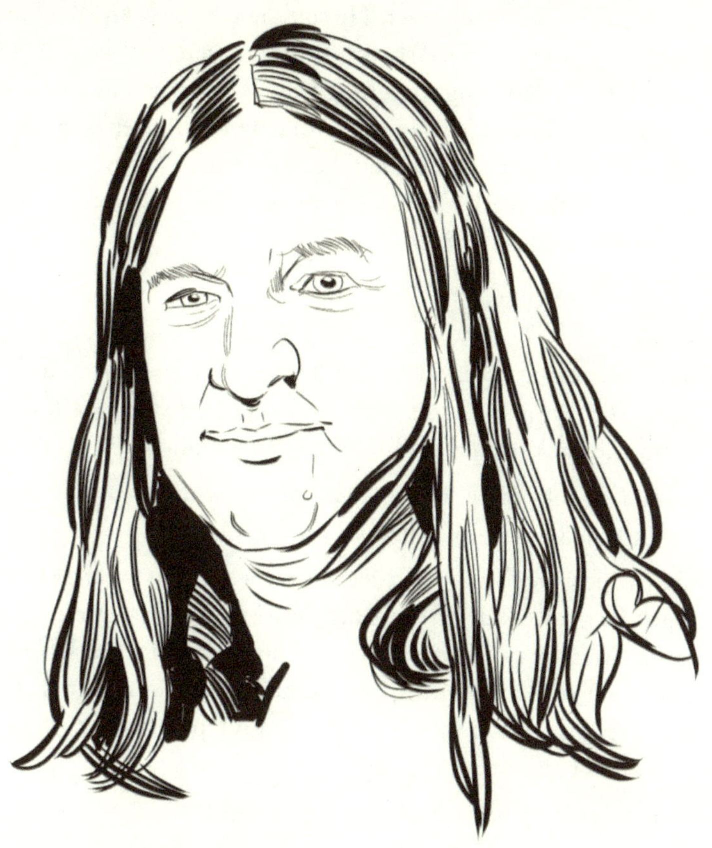

Bob Hannam lives in San Francisco.

He sold merchandise for years on the road for various acts ranging from the Stooges to Neil Young and beyond. He owns a merchandise company called Revolve and he was one of the two guys who made the recent Melvins documentary, *Colossus Of Destiny.*

Bob Hannam originally lived in England but has been here in the states as a U.S. citizen for a long time. I am not aware how I met him, but I think it came from his friendship with Dale Crover first, and then the Melvins later. When I talked to him about his life I realized that he had done years and years of cool stuff that I wasn't aware of whatsoever. He sold merch for both Blondie and the Stooges when the Asheton brothers were still here. He sold merch for Neil Young for a long time. I bet that was interesting. These days, he has settled into working for himself and starting his own company for merchandise and other things. I like Bob a lot, and underneath a slightly gruff exterior, lies a pussycat with a heart of gold. Ha ha ha….

Bob: I first came over to New York in 1996. I overstayed for three years. But I am a citizen now. So I will just say….well, do you want the background from being in England?

Brian: Yeah, of course. I have no context of what it was like to grow up in England or any other country, really.

Bob: I will start when I was a teenager. I wasn't the greatest student, I got in trouble all of the time and I was the class clown. My grades were pretty terrible. So at the age of sixteen, I left school and went to a local college so I could redo some exams. And I was getting pushed by job people and my parents to try and get a job in a bank or something.

Brian: It is funny because almost anything I have seen about British Culture, the two things that seem to be the classic thing to rebel against are either working in a factory or getting a job in a bank… almost like there are no other jobs in England or something.

Bob: Right. Well, at the time I was a teenager in 1986, Margaret Thatcher pretty much decided she wanted to get rid of all of the factories. And all of the coal mines. I am from the north of England, and the main city next to me was Bradford. Bradford was the wool capital of the world. There were hundreds of wool mills. My dad worked in a wool mill, my grandad worked in a wool mill. Seeing all of the mills get shut down and seeing my dad lose his job, it wasn't like the Judas Priest guys who had to go and work in a steel mill factory or something, there was none of that stuff left. Thatcher was getting rid of it all, so you needed to get a job in a bank. Or in an office.

I got a job at a big grocery store on a few nights when I was still in college. I picked up more hours because I wanted to make more money. And then I got a job working in a office, the most mundane fucking job you could imagine. I hated it. I was probably eighteen years old. At this time I was obsessed with music. Like every other kid, I wanted to be a rock star. I would go to shows and think, "I want to know what is going on on the other side of that railing." I wanted to be part of that, I always had this aspiration to be a part of the rock and roll circus. And a friend of mine from my hometown started working for this local band. I started to hang out and eventually became a roadie, I would drive the van down to London and back. I just started working with small bands, setting up drums, guitars.

Brian: What was the musical climate back then?

Bob: I grew up as a heavy rock metal kid. I liked ELO and Queen, then AC/DC and everything else—Motörhead, early thrash metal. I grew up around punk, you really couldn't miss it. So I saw all of those bands, and even though I didn't wear a Stranglers shirt, I loved the Stranglers. I loved the Buzzcocks, all of that post punk stuff. It was in the charts, it was in the top forty in England. Every week, all of those bands.

Brian: That sounds crazy to me. Maybe because England is much smaller.

Bob: I am very proud that I grew up in England at that time. From like '77 to '83. This music basically was like really good three minute pop songs. No matter what you wanted to call it.

Brian: What do you think of England now?

Bob: One of my problems about going back to that little thing is that I wanted to get out of that area that I grew up in, and I didn't feel that there was anything there for me. I had long hair and I would get shit from people for having long hair still, even to this day, I could go back to certain areas of Yorkshire where I grew up, and you will hear a snide comment about my hair. It's like, "you people have not evolved at all, have you?"

Brian: Like people here that live in a small town and think they know everything but haven't moved away from the fifty mile radius where they were born. That is kind of what [bassist] Gareth Turner said about England. He said that there was still a lot of great things about living in England but there is this attitude that if anyone does anything for themselves outside of the norm, they have to be knocked down for getting too uppity, for not knowing their place.

Bob: That is right, you can't have any dreams or aspirations or anything like that. If you do that, you are a freak. But that's the same everywhere. Now it might be a little bit different over there—you can get better food if you want—but the attitude I always got when I was growing up was "when are you going to grow up." I think I have done a good job growing up.

So I started working with bands and ended up in Leeds. Leeds is a big university town. I got a call and ended up working with these two bands that went around Europe for a month. One was called Tub and one was called Fur. The third band that was on this tour went back to New York. I got pretty friendly with a couple of members from each band—this was March of 1996. I was invited to go to New York and hang out afterwards. So, when I finally got paid for that work, I bought a ticket to New York.

My plan was just to hang out for a couple of weeks. I saw Kiss with the original band in makeup, which was a childhood dream. Then I went to New Jersey to see The Cure, I knew a guy who was a guitar tech for them at the time. I was introduced to a guy named Ginger. He used to do merch for bands likes Siouxsie and the Banshees and Depeche Mode. He had this job at Polygram. The merch company. And at the time they had the biggest bands of the world. He asked how long I would be over here and I told him until my money ran out. Then he asked me if I wanted some money. He told me to call this guy at a print shop in New Jersey, he needed a hand. And that is how I fell into merchandise.

And then a few weeks after that, my friend, who was a guitar tech for The Cure, called me up at the print shop in New Jersey. I was asked if I could fly down to New Orleans to replace the bass tech, who had to fly home because his wife was having their baby.

So I ended up flying to New Orleans and went on tour with The Cure for five weeks, seeing and doing all of this stuff that I never thought would ever happen. I always liked The Cure, they always had great pop songs.

So after that I started to work for Polygram and Ginger asked me if I wanted to keep going out on tour. So I went out on these tours of all of these bands that came from England. I did PJ Harvey, Massive Attack, Chemical Brothers,I toured with a whole bunch of bands and then Polygram got bought out by a Universal. And for whatever reason, they just canned the whole merchandise side of that company. The internet had just arrived, so they shifted to that. Ginger said that there wasn't any work left for me so I went back home to England. I went back with my tail between my legs. I didn't want to be there. And going back to your point earlier, England is very small. As well as small minded people, it's tight. The roads are tight. The houses are tight. You get a little claustrophobic there. And that was what I loved about New York and America. It's so big. I don't feel trapped. So going back to Northern England where there was no work, and people that I knew for a long time, looking at me like, "Oh, you failed. Now you have to get a real job."

But I just laid a whole new career. Something will come around. And within six months I was working down in London at all of these festivals for Ginger's brother. And then I got a call from this woman in New York who told me that I was recommended to her. She wanted me to go on tour with Blondie. Okay. Great band.

Then it was the Pretenders. And then Iggy Pop. And then it was Neil Young and Crazy Horse in Europe. I was going all over the world.

I went back to New York for six months, she got me a working visa and I ended up with a green card. Because I wanted to live here, I loved New York at the time, but then it changed and I had to get out so I moved to California.

Brian: When did you start working for Neil Young and Crazy Horse? I guess this must be when you moved out to California.

Bob: I did some European shows for the Crazy Horse tour—I think it was 2001. I was working in Europe and I did a little European tour with Crazy Horse. And after that, Neil went away and did the *Greendale* album, and they toured that *Greendale* thing and thankfully I had nothing to do with that. (laughter)

Brian: I am a huge fan of Neil Young. And I appreciate the fact that he just does whatever the fuck he wants, and follows his muse. I just wish that, as a fan, it was more consistent with what I like about him.

Bob: The thing about Neil is, if you tell him to do something he is not going to do that. Just so he could say, "nobody tells me what to do." I am sure at the time in '92 people were saying, "Yeah, you should make a really good Crazy Horse album like *Rust Never Sleeps*." And he would say, "Oh, I got this concept album."

Brian: Well, then people should just use reverse psychology, like "You should make a *Greendale* box set!"

Bob: Ha ha ha ha!

Brian: What was he like as a person? 'Cause I read that book *Shakey* and that seems like a pretty good snapshot of what he is, warts and all. An eccentric, driven guy.

Bob: Let me just go back a little bit and I will go more in depth about that. So it was 2006. I was doing the David Gilmour solo tour, the first tour he had done in a long time. *On an Island*. And it was great, Rick Wright was there.

Brian: They played "Echoes," which starts off with Rick Wright making that piano note.

Bob: Right. And Phil Manzanera from Roxy Music was there, he was playing second guitar. I was never a huge Pink Floyd fan. I knew one day I would get it but that time had never come. But seeing that David Gilmour tour, it really hit me. I thought that it was really fucking good. Seeing them play "Echoes"...

Brian: "Echoes" is a great song. Richard Wright was totally underrated.

Bob: Just hearing him sing "desperation is the English way." The way he sang that, it was like "Fuck! This is cool." So, on the record David Crosby and Graham Nash did some backing vocals on a couple of the songs. So every now and then, Crosby and Nash showed up and they would do a couple of songs. And I think the last shows of the Gilmour tour, we did one night at the Hollywood Bowl, the next night was at Universal Studios. I was in the corridor talking with my other boss, Norman, from the company in New York, and Graham Nash came by and he said, "Norman...I will talk to you soon. And Bob, it has been great seeing you again. And I guess I will see you in the summer."

And I was, "Uh, okay. See you Graham." And I said to Norman, "What did he mean by that?" And he said, "I guess you are doing the CSNY tour." Alright. Great.

And the CSNY tour was a big deal, because they hadn't done a tour in fifteen years I think. Maybe more. So I went on the CSNY tour, that is when I kind of really got to know the people in Neil's world. Hanging out with his son, Ben, who is in the wheelchair with cerebral palsy, and it was interesting seeing the two camps. There was the CSN camp and then there was the Y camp. And I think I was in the Y camp.

Brian: And that is general perception for most people, they are in the Y camp, ha ha. I was never a fan but I do think that David Crosby has a nice harmony voice. I guess you can say the same thing for Graham Nash, and he seems like a nice guy.

Bob: Graham Nash, out of all of them, Graham Nash is a sweetheart. He is such a nice guy, really friendly. Crosby is a miserable fuck.

Brian: That doesn't seem too surprising. And Steven Stills?

Bob: Stills is fucking crazy. He is just crazy, He has done way too many drugs in his time and he is just fucking crazy. And Neil? Neil is just Neil. He is like all of those three. He can be a real asshole when he wants to be. He can be really sweet when he wants to be. And there is a craziness to him as well.

It is kind of like the same with Iggy Pop, there is two people. There is Jim. Jim is the guy that you hang out with the whole day at the hotel and then he goes to the gig and then you have forty five minutes left of Jim and then he turns into Iggy, this monster. You don't want to meet Iggy Pop. I did meet him once, I did naively meet him early on, I had to get his opinion on something and I had to knock on his dressing room door like twenty minutes before the show. He was sitting down in this stillness with his head down and then he kind of looked up and said, "Not now, Bob. I am thinking things." "Okay. Sorry." (laughter) I never did that again. Just the look in his eyes... The beast was ready to come out. You don't want to get clawed in the neck by this guy.

And Neil could be a little like that. When he gets onstage, he gets pretty angsty with that fucking old black guitar. He is in a trance and sometimes you can see in his eyes that this guy meant business. So I really got to be part of that family for awhile. With his son and Pegi, his wife, and some of the other crew guys. And when I moved out to California, they wanted me to move up near them, right below San Francisco. One of Pegi's best friends had a guest house so I moved into that and became part of that little world for a bit. I would go to hockey games with Neil and Ben, Neil was driving the car, it was just fucking bizarre. This was kind of a surreal fucking life. And it was great, I loved it. He is probably one of the most selfish people on the planet but I don't know...there was something about him. He is a legend. I think that is probably why because he was so selfish, telling the record company that he wasn't going to do things their way and he didn't care if it was going to piss some people off. That was the punk rock attitude of Neil. And to have gotten away with it for so long still is pretty admirable.

Brian: So how many years did you work for Neil Young all in all?

Bob: I probably did it for like eight or nine years.

Brian: What was it that made you decide to step away from that?

Bob: The company, Anvil, got bought out by LiveNation and they bought three companies—one in London, one in New York, and one in San Francisco. I worked for Neil, and when Neil wasn't touring, I worked for Blondie. The touring aspect just started to grind me a bit. I was getting a bit moodier and one of the guys on the Blondie crew, I wanted to punch out one night. And afterwards, I decided that I needed to take a break from all of this. I went out on a road trip and hung out with the Melvins in Las Vegas.

Brian: Do you still have a relationship with Neil Young or any of his people?

Bob: Yeah. I still live up near some of his people. He is living with Daryl Hannah down in Malibu. I would still see him at the concerts. But I wasn't enjoying it and his manager kind of gave me grief for no reason.

Brian: Elliot Roberts?

Bob: Elliot Roberts. He has been with Neil for fucking ever. For fifty years. And I see what Neil could be like and Elliot has to take that every day. Neil gives him the shit, and Elliot is on the tour and he shouldn't even be on the tour. He is too old. He is out there, and I almost felt like he needed to take that angst out on someone else and I was the lowest on the pole and he would just give me shit. I would just get blamed for things that weren't my fault, things that weren't right. And eventually I was like, "Fuck this."

We were going to Australia, and for whatever reason Warner Brothers didn't want to pay for me to go to Australia. And I just decided that this wasn't going to work anymore.

Brian: So besides being burned out on touring anyways, you were sort of being a scapegoat for Neil Young's manager.

Bob: Me and my partner Jamie—he worked for the company in San Francisco that was bought out by LiveNation—and this is a big part of the story, because I am almost freelancing touring, but there is this dark corporate cloud hanging above. Jamie was getting bored, these corporate people would come in, he was doing more work, more hours, he wasn't getting paid any more and he was just feeling the same way, that he wasn't enjoying this anymore.

And so me, not being in that frame of mind with touring, we met up somewhere and I said, "you know, between what you do in the office and what I do on the road, I think that we could do something ourselves." He said he wanted to think about it, and maybe a year passed, and then I got a call from him and he wanted to do it. He said he was tired of all of the LiveNation bullshit and that he didn't get into the business to work for people like this. So we decided to do our own company. So we started Revolve. It felt like we were working for Warner Brothers now, and I didn't want to be a part of that. So that all fell into place.

Brian: So the Melvins friendship...

Bob: Yeah. I remember there were these two boxes of Melvins t-shirts in this warehouse in New Jersey where I worked at. I saw them a bunch of times. A week later I went to Ozzfest in New Jersey and found Buzz and gave him the shirts. A few years later, I went to see them in London and I bumped into Buzz outside the venue and he remembered me. I met Dale a few years later, whenever that Jello Biafra tour was. I remember when I was with the Stooges at All Tomorrow's Parties in England and the Melvins played. They nicknamed me "Stooges Bob," and we got friendly. I moved to Los Angeles in 2008 and started to hang out with Dale a lot more.

Eventually I brought up a conversation with them about why no one had ever made a film about the band? Because they had such a great story. And then Dale had said that people always said they were interested in that but that nothing had ever come of it. And I thought that was bullshit, and that someone had to make it. And then Dale said, "well, why don't you do it?" And I said, "Okay, I will."

And I think it was a year later, I didn't have any touring going on, and I was going to go back to England to visit my folks, and I think I had a conversation with Buzz where he said, "Why don't you just come out on tour with us in Europe? We are doing three weeks, you can sell merchandise." I bought a camera thinking, "Well, if I am going to do this, I guess it should start now on this tour." So at every opportunity I just started to film those guys for the next three or four years.

Brian: I met Ryan Sutherby somehow, but I don't remember when.

Bob: I was stockpiling stuff. And then one day Dale said, "hey you better hurry up with that film because there is a guy in Portland making one. This guy who is a friend of [former Melvins drummer] Mike Dillard. And Ryan had already been down to L.A., They were recording the *Tres Cabrones* album and Dillard told him to come down there. So Ryan came down and interviewed them. And then later that year the Melvins did two shows in Seattle and I came up for that and you and Dan Raymond said, "Hey, the guy who is making the Melvins film is here."

Brian: I do remember that. And we said that you better talk to him.

Bob: We were outside the venue. You asked him how the movie was going, and Dan asked him how far he was into it. I was just listening, I wasn't saying anything. Then a few months later the band played in San Francisco with Redd Kross and Ryan was there. After the show I went up to him and introduced myself and asked if he was the guy making the Melvins film. And I said, "Here is the deal. I have been filming these guys for the last six years and I have been wanting to make a documentary about them. I don't know how far into this you are, but if you want to do this on your own, tell me now and I will back off and you can do what you need to do. If not, I would love to hear where you are at and where I am at and maybe we can pull together and do this." And he said, "Yeah, let's talk about it." And it was good to have both of us nudging each other towards making this happen.

I took the helm a little bit more because Ryan had a job and I was my own boss, so I decided to take half of the day each day to try and put this shit together and get an editor. I just had more time and more access to the tools that you need to use to make a film, and that is kind of what it is. I mean, it is Ryan and my film, there is no argument there. But I think I needed to take a little bit charge of it if it was going to get done. There were a few disagreements about stuff but, all in all, I think it's a really good film. The best part is that the band liked it. And I have heard them say it to people, which is great. And I am proud of it, and I hope Ryan is, too. Ryan is not one to really lay his cards on the table. I think he is proud of it. We don't really chat too much anymore but whatever little money comes in from it I send it to him. I am still trying to get a distribution thing for it if I can. The only problem is that it is a fucking long film and there are a few sound issues in there. I don't know...two weeks ago I was watching a film about Agnostic Front. And one about GG Allin, and it's like fuck... these guys should put the Melvins film in there. So we will see. I am working on that. But it was great. We made a good film.

LOU BARLOW

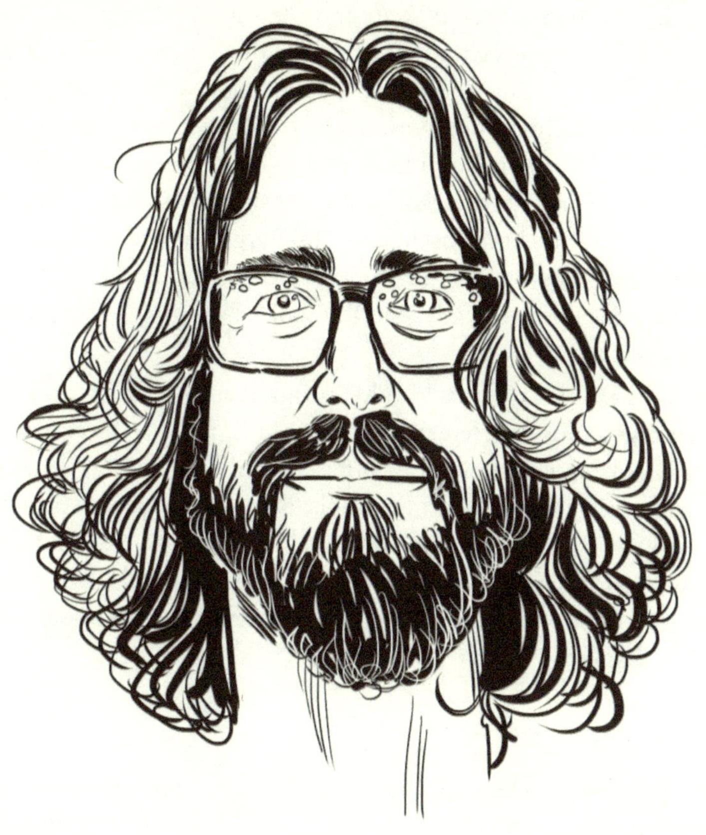

Lou Barlow is someone whose name goes back a long way with me. As the bassist of Dinosaur Jr., he played this overdriven Lemmy-style strumming bass on that band's immortally unfuckable second album, *You're Living All Over Me.* When he was booted from the band, it was never the same again. He started Sebadoh, and lo and behold, the band was not only very popular, but Lou hit his stride as a very good songwriter with classic records like *Sebadoh 3* and *Bubble And Scrape.* He has never stopped, and yeah, Dinosaur Jr. even happened again.

But what I also really like about Lou (as well as J [Mascis] and Murph) is his unabashed background in early eighties hardcore punk, *Maximum Rock N Roll,* and the acquiring of all of those weird little seven-inches that came out during that period. Hell, before Dino Jr, Lou and J. did time in the now legendary Deep Wound. Hailing from Western Massachusetts, Deep Wound recorded their own weird little raging hardcore seven-inch that fits in quite nicely with that world, for sure. Plus, they can name drop Neos, Mecht Mensch, and Discharge and yet still endorse Greg Sage, Gene Clark, or Mick Taylor-period Stones. So, Lou Barlow and the other guys in Dinosaur Jr. are guys I think I can hang out with.

Lou has relocated back to his original stomping grounds, in part due to family. He has a bunch of kids, three to be exact. He also has been working his ass off. Seems like he is always on tour with either Dinosaur Jr., Sebadoh, or some solo acoustic gigs. Lou knows a thing or two about being self-motivated and self-employed. I have always enjoyed talking to Lou and I was happy to get him on the phone a while ago to talk with me about a lot of different topics.

Lou: I remember when you first started talking about this book and posting stuff, it was like, "Oh, wow." I mean, it was funny because I could just see you weighing this career, like, "I am going to do this," making these drawings—and you got a kid. I kind of equate to, when you have a kid, all of a sudden you have to sort of reign in all of your shit. Your time becomes so much more valuable and you realize what you have to do. And to see you going through that, I went through that not too long ago.

Brian: You have three kids.

Lou: Yeah.

Brian: I think back to what life was like before I had children. I had all of the time in the world and it is like, what exactly did I do with all of that time? Let's say you have this idea for something, a melody for a song, or whatever. You have to wait. You have to wait till eight thirty or nine o'clock and by that time, you may not even have the inspiration anymore. It's almost like catching something in a bottle and trying to hold on to it.

Lou: Omigod. It's funny because my wife now, my second wife, she is a designer and so she has had this creative life. My third child is her first child, so I am seeing this creative person going through a birth of a child and going, "Oh, god." (laughter) Because so much of what you do is inspiration-based, and when you realize that your time is so segmented and compartmentalized, you can't breeze it off and go somewhere. It's not even your fucking house anymore, unless you are an asshole.

Brian: Unless you are a horrible parent.

Lou: Or unless you have a partner. I imagine there are some people who have a partner that goes, "That's cool, honey! Just go into your office, I will be out here taking care of the kids!"

Brian: "It's okay. I am not going to be bitter."

Lou: Maybe there are people who have that kind of arrangement. I would know nothing about that. I have been a father for thirteen years and I feel like I am only just now fucking figuring it out. The kind of cool part, though, is that it has taken such discipline. It's made me discipline myself in ways that have seemed almost insurmountable for me for most of my life. My life is kind of split up—I have my domestic life, and I can feel like it's in order, but then I go on tour for a fucking month and I come back home and my whole thing is like, "What was I doing again?" and then I have to recreate my domestic life. It's hard. I am having a really hard time with that.

Brian: It is usually because of children. For instance, I talked to Dale Crover the other day and Dale said that you two hit it off, and part of that was because there was no one else around him that was in the same situation as you guys both having children.

Lou: I have to say, out of everyone that I have ever met who has kids and does the same things that we do, I have never met anybody so similar. The way that we interacted with our families was very similar, and even though I ended up becoming divorced for a while, my relationship with my first wife was when I met Dale. I mean, we were a couple working together really hard trying to figure things out. It didn't work out ultimately, but you are willing to try and work things out. Dale is a really sensitive guy in a really cool way and he is really trying to do the best that he can.

We were so similar. We exist half on the road, half at home, we are trying to balance these kids, my kids are so similar in age to Scarlett and Cassius, and it was cool. Getting to know Dale in that context and then finally starting to work with him—and the fact that the band was going to work around his kids—that was really cool to see because there are ways to do this.

Brian: Those guys have a good thing going, obviously.

Lou: They kind of strike me as friends. I don't really have that with my long-term bandmates. But there is something with Dale and Buzz, I know that feeling so well. They know each other on this kind of level that could be hard to maintain for that long. Their personalities are so consistent in a way. Buzz is a pragmatic guy but also I find him to be a warm person. There is a warmth to him.

Brian: I totally agree.

Lou: Dinosaur Jr kind of works on that level. J and I hooked up at a similar age to Buzz and Dale. We don't have that kind of chemistry that Buzz and Dale have, but still over the years there are these things that, when they work, you realize it. J has a lot of people around him that he is very loyal to. It does come down to who you like, and who you want to hang out with. It really comes down to the quality of your experience when you are on the road together and you are sharing that time together. You just can't arbitrarily choose people.

Brian: I couldn't help but notice that you guys have spent a lot of time with John Brannon and all of those guys from his bands.

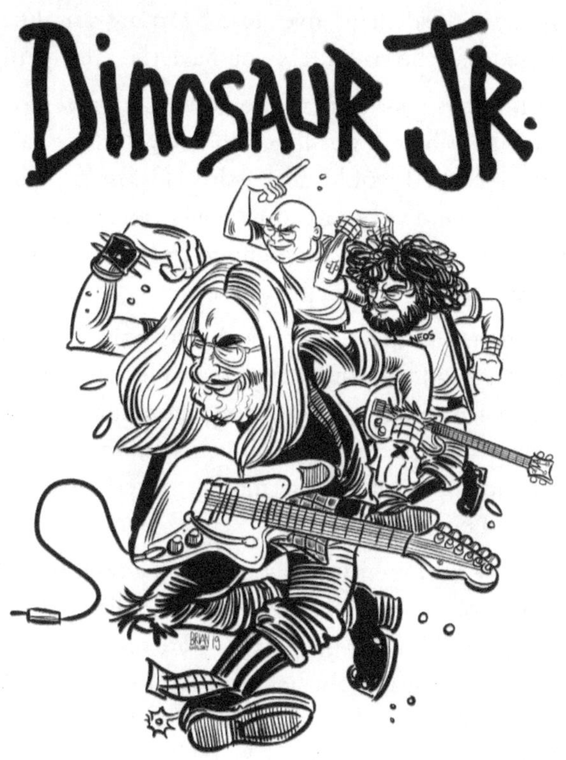

Lou: We have spent so much time with them, the last couple of years. They are fucking great. They are so funny. The warmth between those guys—they really watch out for each other, they have these little show rituals that they all do together. Harold [Richardson] makes tea for them every day. They make sure that they are taking their medication. (laughter) They really work well together and it was really enjoyable to hang out with them. None of those guys have children, except for the drummer. The youngest guy in the band has grandchildren. (laughter) The drummer has a twenty year old who has a kid and Harold and Ron and John are just like rockers, you know. Harold and Ron have real jobs. John is a cook. It's funny. They are so much fun. I really enjoy those guys.

Brian: So you moved back east and have three children. I think I already mentioned that I live close by to my daughter's mother, who lives down the street. Do you have the same thing?

Lou: Yeah. She is less than a mile away. Like real close. When I first moved out here it was like, "So, are your kids back in L.A.?" I am like, "NO." I would never; this is it, man. Wherever they are, I have to be. I've got to co-parent. I can't even imagine. I am taking this in the face, I am going to figure it out. (laughter) It's fucking hard.

Brian: Being a parent in a regular healthy situation is difficult. And when you add anything even the tiniest bit different to that, everyone that you knew beforehand pretty much disappears. And then they get this weird idea that you wouldn't want to see them because you are so busy. "No, motherfucker! Give me a call and come over! Let's hang out!"

Lou: It's really funny. I kind of wish that I stayed in L.A. and just figured shit out because I had developed a little bit of a support group, people I know or people that were my peers, like Dale and other people. Coming out here, though, I was like, "I gotta go back! I can't live in L.A.! I gotta be closer to Dinosaur Jr, I gotta go back to my roots! L.A. is too hard." And then I come back here and it's like, wow. Start from scratch. It's funny.

When I got divorced, I was looking down the barrel of a fifty-fifty split of all my assets with her, which is, you know, I have no problem with that. That was fine. Whatever I had to do to sacrifice and keep my ex secure or anything like that, that was totally fine and nothing that I could complain about. But I cannot support two households in Los Angeles. I can't do this, it is too much. So I had to sell my house and go back home. I decided that I needed to change my life and I had to do that for all kinds of reasons, including artistic reasons, health reasons, and all kinds of shit that I had to do to get my life in order—especially after having children—in order to be strong enough to face the challenges of raising kids. If I have to do this, I am going to do this because it will be the best for my kids. We will have more support because my ex's family lives close by, my kids are close to their grandparents now, I have a sister out here, too.

It's nice to have that as a part of my life.

Brian: So obviously you are no stranger to hustling and being self employed, right?

Lou: Yeah. I am employed though, because I am an employee of Dinosaur Jr. I mean, that is part of what I do. It goes in and out, obviously.

Brian: And they have a manager.

Lou: J has had an accountant that he has worked with since the late eighties or early nineties. He has management that adores him. Brian Schwartz, he really works for the band, for J, and cares about us. J kind of figured out some stuff a long time ago. He understands shit that people say, like, "You gotta make your brand—you gotta do the same thing over and over again, you gotta be consistent, you gotta lay doing the rules right away," and he did it. He laid down all of the shit right away, and he lived by that and he has lived by it since the eighties. It's impressive. He has more of a parachute, let's say. More of a safety net, more support.

Brian: You have Sebadoh, and your solo stuff, and you tour, it seems like you tour a whole lot. All the time, and you are self-managed. You are a pretty busy guy. How do you balance all of that out?

Lou: I gotta say that every year is almost an improvisation. I don't know, one thing that I have working in my advantage that I don't see in a lot of other people, I have always had a lot of self preservation. I know that I have to keep moving on some basic level, and then it has to be about the music. I have to be creating, I have to be thinking towards some body of work. One of the great, for a lack of a better word, passions in my life is creating a catalogue of my own. It's this big sort of messy fucking collection of all the music I have made while I am on this planet.

It may not be important, or even important to other people,

but it is important to me. When I was young, if I had a vision at all, it was that I wanted to be part of making music. I wanted to be part of this flow. So I always think about the thing that I will have to do next, musically. If I am playing with Dinosaur Jr, the next thing that I want to do is play some acoustic music. I feel compelled to make another step, and if I rely on that, if I rely on what I am compelled to do, they go in circles. If I am in Dinosaur Jr and everything is going great then I have to think about what I am going to be doing next year. I gotta start doing it now. I am always trying to think a year in advance.

I start off by imagining myself in the worst possible scenario ever, and then I think about how to prevent that. And that is the way I live. I am raising kids, so I want to make sure that I am feeding them good food. I want to have a house so I can find a corner of it to go and scream into once in a while. I have all of these domestic inspirations, things I want to do domestically and things I want to do to provide for my family. If that means that I have to, you know, spend too much money on fucking organic groceries, then that is what I am going to do. I am going to maintain a life for my family.

Brian: It is interesting to hear that. For me, there is this thing where I just don't have any faith in anything that I do and that I think one day, the jig is going to be up. So I am motivated by fear. But I am also motivated by the fact that this is still want I want to do, drawing stuff. It's also the only thing I can do that makes me feel like a somewhat normal person. And it turns out that I can make enough money to eke out a sort of living doing it.

The thing about Dinosaur Jr that I always enjoyed was that you guys were never strangers about displaying your love for early eighties punk rock and hardcore. Like, you bought *Maximum Rock N Roll* when it was a new and exciting magazine, name dropping or referencing the Neos or Discharge. I always liked that, maybe because Dinosaur Jr. is basically a step away from that, playing weird really loud rock music instead of hardcore.

Lou: I have been home for like a month, so one of the things I wanted to do was set up this little station. I needed some place in my house to play cassettes, and if I like what I am hearing I have to have something to capture it, to record it on to something and save it. So I am going through all of these insanely old cassettes that I made when I was in high school and they are a little bit of these song ideas and then, randomly, there is thirty seconds of a Mecht Mensch demo or Die Kreuzen. So, here I am playing acoustic guitar and developing the basic ideas of my really early Sebadoh stuff—like a strumming style of usually four strings on a guitar in an open tuning kind of thing. I am doing that, but I am listening to hardcore.

The thing that I just love about that stuff was that at that time, just to hear something so explosively sloppy, every hardcore band had a different kind of stroke to it, every band had a sort of idiosyncratic sound, you know? That changed, obviously. In every band, you had a guitarist who did his approximation of, like, Black Flag, Dead Kennedys… you know, whatever. You had some kid trying to, in his way, trying to replicate that. All of those early hardcore bands, each of those bands had a guitarist that was distinctive. Black Flag, obviously. The early Meat Puppets. Every band had somebody's fucking crazy explosive take on whatever they thought Johnny Ramone was doing, or maybe what the Germs were doing. So that approach to the guitar, that absolutely fucking totally spastic male young frustrated energy was just directed into this spray. Every band had its own distinctive thing. Even the drum beats. It really inspires such joy in me, like this is my fucking polka music. I want to hear this shit when I am eighty five years old. I love it.

Brian: All of the hardcore that I thought was really good back then, I can still put it on as a fifty three year old. Granted, I am not doing that every day of course, but I will be reading a good night story to Willow and I will be thinking of the Tar Babies *Face The Music* twelve-inch.

Lou: I can always tell when you go on tour because you start posting a lot about music, because that is when you can finally fucking listen to music. So I will do that with Dinosaur Jr. We got this guy on tour with us named Steven [McBean]. He is in this band Black Mountain. He is, like, a veteran of the Vancouver/Victoria hardcore scene. So this guy saw the Neos when he was a kid but he is an accomplished rock musician now. He is really good seventies rock guy, but he grew up hearing, like, the Dayglo Abortions and all of those bands. And we had one night when he was on tour with us where we all sat around and listened to the Neos, and it was even better than what I remembered. I couldn't believe it.

Brian: The Neos are pretty bizarre and isolated and it's pretty astute for a bunch of sixteen year old Canadians. It is like, "Here is our stance against things that we have no real life experience with," but it is still astute, and brings out the geeky brainy nerd in you. (laughter)

Lou: Oh yeah. That first pressing of the *Hassibah* record is like this huge stack of paper and writing and it's like, "What the fuck?" But the music itself, I think, is really musical, and the way that they work together, it was such a beautiful artifact. What a wonderful thing to put out in the world, you know. What a great use of time for these guys. (laughter)

Brian: I totally agree! So yeah, I always appreciated that you paid lip service to this stuff, it was great.

Lou: I know what the lineage is. Every time I pick up the bass and play in Dinosaur Jr, I feel totally back to that because of the way I play the bass and the kind of attack I use on the bass is totally what remains in me of the capabilities I had playing hardcore. Because I can't play the way I used to play when I was a kid. I wasn't even able to do it when I turned twenty five.

Brian: You mean like your guitar style in Deep Wound?

Lou: Yeah. It was such dexterity, like the way that I strummed—like, I double strummed everything. It was so much a product of me being fifteen, sixteen years old. And I can't do it now. I can certainly play the same chords and all of that at the same speed, but I could never really do it.

Brian: Well you know, the drummers are always the first to go in hardcore.

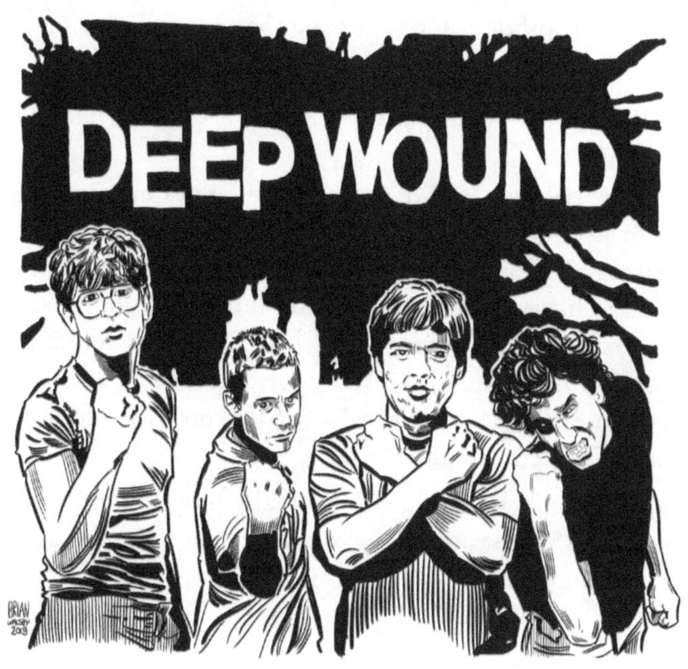

Lou: That's right, especially the ones that are really good. J has very particular ideas about drums. You know, in the Bill Stevenson interview, where he is talking about Robo playing the hi hats? That is the kind of details that we talk about, that J talks about. That is like Dinosaur Jr topics of discussion, you know, Robo's unique style or the origination of the D-Beat.

Brian: I don't want to talk too much about you exiting Dinosaur Jr, but when you first got Sebadoh going you had a really weird and eclectic spread that came out in all of these really weird records. There was a bit of a sense of humor there too, with the single "Just Gimmie Indie Rock" and stuff like that. It all culminated for me when I saw you guys after *Bubble And Scrape* came out.

For whatever reason, that is my favorite Sebadoh record. Not just your songs but the other guys songs too.

Lou: Me too. No, I like it. That is one of the only ones when I hear it now I can actually listen to it and I don't critique it much. It is the best snapshot of the rock band that we were trying to create at the time.

Brian: What about *Sebadoh III*? That's the other one that I was really into.

Lou: I love *Sebadoh III*. We really spent a lot of time capturing Eric Gaffney's songs at that time, which were really hard to get. He was really hard to pin down but we had him in a studio for a couple of days and we did a lot of stuff. So I think all of the electric stuff that we did on the record—which although is a very produced version of Eric Gaffney—is still great. And I think all of my stuff was sort of the pinnacle of what I could do with a four track. I kind of peaked. (laughter)

Brian: Sebadoh ended up being a really popular and successful band. Was that satisfying for you after, you know, being kicked out of Dinosaur Jr.?

Lou: Oh yeah, it was amazing. Overall, I think that, unfortunately, the band getting more popular gave us all of these new challenges to face, and we didn't face them very well to be perfectly honest, The initial thing with Eric and Jason [Loewenstein] and I, we played shows that I thought were so much fun. Unfortunately, you can have one bad night and it will erase any good vibe you had over the course of ten shows. And that is who you are, that is who you will become, and that is what I became. The band was really mercurial because we stepped on stage every night and were totally reacting from the gut, every night. To the point of, if we didn't feel like playing songs, we would make a bunch of fucking noise. Or, "Fuck, we are too high to play. Oh, well." (laughter)

We were like these young kids just showing up in this van every day, and whatever went on that day came out on stage. If there were some tensions brewing, then there was a really good chance that it could be displayed on stage. And to me, that was like, that is what you want to do. Because that was, like, hardcore to me as well. Because every band that you would see—touring bands like Flipper or SS Decontrol, who just commanded by sheer brute force, or the Big Boys would be this truly unbelievably welcoming band, or Hüsker Dü or the Minutemen or Black Flag, those were really personal experiences—you felt like, when a band like that stepped on stage, that you as an audience member were almost vulnerable, you know? And when Sebadoh started playing, especially after Dinosaur Jr, I was still on that tip. If I want to say some wise ass shit about this club tonight, or if the sound guy is a dick, then everybody's going to know about it.

Brian: I have to ask about that book that Michael Azerrad wrote with the Dinosaur Jr chapter, *Our Band Could Be Your Life*[1]. Your chapter just totally dominated the whole book. It was very personal, an explanation of the dynamic. Was it weird afterwards to have all of that stuff out there in the world for everyone to read?

Lou: No. No, I pursued that. When Michael Azerrad came to me and asked me to tell my story I was like, "Fuck yeah!" For me as a music fan, I want all of the shit, I don't want any soft-pedaled stuff, I want to know about stuff. That's it. I just read a Joni Mitchell book and the thing that I pulled away from it that I am really the happiest about, is that Joni Mitchell was totally into coke. And she was a real asshole, really into coke. And that is a great thing to know about Joni Mitchell. I am glad that I know that. It explains things.

So when I was given that opportunity, you know, I was experiencing a ton of success with Sebadoh and had felt totally vindicated in a lot of ways. But I still seized on this opportunity to just talk shit about J. And when I did, and when that book came out and I read that fucking chapter, it depressed me to a degree that was hard to describe. I was like, "Oh no." It was almost like a wake

---

1 https://www.hachettebookgroup.com/titles/michael-azerrad/our-band-could-be-your-life/9780316787536/

up call, like when an alcoholic hits rock bottom, like waking up in a hospital after a binge or something.

I was like, "Oh no. This sucks." Even if it was the truth, that shit is ugly, you know?

But the kind of cool thing was, in the ensuing year or so after it came out, our circles started to cross over a little bit more, and then I ended up in the position of being asked to be back in the band again, and I said yes. I have got to re-do this, this is bullshit. This cannot be the ending. If I go to the grave with this idea that J Mascis really hurt me, or that I shouldn't have been kicked out, who gives a shit? I was so appalled by what I said, it was difficult to read. And the book was pretty popular.

Brian: In some weird way, maybe the end result of the book is what got the original band back together.

Lou: For me it was, I don't think it was anything J was interested in, or anything like that. When the first three records were getting reissued there was some promotion, and what better thing to do then get the band back together. J said, "I am not into that at all." And then he laid out the terms he would need to do it, and they presented those terms to me and Murph, and we both said, "Sure, we will do it." (laughter)

Brian: I thought you guys must have known that it was a good thing and worth it to keep going. You started to make new records. And a lot of times when you see a band get back together, the only people that show up are the people the same age from back then. But there were all of these kids at those shows.

Lou: The really cool thing about that to me is that you have become… I am going to use the word "iconic." To me, I equate that with the Ramones—You have this band that has this sound, and every time that you put the record on, that sound comes out, and that is the Ramones and you stare at the cover. That is such a unique and cool thing, to be in a band that is regarded that way. That checks a huge box of life achievements for me. I don't know where else to go with that, to be perfectly honest with you,

"Wow, I was in a kind of iconic punk band." Like, what else is there, really? I mean, I wish that was enough to completely hang my hat on. It's not enough to do that, it's not enough to live the life that I want to live, with my family and all of that stuff, but it's fucking cool.

And you kind of see it with the Melvins as well. We are old enough to know what we need to do, we know enough about music to survive. We are not going to be the Ramones. J has this amazing quote, "Who wants to be the Ramones? A bunch of guys in a van who hate each and get cancer and die." (laughter)

Brian: Wow.

Lou: But, you know what I mean? You figure a way to do that so that you are not that. There are people that never overcome that lifestyle, of being in a van with a bunch of people that they hate. I swear to god, it's weird. You meet older people that live that lifestyle and it is shocking. But the guys who have survived that are our age now, which includes the Negative Approach guys and the Melvins and, I think, Dinosaur Jr as well. You have these people that know well enough to stay out of each other's way, who do not wage constant psychological warfare against each other, which men often do. If you get some men in an enclosed space, they can do heavy damage to each other through these games that they do. I have seen older guys that should know better doing that. You gotta figure a way to spend time with these people who you may not love, but who you appreciate it some way.

Brian: I gotta ask you about the tour you guys did where you took Henry Rollins with you and he interviewed you onstage every night. Was that his idea or your idea?

Lou: Neither. It was the management's idea. You know, back in the day, if you were a band and doing pretty well, you could be sure that someone was going to assassinate your character in some fucking fanzine, that someone was going to call you on your bullshit at any point. But with Dinosaur Jr, we go through these points— like three years ago, we went through this thing where we played a bunch of nights at the Bowery Ballroom where we celebrated the thirtieth anniversary of our first record. We had all of these guests, and it's really funny because it was sort of the hallmark of this reunion thing with the band and the management. Maybe the management first, because certainly J—he's truly amazing, he is like a combination of extremely ambitious and almost totally disconnected. It's an amazing combination. I mean, he is a genius, I have never doubted that. But anyways, so the band was like, "Wow! Let's play the entire *Bug* album!" And Henry is obsessed with J…

Brian: Henry impresses me a lot because of just how he has ended up being a spokesperson for whatever you want at any given moment. (laughter) I think that is an amazing talent.

Lou: I know. I agree. I actually found that whole thing really surreal. The interviews were insanely awkward, and Henry really wants to make sure that he shows his modesty, so he becomes deferential. In the midst of that tour, we would do these interviews where he would be like really very carefully taking his persona down in order to be deferential to this whole legacy of Dinosaur Jr. So he was doing that, and one of the nights on the tour he actually did a show, where he stood up and talked, and he was fantastic. He is sort of a complicated character, he is extremely hard on himself, that is what I picked up with him. And we were, like, living with him. He was on the bus, and we were waking up with Henry and going to a Starbucks with Henry. (laughter)

He is a lot like these old punk rocker guys who almost feel like they can't stop talking. Mike Watt is like that, Henry is like that…

Brian: Jello…

Lou: Yeah, from what I heard, Jello too. There is a funny story of him being locked in Dale's garage for talking (laughter). I totally believe it, too! Ian MacKaye talks a lot to, Ian is nice. He is definitely the most normal guy that I have met of that caliber. John Brannon to a degree, too. We saw those guys and we were just compelled to just stand near them, and people would ask them questions, so these guys *are* like spokespersons.

I think it is hard for Henry, and it is hard for Watt, those guys. Knowing them and spending some time with both of them on tour, it's like they take on a lot of energy, and they are really hard on themselves. It's like we were just talking about—you can't subject yourself to how you lived when you were in your twenties or with that kind of scrutiny.

DOUG DOBEY

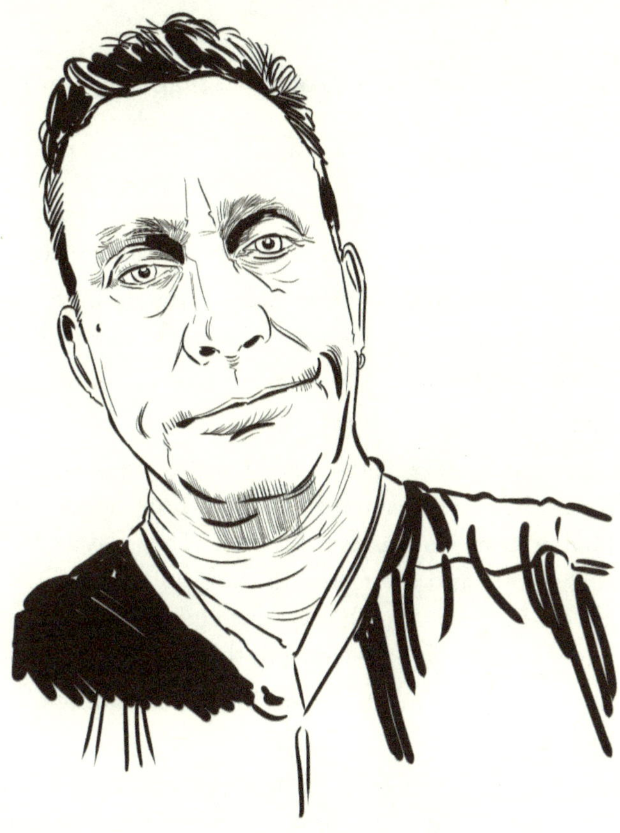

Doug Dobey is a self-employed graphic designer who lives in Richmond, Virginia. He used to be one of those wacky slam dancing punk rockers (in between going to school to learn his craft) in the early eighties. He did a lot of flyers for punk shows and really stood out as the dude who did all of the graphic work for the band Honor Role, who are one of my top ten favorite bands on earth. It's his work all over that bands albums, singles, and flyers.

That is the main reason I wanted to talk to him and include him in all of this. Plus he is a nice guy. He keeps on working and has carved out a comfortable life using some of the DIY work ethic that he learned decades ago. So take it away Doug.

♫

Brian: Chip Jones was the one that suggested that I should talk to you.

Doug: Good old Chip.

Brian: I don't know a whole lot about you and your path but I was a big fan of your graphics for the Honor Role stuff.

Doug: That is kind of weird because my desire to have a career with graphic arts started with all of the Honor Role stuff and going that route.

Brian: Were you doing stuff before that?

Doug: I had done some flyers and some record covers for some other bands, but when I started doing stuff for Honor Role, they just kind of let me do whatever I wanted. They trusted me to interpret their music and their view in the graphics, and they were just awesome about it. And I just wanted to put the best shine on it that I could. I am still very happy to this day with that body of work.

Brian: You pretty much did everything, including the first seven-inch, right?

Doug: Let's see, the first seven-inch was *It Bled Like A Stuck Pig*, that was a stencil and spray paint illustration that I did for that, yeah.

Brian: Did you do something for Pen Rollings' other band, Butterglove?

Doug: I didn't do Butterglove but I did the Breadwinner records. And I did the Honor Role compilation CD for Merge Records.

Brian: What other bands did you do besides Honor Role back then?

Doug: I did the original White Cross logo. Crispy [Richard Cranmer], their singer, was a graphic designer also, he put together the record covers. But I cut that original stencil and it ended up being their logo.

Brian: You kind of came of age during the punk rock explosion of the late seventies.

Doug: Yeah, I came to Richmond in 1978 when I was eighteen years old to go to school. I went to Virginia Commonwealth University to take communications art classes and design art classes.

Brian: So you went to school in the day and began to go to shows at night.

Doug: Yeah. October of the first semester that I was there, I was on the concert committee of VCU and when the Ramones played there for Halloween, I did a flyer for that show. Looking back at it today, it was awful. I remember it being the first job that I got paid for, so it was a big big deal. I think that I got five bucks and all of the beer that I could drink. But I wasn't drinking then so... You know how it is—I spent hours and hours and hours on something that I got five dollars for, but it wasn't about the money. It was just about being excited to do something.

Brian: I know a thing or two about that. (laughter)

Doug: I bet you do. During the VCU years, I segued into punk rock and ended up... I don't know if I should say I was "living that lifestyle," but the outside world became more important than VCU did. I ended up quitting once and going back again and quitting without actually graduating.

Brian: Were you super close to graduating, like a lot of people who suddenly do that?

Doug: I was one semester away. (laughter) And then my father, bless his heart, when it was time for him to retire, he called me and told me that he was going through all of his money and told me that if I ever wanted to go back to school and finish up, that he would pay for it. And that was eight years after I had quit school. I just got tears in my eyes. Like, how fucking amazing is that? When someone gives up on college, that must have broken my parents' hearts, that I quit like that. But I didn't. I was already working in the field and didn't think that I needed to go back, but it was super sweet of them.

Brian: Totally, Yeah. I always see you online posting some really good music and saying something like, "Deadline Music" or whatever. What do you do these days?

Doug: I am totally a freelancer. Self independent. I work from my house, I have an office upstairs but I swear to god most of the time I am sitting in the comfy chair in the living room with a laptop and do everything with just a trackpad. No mouse or tablet or anything like that. I can go work in a coffee shop and not have to drag a bunch of stuff around.

Brian: How long have you been self-employed? Have you been self-employed this entire time?

Doug: No. My first job out of VCU was at an engraving shop, back when they used to burn negatives and make halftones. I was a camera operator and did some photo stripping and airbrushing and stuff like that. And at that job, I am sure that I learned more, doing that, than I did at VCU. I learned more about the process—from an idea to a finished product, through lots of trial and error and work. It was really good for me. That is where I did a lot of the flyers that I did, and I did a lot of it after hours. I had a key because I was the first one in in the morning. I would get there at seven thirty in the morning. So, since I had a key, I would go in there at one in the morning and stay there until three in the morning working on punk rock flyers. And, of course, I got caught eventually. My boss found a boxful of exposed film and stuff that I had used to make flyers. I actually did the Honor Role *The Pretty Song* album cover at that shop after hours.

So my boss called me into his office and he had the box there. And he asked me, "How much do you like this job?" And I said, "Um…a lot?" And he said, "I am going to charge you for the film that you used, not for the time." And he made me pay sixty bucks—which was a fortune back then—and then he sent me home and said, "I want you to think about how important this job is to you." (laughter) I went home and I would like to think that

I went back to bed, but I was probably sweating all day, worrying that I was going to get fired. I came back the next day and he said something about me never doing that again.

Brian: Did you honor that? It almost sounded like you are being scolded like a parent would do. "I am not mad, I am just disappointed."

Doug: I still did some stuff but not as much. It was awesome that I got to keep the job but I made it a point to make sure I carried everything out at the end of the night.

Brian: He must have liked you.

Doug: Yeah, he did. He was basically a really good guy. He definitely let me off the hook. But that was where I did a whole lot of my early stuff. After that I worked at the Virginia Museum of Fine Arts, in their publication department. I put together magazines and catalogs and things like that. It was a really nice, do-no-harm kind of job. I was working for the arts, not really selling anything, so it felt really good working there.

After that I was an art director at a regional art magazine up here. And that was kind of a big deal, and I was kind of on my career ladder, or whatever. I was making decent money and it was a prestigious job and it was fun and I got to work with a good friend of mine. So that was pretty cool.

And during that period, I got married and we had a daughter. But during all of this time, during all of these things, I was always doing freelance jobs. After hours, it was usually music industry stuff. There is a list of record covers that I have done[1].

At some point, I realized that I wanted to be home more, and I wanted to freelance, and work at home, and be around my daughter a lot more. And I can't remember the time frame of when exactly that was but it was a really good decision. I have two gigs that are kind of my constants, and then I have clients that sort of come and go. Currently the two big things I have been working

1 Record covers designed by Doug Dobey: https://dobeydesign.myportfolio.com/music

on in the last few months are a new restaurant that is opening up where I did the logo design for them, and all of their menus and advertising and stuff like that. And then there is a brewery that is about to open up here in Richmond, where I designed their logo and am doing beer labels for them. I got Ed Trask to paint my logo on their building. It looks amazing and I am really happy with it.

Brian: Sounds like you kind of got it made.

Doug: You know, I joke about it but I feel successful when the mortgage is paid and the lights are on. I am not making tons and tons of money. I think everyone would like to have more money but things are pretty comfortable and things are going okay. And like I said, I am paying the mortgage.

Brian: I remember not too long ago that the Descendents came through Richmond. I am friends with the guy who does all of the artwork, Chris Shary. He does a lot of stuff and his wife Lori does a lot of art as well. Any time the band plays anywhere, they have Chris do some sort of limited t-shirt that has something to do with the town they are in. And when they came to a Richmond and Chris made a shirt, they took some of your work for that Honor Role graphic and they put a Milo character in there.

Doug: Yeah! That knocked everybody out. Yeah, I went to that show with Pen and we were just knocked out by it. Honor Role, I went on tour with them once, and we ended up staying with the Descendents in... I want to say Manhattan Beach, I am not sure. It might have been Hermosa, Manhattan, but it was one of those beaches. So we stayed at their place and everyone got along really well, but, you know, it was a million years ago. There was kind of a connection, I think, from that. The Descendents, or at least Billy Stevenson, were fans of Honor Role. I didn't know about that t-shirt until I came to the show that night and I was knocked out by it. What a fucking honor, for a band of that stature to ape and incorporate the Honor Role stuff into their thing. He did another one for Corrosion Of Conformity for their thing, right?

Brian: Yes, he did.

Doug: That was cool because we used to hang out with COC and you Raleigh folks.

Brian: The band I hold in the highest regard that came out of this region of the East Coast was Honor Role. More than what was in Raleigh, more than anything from D.C.—and I loved all of the stuff that came from both places.

Doug: Yeah! Honor Role were bizarre, Brian. I was really lucky because they were friends of mine. So I try to separate myself from it, but very few bands moved me the way Honor Role did, I mean they were so fucking good. Live, they were just ridiculous. The amount of times that I saw them and I never once got bored.

I thought about something else: you were talking about your friend Chris doing the Descendents t-shirt with the Honor Role nod—I did the logo for Loincloth, that upside down cross logo for Pen, and Away from Voivod did a redesign of it in his fucked up techno-spacy style that he does. It was just like the Descendents thing, like, "Wow, someone thought enough about this to want to mess with it." And I thought, "Man, that is really cool." It was a big deal, because Voivod played here in Richmond and I was hanging out with Pen and we went and talked to Away and there was this mutual admiration thing. He was saying, "No man, your logo was so great and all of your Honor Role stuff is so great."

I was like, "Jesus…" He was really nice.

John Reis, he is a big fan of Honor Role and he is a big fan of my artwork; Henry Owings of *Chunklet* magazine, we share a mutual admiration; Chris Bald, he was from Dischord, and people like that, are getting in touch, talking fan shit with me, talking about design work, mostly the Honor Role stuff. And it is years and years later. And it just blows me away.

We all came up from the same scene so just to hear peers twenty or thirty years later, it absolutely knocks me out. It was a really cool time to be in, too.

SCOTT RADINSKY

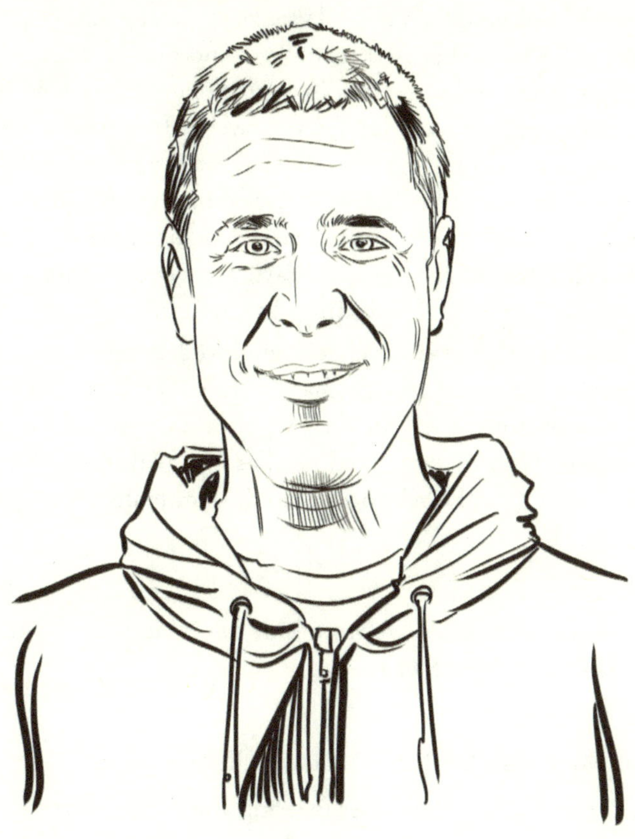

In terms of this book, Scott Radinsky is probably my oldest friend. We met in Simi Valley when we were both kids. I met Scott along with Dennis Jagard around the same time. They had a little punk rock junior high school band that turned into Scared Straight, which eventually added me to drums after Scott quit his position and I took over behind the kit while he went to singing. We played together from the end of 1984 until the end of 1985. I went on two tours with Scared Straight and it was a lot of fun, sort of the most exciting band I was ever in solely because it was the first one.

Scott had two things going on–the first was that, rather sadly, his father had passed away while we were playing music in Scared Straight. And if that isn't traumatic and bizarre enough to go through, it sort of lit this idea in Scott to pursue baseball. Which he did very quickly and he did very well. He is still involved to this very day, in one form or another. He sang in various bands in the off-season of his baseball career since the beginning–first in Scared Straight, then after the band changed the name to Ten Foot Pole, then in the band he started afterwards called Pulley, Scott has a long list of recordings behind him.

Scott obviously was never self employed, but his story is still interesting and weird enough that I wanted to talk to him. He has always been a really decent sort of guy and I wanted him in here regardless. How many retired pro baseball players do you know who sing in a punk rock sort of band? Not many I am certain.

♫

Brian: I met you when we were kids and you were in the band Secure Our Future, S.O.F.

Scott: At the roller rink!

Brian: Holiday Roller Rink in Simi Valley.

Scott: That is how I remember meeting you for the first time. You were drawing shit and you said, "Man, you guys are really cool. I will draw some pictures for you."

Brian: What grade were you in? Were you in high school yet?

Scott: It was the summertime, and it was just before school had started, before I started high school.

Brian: Were you already interested in baseball at that point?

Scott: Well, the interest in baseball, that was just from being a kid and being exposed to it when I was young. And I was good with it so I would sign up for the next year. I had tried basketball. I didn't really try football. I liked sports in general and my dad never really pushed us but it was always offered. So baseball just seemed to be the one thing that I continued staying with that was maybe a little easier than shooting a basketball or kicking a soccer ball. Both my parents didn't push it, they just supported it.

Brian: So by the time the band Scared Straight had formed, you were playing drums That was early '84, I think.

Scott: The original S.O.F. probably started at some point in '82 or '83. We were a band for a year before we played that battle of the bands thing. We played at the junior high when I was in ninth grade still.

Brian: What junior high school? Valley View?

Scott: Yeah, that was our first gig.

Brian: How did that go?

Scott: It was amazing, man. I think we blew everyone away. They had no idea, punk rock was totally new, hardly anyone knew about it. It was cool. And Dennis [Jagard] … having a guitar player whose father was in the sound business was amazing, he just brought in this insane sound system and we just blew the junior high away.

Brian: So when I started to pal around with you and desperately wanted to be your friend, and when you all finally allowed me to join Scared Straight, was that when your interest in baseball started to pick up? I didn't even play with you for a whole year, but it just seemed like it was such a longer amount of time—because that is how time is when you are young, it seemed like three years but it was in reality not even one.

Scott: In tenth grade, I was starting off the season with the team. I didn't practice with the team a whole lot, my dad was going through his illness. I think at one point I was getting ready to move to Hollywood with my friend, Rob. I started another year, my dad was still sick, and it was getting close to the end for him.

My high school coach walked up to me in the middle of the

school during lunchtime and said, "Hey, Radinsky. Aren't you in my class?" And I looked at him and said, "Yeah." "Well, when are you going to show up?" "My dad just died a few days ago. I will be there tomorrow." I was in eleventh grade, and I started pitching. And that is when it really started taking off. My dad had just died, so if I didn't have a chip on my shoulder before that, as sort of an angst-ridden punk rock kid, now I was just... it sounds kind of corny, but...

Brian: No, it doesn't. I remembered your dad. That was a traumatic thing, but also we were kids so I don't think anyone knew what to say during that time, hanging out with you.

Scott: I just channeled all of that. It was crazy because at the time, that is pretty much the worst thing that can happen to you—what happened to me—but it was also one of the best things that happened to me because, and I don't mean this in that way, but I just channeled it one hundred percent into my left fingers and my arm, with really the utmost hate. And to compete, in front of a person who is holding a bat, I was blowing it all out, letting it all hang out. Every pitch was just hate after hate after hate. And for some reason it just clicked. And that was that.

Meanwhile the band was like an extreme high. We were playing all kinds of killer gigs, we were getting on some good shows and there was a lot of good energy, and the band members got along and were having fun. It was pretty good. And baseball was going pretty good. And towards the end of that season in eleventh grade, I asked my high school coach something like, "Isn't there a chance I could go to college doing this?"

He said that he thought that I could do much more than just that. And then that is when I started to take it seriously. Losing my dad made me give a hundred percent focus, and so I took advantage of that. Because of that hate, I was able to beat that other guy. I had an extra ingredient that made me better, that maybe some of those other guys didn't have. And it wasn't necessarily talent, it was motivation. So that is what I mean about what happened to my dad and to me being the worst thing to happen but also the best thing that happened to me, because it put me on the right path.

Brian: I still remember the tours that we went on, and when I look back on it, I think it was pretty amazing that our families let all of us go on them when we were so young.

Scott: It is crazy when you think about what things were like back then. The times were a little bit different. We literally went from one coast to the other and all of our parents knew that we were doing it. And there was really not anyone much older than us doing it. I always thought that the one show we did—where we went swimming and then played that brick warehouse in Lincoln, Nebraska—for that tour, that was like the high point of that. It was a great show, great people.

Brian: I totally agree, that show in particular was really good. A bunch of fucking kids came out, it was the climate where you didn't have to be great, and I mean, we were pretty good but we weren't like, you know, Minor Threat or Black Flag. But it was still new enough and young enough where people would just go out and see anybody and everybody. It was very exciting.

Scott: And those times will never happen again. That was sort of the way it was. To be able to be that age and to have our parents let us do that, and to have experienced that back then—to be able to watch Power Of The Spoken Word, or to play outside at a skate ramp—I don't think that stuff will ever happen again. Maybe it still does. Maybe I am totally wrong in saying that but back then, it was so fresh. It was a big part of knowing that you were sort of blazing a trail.

Brian: Definitely. So, after I moved away, the band evolved and your baseball career began at the same time. What year was that?

Scott: Okay, we did that tour and you ended up staying in North Carolina. Then we came back and we went out and got a drummer. It was probably one of the biggest periods of Scared Straight, as far as what we got. We had good shows and we started to get some recognition, it was pretty cool. So in my senior year, the baseball thing started to really take off. There was a lot going on then. I got drafted by the White Sox out of high school. Dennis went away to college. There became this normal routine: during the wintertime I would come home after baseball and there was five months off and that was when we continued to play. Then I would go to baseball and Dennis went to school and Steve (Carnan) had a business. We would all do our thing and then we would all get back together again, play shows, record. We always kept it going, we always kept the band.

I would say about four years after high school, when Dennis graduated and when I got to the big leagues, we were all back in the same area again and there was a whole new scene. We changed the name of the band to Ten Foot Pole. We just kind of slid into it, there was a whole new musical thing, it obviously became a little more melodic, we became better as players, the songwriting got better. And that was right around 1990.

Around 1994 we hooked up with Epitaph Records, and that is when things really changed. All of a sudden we were exposed to an incredible audience in the States, and really the whole world. And we had support from one of the best punk rock record labels that you could be on at the time.

Brian: Plus, It has to be pointed out that, all of a sudden, you could be in a punk rock sort of band and sell records, people would buy lots of these records and that certainly didn't really fucking happen back when we were kids. There wasn't a business model for that back then.

Scott: No. It got to a point where people could actually make a living at it. I think that was what happened to my band, and what they got caught up in. We had a normal four month run, then shit got ridiculously huge, and I think that they were awestruck with that because you could quit your job and possibly make a living. And there were a lot of people back then who did this and went for it, a lot of my friends did. It worked out for some and it didn't work out for others. But the potential was there. And then of course it got absolutely saturated. And then the internet came in and made it what it is today. (laughter)

Brian: You just summed all of that up beautifully. You have always said that you felt like you never had a lot in common with most of the people that do what you do and are in the baseball world with you. Why exactly is that?

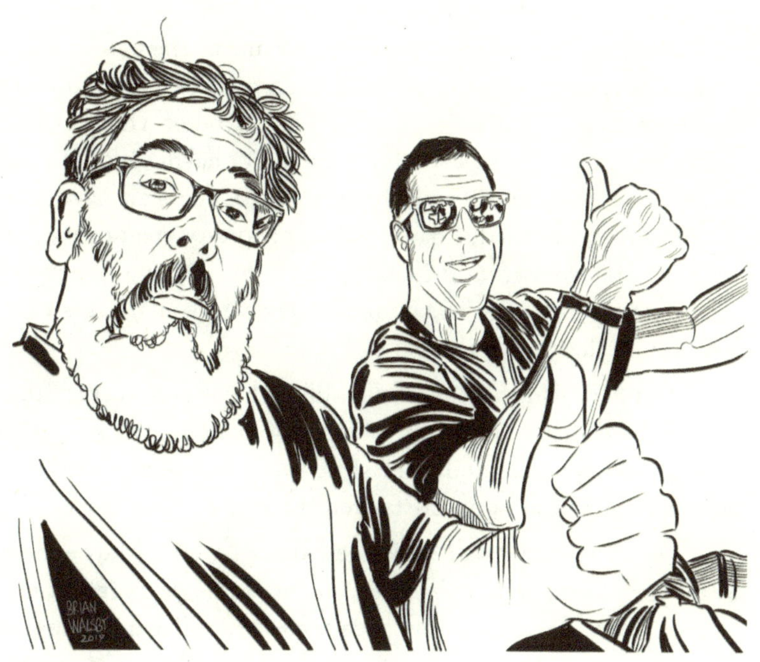

Scott: Um, well I definitely think that at the time when I was eighteen years old and signed up into the world of professional baseball and going to Florida and being exposed to all of these other so called jocks and college guys, I mean, my background is completely different. There was not even one person on any team that I have played with that went into a smoky basement club in Hollywood and watched Raw Power (the famous Italian hardcore band), or knew about *Maximum Rock N Roll*—just a totally,

totally different world. I would enjoy getting on my skateboard and cruise around, they would all laugh at me. They just wanted to drink beer and my lifestyle was just different than maybe the typical major league type of lifestyle.

But as the years have gone on, and when I became a coach, I realized that, you know, we were all different people. I don't want to say that I didn't get along with everybody, because I did, but we were all different people. When you go to work, and then you leave work, you realize that you are on a team with twenty five guys. But I am really by myself for six months. I guess it is kind of like bands that go on tour and how some of the people don't really like each other and they kind of go their own separate way and have their own dressing room. That is kind of what baseball is like, in a sense. I was just talking about not having a lot of stuff in common, but you can make friends. And as the years have gone by and I have matured, I have made some pretty great friends in baseball. But away from the field, away from work, not too many of them are going to go to a punk rock gig with you. That is what I meant by that whole thing.

Brian: You have had this sort of dual life of having this career, this day job, and then having time off to sing in a punk rock kind of band. You have been doing the same thing for twenty five years so there must be a lot of satisfaction there.

Scott: I never missed a year where we didn't play gigs. Maybe some years there were only a few gigs, maybe some years it was the opposite, but there has always been some sort of live music input. That in itself is amazing, just to be able to do that. And since I have been able to take care of myself and sustain my health to be available to do my job for eight straight months with no days off year after year after year, and to pull that off, are you kidding me? And on top of that, having a skateboard park business for twenty years, and to do that for a living? I don't know who to thank for that. There are no words to describe how blessed I am, you know?

BUZZ OSBORNE

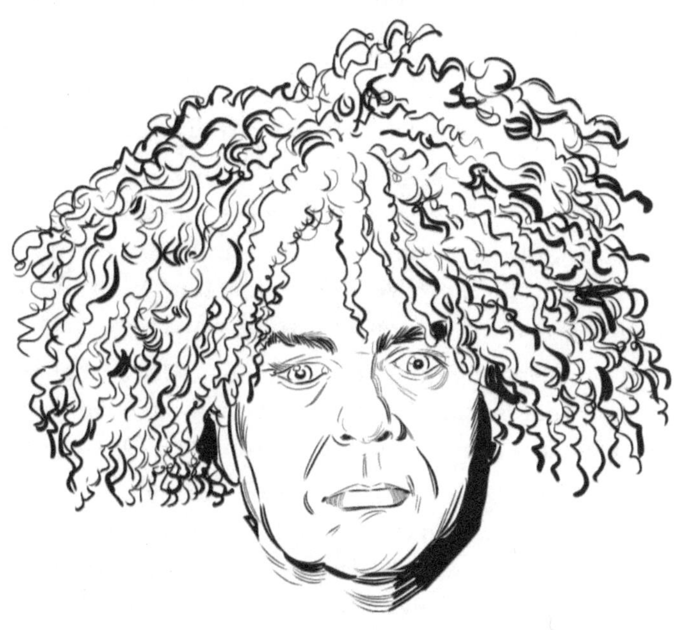

Buzz Osborne is actually a real softie in real life. He cares a lot about who he chooses to have as friends. I am fortunate to be one of those people, and I have benefited a lot from that kind of generosity, which doesn't come along every day.

That may not be something that comes across a lot when you read an interview with him, but Buzz is a great guy and one of the smartest people I have ever met in my life, if not the smartest. I have learned a lot, and marvel at how he plays his cards close to the vest.

He understands himself and his place in the world very well, and he works harder than any ten people that I can think of. *Driven* is definitely the word I would use to describe him. I don't completely understand where it all comes from but it is always there. And in all of the years of being the leader of the Melvins, he continues to work hard and make things work for himself and the rest of the people that he allows along for the ride. Like Jeff Pinkus once said about Buzz, "we are pretty lucky to be in this position where we can all benefit from this guy's obsessive qualities."

♫

Brian: What are a few people that make art that you are inspired by?

Buzz: I think the greatest artist of the 20th century was Andy Warhol. That's who we're modeling everything we do after. On his model, his work ethic. His drive and his ability to handle criticism are all things I've learned from him. Without question, vision is paramount even in how we all view a rock concert today.

Brian: I remember talking to you about Andy Warhol and how I didn't understand him. You made me watch this four hour documentary about him and then I was like, "Oh, I get it now."

Buzz: A lot of people think he was a meaningless hack. Only a brainless fool with no eyes could think something that stupid. When you look at what he accomplished, I don't know how you could think he was anything other than a genius. People who don't recognize this are idiots. I'm not sure what they're looking for when they enjoy art.

Another artist I admire is the director John Huston. I love his work ethic, I love all of the work he did. He didn't become successful at all until he was in his mid thirties. I find that to be very inspiring. His movie, *The Treasure of the Sierra Madre,* is the greatest movie ever made. He's another person that people disagree with me about and usually the disagreements come from people who are only vaguely familiar with his work.

Anyways, those are the two I find the most important to me and my work ethic.

Brian: How did you view work as a kid?

Buzz: From the time I started working as a teenager, I viewed working a job as something I had to do to survive. I needed money and working was the only way I was going to get it. My parents had very little and I certainly didn't expect them to fork over cash every time I wanted something extra. I wanted to work. I had a younger brother who never worked at all until he got out of college—never had a job and also never did a thing except sit at my parents' house until he went away to school, which my parents took out loans to pay for. Basically, he was broke until he was in his mid twenties. I thought that was crazy. He sat around broke until he got a college degree which got him a job where he basically still sits around broke except now he has a mortgage to pay off. Good plan. I did tons of odd jobs and started applying for real jobs as soon as I was old enough. I never had an easy time finding employment, but I looked constantly. I remember Krist Novoselic and I driving all the way to Tacoma and taking a two day seminar which was required if you simply wanted to APPLY for a job at the Post Office. There were hundreds of people there. After two days of sitting and listening to dull lectures and filling out an absolute TON of paperwork, we each did a one-on-one "interview" with a staff member and we were both told separately that unless we were women, black, Indian, or a veteran we could forget about ever getting hired by the Post Office. That was an eye opener. We applied nonetheless. Weeks later we received word that our applications were passed over but we HAD been placed on a callback list. It's been 37 years and I'm still waiting for that call. I never had any luck with employment of that nature. I never had what you'd call a "real" job. I only had shit jobs, but I have a lot of respect for low skill, low pay work. That kind of work has saved my ass more than once.

However, once you become an employer, then all of your rights go out the window. As an employee, you have every right to quit, or not show up whenever you feel like it. As an employer, you aren't afforded that same kind of right. If you're allowed to quit whenever you want and for whatever reason you decide, then I should be allowed to can your ass whenever I want and for anything. For some insane reason the two are viewed very differently. I've never understood it. An employer can be sued for unlawful firing. What the fuck is that? Would they have us believe that a third party who has nothing at stake can better decide if you're a shitty employee or not? What a load.

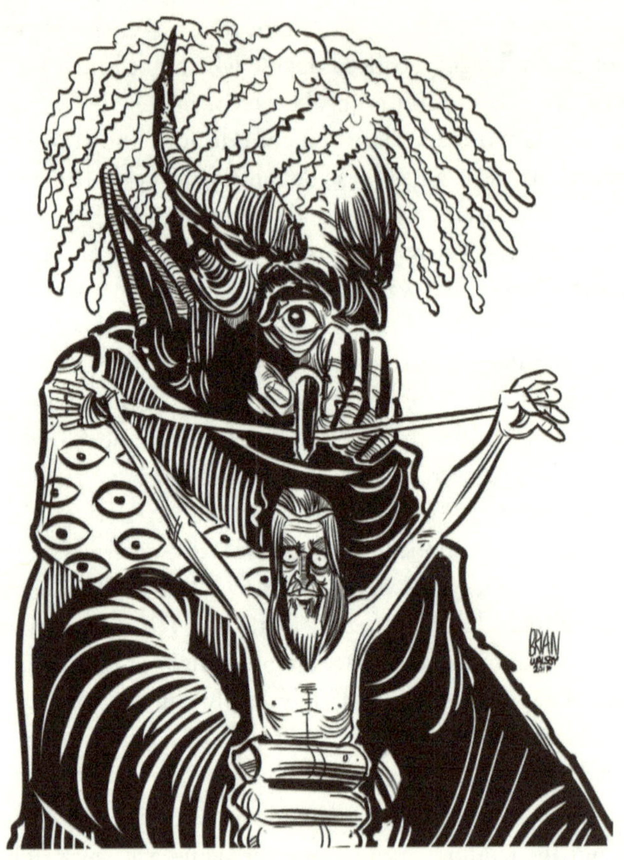

Brian: You are on the other side of the coin, though, because you are an entrepreneur. You have employed me and a big handful of other people over the years, and we have all benefited from your work ethic and the fact that you have three brains going at once, which is something I like to say.

Buzz: As an employer you are always having to face that sort of thing. If someone is a bad employee it's always going to be difficult and you have to be very careful with how you're going to deal with it. In the movie *The Godfather*, there's something Vito says to his son Sonny: "Never tell anyone else what you're thinking." I agree. First off, it's rude. And second, why would you do it? You have nothing to gain by telling everybody exactly what you think. And besides, you could change your mind, so it's better to just leave it. I honestly believe that people dig their own graves in that regard. If you give people every freedom in the world, they'll still want more. Why tell them everything?

Brian: Let's go back to when you and Dale were working at Round Table Pizza in San Francisco, when you guys made the jump to thinking, "Well, we have jobs here, but we can dig in and make the jump to doing the band full time." When was the point where you became the person that was the boss of everything and it was just you working with your booking agent and doing everything?

Buzz: It was the late eighties. There was a short time when we were on a major that we had a manager, but I didn't really like that phase of what was going on. It was during the *Stoner Witch* era so we gave it a shot and it was pretty much what I thought it would be, which was completely useless. To me, a manager is someone who should come up with ideas and do things that are going to further your career and make you some more money somehow, without compromising whatever it is you started out doing in the first place—and that never happened. Most managers just take care of the day-to day-stuff that they're hired to do and then they take a percentage of whatever money comes in off of the top. That's crazy. At best, managers should be paid a percentage AFTER expenses—JUST like the band gets—a percentage of profits and not a percentage of gross. If you're paying your manager a percentage of gross then you're being seriously ripped off. Of course, managers don't see it that way but fuck them. I've never found a manager who I thought was worth a percentage of gross.

When we left our jobs, I quit working in 1988 and it was only as a result of the first royalty check we got from Boner Records which I think was about three thousand bucks. And Dale and I said, "Well, with this we can kind of jump off the cliff and let's see how long we can go without actually having to have jobs." We could always get crappy jobs if this doesn't work out. I never cared what job that was either, you know?

Brian: You certainly haven't had a lot of help from people.

Buzz: No, it's been the complete opposite of that. Not a lot of attention from the hipster labels at any point, even when hipster labels might have mattered. As a result of that we were always very careful, we sort of operate like we would be going to be out of business in six months. As long as you do that, and you're happy with what you get as opposed to what you think you should get, you'll be alright.

Brian: It is funny to think that, at least with all of the Melvins tours that I have gone on, things always stay the same—or there is this continual swell of interest and there is no letup. For a band to make a continual living these days, especially after all of this time, is a really rare thing.

Buzz: Oh we're very careful with that as well. I understand what it takes to keep me on the road—I don't want to be on a bus, I can't be on a bus, I hate buses. I hate bus drivers. I can't make that work. I had to figure out another way to do it, which is why we do shorter drives and stay in hotels every night. That's how you keep me going. I also can't take a lot of musical or business advice from people who don't make their living playing music. Especially musicians who want to talk about how things are for other working musicians when in actuality they have a straight job that doesn't involve music. I can't learn anything from those people. Nothing.

The non-musical people I learn from are guys like Tom Hazelmyer, who's an entrepreneur in a lot of ways. When he talks, people should listen. You should listen to that guy. He knows what he's talking about, you'll always learn something. I am always interested in work stories from people who I think have something that I wouldn't hear otherwise. I want to hear what this person says, I want to listen to them. It could be anyone. How do you know how to do that? How do you make your money? How do you make this work? How do you live? I want to learn from that if at all possible. You can also see how they made their mistakes because I know plenty of millionaires and very few of them are happy. Why? Because money doesn't make you happy. You have to BE happy.

I've already discovered the key to my own happiness which is I know I'll never be happier than when I am lying on the bed with my wife and dogs next to me and we're watching a movie. I have absolutely no debt and I owe no money to the IRS. THAT to me is total happiness.

That's as good as life is going to get for me, and it doesn't matter if I have fifty million dollars or fifty dollars. If you want success and if you want to be completely independent, the best thing to do is to get completely out of debt, as much as possible. That's it. I haven't heard Trump say that. I haven't heard Obama say that. I haven't heard Bush say that, I haven't heard anyone say that. Get out of debt. Get off of that fucking treadmill as fast as possible. Pay your house off, save money, do all of those kind of things. I've always been very careful with my money and I think that's good. I don't take it for granted. Like I said, I operate like I'm going to be out of business in six months. That's how it works best because then you're careful.

Brian: I have used your line quite a few times because it is very appropriate.

Buzz: The only thing you can guarantee is that something will happen.

Buzz: But it will happen, there is no doubt about it. And you should prepare for that kind of stuff and be careful with it. When the band goes out on tour, I am very realistic about what will work and what we can get because I don't want to go back to a place like Athens, Georgia and lose a lot of money and ream them out. I want to go back there twenty times. I want to have a twenty-year relationship with these people. Or longer. The 40 Watt Club in Athens, Georgia, we've been playing there since the late eighties. That's what you want. You want to cultivate the sort of things you can't get by being greedy. I want my relationships with these people to work, I want it long term, and I want people to have a good time when they come and see me play. They aren't going to get that if I'm an arrogant prick.

Brian: Have you ever doubted yourself, or been ready to pack it in at any point along the way, since the Melvins have begun?

Buzz: No. I'd come to the conclusion on more than a few occasions that if I'd continued to do it with certain band members then I'd have to pack it in. What I did instead was change the environment by getting rid of those people. The X factor is gone and now I'm a lot better off. Everyone is better off. That's it. And there were a wide variety of reasons for all of those things, most of which doesn't center around music. It's personalities, or extra curricular activities of one form or another, or familiarity breeds contempt. They start thinking they know better how everything band wise should work and I usually disagree. I'm totally open to new ideas and new perspectives but, by and large, successful businesses don't run by committee. If they're so smart and know so much more than I do then they should easily be able to replicate our success or do it better. I have yet to see that happen.

I always understood that I didn't look like Chris Cornell or Kurt Cobain. I'm not David Cassidy. I'll have to do this a different way and I am totally fine with that. I always figured there were people out there that weren't interested in deciding what music to like using those parameters. It won't be millions but I never had any idea that it would be. Not ever did I entertain the idea that we'd sell millions of records. Never. So when you're not thinking that way, lots can happen for you. I wanted to make my living playing music. That's what I wanted to do. I'm doing it. And I didn't want to do it by trying to be someone I'm not. Basically I've had the same ideas and the same opinions and the same thoughts about that stuff since we started. Nothing attitude-wise has changed.

I stopped measuring my dick against other people's when I was in the eighth grade. I don't think of success in those terms. In my world, I don't compare myself to those people because I'm not part of their world. I've watched those people come and go for decades.

Brian: I have noticed that rubs people the wrong way somehow. That you aren't joining in, or how people measure money and success and how that is the most important thing, and not the quality of what you are doing. You guys have always managed to get the credit and accolades over the years, time and time again, and you are somehow never invited to the party.

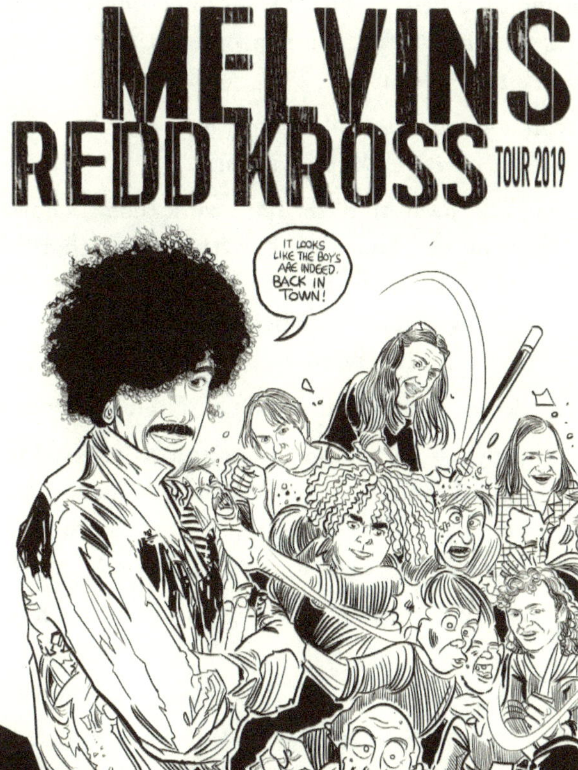

Buzz: I don't want to go to the party. I'm interested in my work, I'm interested in other people's work, but the rest of it I just don't care about. I am not good at that sort of thing and I want to operate without it. If that's what it takes to make it, I'll figure out another way to make it work. I don't want to have anything to do with that kind of insanity. It means nothing to me.

And people look at me and then say that I'm jealous. Brian, you've known me for a long time—jealousy is nothing that ever comes up. I'm very grateful for everything I have. Everything. The tours that we go on are a massive success and they always work, and everyone goes away with something in their hand, and they get paid for what they are doing, and it's a weird way to make a living but I think it's way better than what I was doing before. It's one hundred percent what I want to do musically and artistically, it's art, and there's enough people out there that appreciate it, and that's all I want.

Brian: Yeah, and you know, I don't want to say "lucky" because it really doesn't have a lot to do with luck.

Buzz: If you take away all of the hard work then it's down to pure luck. I fucking hate that shit. I've had people that I've played with say, "Well, not everyone's as lucky as you are." Oh really? Where exactly would the luck be? Was I lucky when I moved to San Francisco with five hundred bucks in my pocket?

Brian: You decided to move down there. No luck involved.

Buzz: I just hopped on a freight train and all of a sudden there I was! And all of a sudden I was just playing guitar in my room and Tom Flynn walked in and said, "I want you to make records for Boner records!" That was it. It was just dumb luck. Whatever.

Brian: Why do you think people don't do their business like the Melvins?

Buzz: Oh, well it depends on what you mean. I think people have a weird idea about how things should work by looking at how other people have done it and they think that's the only way to do it. They can't think outside the box at all. I think the vast majority of people can't do that. I don't know why.

Brian: People have this weird perception of success—that you are either a multi-millionaire or you are a failure.

Buzz: That's what people think about us all the time. There can't be anything in between. I don't believe in that kind of stuff. I don't believe in a lot of the things that people do, like the stock market. Or going to school. I thought going to school was for suckers. Still do. To me, colleges are just indoctrination centers for people who will end up jealous of other people's success. They become victims. Once you decide you're a victim, that's it. You've lost your drive and focus. You've lost your desire to work hard. If I'd have thought that way, I'd be sitting here with nothing. You can't become successful by only working forty hours a week and thinking someone else should foot the bill for your paid vacations, medical benefits, and sick leave. It's not possible. At least I've never heard of that happening. If that's the kind of short-sighted shit you want, then so be it. You'll trade success for a guaranteed wage and a crappy benefits package.

Brian: I have found that working for yourself is way harder than anything that I have ever done. It is very satisfying in many ways but I have to always try and figure things out. So I keep plugging along but it's way harder.

Buzz: If you want to be successful, whatever that means—to answer to no one—you can't do that just working forty hours a week. You can't think you should have the weekends off. That's bullshit. It's never going to work. You're just going to sit there and be mediocre for your entire fucking life and you'll have no one to blame but yourself. End of story. Life's not fair. We're not born the same. I'm an over weight, 5'7 weirdo playing noisy, strange, and hard to listen to music. I know the cards are stacked against me which means I need to work that much harder. Good. I'm up for the challenge.

Brian: You have been friends with Tom Hazelmyer a long time and you work very well together. You seem to have the same temperament and you are both very close. Why do you think you work so well together?

Buzz: Because we see eye-to-eye on how the world works, how wealth works, we understand where money comes from and we understand how things work. We totally get it. And we are very happy with what we get and not with what we think we should have got.

With our limited records, it's art. It's an entry level into art and we make a select few for the people who want something and want to buy it and enjoy it. That's it. If you want just the music, some sucker has already put it up on the internet and there is nothing that I can do about that, it is there for free. But if you actually want a thing in your hand as a result of the way that things are like now, then it is going to cost you. Me and Tom understand that, we both totally get that.

Brian: It seems like you guys got it way before things changed, before the whole music industry thing changed.

Buzz: We could see the writing on the wall a long time ago. I don't know if you remember any of the conversations that we had, but I pretty much had a crystal ball. "Here is what is going to happen. Boom. Done."

The thing is, what we do is very successful on that level and you'd think that someone would notice but no one notices. Nobody does, because they're so stuck in this idea that they have to do things the way they've always been done. That's very very discouraging but oh well, it's business as usual for me.

Brian: The Melvins have obviously influenced a certain amount of people over the years and not too long ago you were invited by the surviving members of Soundgarden to play that concert paying tribute to Chris Cornell. Soundgarden were peers and friends and were a hugely successful band. And I was talking to Dale about it and thought that this might have been the first time outside of interviews and things like that where the Melvins were actually acknowledged to be a part of something that was meaningful. Was that an emotional experience for you?

Buzz: You know, it was nice of them to do that. I just wish it was under better circumstances. I couldn't get past the heaviness of the whole thing. There was no celebration there for me. So it wasn't like, "Yeah! This is great!" I even told those guys that I wish we would have done this when he was alive, instead of now. In hindsight, of course you would think that. They have been through a lot, those guys. You know? Just like the Nirvana guys. You know, you don't always make the right decisions, especially

MELVINS *Beauty and the Beat*

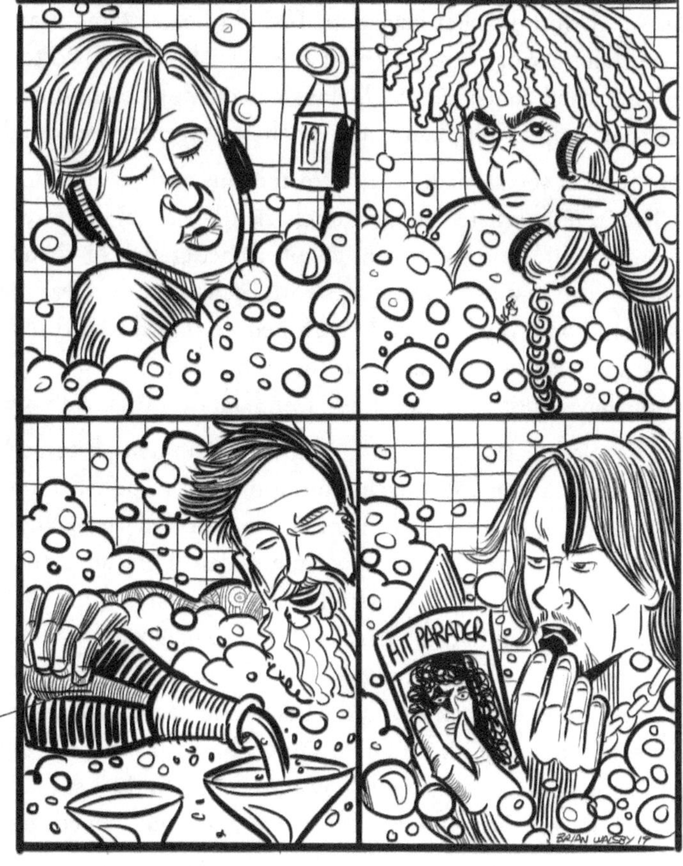

in the Nirvana camp. And I have no idea what motivates people of that nature; I know that is not what I would do. But with the Soundgarden guys, I was always really happy with their success. I always thought that they were fair to us in terms of what I thought we had given them, and as far as what the influence was. And I thought that it was cool that they did really well, that we were influencing stuff that was big on a global level, that was really cool. Now, time moves on, you move on from that whole thing. I am left with all of that stuff and what do you do? You move forward. That is it. You keep moving.

It was cool to do it but I can't say that it was great because it was too fucking hard for me. To think that is what it took to have that happen. I would rather have Kurt Cobain not be famous and be alive, then having it the way that it is. I wish no one had to do a Chris Cornell concert. I would have been happy having a concert like that happen long before one of these tragedies happened.

Brian: I think social media really created this current environment we live in now, where you have to check all of the right boxes and practically audition yourself to people as being pure of virtue and making sure that everyone agrees with each other, whereas before you could actually be friends with people that didn't think the exact same way as you and it was fine. There is a certain arrogance people have these days that I don't understand. It is really weird.

Buzz: People like that never talk to anyone who doesn't agree with them. They are in a feedback loop of mutual respect from other morons. (laughter) First off, people like that don't have any idea what someone like me thinks. I am a realist. I am not a fucking Republican. I am a pro abortion pro death penalty guy. Which party is that? Remind me, because I don't know what it is. I have that with Biafra. When I talk to Biafra I realize really quickly that he doesn't talk to anyone who doesn't already agree with him. He will say something like, "There should be a limit on how much someone can make financially." Who sets this limit? Let's just say it is two hundred thousand a year. Do you just pull something like that out of your ass? What are you talking about? Biafra, when you compare him to the rest of the world, is making too much money, only if you think along those lines.

I personally don't care how much money you have. I don't judge people by that. I also don't view making money as a crime. It's not a crime to make money. It is a crime to do horrible stuff. And the idea that the only way that they could have made this money is by exploiting poor people is insane. (laughter)

Brian: I watched this mini series on HBO about Chernobyl, which sent me down a Stalin era rabbit hole afterwards, I watched this Russian documentary about all of that and how young people in Russia see those sort of things now and all I have to say is I think most people should watch someone like that if only to see that even with all of the problems, things aren't so bad.

Buzz: All you have to do is read this book called *The Big Black Book of Communism*[1] which was written by some French guys. All you have to do is read that. Do you know how many people that have been talking shit about that stuff that I suggested to them that they should read this book? Do you know how many people actually read it? None. Zero.

Brian: I think I don't have all of the answers—I haven't figured it all out yet—and I have changed my mind a lot about things over the years, so I think that when people refuse to check out opposing viewpoints it is because they are scared that maybe something will happen that might challenge their assumptions and the belief system they have had for years and years.

Buzz: They already have the answers that they want so there is no need to look any further. That is it. They are done.

The smartest man I have ever read about is Thomas Sowell. How many black people even know who he is? None. To me, he is the greatest philosopher of all time, and he is thought of as being this right wing idiot. Why don't you try actually reading his work?

---

1 *The Black Book of Communism* by Nicolas Werth, Jean-Louis Margolin, Andrzej Paczkowski, Karel Bartosek, and Jean-Louis Panné (Harvard University Press, 1997) https://www.hup.harvard.edu/catalog.php?isbn=9780674076082

When I have talked to people about their suggestions on things they think I should read, I can tell you that it is a very short list. Generally speaking, it is always books that I have already read. I am not reading the same two people over and over again because they are the only two people you ever fucking suggest to me.

Brian: We both are fans of a lot of music that never seemed to catch on with people. Yet for the Melvins, you have never come close to being one of those bands and have lasted for decades. It never happened to you.

Buzz: Nope. It never will.

Brian: Was there a conscious way to avoid that? You guys worked hard and pretty much created your own luck, while so many other bands—bands that I thought were great—couldn't do that.

Buzz: Well, I quit working in 1988, that was the last time I had a straight job. At that time we put out the *Ozma* record with Tom Flynn, and it actually did okay. That is a really weird record. It sold, out of the gate, like ten thousand copies. For some reason it just hit on that level. I mean, it's a tiny level, it's not big.

Brian: Maybe having an honest person on your side right out of the gate?

Buzz: Yes, that totally helped. Tom Flynn is honest. He paid us everything that we were owed every six months, and he continues to do so to this very day. This has happened for the last thirty years.

Brian: You haven't had a manager for decades—it is just you and a guy from a booking agent.

Buzz: If I have to hire a lawyer to figure out if I can trust you, then I don't want to work with you.

Brian: One of my favorite quotes by you, in terms of business and who you do business with, as a good rule of thumb was if someone you worked with in business did something really unethical—going into business with the type of person who would cheat on their wife, or partner, or whatever—you want to call it.

Buzz: Oh yeah, I have thought that for a long time. If someone is willing to do that to someone in the most intimate relationship they will ever have in their lives, what are they going to do to you? Or to me? I mean, we have been in that situation a few times but, by and large, if that is the kind of behavior that someone is going to do—if that is normal for them—then I probably won't be starting a close business relationship with them. I wouldn't put them in charge of the money. (laughter) I have never personally done that stuff, that is the kind of guy I am. You have been around me for thirty years. I got into this for the music, and I have this idea that I can make a lot more money by treating people fairly than I ever could by ripping people off. And that is the main thing that most people don't understand about capitalism. They think that it usually means grabbing as much money as they can and screwing people over. That is for children. (laughter)

Brian: What about punk rock? How about the influence of punk rock and how about the punk rock of today?

Buzz: I despise hipsters and the hipster mentality. Hipsters spend the majority of their time looking over their shoulder to make sure that everybody else is into what they are into. That's it. They are too cool to do this, they are too cool to do that. They have never been supportive of anything that I have ever done, and I have never forgotten that. I am like a fucking elephant with that stuff. I am not a "good old days" kind of guy. I hate that shit, I fucking hate it. We are a progressive band and we are modern. We aren't an oldies act, we don't fit into that category. We are ten times more punk rock than any of the bands that would be at something like Punk Rock Bowling. They don't see that. Why? Because that is exactly the very reason why we are doing what we are doing. They never have seen that or understood it and it's not my job to make them understand it and I don't care if they ever understand it. I am not there to impress anyone or be a part of anything. I watched that documentary about Fat Wreck Chords, right? Over and over and over, he is in there telling these bands what they should do. "You should do this, you should do that, this song is good, that song is good." You aren't my fucking dad, I will do whatever I fucking want. (laughter) The last thing I need is your advice. Atlantic Records didn't even do that to us. (laughter) He is supposed to be Mr. Punk Rock. If that is punk rock then I am not that. That is worse than everything we set out to be against. You are going to tell bands what is good and bad? Who died and made you a son of a bitch? "Okay Mike, I will do what you say and we will sell a bunch of records. Please tell us what we should do."

I don't get it. I never got it, and don't understand any of it. They are doing one thing, and I am doing another.

Brian: I remember when I met you and did an interview with you guys, you said, "All of you kids out there listening to hardcore might as well start listening to the MC5 and the Stooges now, because you are going to end up listening to them soon anyways." It was the summer of 1986, and it was somehow a prophetic quote, because look what happened a few years later. A lot of punk rockers do this thing where they always show how ignorant they are of other kinds of music, like heavy metal and hard rock music. They pretend that none of that music had any worth and it was only when they heard punk rock that they were suddenly shown the light. I don't trust any of those people at all. One of the reasons I liked the Melvins was because you liked punk rock but had roots in what had happened before and saw the worth in it. I was the same way, I didn't throw out all of my older rock records because of punk rock. It was just, fine, more good music for me to enjoy.

Buzz: I always liked that stuff. We always knew what was good. The stuff I liked at seventeen years old, I still like. I was listening to the MC5 in the seventies. I found out about all of that stuff through the Sex Pistols. Because they did that song "No Fun" which led me to The Stooges which led me to the MC5. I was a lot younger than, say, Legs McNeil. (laughter) I certainly had no cool older brothers. I found out about all of that stuff on my own.

If a band was good, we were going to like it, no matter who

it was. We were the type of people that would go see Black Flag and Van Halen in the same week. People made fun of Van Halen, and they were wrong. They were fucking great. Wrong would be the word that I would use, because if you saw Van Halen on the *Woman And Children First* tour, you would be wrong, because they were fucking amazing. With no hint of irony whatsoever.

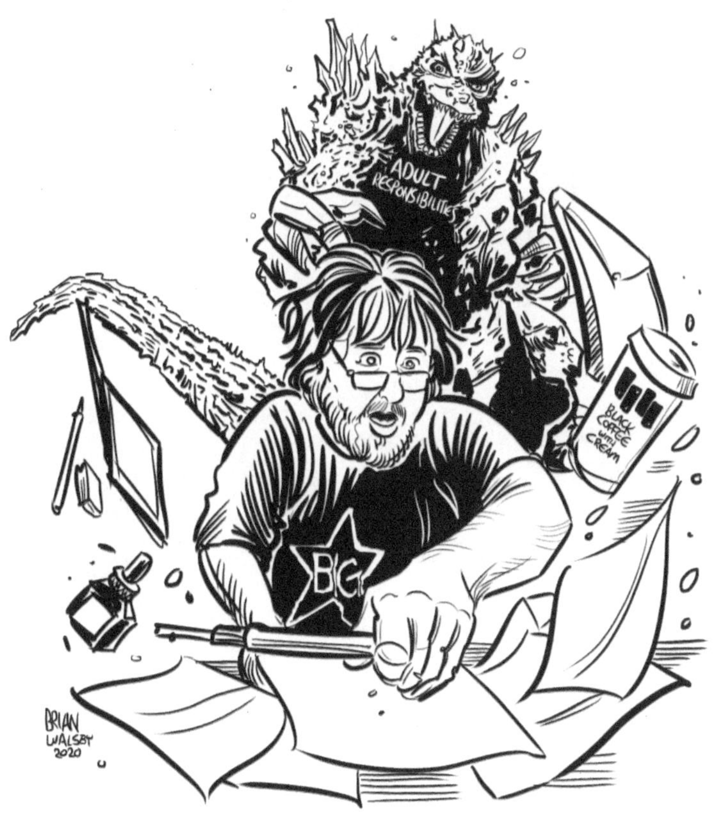

THANKS

Kristin, Willow, Bel, the Melvins, Charles Cardello, Bifocal Media, Mark Givens, Bob Durkee, everyone I have interviewed in this book and anyone else who has supported me in my quest for "SELF EMPUNISHMENT" in the last twenty years.

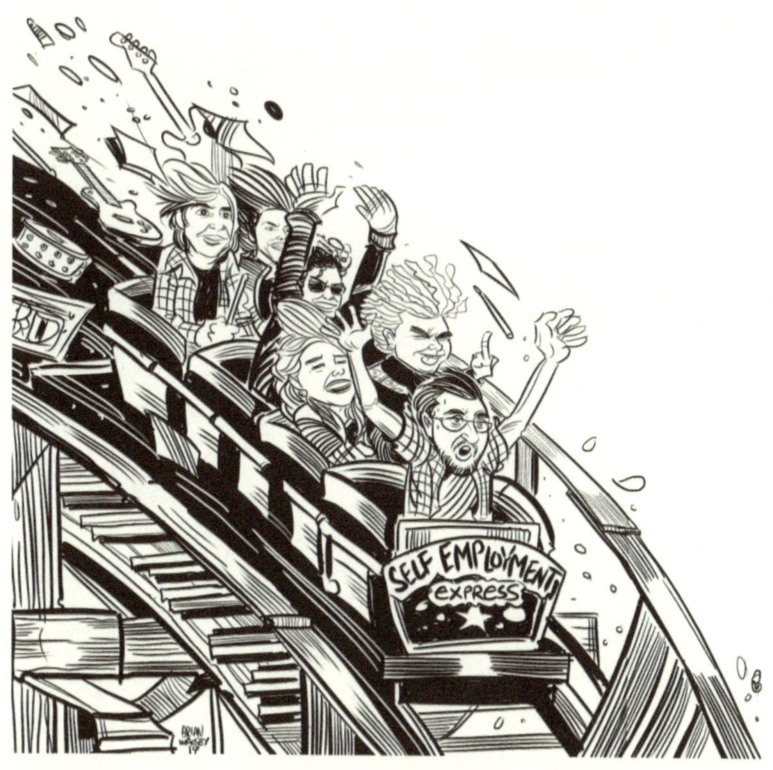

INDEX

BANDS

COMPANIES

FIRST JOB (AND OTHER JOBS)

INSTRUMENTS

INTERVIEWS

MOVEMENTS

PEOPLE

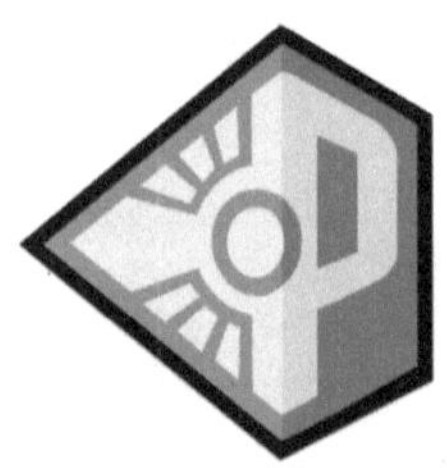

112 Harvard Ave #65

Claremont, CA 91711 USA

pelekinesis@gmail.com

www.pelekinesis.com

Pelekinesis titles are available through Small Press Distribution, Baker & Taylor, Ingram, Bertrams, and directly from the publisher's website.

www.ingramcontent.com/pod-product-compliance
Lightning Source LLC
LaVergne TN
LVHW041053080826
845145LV00007B/1564

* 9 7 8 1 9 4 9 7 9 0 4 2 9 *